D0232606

PLUTARCH

THE AGE OF CAESAR

FIVE ROMAN LIVES

OTHER TRANSLATIONS BY PAMELA MENSCH

Histories: Herodotus

Lives That Made Greek History: Plutarch

The Landmark Arrian: The Campaigns of Alexander

Alexander the Great: Selections from Arrian, Diodorus, Plutarch, and Quintus Curtius

ALSO BY JAMES ROMM

Dying Every Day: Seneca at the Court of Nero

Ghost on the Throne: The Death of Alexander the Great and the War for Crown and Empire

Herodotus

The Edges of the Earth in Ancient Thought

PLUTARCH

THE AGE OF CAESAR

FIVE ROMAN LIVES

TRANSLATED BY PAMELA MENSCH

EDITED, WITH PREFACE AND NOTES, BY JAMES ROMM

INTRODUCTION BY MARY BEARD

W. W. NORTON & COMPANY

INDEPENDENT PUBLISHERS SINCE 1923

NEW YORK | LONDON

Printed in the United States of America
First Edition

For information about permission to reproduce selections from this book, write to Permissions, W. W. Norton & Company, Inc., 500 Fifth Avenue, New York, NY 10110

For information about special discounts for bulk purchases, please contact W. W. Norton Special Sales at specialsales@wwnorton.com or 800-233-4830

Manufacturing by Quad Graphics, Fairfield
Book design by Chris Welch
Production manager: Louise Mattarelliano

ISBN: 978-0-393-29282-4

W. W. Norton & Company, Inc.
500 Fifth Avenue, New York, N.Y. 10110
www.wwnorton.com

W. W. Norton & Company Ltd.
15 Carlisle Street, London W1D 3BS

1 2 3 4 5 6 7 8 9 0

For our teachers at the Latin-Greek Institute

CONTENTS

MAPS

PLUTARCH: FIVE ROMAN LIVES

PREFACE

JAMES ROMM

By 31 BCE, after serving as a battleground for Rome's civil wars for more than a decade, the cities of mainland Greece were exhausted and starving. In rapid succession, the great generals and political leaders of the age, Pompey, Julius Caesar, Brutus, and Octavian, had despoiled the region's food stocks to feed Roman troops. Finally, in flight from Greece after his defeat at the battle of Actium, Mark Antony tried to extract one more shipment of grain from the citizens of Chaeronea, the smallish city-state in Boeotia, near the oracular site of Delphi. Greeks who lived there were whipped by Antony's soldiers as they carried loads of grain across nearly twenty miles of rough terrain, to the Gulf of Corinth, where the retreating ships of Antony and his lover, Queen Cleopatra of Egypt, were waiting.

Among those pressed into this ignominious service was one Nicarchus, the great-grandfather of Plutarch. "They had made one trip of this kind, and when the second load had been measured out and they were about to put it on their shoulders, news came that Antony had been defeated, and this saved the city; for Antony's stewards and soldiers immediately fled, and the citizens divided the grain among themselves," Plutarch records in *Antony*, perhaps recalling what he himself had heard, as a child, at his great-grandfather's knee. The episode has little historical importance, but it is the one direct link Plutarch makes between his own experience and the events of the age of Caesar—roughly speaking, the middle third of the first century BCE, the era that saw the rise to power of Julius Caesar, his murder on the Ides of March in 44 BCE, and the subsequent wars among those seeking to claim, or eradicate, his legacy.

The world was a quieter place by the time Plutarch was old enough to understand his great-grandfather's tales. Born around 45 CE, almost a century after Caesar's assassination, Plutarch grew up in the Greek province of a Roman state that had resolved its internal quarrels and subdued nearly all its foes. His life in Chaeronea was untroubled by the depredations of Roman armies; the era of Nicarchus' youth, in which much of the world had been caught up in the rivalries of towering generals, must have seemed far off. Yet it was that era, and the similarly turbulent era three centuries earlier that had seen the rise and fall of Alexander the Great, to which Plutarch gave the most attention in his *Parallel Lives*, the collection of historical biographies for which he is best known today. The age of Caesar furnished him with five of his longest and most compelling *Lives*, superb illustrations of the thesis that governs the collection as a whole: that character—the endlessly varied contours of the human soul—shapes not only destiny for the individual (as a famous Greek maxim maintained), but the history of nations as well.

As a well-off, intelligent youth, studying philosophy at Athens under a teacher named Ammonius, Plutarch had glimpses of the great imperial power that resided in far-off Rome. In the late 60s CE, when Plutarch was in his twenties, Emperor Nero, pursuing the delusion of a singing career, came sweeping through Greece on a concert tour, and the Greeks prostrated themselves before him (even posting an honorary inscription on the pediment of the Parthenon). In 68 and 69, after Nero died without an heir, the Greek world watched nervously as four rivals battled for succession, resulting in a victory for Vespasian, the founder of the Flavian dynasty.

This brief taste of civil war, after a full century of Julio-Claudian rule, served to remind the world governed by Rome of how much was at stake in the stability of its government. It was a lesson Plutarch kept firmly in mind when he later wrote about the far worse civil wars of the age of Caesar. Unlike others who wrote about those wars—the Roman poet Lucan, already dead by this time, had been a contemporary—Plutarch never questioned the legitimacy of the political system that they had produced, the autocracy today known as the Principate (because its rulers were euphemistically dubbed *princeps*, "first citizen," rather than emperor).

Probably during his years in Athens, Plutarch became acquainted with Quintus Sosius Senecio, a high Roman official then governing Greece who later twice rose to the pinnacle of Roman politics, the consulship. The two men developed a warm bond based on pursuit of shared philosophic goals, and Plutarch ultimately addressed to Senecio his *Parallel Lives*, as well as two of his nonbiographical essays. Another powerful Roman, a senator named Lucius Mestrius Florus, later helped Plutarch obtain Roman citizenship, and Plutarch thereafter adopted the man's first and middle name as part of his own. Florus too would later become consul, a second among the nine Romans of consular rank whom Plutarch counted as personal friends. This collegiality with Roman men of affairs says much about Plutarch's breadth and temperament. Not covetous of power himself, he felt at ease with those who were; he no doubt shared with them many dinner parties of the kind he represents in his *Table Talk*, where learned conversation flowed freely in Greek (for Plutarch learned Latin only late in life).

At some point, probably when Plutarch was in his late twenties or early thirties, official business brought him to Rome, the first of several visits he would make over the next two decades. Greek intellectuals were highly sought after there as lecturers and moral preceptors, and Plutarch's talents soon gained him an audience. Important men, including Arulenus Rusticus—another future consul—listened as Plutarch discoursed, in Greek, on ethical topics. At Rome at this time, the teachings of Stoicism, and to a lesser degree Epicureanism, provided the dominant ethical models for upper-class intellectuals in search of the good life. But Plutarch preferred the less earthbound system devised by Plato and revised by his followers over the course of five intervening centuries. Indeed several of his ethical writings take the form of dialogues, in imitation of the works of Plato, or mount defenses of the Platonic system or attacks on rival schools.

These philosophic dialogues and essays later got lumped together, during the Middle Ages, with Plutarch's various other nonbiographical works—rhetorical exercises, antiquarian miscellanies, and personal reflections on family life, education, and proprieties of thought and behavior—into a vast collection called the *Moralia*. This anthology is just as voluminous as the *Lives*, and would be much larger if all of Plutarch's writings had survived; evidence suggests that he wrote many more works than the seventy-eight grouped today under the heading *Moralia* (a few of which are almost certainly the work of other, unknown authors). It's an uneven collection, encompassing lively works that still bear close reading along with others that today feel stale, stiff, or dated. But it has had enormous influence over time, providing a model for modern moral essayists, including Montaigne and Emerson.

It's difficult to date any of Plutarch's writings absolutely or to establish their sequence, but it seems likely that most of the treatises in the *Moralia* precede the *Parallel Lives*. Indeed, one essay in the collection seems to show that, while Plutarch had not yet begun writing biography, he was thinking about the ethical possibilities the genre offered. In a work that taught how to measure one's progress toward virtue, Plutarch tells his addressee, Senecio, that those striving for moral betterment should

> set before their eyes those who are good or who have been so, and ponder "What would Plato have done in this situation? What would Epaminondas have said? How would Lycurgus or Agesilaus have appeared?," and just as if looking in a mirror, compose themselves differently, or change some mode of speech that is unworthy of themselves, or resist some strong emotion. . . . The thought and recollection of good men

> instantly comes to mind . . . and keeps upright those striving toward virtue, preventing their falls.[1]

The passage seems to anticipate the project that still lay ahead for Plutarch, the *Parallel Lives*—especially when we consider that three of the four inspirational models here mentioned later became subjects of those *Lives*, and one was probably the very first *Life* Plutarch undertook. (The paired lives of the Theban general Epaminondas and the Roman general Scipio once opened the collection of *Parallel Lives*; but these lives, along with at least one other pair, were lost in the work's transmission.)

The metaphor of biography as "mirror" —a reflecting medium by which one sees, and improves, oneself—was to become central to Plutarch as he progressed through the *Lives*, and deeply personal. It figures prominently in the opening sentence of the *Aemilius Paulus*, a passage that comes as close as any to being a mission statement for the *Lives* as a whole: "It first occurred to me to start the writing of *Lives* for the sake of other people, but now I stick to it and make myself at home there for my own sake, seeking by means of history to adorn myself, just as though looking in a mirror, and to make my life conform to the virtues of those men."

Plutarch goes on in this prologue to describe his biographical subjects as dining companions, welcomed sequentially into his home and marveled at, as King Priam (in the final episode of Homer's *Iliad*) once marveled at the beauty and power of Achilles. "I take from the deeds of each the principal and finest things that allow me to get to know them," Plutarch writes.

Plutarch's focus on the "finest things" among the deeds of great men might suggest that the *Lives* supply only positive exemplars. But elsewhere, as in the prologue to *Alexander*, Plutarch speaks of "the workings of virtue *or vice*" (my emphasis) as the matter of his narratives, and indeed Alexander was a creature of very mixed parts,

---

1 *Moralia* 85 A–B.

as was Achilles. The *Lives* lean toward the positive in their portrayals of character and occasionally hide blemishes, but they are far from hagiographic, and their ranks include several figures Plutarch does not regard as admirable. Interestingly, the *Lives* of these antiheroes—among the Greeks, Alcibiades, and among the Romans, Mark Antony—are some of the longest and richest of Plutarch's compositions, revealing a deeper engagement on the part of the author than the more positive portraits. "Nothing touches man but [Plutarch] feels it to be his," Emerson wrote in his introduction to the mid-nineteenth-century edition of Plutarch's works overseen by his friend, Arthur Hugh Clough; "he is tolerant even of vice, if he finds it genial." In his journals Emerson quoted approvingly Clough's judgment that *Antony*, the portrait of a dissolute, reckless charmer, was the very finest of all the *Lives*.

Plutarch had most likely returned to his native Chaeronea at the time he began the *Lives*, probably near the end of the first century CE, when he was about fifty. He had read widely in both Greek and Roman history by that time, so as to draw on a wide array of primary sources, some precise and reliable, others gossipy and anecdotal. Plutarch's wide range of source materials, his lack of discrimination in borrowing from them, and his insouciance with regard to the chronology and relative weight of the events he describes, makes the study of the *Parallel Lives* a frustrating pursuit for modern historians. But Plutarch never intended his work as a historical record. His own programmatic introduction to the *Alexander* serves, once again, as a valuable description of his technique:

> I shall make no other preface than to entreat my readers not to object if I fail to present exhaustive descriptions of all the famous actions of these men, but offer, for the most part, abridged accounts of them. For it is not histories I am writing, but lives; and the most glorious deeds do not always reveal the workings of virtue or vice. Frequently, a small thing—a phrase or flash of wit—gives more insight into a man's char-

> acter than battles where tens of thousands die, or vast arrays of troops, or sieges of cities. Accordingly, just as painters derive their likenesses from a subject's face and the expression of his eyes, where character shows itself, and attach little importance to other parts of the body, so must I be allowed to give more attention to the manifestations of a man's soul, and thereby mold an image of his life.

Plutarch would remain in Chaeronea the rest of his long life, serving the town as magistrate and the nearby shrine of Delphi as Priest of Apollo. He married, and his wife, Timoxena, had at least five children, among them four sons and a daughter who died in childhood (the death prompted Plutarch to compose one of his most moving essays, "A Consolation to His Wife"). He lived through the reign of Trajan, Rome's most beloved and successful emperor since the time of Augustus, and into at least the first few years of that of Hadrian. By the time he died, around 120 CE, the Roman empire was well into an era that Edward Gibbon famously termed "the most happy and prosperous" in the history of the world. Happy and prosperous too was the life he had led: a life rooted in study of the past, service to gods and mortals, and the quest for self-improvement through the contemplation of great historical figures, a quest he bequeathed to others by writing the *Parallel Lives*.

Modern readers of Plutarch's *Lives*, however, are usually not seeking the moral self-improvement their author intended, but rather an immersion in the events of the classical past and an encounter with its greatest personalities. For this reason nearly all recent editions of Plutarch's work, including the present one, have split up the paired *Lives* and reorganized them into clusters to highlight different eras of history. This new scheme obscures the *Parallel* part of the *Parallel Lives* and makes Plutarch's *syncrises*—the comparative essays with which he prefaced each pair of *Lives*, highlighting the ways that the characters of their Greek and Roman subjects might illuminate each other—all but irrelevant. But it allows a fuller exploration of a single place, time, and culture, and a richer sense of the historical context that surrounds its subjects, than the original, paired arrangement.

That historically informed reading is very much the experience our *Age of Caesar* seeks to provide. Plutarch's portraits of the five men included here show them to be emblematic of an era when force of character and personal ambition determined the fates of armies, nations, regimes. The conflicts that dominated the period play out, in Plutarch's biographical scheme, as contrasts in character: first between Julius Caesar and Pompey, two proud, stolid warriors striving to master the energies unleashed by Rome's expanding empire and increasingly professionalized armies; then between Caesar and Brutus, the first a restless man of action, the second a pensive philosopher-statesman driven to take up arms by forces beyond his control. Amid these clashes, Cicero and Antony pursued less fixed agendas, ending up on opposing sides and bound, for no inevitable reason, on a collision of their own. These two complex figures—Cicero a politician always looking for self-advancement and Antony a soldier driven by his lusts for combat, pleasure, and finally, ruinously, for Cleopatra—seem to have intrigued Plutarch most deeply; their quirks and (especially in Antony's case) flaws render them vividly, appealingly human.

In our explanatory notes and Appendix, and through a wonderful historical overview of the late Roman Republic by Mary Beard, we hope to make modern readers feel at home in the world of the first century BCE and allow them to follow Plutarch's biographies in close detail. It is hoped that their enjoyment of the five nearly contemporaneous *Lives* contained herein—those of Pompey, Caesar, Cicero, Brutus, and Antony—will not often be impeded by questions of terminology and nomenclature, questions that so often pose a barrier between ourselves and the classical world. The set of maps that precedes the volume will allow readers to locate most of the places mentioned in these *Lives* as the sites of important events, or to follow the course of the military campaigns that dominate their narratives.

There is further justification for presenting these five *Lives* in a single volume, detached from their Greek parallels.[2] As historian Christopher Pelling has convincingly shown,[3] four of the five—*Cicero* excluded—were composed by Plutarch at nearly the same time, based on a common set of source materials. Although the demonstrably earlier *Cicero*, we felt, had to be included because of its subject's historical importance, the remaining *Lives* contained herein form a uniquely interconnected and unified set, bound together by frequent cross-references and by shared events and concerns. The *Lives* of Cato the Younger and Marcus Licinius Crassus, which in Pelling's view may also have been part of this integrated project, were not selected for this volume, but the annotations highlight significant points where those *Lives* overlap with or differ from the ones presented here.

Among his many intellectual talents, Plutarch was a great prose stylist, and each new English version of his *Lives* grapples with the challenge of his complex, highly structured Greek sentences. The team overseen by John Dryden, in the late seventeenth century, succeeded so admirably that their version remains in print today, though many of its idioms are now out-of-date, and the Greek text on which it was based has been revised by subsequent scholars. Pamela Mensch's translation takes a sounder Greek text as its foundation, and brings Plutarch into line with modern usage, while still preserving much of the grace, solemnity, and elegance of the original. It is truly, we hope, a Plutarch for the twenty-first century.

Emerson closed his introduction to Clough's edition of Plutarch in elegiac tones, foreseeing the enduring relevance of the author it enshrined. "Plutarch's popularity will return in rapid cycles," he

---

2 For the record, those parallels were: *Demosthenes* (the companion to *Cicero*), *Agesilaus* (*Pompey*), *Dion* (*Brutus*), *Demetrius* (*Antony*), and, inevitably, *Alexander the Great* (*Julius Caesar*).

3 "Plutarch's Method of Work in the Roman Lives," ch. 1 of *Plutarch and History* (Swansea: Classical Press of Wales, 2011).

predicted. "His sterling values will presently recall the eye and thought of the best minds, and his books will be reprinted and read anew by coming generations. And thus Plutarch will be perpetually rediscovered from time to time as long as books last." It is the hope of the editor and translator of this volume that, even if "sterling values" are no longer at the forefront of our presentation of Plutarch, the publication of our *Age of Caesar* will help make Emerson a true prophet.

INTRODUCTION

MARY BEARD

The assassination of Julius Caesar on March 15, 44 BCE ("the Ides of March" by the Roman system of dating), is the most famous political murder in history. Caesar had recently been made "Dictator for Life" and he was killed in the name of "Liberty" by a group of men that he counted as friends and colleagues. In the aftermath, the assassins issued coins with a design specially chosen to celebrate the deed and press home the message: it featured the memorable date ("EID MAR"), a pair of daggers and the image of the small hat, "the cap of liberty," regularly presented to Roman slaves when they were granted their freedom. This was liberation on a grander scale, freeing the Roman people from tyranny.

All the characters whose biographies feature in this collection had some role in the story of the murder. Julius Caesar was the victim, his dying moments vividly described by Plutarch. In this account there were no famous last words, *"Et tu Brute?"* or whatever; after a futile attempt to fight back, Caesar pulled his toga over his head and took the twenty-three dagger blows that killed him. Brutus was the leading figure behind the assassination, a frankly messy business as Plutarch makes clear (with several of the assassins themselves "caught in friendly fire," accidentally wounded by blows from their own side), and he was soon more or less forced to leave the city. Cicero, the Roman politician, philosopher, poet, wit, and orator, was not party to the plot but was very likely an eyewitness of the murder, and was straightaway consulted by the assassins about what on earth to do next (one of their main problems was that they had not thought ahead). Antony was Caesar's right-hand man, gave the address at his funeral, and tried to take on the role of Caesar's defender and successor—though he soon found an even more powerful rival for that position. Pompey, with whom this collection opens, was already dead by 44. He had been killed four years earlier in a civil war, leading those Romans who had then been prepared to resort to pitched battles to resist the growing power of Caesar. But his shadow hung over the assassination. Caesar was murdered in an expensive new meeting hall whose building Pompey had funded and he fell in front of a statue of Pompey himself, splattering it with his blood. It was as if Pompey was finally getting his revenge.

The death of Caesar has provided the template for assassination ever since, and has been the focus of debate on the rights and wrongs of political violence. In 1865 John Wilkes Booth used the word "Ides" as the code word for the planned date of the assassination of President Lincoln. Shakespeare in his *Julius Caesar*, largely drawing on an early translation of Plutarch's biography, used the events of 44 BCE to reflect on the nature of political power, ideology, and moral conscience. Others have seen the assassination as a useful reminder of the futility of such attempts at direct action. For what did it achieve? If the assassins had really wanted to quash the rise of one-man rule in Rome, if they wanted to kill the tyranny as well as the tyrant, they were strikingly unsuccessful. More than a decade of civil war followed (a major theme in Plutarch's biographies of Brutus and Antony), but the end result was that Caesar's greatnephew—"Augustus," as he was later known—the man who rivaled Antony as Caesar's heir, became the first Roman emperor. He established autocratic rule on a permanent basis: so much for the return of "liberty."

In the long history of Rome, founded, as the Romans themselves calculated it, around 750 BCE, the murder of Caesar, for all its later notoriety, was just one of many political crises that became particularly intense and violent in the second and first centuries BCE. This was a period of expansion, political change, even revolution. It saw vast Roman conquests overseas and, as a consequence, an enormous influx of wealth into the city. Gleaming marble from Greece, rather than local brick and stone, now began to be used for temples and other public buildings in the city; captive slaves started to make up the majority of the workforce; and so many people flocked to Rome that its population topped a million, the only western city of that size until London in the early nineteenth century. But this age also saw repeated outbreaks of civil war at home, political disintegration, mass pogroms of citizens, and the final fracture of what had once been a more or less democratic system of government. As a leading politician, Caesar was almost typical in coming to a violent end. None of the men featured in this book died in their beds, nor fighting some "barbarian enemy." They were killed in conflict with other Romans, by Roman hands or on Roman orders. Pompey, for example, after losing in battle to Caesar, was decapitated by an Egyptian eunuch, ably assisted by a couple of Roman veteran soldiers; Cicero was put to death in 43 BCE in one of the pogroms, on Antony's instructions, his head and hands later pinned up in the center of Rome as macabre trophies, for the crowds to leer and jeer. A little over a decade later, Antony ended up killing himself after he had lost in battle to Caesar's greatnephew and successor.

The Romans described and fiercely debated the stresses and breakdown of their political system, trailing all kinds of explanations and possible solutions. For this period was also one of *intellectual* revolution at Rome, when the rich tradition of Roman literature began. Starting in the early second century BCE, Roman writers for the first time tried to tell the history of their city, to reflect on its problems and on how they thought it should be governed; and they used writing too for political attacks, insults in verse, self-advertisement in public, and for personal letters in which they shared their aspirations, fears, and suspicions. When Plutarch in the early second century CE was writing these biographies, he could base his narrative on plenty of contemporary material from the age of Caesar. Some of this we can still read, including Caesar's own, one-sided account of his campaigns against the tribes of Gaul and later against Pompey (one of the very few eyewitness descriptions of ancient warfare to have come down to us) and volumes of Cicero's political speeches, philosophical treatises, and hundreds of his private letters, made public after his death by his loyal heirs. This writing helps us to understand what underlay all that chaos.

The rapid growth of the Roman empire was one crucial, and destabilizing, factor. For us, *why* Rome grew in a few centuries from a small moderately successful town in central Italy to one with control over more of Europe and the Mediterranean world than any state before or since is one of history's big puzzles. Most modern observers put it down to some unfathomable combination of greed, a highly militaristic ideology, a dose of good luck, and a happy knack of converting those they conquered into Roman citizens, and so into new soldiers for the Roman cause. The Romans themselves were less puzzled on this score, pointing to the support of the gods, their own piety, and a succession of defensive rather than aggressive wars, in which they intervened to protect allies under threat. They were more troubled by the *consequences* of overseas growth for society and politics back home. Despite their popular modern image, Romans were not simply thoughtless and jingoistic imperialists. Some worried that the wealth and luxury, which came with conquest overseas, undermined what they saw as old-fashioned, tough Roman austerity, a few about the cruelty of conquest (there was even one, perhaps not entirely serious, proposal to put Caesar on trial for genocide during his conquest of Gaul). Others faced the question of how to adapt the traditional structures of Roman government to cope with new imperial demands. For how could you control and defend a vast empire, stretching from Spain to Syria, with a power structure and a system of military command developed to run nothing more than a small town?

That was one of the big issues behind the revolutionary changes of this period, and one of the factors that promoted the rise of dynasts such as Caesar. The political traditions of Rome, at least as far back to the end of the sixth century BCE, had been based on the principle that power was only ever held on a temporary basis and was always shared. The citizens as a whole elected the city's officials, who combined both military and civilian duties, held office for just one year at a time, ideally not to be repeated, and never had fully independent decision-making power. The fact that there had always been not one but two consuls (the most senior of these annual officials) is a clear sign of that long established commitment to *power sharing.* But it was a principle ill suited to governing a far-flung empire and to fighting wars that might take place several months distance from Italy; you could hardly travel there and back in the regular year of office. The Romans improvised various solutions to that problem, sending men out to the provinces, for example, *after* their year of office in Rome. But increasingly the Roman people voted more and more power into the hands of ambitious individual politicians on an almost permanent basis—even though those votes were often controversial and sometimes violently resisted.

Caesar was not the first to challenge the traditional model of power sharing. Despite leading the traditionalists against Caesar in 49 BCE, Pompey himself had, only fifteen years or so earlier, been granted unlimited power for years on end across the whole of the eastern Mediterranean, first to deal with the pirates and human traffickers operating on the sea, then to deal with one of Rome's remaining enemies in the East, King Mithradates of Pontus (in modern Turkey). Cicero was one of those who successfully spoke up, in a speech whose text we can still read, to quell the opposition to this grant, which saw it as a dangerous step in the direction of one-man rule. Even Brutus, despite his fine slogans on the subject of "liberty," seems not to have been entirely immune from similar dreams of personal power. The coin celebrating Caesar's assassination may have displayed the daggers and cap of liberty on one side. But on the other was an image of the head of Brutus himself. In Roman eyes, heads of living people on coins smacked of autocratic ambitions: Caesar was the first to risk such a display at Rome, Brutus the second.

So one side of the age of Caesar, richly documented in Plutarch's *Lives*, was a series of "big men," bankrolled by the vast profits that followed imperial conquests, competing for personal power. And that competition often came down to open fighting—whether in the streets of Rome itself, where there was no police force or any form of peacekeepers to maintain order, or across the empire more widely (the final battle in the Roman civil war between Caesar and Pompey was fought in northern Greece, and Pompey himself was brutally finished off on the coast of Egypt). As the coin of Brutus hints, the murder of Caesar came simply too late to put the clock back to old-fashioned power sharing. If Augustus had not established permanent one-man rule, Antony or some other rival would surely have done so.

Another important side of the period were the increasingly intense debates about what we would call "civil liberties." How was it possible to protect the rights of the individual Roman citizen in this violent turmoil? How were the rights of citizenship to be balanced against the safety of the state itself? This came to a head almost twenty years before Caesar's assassination, in 63 BCE. As Plutarch and others described it, Cicero was consul and believed that he had uncovered a terrorist plot, masterminded by a bankrupt and desperate aristocrat named Catiline, to eliminate some of the leading politicians, Cicero included, and to burn down much of the city. Once he had frightened Catiline out of Rome, Cicero rounded up those he believed were his accomplices and had them all executed without trial, even though they were Roman citizens and, as such, had a right to due legal process. *"Vixere"* ("they have lived"; that is, "they are dead"), he said in a particularly chilling euphemism, as he left the jail after supervising the execution.

Not everyone at the time approved. Caesar was one who objected, combining, as many have since, aspirations for dictatorship with a strong sense of popular justice. But in general Cicero was hailed as a hero who had saved the state from destruction. The popularity did not, however, last for long. Despite claiming the protection of an ancient equivalent of a Prevention of Terrorism Act, Cicero was soon banished into exile, on the charge of executing citizens without trial. He was recalled within a few months, but during his absence, his house had been demolished and a shrine to the goddess Liberty had pointedly been erected on the site. The rights and wrong of this case were debated ever after. How far, the Romans wondered, were elected officials allowed, or obliged, to transcend the law to save the state? As we now debate exactly how far the interests of Homeland Security make it legitimate to suspend the rights and protection that citizenship ought to offer, this is one of the causes célèbres that speak to us most directly.

The age of Caesar, then, was a world of political murder, street violence, constant warfare both inside and outside Rome, and fundamental disagreements about how the state should be run, how democracy and liberty might be preserved, while the demands of empire and security were met. It is impossible not to wonder what it was actually like to live through—and not just for the elite, rich, and male political leaders who were the leading characters and celebrity victims in the dramatic conflicts and the focus of all ancient writers. What of the ordinary men and women who were not in the limelight? Did life for them go on much as before, while the big men and their armies fought it out? Or did the violence and bloodshed touch almost everyone?

It is hard to know, and wrong to generalize. Just occasionally Plutarch does take his eyes off those at the very top of the pile and throw a fleeting glance at ordinary people carrying on with their lives more or less as usual in the chaos around them. We meet in passing Cicero's wives and his daughter, Tullia, who like so many women in the Roman world died from complications of childbirth, along with her infant son. We have a glimpse of an enterprising trader from north Italy, a man called Peticius, who in 48 BCE just happened to be traveling in his ship along the coast of Greece when he spotted Pompey, on the run after his defeat by Caesar—and gave him a lift south. And most engaging of all, thanks to information he had picked up from his grandfather, Plutarch gives us a tiny but vivid insight into the practices "below stairs" in the kitchens of the palace in Alexandria that—to the horror of many Romans—Antony eventually came to share with Queen Cleopatra. Apparently, the cooks were so concerned about preparing the wild boar to perfection, whenever the company upstairs decided to eat, that they had *eight* boars roasting, each put on to cook at a different time, so that one would be sure to be just right when dinner was summoned. It is a nice image of ordinary people living in their own world, and dealing in their own way with (and maybe laughing at) the capricious demands of the world leaders they served.

But not all were so lucky. One memorable story told by Plutarch, repeated and made even more famous by Shakespeare in his *Julius Caesar,* tells the fate of an unfortunate poet called Cinna. This man was not quite as ordinary as Peticius or the cooks in Alexandria; he was actually a friend of Caesar but he was not in the political mainstream. A couple of days after the assassination he went to the Forum to see his friend laid out for his funeral, and fell in with a crowd of Caesar's mourning and angry supporters. These men mistook the poet for a different Cinna, a man who had been one of the assassins, and so tore the poor man limb from limb. The message of the story is clear. Assassinations have innocent victims too. Simple cases of mistaken identity (and there must have been many of those at Rome, in the absence of any form of official ID) can leave a blameless bystander dead. Shakespeare's plaintive line "I am Cinna the poet, I am Cinna the poet" is a haunting reminder of the many who must have been caught in the crossfire when the leaders of the Roman world clashed.

MAPS

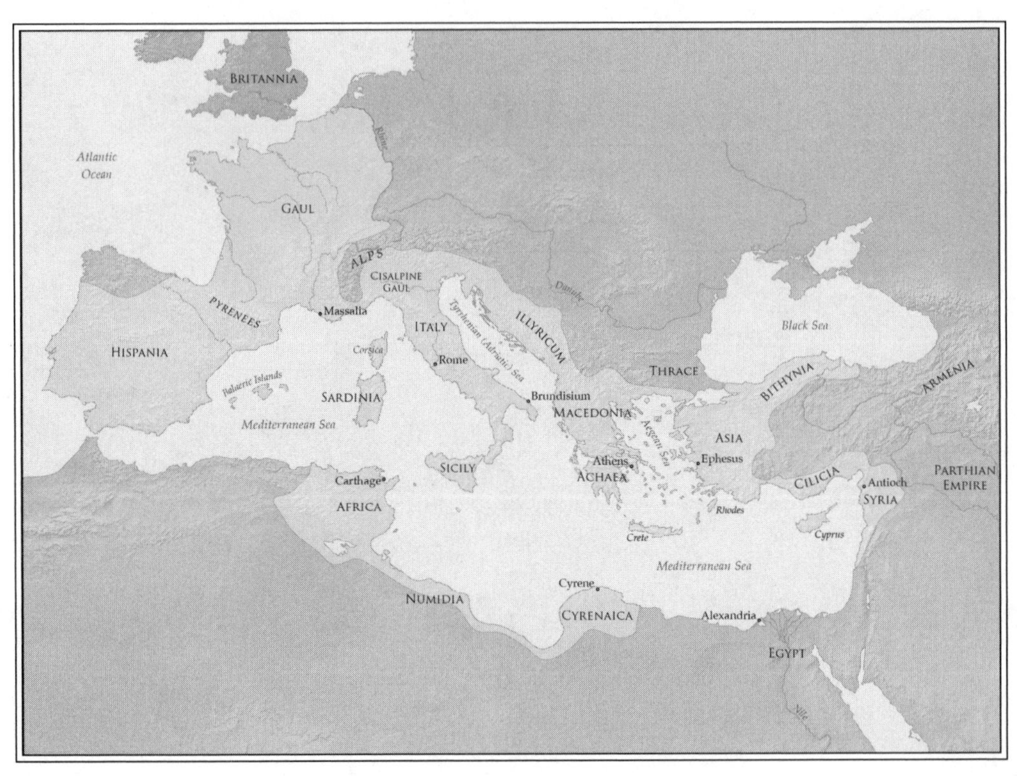

THE ROMAN EMPIRE IN THE TIME OF JULIUS CAESAR

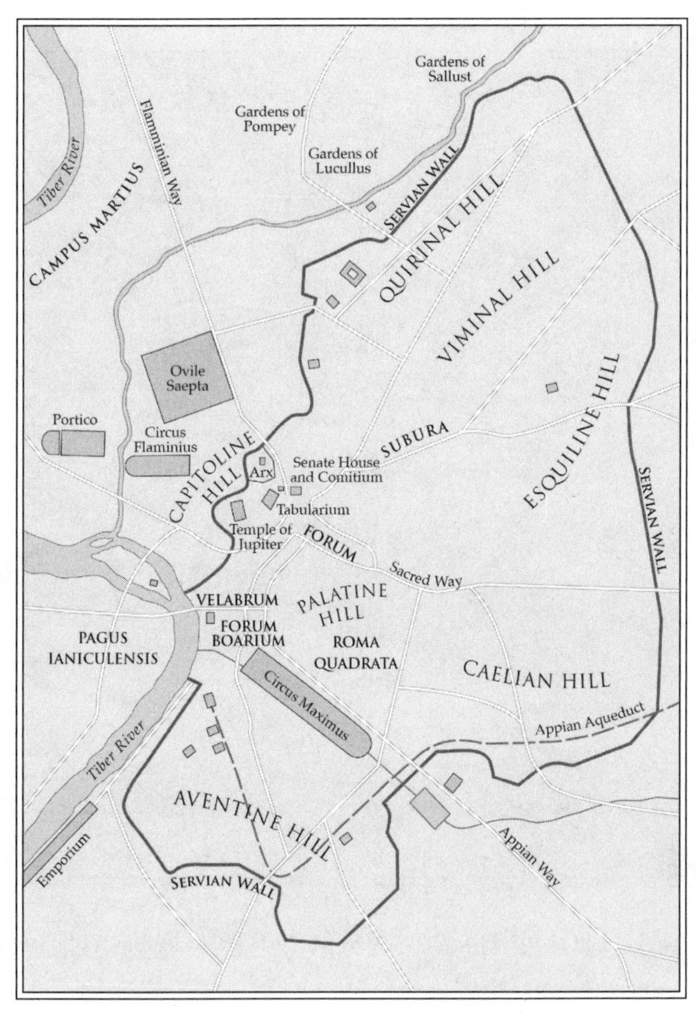

ROME IN THE TIME OF JULIUS CAESAR

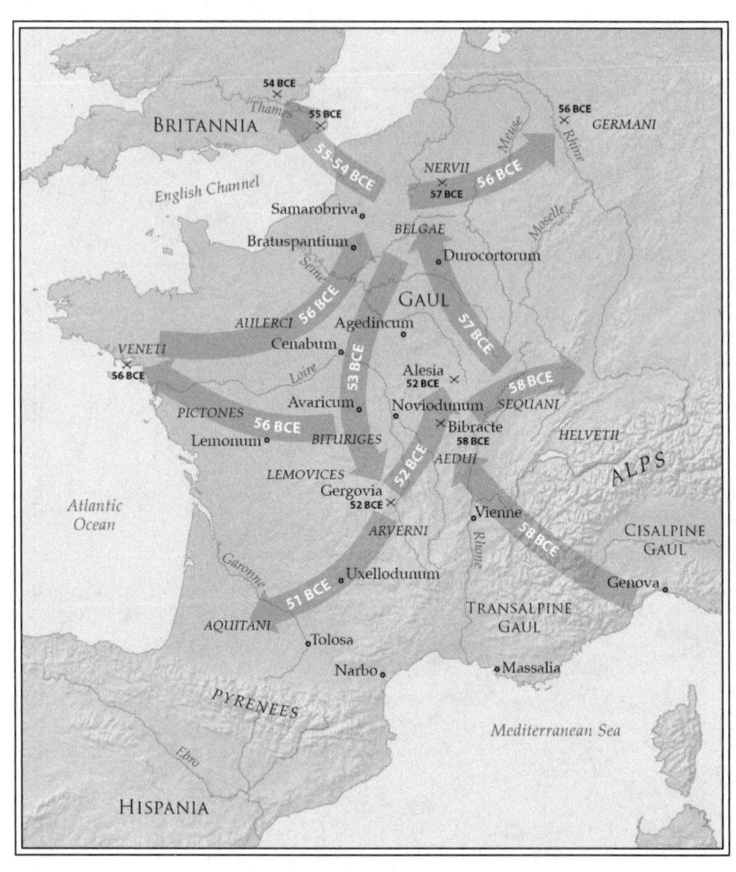

JULIUS CAESAR'S CAMPAIGNS IN GAUL

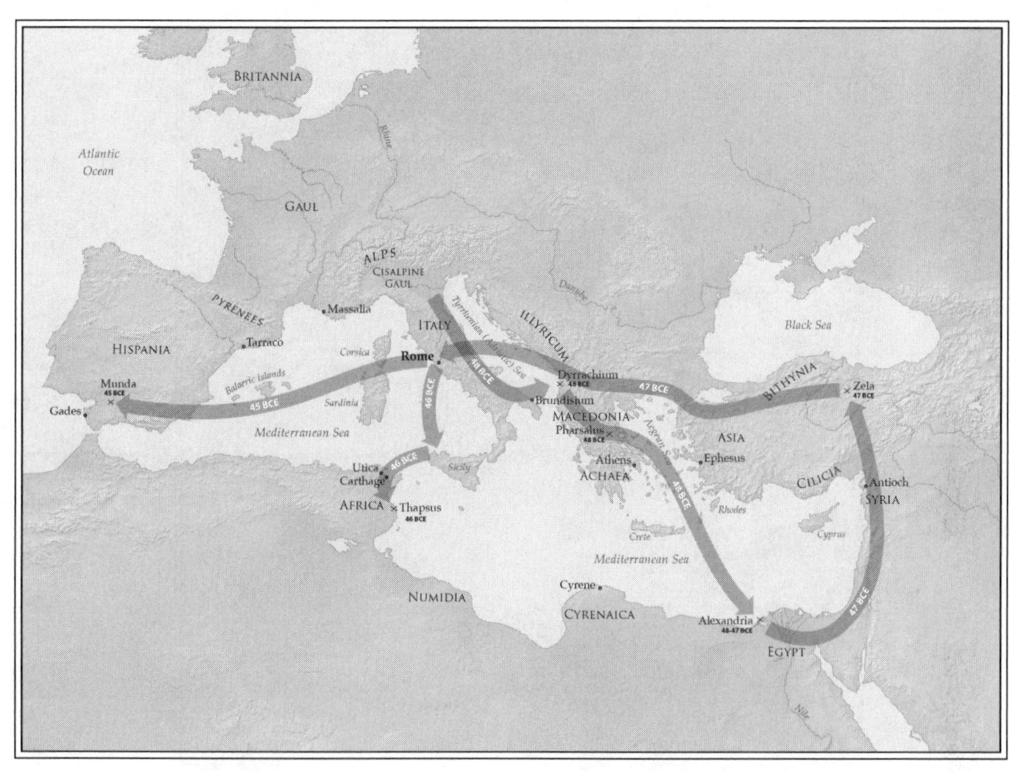

MOVEMENTS OF JULIUS CAESAR IN HIS CAMPAIGNS AGAINST POMPEY AND THE SENATORIAL FORCES

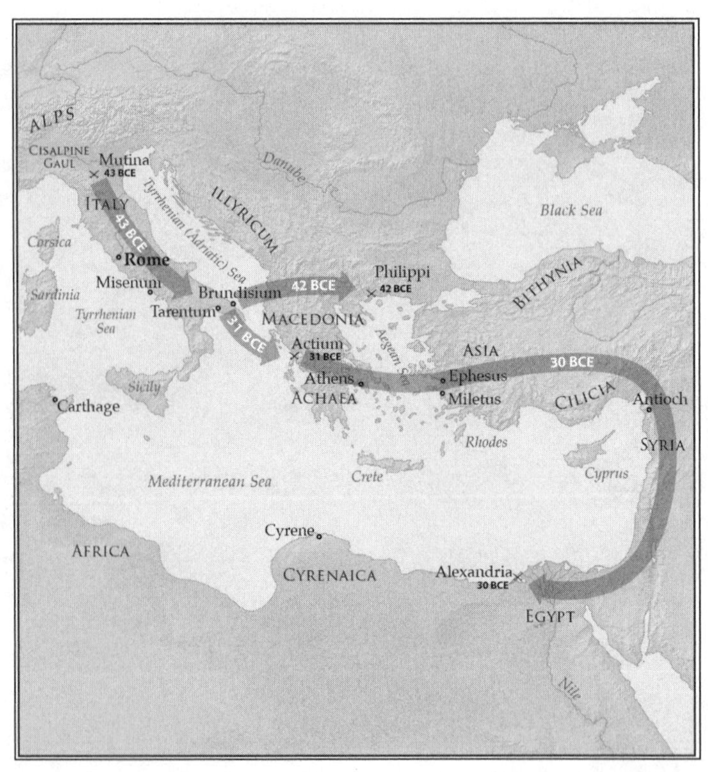

MOVEMENTS OF OCTAVIAN AND ANTONY AGAINST BRUTUS AND CASSIUS (43–42 BCE), AND OF OCTAVIAN AGAINST ANTONY (31–30 BCE)

PLUTARCH

FIVE ROMAN LIVES

POMPEY

The Roman people seem to have entertained for Pompey, from the very start, the same feeling the Prometheus of Aeschylus expresses for Heracles[1] when, after being saved by him, he says,

Most dear to me this child, whose father I hate.

For the Romans had never harbored a hatred so powerful and savage for any of their generals as they did for Strabo,[2] the father of Pompey; while he lived they feared his power in arms (for he was a consummate warrior), but when he died, struck by a thunderbolt, and his body was being carried out for burial, they dragged it from the bier and showered it with insults. Yet no Roman has enjoyed a deeper goodwill, or one that sprang up sooner or reached a greater height when he was prospering, or abided so constantly when he had stumbled, than Pompey. And whereas there was only one cause of their hatred for Strabo, namely his insatiable avarice, there were

---

1 Prometheus, the defiant god whom Zeus orders chained to a mountain crag in Aeschylus' tragedy *Prometheus Bound*, was ultimately freed by Heracles, son of Zeus, as recounted in a lost play, *Prometheus Unbound*, from which Plutarch here quotes.

2 Gnaeus Pompeius Strabo (135–87 BCE), no relation to the geographer Strabo, was a military commander widely reviled for his self-serving part in the Social War between Rome and its Italian allies and the civil war between Marius and Sulla.

many reasons for their adoration of Pompey: his temperate way of life, his military training, his persuasive speech, the trustworthiness of his character, and his affability when meeting people, since no one asked a favor with less offense, or bestowed one with more grace. For in addition to his other talents, he had the ability to give without oppressing, and to receive without losing his dignity.

2. In his youth his handsome looks won him great popularity, and captivated his hearers even before he spoke. His beauty as a boy had something in it of benevolence and dignity, and in the prime of his manhood the majesty and kingliness of his character at once became visible in it. His hair rose in a slight wave from his forehead, and this, with the flickering motion of his eyes, created a resemblance, more talked of than really apparent, to the statues of King Alexander.[3] And for this reason many applied that name to him in his youth; Pompey himself did not decline it, so that some called him Alexander in mockery. And therefore Lucius Philippus, a man of consular rank, when he was pleading in favor of him, said he was doing nothing unusual if, being a Philip, he was fond of Alexander.[4]

It is related of Flora the courtesan[5] that when she was quite old she always liked to recall her former intimacy with Pompey, and used to say that she never went away after sleeping with him without bearing the mark of his bite. She would also describe how Geminius, one of Pompey's companions, fell in love with her and pestered her greatly with his attentions; and when she explained that she had to refuse him because of Pompey, Geminius took the matter up with him. Pompey, accordingly, turned her over to Geminius and never afterward consorted with her, though he was thought to have a passion for her; and she herself did not bear this treatment in

---

3 The portrait busts of Alexander created by Lysippus, and later imitated by others, show a distinctive parting of the hair and an emotional cast of the eyes.

4 A different Philip, Philip II of Macedon, was father to Alexander the Great.

5 Evidently an early lover of Pompey, mentioned again at chapter 53 below.

the manner of a courtesan, but was ill for a considerable time from grief and longing. This Flora, they say, bloomed into such beauty that when Caecilius Metellus was adorning the temple of Castor and Pollux with statues and paintings, he included her portrait among his votive offerings. In his conduct also with the wife of Demetrius, his freedman (who had great influence with him and left an estate of four thousand talents), Pompey acted, contrary to his usual habits, not fairly or generously, fearing that he might appear to be vanquished by her beauty, which was irresistible and widely spoken of. But though he was extremely circumspect and guarded, yet even in matters of this nature he did not escape the censures of his enemies, but was accused of affairs with married women, for whose gratification he is said to have neglected and compromised many public interests.

With regard to his simplicity and plainness in eating and drinking, the following story is told. Once when he was ill and nauseated by food, a physician prescribed him a thrush to eat. But when his servants, on searching, found none for sale (for they were not then in season), and someone said they could be found at the house of Lucullus,[6] since he kept them all year round, Pompey asked, "So if Lucullus were not luxurious, Pompey could not live?" And disregarding the physician, he took something that could easily be procured. But this was at a later time.

3. While he was still a very young man, and serving in an expedition that his father was commanding against Cinna,[7] he had a certain Lucius Terentius as a companion and tentmate. This man, bribed by Cinna, was himself going to kill Pompey, while others were to

---

6 Lucullus was a general and politician of the early first century BCE, famous for his gourmandizing and sumptuous expenditures. Plutarch made him the subject of one of his *Lives*.

7 In the power struggle between the factions of Sulla and Marius, in the mid-80s BCE, Strabo played a shifting role; at this point (87 BCE) he was opposing Lucius Cornelius Cinna, an ally of Marius.

set fire to Strabo's tent. Pompey was informed of this conspiracy while at supper. He was not at all disconcerted, but on the contrary drank more freely than usual and expressed great affection for Terentius. But when he had retired to rest, he slipped out of his tent unnoticed, set a guard about his father, and quietly awaited the outcome. Terentius, when he thought the right moment had come, rose with his drawn sword, came to Pompey's couch, and stabbed many times through the bedclothes, as if Pompey were lying there. After this there was a great uproar, arising from the hatred felt toward Strabo, and an impulse to revolt on the part of the soldiers, who tore down their tents and took up their weapons. The general, fearing the tumult, did not come forward, but Pompey, going about among the soldiers, entreated them with tears, and finally threw himself face-down before the gate of the camp and lay in their way, weeping and bidding those who were marching off to trample on him. At this, everyone drew back out of shame, and all except eight hundred changed their minds and were reconciled to the general.

4. As soon as Strabo was dead,[8] Pompey, as his heir, was put on trial for his father's embezzlement of public property. And though Pompey discovered that most of the thefts had been perpetrated by a certain Alexander, a freedman of his father's, and proved this to the magistrates, he himself was accused of having in his possession some hunting nets and books that were taken at Asculum.[9] These items Pompey had indeed received from his father when Strabo took Asculum, but he had lost them when, on Cinna's return to Rome, Pompey's house was broken into and plundered by Cinna's guards. In this trial he made many preparatory pleadings against his accuser, in which he showed an astuteness and composure beyond his years, and gained great reputation and favor. As a result Antistius, the praetor and judge in the case, took a great liking to him and offered

---

8 By lightning, as mentioned in chapter 1 above.

9 Asculum, the first Italian town to revolt from Rome at the start of the Social War, was captured by Strabo in a siege in 89 BCE.

him his daughter in marriage, and conferred with friends about it. Pompey accepted the proposal, and a private contract was drawn up; but the people came to know of it from the trouble Antistius took to favor Pompey. And finally, when Antistius announced that the judges had voted to acquit, the people, as if a signal had been given, shouted out, "For Talasius!"—the ancient and traditional acclamation at marriages.

The custom is said to have this origin: At the time when the daughters of the Sabines came to Rome to see a spectacle of games, and were abducted by the most distinguished and bravest of the Romans to be their wives,[10] certain laborers and herdsmen of obscure rank were carrying off a tall and beautiful girl. And lest any of their superiors should meet them and take her away, they cried out, "For Talasius" as they ran (Talasius being a well-known and popular figure), so that everyone who heard the name clapped their hands and joined them in the shout, as if they were rejoicing and commending what they were doing. Now, they say, because the marriage proved a fortunate one for Talasius,[11] this acclamation is used humorously as a nuptial greeting at weddings. This is the most plausible of the accounts given about Talasius. In any event, a few days after the trial, Pompey married Antistia.

5. Then he went to Cinna's camp;[12] but alarmed by some false accusation, he quickly departed unnoticed. His disappearance excited suspicion, and a rumor spread through the camp that Cinna had murdered the young man; then all who had long resented and

---

10 The legendary rape of the Sabine women, an event of mythic history dating all the way back to the era of Rome's founding (eighth century BCE). Plutarch retells the same legend about the cry "for Talasius" at chapter 15 of his *Romulus*; the story ultimately derived from Livy (1.9.12).

11 It's unclear why Plutarch speaks here of the marriage to Talasius, formerly portrayed as a fiction, as having actually taken place.

12 Perhaps in an attempt to switch from the side supported by his father, the faction of Sulla.

hated Cinna resolved to go after him. Cinna, trying to flee, was seized by one of the centurions, who pursued him with his drawn sword, whereupon Cinna, falling upon his knees, offered the man his seal ring, an object of great value. But the centurion, retorting insolently, said, "I have not come to seal a guarantee, but to punish a lawless and abominable tyrant," and slew him. Cinna having died in this way, Carbo, a tyrant even more unstable, received and exercised the supreme command. But Sulla was approaching,[13] to the joy and satisfaction of most people, who in their present plight considered a change of masters no small comfort. To such a pass had the city been brought by its misfortunes that, in despair of liberty, it sought only a more tolerable servitude.

6. At that time Pompey was in Picenum in Italy, as he had estates there, though the greater motive of his stay was the liking he felt for the towns in that district, which were affectionately and kindly disposed toward him as his father's son. But when he saw that the noblest and best of the citizens were forsaking their homes and hastening from all sides to Sulla's camp as to a haven, he himself did not think it right to go to Sulla as a fugitive, or with nothing to offer, or requesting his help; instead he should first confer some favor in a way that would gain him honor, and arrive at the head of a body of troops. He therefore solicited the people of Picenum for their assistance. They gladly listened to him and paid no heed to the messengers sent from Carbo. In fact, when a certain Vedius said that Pompey had jumped straight from pedagogy into demagogy,[14] they were so incensed that they fell at once upon Vedius and killed him.

After this, Pompey, though he was only twenty-three, and had not been appointed general by anyone, conferred the command

---

13 On his return from the Mithridatic War in the East, in 83 BCE (see Plutarch's biography of this military leader, *Sulla*, ch. 27). Cinna had died the previous year.

14 A joke at the expense of Pompey's youth. "Pedagogy" in this case refers to the period in which a young boy is overseen by his tutors and guardians.

upon himself. Setting up a tribunal in the marketplace of Auximum, a large city, he issued a public edict, ordering the chief men (two brothers named Ventidius, who were acting against him in Carbo's interest) to leave the city. He then proceeded to levy soldiers, and after issuing commissions to centurions and other officers in proper form, he went around to the other cities, doing the same thing. All of Carbo's partisans yielded and withdrew, and everyone else cheerfully offered Pompey his services, so that in a little while he had mustered three entire legions and supplied them with food, baggage wagons, carriages, and other necessities of war. Then he advanced toward Sulla, not as if he were in a hurry or eager to avoid detection, but halting often on the way to harass the enemy, and doing what he could to wrest from Carbo's control all the Italian territory through which he passed.

7. Three enemy commanders—Carinas, Cloelius, and Brutus[15]—encountered him at the same time, not all head-on, or from a single direction, but surrounding him with three armies in order to overwhelm him. Pompey, however, was not alarmed, but collected all his troops into one body and hastened against the army of Brutus, having stationed his horsemen, among whom he rode, at the head of his forces. And when from the enemy's side the Celtic horsemen rode out to meet him, he himself fought hand to hand with the first and strongest of them, struck him with his spear, and brought him down. The others then turned and fled, threw their own infantry into confusion, and caused a general rout. After this the opposing generals, quarreling among themselves, retired as best they could, and the cities came over to Pompey, thinking that the enemy had dispersed out of fear. Next, Scipio the consul came to attack him; but before their front ranks were within range of each other's javelins, Scipio's soldiers saluted Pompey and came over to him, and

15 Possibly Marcus Junius Brutus—the father of the more famous Brutus, who helped assassinate Julius Caesar—but more likely Lucius Junius Brutus Damasippus.

Scipio took to flight.[16] Finally, Carbo himself sent many troops of horsemen against him by the river Arsis; resisting them stoutly, Pompey routed them, and in the pursuit forced them onto difficult ground, unsuitable for horses, where, seeing no hope of escape, they surrendered to him with their armor and horses.

8. Sulla had not yet learned of these actions, but at the first news and reports grew anxious about Pompey, engaged as he was with so many and such experienced enemy generals, and hastened to his aid. But when Pompey learned that Sulla was near, he ordered his officers to get their men fully armed and draw them up in array, that they might make the finest and most splendid appearance before the *imperator*; for he expected great honors from him, and met with even greater. For when Sulla saw him advancing with a remarkable army of brave young men, their spirits elated and encouraged by their successes, he sprang from his horse, and after being saluted, as was proper, with the title of *imperator*, he in turn saluted Pompey as *imperator*,[17] though no one would have expected Sulla to address a young man, and one who was not yet a senator, with a title that was the object of contention between him and the Scipios and Marii. And all the rest of his behavior was in keeping with these first friendly gestures; he would rise to his feet when Pompey approached, and uncover his head—things he was rarely seen doing with anyone else, though there were many worthy men about him.

Yet Pompey was not puffed up by these things; and when Sulla would have sent him at once into Gaul, a province in which it was

---

16 Lucius Cornelius Scipio was consul in 83 BCE. In his *Sulla*, Plutarch tells the story of the desertion of Scipio's forces, but with Sulla, not Pompey, as the general whom they joined (ch. 28).

17 The honorific *imperator* ("commander") was awarded by a general's troops, or sometimes by the Roman Senate, to commemorate important victories. Sulla here has no right to grant the title, but uses it anyway as a kind of extravagant courtesy.

thought Metellus,[18] who commanded there, was doing nothing worthy of the large forces at his disposal, he said it was not right for him to take a province out of the hands of his senior in command and his superior in reputation; but if Metellus were willing, and ordered him to do so, he was prepared to assist him in the war. And when Metellus accepted the proposal and wrote to him to come, he immediately hastened into Gaul, where he achieved wonderful exploits by himself, and fired up and rekindled that bold and warlike spirit that old age was now extinguishing in Metellus, just as molten bronze, when poured upon that which is rigid and cold, is said to dissolve and melt it down faster than fire itself. But just as an athlete who has gained the first place among men, and carried away the prizes at all the games, takes no account of his victories as a boy and leaves them unrecorded, so it is with the exploits of Pompey at that time, though they were extraordinary in themselves; but because they have been buried in the multitude and greatness of his later wars and contests, I am afraid to recur to them, lest by spending too much time on the deeds of his youth I leave no room for those actions and experiences that were greatest, and that best illustrate his character.

9. When Sulla had gained control of Italy and was proclaimed dictator, he began to reward the rest of his officers and generals by making them rich, advancing them to offices, and granting them freely and without reservation any favors they requested. And, as he admired Pompey's integrity, and thought the man might be of great use to him in his affairs, Sulla was eager to attach him to himself by some family relationship. His wife, Metella, sharing his wishes, they persuaded Pompey to divorce Antistia and marry Aemilia, Sulla's stepdaughter (Metella's daughter by Scaurus), though she already had a husband and was expecting a child.

This marriage, accordingly, was a product of tyranny, and suited the advantage of Sulla rather than the character and habits of

18 Quintus Caecilius Metellus, dubbed "Pius" to distinguish him from a son who bore the same name (but is generally known as "Celer").

Pompey, Aemilia being given to him in marriage when pregnant by another, and Antistia being driven away with dishonor and misery by him, for whose sake she had recently been deprived of her father. For Antistius had been murdered in the Senate house because he was suspected of favoring Sulla for Pompey's sake; and Antistia's mother, on witnessing these outrageous acts, had committed suicide. Hence this misfortune was added to the tragedy of that marriage; and as the crowning blow, Aemilia, as soon as she entered Pompey's house, died in childbirth.

10. After this, news came to Sulla that Perpenna[19] was taking possession of Sicily and making the island a refuge for the survivors of the opposition party, that Carbo was hovering about those seas with a fleet, that Domitius[20] had invaded Africa, and that many other prominent exiles were flocking there—as many as had managed to escape his proscriptions. Against these men Pompey was sent with a large force. Perpenna immediately abandoned Sicily to him. Pompey received its distressed cities, and treated all of them except the Mamertines[21] in Messene with great kindness. When they deprecated his court and jurisdiction, alleging that these were forbidden by an ancient Roman law, Pompey replied, "Will you not stop quoting laws to us who have our swords by our sides?" He was also thought to have treated the unfortunate Carbo with an inhuman insolence. For if there had been a necessity, as perhaps there was, to put the man to death, it should have been done as soon as he was seized, for then it would have been the act of the man who ordered it. But here Pompey commanded a man who had been three times

---

19 The man whom Plutarch mistakenly calls Perpenna was Marcus Perperna Vento, a prominent general of the Marian faction. See Plutarch's *Sertorius* 15 and 25–27.

20 Gnaeus Domitius Ahenobarbus, another Marian general and an ancestor of Nero.

21 A cohort of hardened soldiers, the descendants of a corps of mercenaries first brought to Sicily several centuries earlier.

consul to be brought in shackles to stand before the rostrum, where he himself was sitting in judgment, and interrogated him closely, to the distress and indignation of the audience. Then he ordered him to be led away and put to death. It is also reported that when Carbo had been led to the place of execution, and saw the sword already drawn, he asked that a convenient place and a brief time might be afforded him, as his bowels were giving him trouble. And Gaius Oppius, the friend of Caesar,[22] says that Pompey also dealt cruelly with Quintus Valerius, a man known to be of exceptional learning and science. For when Valerius was brought to him, Pompey drew him aside and walked up and down with him, asked and learned what he wished to know, and then ordered his officers to lead him away and put him to death. But whenever Oppius speaks about the enemies or friends of Caesar, we must not be too credulous.

Pompey was compelled to punish those enemies of Sulla who were especially eminent and whose capture was common knowledge; as for the rest, he let as many as possible escape detection, and even helped some to get away. When, for example, he had decided to punish the city of Himera, which had sided with the enemy, Sthenis, the city's popular leader, asked Pompey for an audience and said he would be acting unjustly if he let the guilty party go and destroyed the innocent. And when Pompey asked him whom he meant by the guilty party, Sthenis said he meant himself, since he had persuaded his friends, and forced his enemies, to do as they had done. Delighted with the frankness and spirit of the man, Pompey pardoned him first, and then all the others. Furthermore, when he learned that his soldiers were disorderly in their journeys, he put a seal upon their swords, and whoever broke the seal was punished.

11. While attending to these matters and arranging the affairs of Sicily, he received a decree from the Senate and a letter from Sulla

---

22 Gaius Oppius, a politician of the mid-first century BCE, authored several now lost historical treatises. Plutarch shows an admirable skepticism in questioning his reliability.

ordering him to sail to Africa to make war upon Domitius with all his forces. For Domitius had mustered an army many times larger than that with which Marius, not long before, had crossed from Africa into Italy and caused a revolution in Rome, making himself a tyrant instead of an exile.[23] Pompey, accordingly, after making all his preparations with the utmost speed, left Memmius, his sister's husband, as governor of Sicily, while he himself set sail with one hundred twenty warships and eight hundred transports carrying provisions, weapons, money, and siege engines. When he had landed with part of his fleet at Utica and with part at Carthage, seven thousand of the enemy revolted and came over to him; the forces that he brought with him consisted of six entire legions.[24]

Something absurd is reported to have happened to him then. Some of his soldiers, it would seem, having stumbled upon a treasure, got a good sum of money. When the incident became public, the rest of the army began to imagine that the place was full of money that had been hidden there by the Carthaginians at some time of misfortune. Accordingly, Pompey was unable for many days to do anything with his soldiers, who were engaged in hunting for treasure. He himself went about laughing to see so many thousands of men digging and turning up the earth. Finally, abandoning their search, they urged Pompey to lead them where he pleased, declaring that they had been punished enough for their folly.

12. Domitius had drawn up his army against Pompey; but there was a ravine between them, craggy and hard to cross; at the same time, a great storm of wind and rain had been pouring down since morning, so that he gave up all thought of fighting that day and commanded his troops to retreat. But Pompey, who had been watching for this opportunity, quickly advanced and crossed the ravine. The enemy was in great confusion and disorder, and not all of them were

---

23 Marius' return to Italy from Africa, in 87 BCE, is described at *Marius* 41–43.

24 About thirty-six thousand troops.

there, nor did they resist with any uniformity; and the wind, having shifted, drove the rain full in their faces. The Romans were also troubled by the storm, since they could not see one another clearly, and Pompey himself, not being recognized, narrowly escaped death; for when one of the soldiers asked him for the password he was somewhat slow to answer.

But having routed the enemy with a great slaughter (for they say that of twenty thousand, only three thousand escaped), they hailed Pompey as *imperator.* And when he said he could not accept that title as long as the camp of the enemy was standing, but that if they thought to make him worthy of the honor they must first demolish *that,* they instantly assaulted the fortifications, and there Pompey fought without his helmet, in fear of his former danger.[25] The camp was thus taken, and Domitius perished. Then some of the cities surrendered at once, and the others were taken by storm. Pompey also captured King Iarbas, a confederate of Domitius, and gave his kingdom to Hiempsal.[26]

Taking advantage of the good fortune and impetus of his army, he invaded Numidia. He advanced through the country for many days, conquering all whom he encountered, and revived the barbarians' fear of the Roman power, which had all but faded away. He even said that the wild beasts of Africa should not be left without some experience of the courage and strength of the Romans. Accordingly, he spent a few days hunting lions and elephants. And it is said that it took him only forty days, all told, to overthrow his enemies, subdue Africa,[27] and settle the affairs of its kings, though he was then only twenty-four years old.

---

25 Referring to the earlier part of this chapter, in which Pompey had briefly gone unrecognized.

26 A king of Numidia and a supporter of Sulla, Hiempsal had earlier been deposed by Iarbas, who took Marius' side in the civil war.

27 "Africa" here translates the Greek *Libya*; both terms referred primarily to North Africa, and usually excluded Egypt.

13. On his return to Utica, a letter was brought to him from Sulla, ordering him to dismiss the rest of his army, but to remain there himself with one legion and await the general who was to succeed him. Pompey himself did not let on how distressed he was at this order, but his soldiers resented it openly. And when Pompey begged them to go home ahead of him, they began to malign Sulla and declared that they refused to forsake their general, and urged him not to trust the tyrant. At first Pompey tried to soothe and pacify them; but when he could not persuade them, he descended from the rostrum[28] and departed to his tent in tears. Then his soldiers seized him and set him again on the rostrum, where a great part of the day was spent in dispute, his men pressing him to remain and command them, and he entreating them to obey and not to mutiny. At last, when they grew even more importunate and clamorous, he swore he would kill himself if they attempted to force him, and even then they scarcely desisted.

The first news that reached Sulla was that Pompey had revolted. Sulla told his friends it was his fate to contend with children in his old age; for Marius too, who was a very young man, had given him a great deal of trouble, and involved him in the utmost danger. But when he learned the truth and saw everyone rushing forth to welcome Pompey and accompany him home with great affection, he was eager to outdo them. He therefore went out ahead to meet him, and after embracing him with great cordiality, hailed him in a loud voice as "Magnus" (which means "the Great"),[29] and ordered those who were present to call him by that name. Others, however,

---

28 Evidently the army camp had a speaker's platform from which Pompey could address his troops. The platform officially termed "rostrum" stood in the Forum at Rome; it was called either rostrum or rostra because it was adorned with the beaks (*rostra*) of captured enemy warships.

29 As indicated here, Plutarch first transliterates the Latin word *Magnus* and then translates it into Greek. Magnus became a kind of surname for Pompey later in life, as Plutarch goes on to say.

say that this title was first given him in Africa by the whole army, but acquired authority and weight by Sulla's confirmation. Pompey himself was the last of all to use it; for it was a long time after, when he was sent as proconsul against Sertorius,[30] that he began to sign his letters and decrees "Pompeius Magnus," since by then the name had become familiar and no longer excited envy.

One should therefore respect and admire the ancient Romans, who did not bestow such titles and surnames as a reward for successful wars and commands only, but also adorned the achievements and virtues of their statesmen with the same tokens of honor. In two instances, at any rate, the people bestowed the title "Maximus," which means "the Greatest": upon Valerius, for reconciling the Senate and people; and upon Fabius Rullus, because he expelled from the Senate certain descendants of freedmen who had been enrolled in it on account of their wealth.[31]

14. Pompey now asked for a triumph,[32] but Sulla turned him down. For the law granted that honor to a consul or a praetor only, and to no one else. And therefore Scipio the elder, who had subdued the Carthaginians in Spain in far greater and nobler contests, did not request a triumph; for he was not a consul, nor even a praetor.[33] And if Pompey, who had scarcely yet grown a beard, and was not of age to be a senator, entered the city in triumph, it would render Sulla's government and Pompey's honor altogether obnoxious. This was what Sulla said

---

30 See 17–21 below.

31 Two examples taken from early Roman history; Marcus Valerius Maximus belongs to the early fifth century BCE, Fabius Rullus Maximus, the subject of a Plutarchan life, belongs to the late fourth.

32 The Roman triumphal procession, in which a conquering general was conducted through the city amid great pomp and festivity, was a potent means of political advancement; the right to hold such triumphs was carefully controlled by the Senate and, in this case, the dictator.

33 Scipio Africanus defeated the Carthaginians in Spain in 210 and 209 BCE, before attaining the consulship in 205.

to Pompey, declaring that he would not grant his request, but would oppose him and thwart his ambition if he refused to obey him.

Pompey, however, did not cower, but urged Sulla to bear in mind that more people worshipped the rising than the setting sun, implying that his own power was increasing and Sulla's on the wane. Sulla did not hear the words perfectly, but seeing, from their looks and gestures, that those who *had* heard him were amazed, he asked what he had said. When he learned what it was, he was shocked at Pompey's boldness, and cried out twice in succession, "Let him triumph." And when many were offended and displeased with him, Pompey, wishing all the more to annoy them, tried to drive into the city on a chariot drawn by four elephants; for he had brought several from Africa that he had captured from its kings. But since the gates of the city were too narrow, he gave up the idea, and switched to his horses. And when his soldiers, who had not received the rewards they had expected, wanted to make trouble and raise a rumpus, Pompey said he could hardly care less, and would rather dispense with the triumph than flatter them. At this, Servilius, a man of great distinction, who had been most opposed to Pompey's triumph, said he now saw that Pompey was truly great and worthy of a triumph. It is clear that Pompey might easily have become a senator at the time, had he wished it.[34] But he was not eager for that, since he was ambitious, as they say, only for honors that were distinctive. For it would not have been surprising for Pompey to serve in the Senate before he was of age, whereas it was exceptionally glorious for him to celebrate a triumph before he was a senator. And this did much to endear him to the people, who were delighted that after a triumph he was still classed among the knights.[35]

---

34 Roman constitutional rules required a minimum age of thirty for appointment as quaestor, a precursor to the Senate (see Appendix). Plutarch implies that the rules could have been bent to allow Pompey into the Senate at a younger age.

35 Under Rome's class-stratified constitution, the knights or equestrians, less

15. Sulla, however, was displeased at seeing to what a height of renown and power Pompey was advancing; but being ashamed to hinder him, he kept quiet—except, that is, when by force and against his wishes Pompey made Lepidus[36] consul, having campaigned for him and got the people to support him by the goodwill they felt for himself. On that occasion, seeing Pompey go off with a crowd through the Forum, Sulla said, "I see, young man, that you rejoice in your victory. For how could it not be a fine and noble thing for Lepidus, the worst of men, to be made consul in preference to Catulus, the best in the city,[37] and all through your influence with the people? Yet you would do well to keep awake and look to your interests; for you have made your enemy stronger than yourself." But the clearest proof that Sulla was not well disposed to Pompey was in his will. For though he bequeathed gifts to other friends, and appointed others as guardians of his son, he wholly overlooked Pompey. Yet Pompey bore this with great moderation and tact; so much so that when Lepidus and some others tried to prevent the body of Sulla from being buried in the Campus Martius, or even from receiving a public funeral, Pompey came to the rescue and saw to it that the rites were performed with all honor and security.

16. Shortly after the death of Sulla, the man's prophetic words were fulfilled, and Lepidus tried to thrust himself into Sulla's position. Taking no roundabout route, resorting to no pretense, but immediately appearing in arms, he once again roused and gathered about him all the ailing remnants of the factions that had escaped the hand of Sulla. His colleague, Catulus, who was followed by the incorrupt

---

wealthy than the senatorial class, were excluded from certain political offices and honors.

36 Marcus Aemilius Lepidus the elder, father of the more famous triumvir mentioned in *Caesar* and *Antony*. The year is 79 BCE.

37 Quintus Lutatius Catulus was in fact elected co-consul along with Lepidus, as the next chapter makes clear, but Lepidus had evidently won a greater number of votes.

and sounder part of the Senate and people, was the man the Romans then held in the highest esteem for wisdom and justice; but he was thought better suited to political than military leadership. The crisis required Pompey, who was not long in deciding how to proceed. Attaching himself to the nobility, he was appointed commander of the army against Lepidus, who had already stirred up a great part of Italy and was holding Cisalpine Gaul with an army under Brutus.[38]

As for the rest of Lepidus' garrisons, Pompey subdued them with ease; but at Mutina, in Gaul, he lay a long time encamped against Brutus. In the meantime Lepidus marched in haste to Rome, and besieging it, demanded a second consulship and terrified the citizens with a throng of followers. But their fear vanished when a letter brought from Pompey announced that he had ended the war without a battle. For Brutus, either betraying his army, or being betrayed when it revolted, surrendered himself to Pompey, and receiving an escort of horsemen, retired to a little town on the Po, where he was slain the next day by Geminius in obedience to Pompey's order. And for this Pompey was severely censured. For at the beginning of the revolt he had written to the Senate that Brutus had voluntarily surrendered himself; and then he sent other letters denouncing the man after he had been slain. The Brutus who, with Cassius, slew Caesar was a son of this Brutus, and was like his father neither in war nor in his death, as is written in his *Life*.[39] Lepidus, as soon as he was banished from Italy, crossed to Sardinia. And there he fell ill and died of sorrow, not for his public misfortunes, as they say, but upon the accidental discovery of a letter proving that his wife had been unfaithful to him.

---

38 See note 15 above. This time "Brutus" refers to Marcus Junius Brutus, the father of the conspirator, although Plutarch is not aware that the earlier Brutus was probably a different person.

39 The death of the elder Brutus, at Pompey's hands, is alluded to at *Brutus* 4, but Plutarch's larger point about the dissimilarity of father and son is not found there.

17. But there remained Sertorius, a general very different from Lepidus, in possession of Spain, and posing a formidable threat to the Romans;[40] into this man, as if for a final disease, the evils of the civil wars had now poured. He had already slain many of the inferior commanders, and was at this time engaged against Metellus Pius,[41] a distinguished man and a good soldier, though he was now thought too slow, by reason of his age, to follow up the opportunities of the war, and likely to be found wanting in the rough-and-tumble of events. For Sertorius attacked him impetuously, like a bandit, and by ambushes and flanking movements confused a man who was used to conventional combat, and who commanded stationary and heavy-armed troops. Pompey, therefore, who kept his army under his command, made it his object to be sent out to assist Metellus; and though Catulus ordered him to disband his forces, Pompey would not do so, but remained in arms near the city, always making some excuse or other, until the Senate, on Lucius Philippus' motion, gave him the command. It was on that occasion, they say, that when one of the senators asked with amazement whether Philippus thought Pompey should be sent out as proconsul, Philippus replied, "No indeed, but as pro*consuls*,"[42] implying that both consuls for that year were utterly useless.

18. When Pompey arrived in Spain, as is usual when a new commander is famous, he inspired the men with hopes, and those nations that were not firmly tied to Sertorius began to waver and change their allegiance. At this Sertorius made various arrogant speeches disparaging Pompey, and mockingly remarked that he would have

---

40 Even though all the commanders under discussion here are "Roman," Plutarch reserves that term for the followers of the Sullan faction in power, led now by Pompey. Quintus Sertorius was the subject of another Plutarchan life.

41 See note 18.

42 In Latin as in Greek, the term Philippus plays on can mean "in place of a consul," such that Pompey is here imagined taking the place of both standing consuls. For Philippus see chapter 2 above.

needed only a cane and whip for the boy, if he were not afraid of the old woman, meaning Metellus. But in fact he kept a close and wary eye on Pompey, and conducted the campaign more cautiously than before. For Metellus, to everyone's surprise, had become extremely luxurious in his way of life and had given himself up completely to his pleasures; indeed, there had been a great and sudden change in his attitude toward ostentation and extravagance. And this very thing gained Pompey a marvelous goodwill and reputation, since he had always maintained a simplicity in his way of life—though this entailed no great sacrifice, for he was naturally temperate and restrained in his desires.

The war had various phases, but nothing annoyed Pompey so much as the capture of the city of Lauron by Sertorius. For when Pompey thought he had him surrounded, and had boasted somewhat about it, it suddenly appeared that he himself was surrounded. As a result he was afraid to move and had to watch while the city was burned before his eyes. But later, in a battle near Valentia, he defeated Herennius and Perpenna (experienced warriors who had fled to Sertorius and were serving under him as generals), and slew more than ten thousand men.

19. Pompey, elated by this victory and filled with confidence, made haste to engage Sertorius himself, so that Metellus might not share in the victory. Late in the day they joined battle near the river Sucro, both fearing the arrival of Metellus—Pompey being eager to fight alone, Sertorius to have only one antagonist. The outcome of the battle proved doubtful, since a wing on each side was victorious; but of the generals Sertorius won greater honor, since he had routed the division posted opposite him. Pompey, who was on horseback, was attacked by a strong man who fought on foot; and when they engaged at close quarters and came to grips, the strokes of their swords fell upon each other's hands, though not with the same result. For Pompey was merely wounded, whereas he cut off the other man's hand. Then, when many rushed toward Pompey together, his own forces being routed, he made his escape unexpectedly by abandoning

his horse to the enemy. For the horse had golden cheek-pieces and trappings of great value. The soldiers fought one another as they divided these spoils, and so were left behind. At daybreak, both generals drew out their forces to confirm the victory; but at Metellus' approach, Sertorius withdrew and his army scattered. For his forces regularly disbanded and then regrouped, so that he often wandered alone, and often appeared again in the field with an army of 150,000 men, swelling suddenly like a winter torrent.

Pompey, then, when he was going after the battle to meet Metellus, and they were near each other, ordered his lictors to lower their fasces in honor of Metellus, as his superior.[43] But Metellus forbade this, and in all other respects behaved very civilly to him, not claiming any prerogative either with respect to his consular rank or seniority, except that when they encamped together the watchword was given to the whole camp by Metellus. But they generally encamped apart. For their inventive enemy[44] used to cut them off and divide them from each other, and was clever at appearing in a variety of places within a short time, and at drawing them from one contest to another. And at last, by cutting off their provisions, laying waste the country, and holding sway at sea, Sertorius drove them both out of that part of Spain that was under his control, and forced them, for lack of supplies, to take refuge in provinces that did not belong to them.

20. Pompey, having made use of and expended most of his private resources on the war, asked the Senate for money, warning that if they failed to send it he would return to Italy with his army.

---

43 The fasces symbolized the power of punishment held by certain Roman officials. It consisted of a bundle of rods tied around an axe. Various numbers of fasces-bearing attendants, called lictors, accompanied officials as they went about in public, and if a higher-ranked official was encountered, the lictors would lower their fasces before that person.

44 Sertorius, who as noted in chapter 17 specialized in quick movements with light-armed forces.

Lucullus was consul at the time, and though at odds with Pompey, was seeking to win command of the Mithridatic War[45] for himself; he therefore took pains to have the money sent, for fear of giving Pompey an excuse to leave Sertorius and march against Mithridates, an antagonist whose defeat would prove honorable and easy to achieve. In the meantime Sertorius died, treacherously murdered by his friends; and Perpenna, the chief among these, undertook to carry on the same enterprises. He had the same forces and equipment, but lacked the same judgment in the use of them. Pompey therefore marched at once against Perpenna, and finding that he acted erratically in his affairs, had a decoy ready for him, having sent a detachment of ten cohorts with orders to scatter up and down the plain. Perpenna routed these cohorts and was in pursuit of them, when Pompey appeared suddenly with his army, joined battle, and won a complete victory.[46] Most of Perpenna's officers were slain in the battle, but Perpenna himself was brought to Pompey, and by his orders was put to death. In this Pompey did not show ingratitude, nor was he unmindful of what had occurred in Sicily, as some have charged, but exercised great intelligence and judgment for the security of his country. For Perpenna, having in his custody all of Sertorius' papers, offered to produce letters from the greatest men in Rome, who, eager to subvert the established order and change the form of government, had invited Sertorius into Italy. And Pompey, fearing that these might occasion greater wars than those that had now ended, had Perpenna put to death and burned the letters without reading them.[47]

21. After this, Pompey remained in Spain long enough to suppress the greatest disorders, and to allay and settle the most inflammatory

---

45 Mithridates of Pontus had raised an anti-Roman rebellion in the East, and had fought a series of wars with Rome starting in 88 BCE.

46 In other words, Pompey lured Perperna into overconfidence and carelessness by giving him the appearance of an easy victory.

47 In order to protect the identity of Sertorius' partisans and prevent a purge.

of affairs there; then he led his army back to Italy, where by chance he arrived at the height of the Slaves' War.[48] Accordingly Crassus,[49] the commander in that war, expedited the battle at great risk, and was successful, slaying 12,300 of the insurgents. Yet even here, fortune somehow or other reserved for Pompey some share in the success of the war; for 5000 fugitives from the battle fell into his hands, all of whom he slew, and then anticipated Crassus by writing to the Senate that Crassus had overthrown the gladiators in a pitched battle, but that *he* had plucked up the whole war by the roots. And it was pleasing to the Romans both to say this and to hear it said, so fond were they of Pompey. But with regard to Spain and Sertorius, no one, even in jest, would have given the credit for their subjugation to anyone but Pompey.

Nevertheless, all this expectancy and reverence for Pompey were mingled with suspicion and fear that he might not disband his army, but would make his way by force of arms and absolute authority straight to the seat of Sulla's power. Accordingly, among those who ran out to greet him on his arrival, as many went out of fear as affection. But after Pompey had dispelled this suspicion by declaring beforehand that he would discharge his army after his triumph, there remained only one complaint among those who envied him, namely that he courted the common people more than the Senate, and had decided to restore the authority of the tribunes[50] that Sulla had abolished, and thereby gratify the people, which was indeed the fact. For there was nothing that the people of Rome were more wildly eager for, or more passionately desired, than to see the tribunate restored. Pompey therefore considered himself extremely for-

---

48 The slave rebellion led by Spartacus, which raged between 73 and 71 BCE.

49 Marcus Licinius Crassus is the subject of another Plutarchan life. For the episode here recounted, see *Crassus* 11.

50 Under Sulla's constitution, the tribunes, guardians of the interests of the lower classes, had been stripped of most of their power, including the power to veto acts of the Senate.

tunate in this opportunity, because he could have found no other means (if someone else had anticipated him in this) of adequately repaying the goodwill of his fellow citizens.

22. Though a second triumph was decreed him, and a consulship,[51] it was not for these honors that men thought him remarkable and great; instead they regarded as proof of his brilliance the fact that Crassus—the richest man of his day, the most eloquent, and the most important, who looked down on Pompey himself and everyone else—did not dare to run for the consulship before he had requested Pompey's support. And Pompey was overjoyed, since he had long sought an occasion to do Crassus some friendly service; he therefore campaigned for Crassus, and entreated the people heartily, declaring that he would be no less grateful to them for such a colleague than for the consulship. Yet when they were elected consuls, they disagreed about everything and constantly opposed each other. In the Senate, Crassus carried more weight; but among the people the power of Pompey was great. For he had restored their tribunate and permitted the courts to be transferred back to the knights by a new law.[52] But Pompey himself furnished them with the most agreeable of spectacles when he appeared and requested a discharge from military service.

It was the custom for the Roman knights, when they had served out their appointed time, to lead their horses into the Forum before the two officers called censors, and after listing the commanders and generals under whom they had served, and giving account of their own service, to receive their discharge, each man with honor or disgrace, depending on his conduct. On the present occasion, then, the censors Gellius and Lentulus were sitting in state, examining the knights who were passing in review, and Pompey was seen coming

---

51 In 70 BCE.

52 Another reversal of Sulla's reforms, which had given authority over all extortion trials to juries composed only of senators. On the knights, or *equites*, the property class below that of the senators, see Appendix.

down into the Forum with all the ensigns of his office, but leading his horse in his hand. When he came up and could be recognized, he ordered his lictors[53] to make way for him, and led his horse up to the rostrum. The people were amazed and fell silent, and the magistrates regarded the sight with awe and delight.[54] Then the senior censor examined him: "Pompeius Magnus, I ask you whether you have performed all the military services required by law." "Yes," replied Pompey, "I have performed them all, and all under myself as *imperator*." On hearing this, the people gave a great shout, unable to contain their joy; and the censors rose up and accompanied Pompey home to gratify the citizens, who followed them with applause.

23. Pompey's term of office was now expiring, and his differences with Crassus were increasing, when a certain Gaius Aurelius, who belonged to the equestrian order but had never engaged in public affairs, mounted the rostrum at an assembly, came forward, and said that Jupiter had appeared to him in a dream, commanding him to tell the consuls not to lay down their office until they were friends. After this was said, Pompey stood silent, but Crassus, taking the initiative, clasped Pompey's hand and said, "I do not think, fellow citizens, that I do anything base or dishonorable in yielding first to Pompey, whom you were pleased to call 'the Great' before he had grown a beard, and to whom you voted two triumphs before he was a senator." At this they were reconciled, and laid down their office.

Crassus resumed the way of life he had chosen from the start; but Pompey, for the most part, gave up representing parties in lawsuits, and gradually withdrew from the Forum, showing himself rarely in public, and then only with a large entourage. It was no longer easy to meet or even see him without a crowd of people around him; instead he was most pleased to make his appearance in the midst

---

53 See note 43.

54 Although a knight, Pompey was exempt from this review process because of his roles as army commander and consul, but he submitted himself nonetheless.

of a large company, as though he wished to maintain in this way his pomp and majesty, and as if he thought he ought to preserve his dignity from contact with the overtures and conversation of the common people. For life in a toga[55] is apt to lower the reputation of men who have grown great by arms, and who are ill suited for civic equality. These men expect to be treated as the foremost in the city, as they were in the camp, whereas men who have *not* distinguished themselves in war think it intolerable if in the city, at any rate, they are not to have any advantage. And so when a warrior renowned for military success and triumphs takes part in the life of the Forum, people try to abase and humiliate him, whereas if he renounces and withdraws from such activity, they maintain his military honor and authority beyond the reach of envy. Events themselves soon revealed the truth of this.

24. The power of the pirates was based in Cilicia at first,[56] and in its early days was precarious and obscure, though it gained confidence and boldness during the Mithridatic War, since it was employed in the king's service. Afterward, while the Romans were embroiled in their civil wars near the gates of Rome, the sea was bereft of a guardian, which gradually enticed and drew the pirates on not only to attack merchants and ships, but also to lay waste islands and coastal towns. So that now men of wealth and noble birth and superior abilities embarked on pirate vessels and shared their exploits, as if the occupation brought a certain renown and prestige. They had various piratical harbors and fortified beacon towers, and fleets put in that were well manned with the finest crews, well navigated by the most expert pilots, and composed of light, swift-sailing vessels adapted for their special purpose. In fact it was not their being so

---

55 That is, a life of civilian politics.

56 Plutarch moves abruptly to a new sphere of Pompey's career. Piracy in the Aegean and Adriatic had been a problem for Rome for decades, but had grown much worse in the 80s BCE, after Mithridates of Pontus started supporting the pirates.

formidable that excited indignation; more odious still was their ostentation. For their ships had gilded stern masts, and purple awnings, and silver-plated oars, as if they reveled and gloried in their iniquity. Their flutes and harps and drinking bouts along every coast, their abductions of high officials, and their ransomings of conquered cities were a reproach to the Roman supremacy. There were more than a thousand of these pirate vessels, and they had captured four hundred cities. They attacked and despoiled refuges and temples that had never been violated, such as those of Claros, Didyma, and Samothrace; and the temple of the Earth in Hermione, and that of Asclepius in Epidaurus, and those of Poseidon at the isthmus, at Taenarum, and at Calauria; those of Apollo at Actium and Leucas; and those of Hera at Samos, at Argos, and at Lacinius. They themselves offered strange sacrifices on Mount Olympus and performed certain secret rites, among which those of Mithras have been preserved to this day, having been first instituted by them.[57]

But they inflicted most of their insults on the Romans, even going inland up their roads, plundering and destroying their country houses. Once they seized two praetors, Sextilius and Bellinus, in their purple-bordered togas, and carried them off together with their attendants and lictors. They also captured a daughter of Antonius, a man who had celebrated a triumph, as she was traveling into the country, and exacted a large ransom for her.[58] But their most outrageous insult was this: Whenever a captive cried out that he was a Roman citizen,[59] and told his name, they would pretend to be petrified, and would strike their thighs and fall down before him, beseeching him to pardon them. The captive, seeing them so hum-

---

57 The rites of the god Mithras had increasingly made their way from Mesopotamia and Iran into the Greco-Roman world in Plutarch's time.

58 At *Caesar* 2, Plutarch relates how Julius Caesar also was kidnapped and held for ransom by pirates.

59 Ordinarily the cry "*civis Romanus sum*" ("I'm a Roman citizen") was expected to secure humane treatment for Romans traveling abroad.

ble and suppliant, would believe they were sincere. Then some of them would put *kalkioi* on his feet,[60] and others would throw a toga around him, so that he would not go unrecognized again. After carrying on this charade for a considerable time, and getting their fill of mocking him, they would at last let down a ship's ladder in the middle of the sea and tell him to disembark, wishing him a pleasant journey; and if he resisted, they would throw him overboard themselves and drown him.

25. This power had spread throughout our Mediterranean Sea, making it unnavigable and closed to all commerce. And this is what chiefly inclined the Romans, who found themselves short of provisions, and expected a great scarcity,[61] to send Pompey out to recover the seas from the pirates. Gabinius, one of Pompey's associates, drafted a law that gave him not just a command at sea, but an outright monarchy and a power over all men for which he would not be held accountable. For the law gave him absolute authority over the sea within the Pillars of Hercules[62] and in the adjacent mainland to a distance of fifty miles from the sea. There were very few regions in the Roman world that fell outside of that compass; and the greatest nations and the most powerful kings were included in it. Furthermore, by this decree he was authorized to choose fifteen legates from the Senate, and to assign a theater of operations to each, and to take from the public treasuries and the tax collectors as much money as he pleased, and to have two hundred ships, with power to levy as many soldiers and seamen as he required.

When these provisions were read in the assembly, the people received them with great pleasure; but the chief and most influential

---

60 Plutarch here uses a transliteration of the Latin *calcei*, the distinctive closed-toe shoe worn by the Romans.

61 Since Rome depended on grain shipments from Egypt and Sicily to feed its huge population, piracy in the Mediterranean threatened to starve the city.

62 That is, the Mediterranean, a body of water for which the Romans had no proper name. The Pillars of Hercules are the modern Straits of Gibraltar.

men of the Senate thought that such uncircumscribed and unlimited power, though it was beyond the reach of envy,[63] ought to be feared. Hence they all opposed the law except Caesar. He endorsed it not because he cared in the least for Pompey, but because from the start he courted the favor of the people and sought their support. The rest inveighed strongly against Pompey. And when one of the consuls told him that if he emulated Romulus he would not escape Romulus' end,[64] the man was in danger of being destroyed by the multitude. Yet when Catulus came forward to speak against the law, the people, out of respect, were quiet for some time. And when, after he had said much in praise of Pompey, and nothing invidious, he advised them to spare such a man and not expose him to a succession of dangers and wars, saying, "Who will you have if you lose him?," they all cried out with one voice, "*You!*" And so Catulus, when he could not persuade them, withdrew, and when Roscius came forward, no one would listen to him. He therefore made signs with his fingers, indicating that they should choose not Pompey alone, but should choose a second Pompey to accompany him.[65] At this, it is said, the people, being extremely incensed, raised such an outcry that a raven flying over the forum was stunned, and dropped down among the crowd. (Hence it would appear that the cause of birds falling to the ground is not any rupture or division of the air causing a vacuum, but the actual impact of the voice, which, when it is carried up with great volume and strength, raises a sort of surge and billow in the air.)

26. The assembly then broke up; and when the day came on which they were going to hold the vote, Pompey departed for the country. But on hearing that the bill had been passed, he entered the city by night to avoid the envy that might be awakened if peo-

---

63 This was not in fact true, as the next chapter reveals.

64 According to one legend, Romulus was torn to pieces by a Senate resentful of his power.

65 Meaning Catulus himself.

ple flocked to meet him. In the morning he came forth and offered sacrifice; and when an assembly was held for him, he succeeded in obtaining many other things besides those that had already been granted him, and almost double the preparation. For five hundred ships were manned for him, and an army raised of 120,000 men-at-arms and 5000 horsemen. Twenty-four men who had held command or served as praetors were chosen from the Senate by him, and two quaestors were included. And the price of merchandise immediately fell,[66] which delighted the people and moved them to say that the very name of Pompey had ended the war.

Yet, after dividing the Inner Sea[67] and its coastal areas into thirteen districts, he allotted to each a commander and a squadron of ships; and with his forces thus dispersed into all quarters he surrounded whole fleets of pirate ships that fell into his hands, and immediately hunted them down and brought them into his harbors; others, anticipating him, dispersed and escaped, hastening from all sides into Cilicia, as if into their hive; against them Pompey himself planned to proceed with his sixty best ships. But he did not sail against them until he had cleared of all their pirates the Tyrrhenian Sea, the Libyan Sea, and the sea near Sardinia, Corsica, and Sicily;[68] this he accomplished in the space of forty days by his own inexhaustible industry and the zeal of his officers.

27. But in Rome the consul Piso, out of anger and resentment, was damaging Pompey's naval equipment and discharging his seamen; Pompey therefore sent his fleet around to Brundisium, while he himself went up through Tuscany to Rome. No sooner had the people learned of this than they all streamed out onto the road, as if they had not sent him out only a few days before. What excited their

---

66 See note 61.

67 The Mediterranean.

68 The Tyrrhenian Sea—not the one we know, but the Roman name for the modern-day Adriatic—lies between Italy and Greece; the other seas mentioned here are different sectors of the Mediterranean.

joy was the unexpectedly rapid change, the market now overflowing with an abundance of provisions. As a result Piso was in danger of being deprived of his consulship, Gabinius having already drafted a law for that purpose. But Pompey prevented this, and after transacting all his other business with great moderation, and getting what he needed, he went down to Brundisium and sailed off. And though he was pressed for time, and sailed in haste past other cities, yet he could not pass Athens by, but went up to the city, sacrificed to the gods, and made an address to the people. And just as he was leaving the city, he read two inscriptions, each of a single line, addressed to him; one inside the gate:

Inasmuch as you know you are mortal, you are a god;

the other outside:

We awaited you, we bowed before you, we saw you, and now we send you on your way.[69]

Now some of the pirates who were still roving in bands about the seas begged for mercy; and since he treated them decently, seizing their ships and taking them prisoner, but doing them no further harm, the rest, becoming hopeful of mercy too, fled from his other commanders, went to Pompey with their wives and children, and surrendered to *him*. He spared all who came to him, and it was chiefly by their help that he tracked down, seized, and punished those who, aware that their crimes were unpardonable, were still lying low.

28. But the greater number of pirates, and the most important ones, had conveyed their families and treasures, with all their people who were unfit for war, to forts and strong citadels near the Taurus

---

69 The tone of studied indifference is meant to illustrate the Athenians' lack of regard for power and pomp.

mountain range,[70] while they themselves, having manned their ships, awaited Pompey's attack at the promontory of Coracesium in Cilicia; in the ensuing battle they were defeated and then besieged. At last, having sent him submissive messages, they surrendered themselves and the cities and islands under their control, all of which they had so fortified that they were hard to get at and virtually impregnable. The war was therefore ended, and all piracy driven from the sea in the space of three months; and along with many other ships, Pompey received ninety that had bronze beaks.[71] As for the men themselves, who numbered more than twenty thousand, he never so much as thought of putting them to death; yet he did not consider it right to let them go, either to disperse or reunite, since they were numerous, poor, and warlike. Reflecting, therefore, that man by nature neither is nor becomes a wild or unsociable creature, but by vicious habit makes himself what by nature he is not; but that he may be tamed and civilized by a change of place, occupation, and manner of life; and that even wild beasts lay aside their savage ways when they are domesticated and treated more gently—with this in mind he decided to transfer these men from sea to land, and give them a taste of a decent life by accustoming them to living in cities and working the land. Some of them, accordingly, were admitted and assimilated into the small and somewhat desolate towns of Cilicia, which acquired additional territory; and after he had restored the city of Soli, which had recently been laid waste by Tigranes, the king of Armenia, he settled many there. But most of them were settled in the Achaean town of Dyme, which was then bereft of men and had plenty of fertile land.

29. His critics found fault with these proceedings,[72] and his treatment

---

70 High, rugged mountains of southeast Turkey.

71 Bronze ramming beaks made ships much more formidable to their enemies.

72 That is, they wanted harsher treatment of the pirates rather than an amnesty.

of Metellus in Crete was disapproved of even by his closest friends. Metellus, a kinsman of that Metellus who had been Pompey's colleague in Spain, had been sent as general to Crete before Pompey was assigned his command of the seas;[73] for Crete was the second source of pirates after Cilicia. And Metellus had shut up many of them in their strongholds there, and was slaughtering and destroying them. But those who still survived and were besieged sent supplications to Pompey and invited him to the island, alleging that it was part of his precinct, and that every part of it fell within the distance from the sea specified in his commission. Pompey accepted the invitation and wrote to Metellus, commanding him to stop the war. He also wrote to the cities, urging them not to pay heed to Metellus, and sent them one of his lieutenants, Lucius Octavius, as general, who entered the fortifications of the besieged and fought on the pirates' side, thus rendering Pompey not only odious and oppressive but even ridiculous, since he lent his name to impious and godless men, and sought to shield them with the magic power of his reputation, merely out of envy and jealousy of Metellus. For not even Achilles was thought to be acting like a man, but rather like a boy utterly senseless and all in a fever for glory, when by a gesture he prevented the other Greeks from striking Hector,

Lest someone striking first should win honor, and he come second;[74]

whereas Pompey actually fought to save the common enemy, that he might rob a Roman general, after all his efforts, of a triumph. Metellus, however, would not give in, but captured the pirates and

---

73 The two Metelli referred to here are, respectively, Quintus Caecilius Metellus Creticus and Quintus Caecilius Metellus Pius; the latter is the same man as the Metellus in chapter 8 (see note 18).

74 *Iliad* 22.207, in an episode where Achilles, the lead fighter of the Greek army at Troy, waves off his fellow Greeks from attacking Hector, the Trojan hero.

punished them, and dismissed Octavius after insulting and abusing him in camp.

30. When the news came to Rome that the war with the pirates was at an end and that Pompey, at leisure now, was visiting the cities, Mallius,[75] a tribune of the people, proposed a law that Pompey should receive all the territory and forces that Lucullus[76] commanded, together with Bithynia, which Glabrio held; and that he should wage war upon Mithridates and Tigranes,[77] retaining the same naval forces and the sovereignty of the seas as before. But this meant placing the Roman empire in the hands of one man; for the only provinces that seemed to be excluded from his domain by the former law—namely Phrygia, Lycaonia, Galatia, Cappadocia, Cilicia, Upper Colchis, and Armenia—were all added to it, together with the troops and forces with which Lucullus had defeated Mithridates and Tigranes. Though Lucullus was thus robbed of the glory of his achievements, and his successor would gain the triumph without the combat duty, this was of less concern to the aristocratic party; yet they did think that the man was treated unfairly and ungratefully. But they were troubled by the power of Pompey, thinking it constituted a tyranny, and exhorted and encouraged one another privately to attack the law, and not to give up their liberty. Yet when the day came, they lost their nerve through fear of the people, and all remained silent except Catulus,[78] who boldly denounced the

75 His name was actually Manilius. Cicero, who was praetor at this time, composed an important speech (the extant *Pro lege Manilia*) in defense of the law here referred to.

76 Lucius Licinius Lucullus, a politician and highly successful general of the late Roman Republic, and the subject of another Plutarchan life.

77 On Mithridates, see note 45. King Tigranes II of Armenia was Mithridates' son-in-law. Lucullus had led an invasion of Armenia some years before this in an effort to capture Mithridates, who had fled there for refuge, but after initial successes the effort ended in a mutiny of Lucullus' troops.

78 See chapter 15 above and note 37.

law and the tribune who proposed it; and when he could persuade no one, he shouted from the rostrum, urging the Senate again and again to seek out some mountain as their forefathers had done, and flee to the rocks where they might preserve their liberty.[79] The law was passed, as it is said, by all the tribes, and Pompey, in his absence, was made master of almost all the power that Sulla had wielded after vanquishing the city by force of arms. When Pompey had received his letters and learned what had been decreed, it is said that in the presence of his friends, who came to congratulate him, he frowned, struck his thigh, and exclaimed in the manner of one who was already oppressed and weary of command: "Alas, for my unending labors! How much better to have been a nobody, if I am never to end my service as a soldier, or escape people's envy and live at home in the country with my wife." But not even his dearest friends could endure this posturing, aware as they were that his enmity toward Lucullus, rekindling his innate love of honor and power, gave him ever greater satisfaction.

31. And of course his actions soon unmasked him. For he issued edicts everywhere, commanding the soldiers to join him, and summoned all the subject kings and princes within his domain. And as he advanced across the country, he left nothing unchanged that had been done by Lucullus. He commuted many punishments, and confiscated rewards, and acted in all respects as if he aimed to show the admirers of Lucullus that their favorite had no authority whatsoever. Lucullus protested through his friends, and it was thought proper that they should meet; and so they met in Galatia.[80] And as they were the greatest and most successful generals, their lictors had their rods wreathed with laurel when they met.[81] But Lucullus was

---

79 In several episodes of early Roman history, according to legend at least, the common people had seceded and left Rome, fleeing to nearby mountains, in order to protest abuses of power by the patrician class.

80 See *Lucullus* 36 for a different account.

81 See note 43 above on lictors and the rods they carried. The rods of the

advancing from green and shady regions, while Pompey's march was through a parched and treeless country. Accordingly, Lucullus' lictors, when they saw that Pompey's laurels were altogether withered and dry, helped him to some of their own, which were fresh, and adorned and crowned his rods. This was thought to be an omen that Pompey was coming to take away the reward and honor of Lucullus' victories. Lucullus had been consul before Pompey, and was the older man; but Pompey's two triumphs[82] gave him greater prestige. Their first interview was conducted with the greatest tact and cordiality. Each magnified the other's exploits and congratulated him on his successes; but in their subsequent talks they came to no fair or reasonable agreement; they even reproached one another, Pompey charging Lucullus with love of money, and Lucullus charging Pompey with love of power, so that their friends had difficulty separating them.

Lucullus, while in Galatia, distributed the territory he had captured, and gave gifts to whomever he pleased, while Pompey, encamped not far from him, tried to prevent any obedience to Lucullus' orders, and sent away all his soldiers, except sixteen hundred, whom he regarded, in light of their stubbornness, as useless to himself and hostile to Lucullus. In addition, he would disparage the achievements of Lucullus, saying that he had waged war against make-believe and shadow-play kings only, while to himself there was left the struggle against a genuine and tested army, since Mithridates was now resorting to shields, swords, and horses. Lucullus, for his part, retorted that Pompey was marching forth to fight an image and shadow of war, accustomed as he was to landing like a lazy bird of prey on bodies others had killed, and to pulling to pieces the remnants of wars. For it was in this way that Pompey had claimed credit for the victories over Sertorius, Lepidus, and the insurgents under

---

fasces were topped with laurel wreaths for commanders who had received the title *imperator*.

82 See chapters 14 and 22 above.

Spartacus, though they had actually been won by Metellus, Catulus, and Crassus. So it was no surprise that he was trying to appropriate to himself the glory of the Pontic and Armenian Wars[83]—a man who had contrived in some way or other to thrust himself into the honor of a triumph over runaway slaves.[84]

32. After this, Lucullus went away, and Pompey, having distributed his whole fleet as a guard over the sea between Phoenicia and the Bosporus, marched against Mithridates, who had a phalanx of thirty thousand foot soldiers and two thousand horsemen, but dared not offer battle. At first the king had encamped on a strong mountain that would have been hard to assault, but abandoned it, thinking it had no water. Pompey then occupied it; and judging by the nature of the vegetation and the configuration of the ground that the place had springs, he ordered his men to sink wells everywhere. Soon his camp was abundantly supplied with water, so that people marveled that during all the time of Mithridates' encampment there the man had remained unaware of this possibility. Then Pompey besieged the king's camp and walled him in. But after enduring a siege of forty-five days, Mithridates managed to escape in secret with the strongest part of his force, having first put to death the sick and unfit. Pompey, however, overtook him near the river Euphrates and encamped close by; and fearing that the king might cross the river and give him the slip, he drew up his army to attack him at midnight. At that very time Mithridates, it is said, had a dream foreshadowing what would come to pass. He dreamt that he was sailing in the Pontic Sea[85] with a favoring wind, and was just in view of the Bosporus, conversing pleasantly with the ship's company as though overjoyed at his evident and certain deliverance; but suddenly he

---

83 The Pontic War refers to the contest with Mithridates; the Armenian, with Tigranes II.

84 Referring to Pompey's victory over the Spartacus rebellion (see chapter 21).

85 The terms "Pontic Sea" and "Pontus" denote the Black Sea.

saw himself deserted by everyone, and floating on a small piece of wreckage. In the course of this harrowing dream, his friends came and awakened him with the news of Pompey's approach. He was therefore compelled to fight in defense of his camp; and his commanders led out their forces and placed them in array. But when Pompey noticed their preparations, he hesitated to risk a battle in the dark, and thought it necessary only to surround them, lest they escape, and to attack with the advantage of numbers the next day. Pompey's oldest officers, however, by entreating and encouraging him, persuaded him to attack at once; for it was not completely dark, but the moon, which was setting, still gave enough light to discern bodies. And this, more than anything, put the king's troops at a disadvantage. For the Romans were attacking with the moon at their backs; and since it was very low and about to set, the shadows cast by their bodies were thrown far in advance and fell upon the enemy, who were unable to estimate accurately the distance between themselves and the Romans; imagining them to be near at hand, they threw their spears to no effect and hit no one. The Romans, seeing this, ran up to them with a great shout, and the barbarians no longer ventured to stand their ground, but fled in a panic and were cut down; many more than ten thousand of them perished, and their camp was taken.

Mithridates himself, at the outset, charged and cut through the Romans with eight hundred horsemen; but all the rest soon dispersed, and he was left with three persons. Among them was Hypsicrateia, a concubine, who was always of a manly and daring spirit; hence the king called her Hypsicrates.[86] On this occasion she was dressed and mounted like a Persian; she was neither exhausted by the long journeys, nor did she tire of attending the king in person and looking after his horse until they came to an estate, Sinora, that was full of the king's money and treasure. From there Mithridates took expensive garments and distributed them to those who had hastened

---

86 A male name in place of her female one.

to him in his flight. He also gave each of his friends a deadly poison, so that none of them might fall into the hands of the enemy against his will. From there he set out to Tigranes in Armenia; but Tigranes forbade him to come,[87] and proclaimed a reward of a hundred talents for his capture; Mithridates therefore passed by the sources of the Euphrates and fled through Colchis.

33. Pompey then invaded Armenia at the invitation of the young Tigranes,[88] who was now in revolt from his father and met Pompey near the river Araxes,[89] which rises in the same region as the Euphrates, but turns eastward and empties into the Caspian Sea. These two men marched together through the country, receiving the submission of the cities they passed. But King Tigranes, who had recently been crushed by Lucullus, had learned that Pompey was a gentle and mild-mannered man; he therefore agreed to accept a garrison in his palace, took with him his friends and kinsmen, and went in person to surrender himself to Pompey. When he arrived on horseback at the Roman camp, two lictors of Pompey came to him and ordered him to dismount and go on foot; for no man had ever been seen on horseback in a Roman camp. Tigranes obeyed this order; he also unloosed his sword and handed it over to them; and finally, when he came into the presence of Pompey himself, he took off his tiara, and tried to lay it at Pompey's feet. And what was most humiliating of all, he would have fallen prostrate at his knees had Pompey not prevented it, taking him by the hand and leading him forward. After placing Tigranes on one side of him and the man's son on the other, Pompey told the king that the rest of his losses were attrib-

---

87 This sudden reversal of Tigranes II's former support for Mithridates is unexplained, unless the victory of Pompey in the night battle had simply made Mithridates' revolt a lost cause.

88 Tigranes III (the "young Tigranes") had at this point largely taken over from his father, Tigranes II. This new ruler had changed Armenia's foreign-policy course and opted for collaboration with Rome.

89 The modern-day Aras River.

utable to Lucullus, who had dispossessed him of Syria, Phoenicia, Cilicia, Galatia, and Sophene;[90] but all that he had preserved until that time he should keep, paying the sum of six thousand talents as a penalty for injuries done to the Romans, and that his son should be king of Sophene.Tigranes himself[91] was delighted with these terms, and when the Romans hailed him as king, he was overjoyed and promised to give each soldier half a mina of silver, each centurion ten minas, and each tribune a talent. But his son was displeased and, when he was invited to supper, said that he did not need Pompey for that sort of honor, for he would find another Roman to entertain him. At this he was put in shackles and reserved for the triumph. Not much later Phraates the Parthian sent word to Pompey and demanded to have the young man, being his son-in-law, given up to him, and proposed that the Euphrates should be the boundary of their empires. Pompey replied that the young Tigranes belonged more to his father than his father-in-law, and as for the boundary, the just one would be adopted.[92]

34. Leaving Afranius in charge of Armenia, Pompey himself went in pursuit of Mithridates, and was forced to march through the nations that inhabited the Caucasus Mountains. Of these nations the Albanians and Iberians are the greatest. The Iberians extend as far as the Moschian Mountains and the Pontus;[93] the Albanians lie to the east as far as the Caspian Sea. The Albanians at first granted

---

90 A region of what is today eastern Turkey, between the Black and Caspian Seas.

91 That is, the elder ruler, Tigranes II.

92 Phraates III, who had come to the Parthian throne in 70 BCE, had formerly allied with Pompey against Mithridates and Tigranes II, but that alliance has now clearly broken down.

93 The people referred to here as Iberians and Albanians are today called Caucasian Iberians and Caucasian Albanians (that is, those dwelling near the Caucasus Mountains), to distinguish them from the separate but probably related groups in modern Iberia and Albania. For the Pontus, see note 85

Pompey's request for a safe-conduct; but when winter had overtaken his army in their country, and the soldiers were busy celebrating the Roman festival of Saturn, they mustered a body of no fewer than forty thousand men and attacked the Romans, having crossed the river Cyrnus, which rises in the Iberian mountains, receives the river Araxes as it flows from Armenia, and empties by twelve mouths into the Caspian. (Others, however, say that the Araxes does not join this stream but follows its own course, and empties near it into the same sea.)[94] Though it was in Pompey's power to obstruct the enemy's passage of the river, he let them cross it undisturbed; and then leading his forces onward and giving battle, he routed and slew great numbers of them. But when their king sent ambassadors and begged for mercy, Pompey pardoned the offense and made a treaty with him. Then he marched against the Iberians, who were not less numerous than the others and more warlike, and highly eager to gratify Mithridates by driving out Pompey. For the Iberians had never been subject either to the Medes or the Persians, and they likewise escaped the dominion of the Macedonians,[95] since Alexander departed in great haste from Hyrcania. Yet Pompey routed this people too in a great battle, where nine thousand were slain and more than ten thousand taken prisoner. From there he invaded Colchis, where Servilius met him by the river Phasis, bringing the fleet with which he was guarding the Pontus.

35. The pursuit of Mithridates, who had thrown himself among the tribes near the Bosporus and Lake Maeotis,[96] presented great difficulties. News was also brought to Pompey that the Albanians had

---

94 Herodotus (1.202) was the main proponent of this opinion.

95 The Medes and Persians, centered in what is now Iran, subjugated most of the Near East in the period from about 650 BCE to 331 BCE; thereafter, the Macedonian king Alexander the Great and his successors took over the lands the Persians had ruled. The rugged, wintry country south of the Caspian was able to maintain independence from both empires.

96 Lake Maeotis is the modern Sea of Azov, bordering the Crimean peninsula.

again revolted. Turning back against them, angry and determined to overpower them, he crossed the Cyrnus again, this time with great difficulty and danger, since for long stretches the barbarians had fenced off its banks with a palisade. Then, as he had to make a long march through a waterless and difficult terrain, he ordered ten thousand skins to be filled with water, and with this supply advanced toward the enemy. He found them drawn up at the river Abas, sixty thousand horsemen and twelve thousand foot soldiers, poorly armed, and most of them wearing the skins of wild beasts. They were commanded by Cosis, the king's brother, who, as soon as the battle was joined, charged at Pompey himself and hurled his javelin at the flap of his breastplate; but Pompey ran him through and killed him.

In this battle it is related that there were also Amazons fighting on the side of the barbarians, and that they came down from the mountains by the river Thermodon. For after the battle, when the Romans were stripping the enemy corpses, they came upon Amazonian shields and buskins; but no woman's body was seen. The Amazons inhabit the parts of the Caucasus that reach down to the Hyrcanian Sea; they do not share a border with the Albanians, since the Gelae and Leges lie between. They consort with these people every year for two months near the river Thermodon; then they go off and live by themselves.[97]

36. After the battle, Pompey was eager to advance to the Hyrcanian and Caspian Sea[98] but was forced to turn back when he was a three days' march from it by a multitude of deadly serpents, and retreated into Lesser Armenia. There the kings of the Elymaeans

---

97 The river Thermodon, in eastern Anatolia, was traditionally associated with the tribe of legendary warrior women known as Amazons, as was the region bordering the southern Caspian. There were indeed nomadic tribes in these regions that (to judge by their burials) gave women more prominent roles in battle and in the hunt than did Greco-Roman society, though no tribe is known to have excluded males, as the Amazons were thought to do.

98 A single body of water is here called by two names.

and the Medes sent ambassadors to him, to whom he made friendly replies by letter; but against the king of Parthia, who had invaded Gordyene and was despoiling the subjects of Tigranes, he sent an armed force under Afranius, which drove the Parthian king out of the country and pursued him as far as the district of Arbela.

Of all the concubines of Mithridates who were brought to Pompey, he lay with none himself but sent them back to their parents and kinsmen. For most of them were the daughters and wives of generals and princes. But Stratonice, who was held in the highest esteem by the king and had custody of his richest fortress, had been, it seems, the daughter of a harpist, an old man of no great fortune; and when she played for Mithridates at a drinking party, she so captivated him that he immediately took her to his bed and sent away the old man much dissatisfied at not having received so much as one kind word. Yet when the man woke in the morning, and saw tables in his house covered with gold and silver goblets, and a large crowd of servants, and eunuchs, and slaves bringing him costly garments, and a horse standing by the door adorned like those of the king's friends, he regarded the whole thing as a mockery and a joke, and tried to run away. But when the servants laid hold of him and told him that the king had bestowed on him the house of a rich man who had recently died, and that these were only the small first fruits[99] and specimens of other riches and possessions to come, he was persuaded at last with much difficulty to believe them. And donning his purple robe and leaping upon his horse, he rode through the city, shouting, "All this is mine." To those who laughed at him he said there was nothing surprising in this; the surprising thing was that he did not throw stones at all he met, he was so mad with joy. Such was "the parentage and blood"[100] of Stratonice.

She now surrendered this fortress to Pompey and offered him

---

99 An analogy to the custom of giving an initial portion of the yearly harvest as an offering to the gods.

100 *Iliad* 6.211.

many presents, of which he accepted only those that might adorn the temples of the gods and add splendor to his triumph; the rest he ordered Stratonice to keep and enjoy. And likewise when the king of the Iberians sent him a couch, a table, and a throne, all of gold, and begged him to accept them, he delivered them all to the quaestors, for the public treasury.

37. In the garrison of Caenum, Pompey found and read with pleasure some private writings of Mithridates, containing much that threw light on the king's character. For there were memoirs from which it appeared that he had poisoned many persons to death, including his son Ariarathes, as well as Alcaeus of Sardis, for having beaten him in a horse race. There were also interpretations of dreams, some dreamt by himself, some by his wives, and an exchange of love letters between him and Monime. Theophanes says that there was also found a speech of Rutilius, in which he tried to incite the king to the slaughter of the Romans in Asia.[101] But most people justly conjecture that this was a malicious invention of Theophanes, perhaps because he hated Rutilius (a man not at all like himself), but probably also with an eye to gratifying Pompey, whose father had been described as a scoundrel in Rutilius' histories.[102]

38. From there Pompey went to Amisus,[103] where his love of glory was justly punished. For though he had often reproached Lucullus because, while the enemy was still living, he would issue decrees and distribute gifts and honors, as conquerors usually do only when a war has been brought to an end, yet now he himself, while Mithridates

---

101 In 89 BCE, Mithridates ordered the slaughter of all Romans living in the province called Asia (roughly, the western portion of modern Turkey), with the result that tens of thousands were killed in a single night.

102 Theophanes was a Greek historian traveling in Pompey's train; Plutarch used his writings when researching *Pompey*. Publius Rutilius Rufus was a philosopher and historian as well as a general. His history of Rome, written in Greek, does not survive, and it is unclear whether Plutarch had read it.

103 On the Black Sea coast.

was master in Bosporus and had collected a powerful force, as if all hostilities had ended, was doing the same thing—regulating provinces and distributing gifts; for many commanders and princes, and twelve barbarian kings, had come to him. So to gratify these other kings, he would not condescend, when replying to a letter from the king of Parthia, to address him as King of Kings, as others used to do. Besides, a desire and zeal possessed him to recover Syria, and to march through Arabia to the Red Sea so that he might extend his victories to the Ocean that surrounds the inhabited world.[104] For in Africa he had been the first to advance his victories to the Outer Sea; and again in Spain he had made the Atlantic Ocean the limit of the Roman empire; and thirdly, in his recent pursuit of the Albanians, he had nearly reached the Hyrcanian Sea.[105] Intending, therefore, to bring the Red Sea within the circuit of his expedition, he broke camp. For he saw that it was difficult to hunt for Mithridates with an army, and that the man would be harder to deal with when he fled than when he fought.

39. Hence Pompey, after declaring that he would leave behind him for this man an enemy mightier than himself, namely famine, stationed a guard of ships to lie in wait for the merchants who sailed to the Bosporus, death being the penalty for those who were caught. Then, taking the greatest part of his army, he marched forth. And when he came upon the still unburied corpses of those who were slain with Triarius in his unfortunate engagement with Mithridates, he gave them all a splendid and honorable burial.[106] (The neglect of

---

104 The Indian Ocean (here referred to, according to the usual Greco-Roman terminology, as the "Red Sea") was thought to be a portion of Ocean, the body of water that, as was thought, encircled the three continents known to the Greeks and Romans.

105 The Caspian (or Hyrcanian) Sea was thought by most ancient geographers to open out into Ocean at its northern end, making it another boundary of a "universal" empire.

106 Triarius, a subcommander serving under Lucullus, had led a disastrous attack on Mithridates some three years earlier. Thousands of Roman slain had gone unburied in the interim.

these men seems to have been the main reason Lucullus was hated by his soldiers.) After subduing, by means of his forces under Afranius' command, the Arabians near Amanus, he himself went down into Syria; and since this country had no legitimate kings he declared it a province and possession of the Roman people. He also subjugated Judaea and arrested its king, Aristobulus.[107] Some cities he rebuilt, and to others he gave their liberty, punishing their tyrants. But he spent most of his time administering justice and settling the disputes of cities and kings; and where he could not be present in person, he sent his friends. Thus when the Armenians and Parthians referred to him the judgment of a territorial dispute, he sent them three judges and mediators. For the fame of his power, no less than that of his virtue and clemency, was immense, and served as a veil for most of the offenses committed by his friends and intimates, since it was not in his nature to restrain or punish wrongdoers; but he always treated those who had dealings with him in such a way that they were willing to endure the avarice and harshness of his friends.

40. The one who had the most influence on him was the freedman Demetrius, a youth of good understanding in some respects, but somewhat too insolent in his good fortune. The following story is told of him. Cato the philosopher,[108] when he was still a young man, but already of great reputation and noble mind, went up to Antioch at a time when Pompey was not there, desiring to see the city. He himself, as always, went on foot, while his friends accompanied him on horseback. And seeing before the gates of the city a crowd of men dressed in white—the young men on one side of the

---

107 Jewish high priests and kings often had Greek names in this era. Aristobulus was deposed by Pompey in favor of his more tractable brother, Hyrcanus.

108 Plutarch here calls the younger Cato a "philosopher" because of his staunch adherence to Stoic principles. The same incident recounted here is retold in chapter 13 of Plutarch's *Cato*, with the additional epilogue that Cato himself found the story funny later in life.

road, the boys on the other—he was annoyed, thinking this was done in his honor, though he had no wish for such demonstrations. Nevertheless, he urged his friends to dismount and walk with him. But when they drew near, the master of all these ceremonies met them, holding a garland and a wand,[109] and asked them where they had left Demetrius and when he would arrive. At this, Cato's friends burst out laughing, but Cato said only, "O the miserable city!" and passed by without any other answer.

Yet Pompey rendered Demetrius less obnoxious to others by enduring his haughty behavior without taking offense. For it is reported that often at his entertainments, when Pompey was awaiting and receiving his other guests, Demetrius would be already reclining in a lordly manner, with the hood of his toga pulled over his ears.[110] Before his return to Italy, he had purchased the most delightful country houses near Rome, and the most beautiful pleasure grounds; and there were sumptuous gardens, called "Demetrian" after him; and yet Pompey himself, until his third triumph, inhabited a modest and simple house. Afterward, it is true, when he had erected his famous theater,[111] he built, as a sort of annex to it, a house more splendid than his former; yet even this did not excite envy, since the man who became its owner after Pompey, when he entered it, expressed surprise and asked where Pompey the Great used to take his supper.[112] So runs the story.

41. The king of the Arabs near Petra, who had formerly dispar-

---

109 Suppliants seeking the help of gods and rulers traditionally wore garlands and carried ritual wands called *thyrsi*. Demetrius was known to have great influence with Pompey, so the citizens of Antioch were preparing to ask him to intercede on their behalf.

110 Wearing the toga in this way showed a leisurely, casual demeanor.

111 The Theater of Pompey, the first stone theater built at Rome, was completed in 55 BCE. Its ruins are still the site of dramatic performances today.

112 That is, the house had no room large or sumptuous enough to be an obvious banqueting hall.

aged the power of the Romans, now took fright and wrote that he had resolved to obey and carry out all orders. Pompey, however, wishing to confirm him in that intention, marched toward Petra, an expedition not wholly blameless in the eyes of most of his followers. For they considered it an avoidance of their pursuit of Mithridates and thought Pompey should turn against their inveterate antagonist, who was now rekindling the war and reportedly making preparations to march an army through Scythia and Paeonia against Italy. But Pompey, judging it easier to destroy the king's forces in battle than to seize his person in flight, was unwilling to wear himself out in a vain pursuit, and therefore sought other ventures in the interval, which he chose to prolong.

But fortune resolved the difficulty. For when he was not far from Petra, and had pitched his camp for that day and was exercising on horseback nearby, couriers rode up from Pontus bringing good news. Such messengers are recognized at once by the heads of their javelins, which are crowned with laurel. As soon as the soldiers caught sight of them, they flocked to Pompey. At first he wished to finish his exercise, but at their shouts and entreaties he dismounted, took the letters, and led the way to camp. There was no rostrum, nor had there been time to build the military substitute, which the soldiers make by cutting up thick clods of earth and heaping them one upon the other; but in their eager impatience, they created a mound by piling up pack saddles. Standing upon this, Pompey announced to them that Mithridates was dead, having killed himself when his son Pharnaces revolted from him, and that Pharnaces had come into possession of everything there, and was acting, as he wrote, on his own behalf and that of the Romans.[113]

42. At this the army, filled with joy, as was natural, fell to sacrificing and feasting as if in the person of Mithridates ten thousand of their enemies had perished. Then Pompey, who had brought his ventures and expeditions to an unexpectedly easy conclusion,

---

113 In 63 BCE.

immediately left Arabia, and passing rapidly through the intervening provinces, reached Amisus. There he received many presents brought from Pharnaces, with several dead bodies of the royal family, and the corpse of Mithridates himself, which was not at all recognizable from the face (for the embalmers had neglected to melt away the brain);[114] but those who asked to see him knew him by the scars. Pompey himself could not endure to see the body, but to ward off divine jealousy sent it away to Sinope.[115] He marveled at Mithridates' garments, and the size and splendor of his armor; but the sword belt, which cost four hundred talents, was stolen by Publius and sold to Ariarathes;[116] his tiara also, a piece of admirable workmanship, was secretly given by Caius, the foster brother of Mithridates, to Faustus, the son of Sulla, at his request. This escaped Pompey's notice at the time, but Pharnaces, learning of it afterward, punished the thieves.

After arranging and settling matters there, Pompey embarked on his homeward journey in greater ostentation and with more festivity. For example, when he came to Mitylene, he gave the city its liberty, for the sake of Theophanes,[117] and viewed the traditional contest of poets, which had as its only theme his own exploits. Pleased with the theater there, he had sketches and plans drawn of it, intending

---

114 According to Herodotus (2.86), removal of the corpse's brain was normally the first step in mummification. If the brain was left intact, its decomposition would cause the face and skull to rot.

115 Pompey's assumption is that the corpse, as the token of his complete victory, might incur the ill will of divinity. Less pious commanders often abused the corpses of great enemies or impaled their severed heads. Sinope is a Greek city on the north shore of Anatolia and the burial place of others in Mithridates' family.

116 Not the Ariarathes mentioned in chapter 37, Mithridates' son, who was already dead by this time, but presumably the son of Ariobarzanes, the ruler of Cappadocia.

117 On Theophanes, who was a native of Mitylene, see note 102. To "give a city its liberty" meant exempting it from taxes and other obligations to Rome.

to build one like it in Rome, only larger and more magnificent.[118] In Rhodes he attended the lectures of all the sophists, and gave to every one of them a talent.[119] Poseidonius has actually described the disputation that he held in Pompey's presence against Hermagoras the rhetorician on the subject of the Principles of Invention.[120] In Athens he treated the philosophers in like manner, and gave the city fifty talents toward its restoration. He hoped to return to Italy in the greatest glory possible to man, and find his family as eager to see him as he was to see them. But that supernatural agency that always takes care to mix some ingredient of evil with the greatest and most glorious goods of fortune[121] had for some time been secretly busy in his household, preparing him a painful welcome. For Mucia[122] had been unfaithful to him during his absence. While abroad at a distance he had disparaged the report; but when he drew near to Italy, where he had more leisure to look into the charge, he sent her a bill of divorce, though he neither wrote at the time nor afterward stated on what grounds he divorced her. But the reason is mentioned in Cicero's letters.[123]

43. All sorts of stories about Pompey continued to reach Rome ahead of him, and there was considerable uproar there, people assuming that he would at once lead his army against the city

---

118 The later Theater of Pompey (see note 111).

119 "Sophists" is the term Plutarch uses for rhetoricians and philosophers of many stripes.

120 Poseidonius, the brilliant Greek polymath and writer (whose *Histories* are partly extant) opposed the doctrines of Hermagoras, a teacher of rhetoric and author of various treatises, regarding what Romans called *inventio*, the stage of composition in which an orator seeks out lines of argument.

121 The doctrine that the divine requires a "mixture" of good and evil fortune in human life is deeply rooted in Greek religious thought.

122 Pompey's first wife and mother of three of his children.

123 The only surviving mention of the divorce in Cicero's letters (1.12.3) does not in fact speak of the cause.

and that a monarchy would be firmly established. Crassus,[124] taking his children and his money, stole out of the city, either because he was really afraid, or, as is more probable, because he wished to give credit to the accusation and exacerbate the people's resentment. Pompey, accordingly, after crossing into Italy, assembling his soldiers, and delivering a suitable and kindly speech, commanded them to disperse to their respective cities and return to their homes, remembering to come together again for his triumph. When the army disbanded, and everyone had learned about it, an astonishing thing happened. When the cities saw Pompey the Great passing through the country unarmed, and with only a few friends, as if he were returning from a trip abroad, their inhabitants came pouring out to show their affection for him, escorting and conducting him with a larger force to Rome, where, had he intended to foment unrest and revolution, he would have had no need of his army.

44. Since the law did not permit a commander to enter the city before his triumph, Pompey sent word to the Senate, entreating them as a favor to him to postpone the consular elections so that he might personally assist Piso in his campaign. Cato opposed the request, however, and Pompey did not get what he wanted.[125] But as he admired Cato's frankness and the firmness that he alone dared to use in defense of law and justice, he conceived a desire to attach the man to him in some way. Since Cato had two nieces, Pompey wished to wed one of them himself, and marry the other to his son. But Cato suspected the overture, believing Pompey aimed to corrupt him, bribing him in some way by a family alliance, though his wife and sister were vexed that he would reject a connection with Pompey the Great. Meanwhile, as Pompey wished to have Afranius

---

124 See note 49. Pompey and Crassus had become antagonists when both were consuls in 70 BCE.

125 See *Cato* 30 for another account of this episode, from Cato's perspective. The point at issue was the independence of the Senate and the inviolability of constitutional procedure.

made consul, he lavished money among the tribes for their votes, and the people went down to his gardens to receive it. As a result the affair became notorious and Pompey was maligned. For the office of consul was their highest; and he had gained it by dint of his successes, but was making it something to be purchased by those unable to gain it by their own merits. "In these reproaches," said Cato to the women, "we would have had to share, had we become allied to Pompey." And on hearing this, they acknowledged that his judgment of what was right and proper was better than theirs.[126]

45. The magnitude of Pompey's triumph was such that, though it was held over the space of two days, yet the time did not suffice, so that of what had been prepared for the spectacle there was as much withdrawn as would have dignified and adorned another triumph. Ahead of the procession were carried tablets inscribed with the names of the nations over which he had triumphed. These were Pontus, Armenia, Cappadocia, Paphlagonia, Media, Colchis, the Iberians, the Albanians, Syria, Cilicia, Mesopotamia, Phoenicia, Palestine, Judaea, Arabia, and all the power of the pirates who had been overthrown by land and sea. And in these countries no fewer than a thousand strongholds had been captured, and not many fewer than nine hundred cities, together with eight hundred pirate ships; and thirty-nine cities had been founded. In addition, these tablets recorded that whereas the public revenues from taxes had been fifty million drachmas, the Romans were receiving from *his* acquisitions a revenue of eighty-five million; and that he was bringing into the public treasury coined money, gold and silver plate, and twenty thousand talents of silver, over and above what had been distributed among the soldiers, of whom the man who got the smallest share received fifteen hundred drachmas. The prisoners of war

---

126 At *Cato* 30, Plutarch tells the same anecdote but adds a personal observation that Cato's rejection of Pompey's suit proved ill advised, in that it drove Pompey closer to Julius Caesar, whose daughter he married instead (see chapter 47 below).

who were led in triumph, besides the chief pirates, were the son of Tigranes the Armenian with his wife and daughter, and Zosime, a wife of Tigranes himself, Aristobulus, king of Judaea, a sister and five children of Mithridates, Scythian women, and hostages given by the Albanians and Iberians and by the king of Commagene;[127] there were also vast numbers of trophies, one for every battle in which Pompey had been victorious either in person or through his lieutenants. But what redounded most to his glory, and had never been attained by any other Roman, was the celebration of his third triumph over the third continent. For others before him had celebrated three triumphs; but he celebrated his first over Africa, his second over Europe, and this last over Asia, so that he seemed in a sense to have brought the whole world under his power in these three triumphs.[128]

46. As for his age at that time, those who compare him in every respect to Alexander, and insist on forcing the parallel,[129] maintain that he was not quite thirty-four, though in truth he was near forty. And how well it would have been for him had he ended his life at that point, while he still enjoyed the good fortune of Alexander![130] For the years that followed brought him only successes that excited envy, or failures too great to be remedied. For the authority he had gained in the city by his merits he used to support the unjust doings of others, so that by advancing their fortunes he detracted from his own reputation, until he was finally overthrown by the strength and magnitude of his own power. And just as the strongest citadel or fort in a town, when it is taken by an enemy, affords him its own

---

127 These hostages were pledges of good behavior and signified subservience to Rome.

128 The Greeks and Romans of course knew of only three continents. The first two triumphs of Pompey are related at chapters 14 and 22 above.

129 An interesting criticism coming from Plutarch, who specialized in parallels both genuine and forced.

130 Alexander the Great died at age thirty-two, without having lost a battle.

inherent strength, so Caesar, after Pompey's influence had made him strong enough to defy the city, ruined and overthrew the very man who had strengthened him against others. This came about as follows.

Lucullus, when he returned from Asia, where he had been treated insultingly by Pompey,[131] was received with splendid honor by the Senate; and after the return of Pompey, whose ambition they wished to curb, they encouraged Lucullus to take part in politics. By then Lucullus had grown cold and disinclined to engage in public affairs, having given himself up to the pleasures of ease and the enjoyment of his wealth; but he immediately leapt upon Pompey, and by attacking sharply, succeeded in having his own decrees, which had been repealed by Pompey, reestablished, and gained the advantage in the Senate with the assistance of Cato. Pompey, thus rejected and humbled, was forced to flee to the tribunes of the people for refuge, and to attach himself to young men.[132] Of these the vilest and most impudent was Clodius, who took him about and demeaned him in public, dragging him here and there among the throngs in the Forum to promote those laws and speeches that he made to gratify and flatter the people. He even demanded of Pompey a reward for his services, as if he were not disgracing but benefiting him, and this reward he later exacted in the betrayal of Cicero, who was Pompey's friend and had done more than anyone to support his policies. For when Cicero was in danger and begged his help, Pompey would not even see him, but shut his door to those who had come to intercede for Cicero, and slipped out by another. Cicero, fearing the result of his trial, departed secretly from Rome.[133]

47. At that time Caesar, having returned from military service,

---

131 See chapter 31.

132 The implication here is that younger members of the Roman political class were more open to defiance of the Senate and changes in the established order.

133 See *Cicero* 30–31.

had adopted a policy that brought him great favor for the present and power for the future, and proved extremely harmful to Pompey and the city. He was running for his first consulship;[134] and observing that while Crassus and Pompey remained at odds, if he attached himself to one he would make the other his enemy, he exerted himself to reconcile them, an object that was honorable in itself and tending to the public good, though he undertook it for a shady reason and with the cleverness of a schemer. For the opposing forces that, as in a ship, kept the city evenly balanced, combined and came over to one side, and thus created an irresistible surge that overpowered and overwhelmed their entire commonwealth. Cato, at any rate, when people said that the city had been overturned by the quarrel that later arose between Caesar and Pompey, said they were mistakenly laying the blame on what happened last; for it was not their discord and enmity but their unanimity and concord that gave the first and greatest blow to the city. For Caesar was elected consul; and he began at once to pay court to the poor and indigent by proposing laws for the founding of colonies and the distribution of lands, thereby debasing the dignity of his office and turning the consulship into a sort of tribuneship.[135] And when Bibulus, his colleague, opposed him, and Cato was prepared to assist Bibulus with all his might, Caesar brought Pompey to the rostrum, and addressing him in the sight of the people, asked him if he approved of the laws. And when Pompey said he did, Caesar said, "Then if anyone resists the laws, will you come to the aid of the people?" "Certainly," replied Pompey, "I will come, and against those who threaten the sword, I will appear with sword and shield." Until that day, Pompey had never, it was thought, said or done anything more vulgar, so that even his friends apologized for him and said that the

134 The consulship of 59 BCE. See *Caesar* 13–14.

135 The office of tribune had been reserved for nonpatricians by the Roman constitution. Consuls were members of the senatorial class and were expected to uphold the interests of that class.

words had escaped him on the spur of the moment.[136] Yet it was clear by his later behavior that he had wholly devoted himself to Caesar's service. For to everyone's surprise he married Julia, Caesar's daughter, though she was engaged to Caepio and was to be married within a few days; and to soothe Caepio's wrath, Pompey promised him his own daughter, though she was engaged to Faustus, the son of Sulla. Caesar himself married Calpurnia, the daughter of Piso.

48. After this, Pompey filled the city with soldiers and managed all things by force. As Bibulus the consul was going down into the Forum with Lucullus and Cato, Pompey's men fell upon him and broke his fasces;[137] and somebody even threw a basket of manure on the head of Bibulus himself; and two of the tribunes who escorted him were wounded. When they had thus cleared the Forum of their adversaries, they passed the law for the distribution of lands. And the people, caught by this bait, became docile and obedient; never meddling, they silently cast their votes for whatever was proposed. Accordingly, they confirmed the decrees that Lucullus had opposed; to Caesar they granted both provinces of Gaul, together with Illyria, for five years, and four complete legions;[138] and as consuls for the following year they elected Piso, the father-in-law of Caesar, and Gabinius, the most outrageous of Pompey's flatterers.

Throughout this time, Bibulus shut himself up at home, and did not appear in public for the eight months remaining of his consulship, though he issued edicts full of slanders and denunciations against both Caesar and Pompey; Cato, as if inspired and possessed by Phoebus, foretold in the Senate what the future held for the city and for Pompey; Lucullus retired to a life of ease, claiming that he

---

136 Pompey's undisguised reference to the use of military force was inappropriate to the civilian political context.

137 See note 43.

138 See *Caesar* 14, where the opposition of Cato is stressed.

was too old for public affairs; it was then that Pompey said that luxurious living was more unseasonable for an old man than public service. Yet Pompey himself soon grew soft; indulging his passion for his young wife, he devoted most of his time to her, passed his days in country houses and gardens, and paid no heed to what was happening in the Forum, so that even Clodius, who was then a tribune of the people, began to despise him and to engage in the most audacious attempts. For when he had banished Cicero, and sent Cato away to Cyprus on the pretext of military duty, and when Caesar had left for Gaul, and when he saw that the people now looked to him as the leader who did everything to please them, he at once tried to repeal some of Pompey's decrees; he took Tigranes, the captive,[139] out of prison and kept him about as his companion; and he prosecuted several of Pompey's friends, thereby making a test of Pompey's power. At last, when Pompey appeared at a trial, Clodius, accompanied by a crowd of unruly and contemptuous ruffians, stood up in a conspicuous place and put questions to them as follows: "Who is a dissolute *imperator*?" "What man seeks another man?" "Who scratches his head with one finger?"[140] And they, at a shake of his toga, like singers making responses in a chorus, would answer each question by shouting, "Pompey!"

49. This was indeed annoying to Pompey, who was unaccustomed to hearing himself maligned, and was inexperienced in this sort of battle; he was even more vexed when he noticed that the Senate was delighted to see him smeared and paying a price for his betrayal of Cicero. But when it came even to blows and wounds in the Forum, and one of Clodius' servants was caught creeping through the crowd toward Pompey with a sword in his hand, Pompey made this his excuse (though he was also afraid of Clodius' insolence and abuse), and never came again into the Forum during all the time Clodius

---

139 For the capture by Pompey of the younger Tigranes, see chapter 33.

140 A gesture the Romans found effeminate or foppish.

was tribune, but stayed close to home and consulted with his friends about how he might allay the anger of the Senate and the nobility against him. To Culleo, who urged him to divorce Julia and abandon Caesar's friendship for that of the Senate, he would not listen; but he was readily persuaded by those who thought he should call Cicero home from banishment—a man who was the greatest adversary of Clodius and the most beloved in the Senate. He therefore brought Cicero's brother into the Forum, attended with a large force, to petition for his return; and there, though some were wounded and some slain, he got the better of Clodius.[141] And when by decree Cicero returned home, he immediately reconciled the Senate to Pompey; and by speaking in support of the corn law, he again, in effect, made Pompey master of all the Roman possessions by land and sea. For this law placed under his authority harbors, trading stations, storehouses, and, in short, all the concerns both of the merchants and the farmers.

Clodius charged that the law had not been made because of the scarcity of grain, but the scarcity of grain was made so that the law might be proposed—a law whereby the power of Pompey, which was now, as it were, dying away, might be rekindled and recovered in a new office. Others maintain that this was a stratagem of Spinther, the consul, who sought to confine Pompey in a higher office so that he himself might be sent out to assist King Ptolemy.[142] But in the end Canidius, the tribune, proposed a law to send Pompey, without an army and attended by two lictors, as a mediator between the king and the people of Alexandria. Pompey appeared to consider the law by no means unacceptable, but the Senate rejected it on the specious grounds that it feared for his safety. Yet writings were found scattered about the Forum and near the Senate house suggesting

---

141 See *Cicero* 33.

142 Ptolemy XII of Egypt, nicknamed Auletes or "Flute Player" for his musical pretensions, was at this time living in exile at Rome, having been ousted by a popular rebellion. Spinther and Pompey were two of several Roman leaders vying for the right to invade Egypt and restore him.

that Ptolemy wished to have Pompey assigned to him as a general instead of Spinther. And Timagenes even declares that Ptolemy went away and left Egypt not out of necessity, but persuaded to do so by Theophanes,[143] who was eager to give Pompey the opportunity to enrich himself in a new command. But Theophanes' turpitude does not go so far to make this story credible as does Pompey's own nature—which was averse, with all its ambition, to such base and sordid conduct—to render it *in*credible.

50. Having been appointed to administer and manage the corn trade, Pompey sent his agents and friends in many directions, while he himself sailed to Sicily, Sardinia, and Africa and collected grain. He was about to sail home with it when a great storm arose at sea, and the helmsmen hesitated to put out. But Pompey led them aboard, told them to weigh anchor, and shouted, "To sail is necessary; to live is not." By this zeal and courage, accompanied by good fortune, he filled the markets with grain, and the sea with ships, so that his surplus provisions sufficed also for foreign peoples, and there was an abundant flow, as from a spring, for everyone.

51. Meanwhile, the Gallic Wars raised Caesar to greatness; and whereas he appeared to be far distant from Rome, engrossed in the affairs of the Belgae, Suevi, and Britanni, he was working cleverly and in secret in the midst of the people, undermining Pompey in all political matters of most importance. Caesar, enveloping himself in his military force as if it were his own body, was training it thoroughly, not merely for the conquest of the barbarians, but as though his contests with them were mere exercises, akin to hunting and the chase, and making it invincible and terrifying. In the meantime, he was sending to Rome the gold and silver and other spoils and treasure that he took from the enemy in his many wars; and by tempting people with bribes, and supporting aediles,[144] prae-

143 On Theophanes see note 102. Timagenes was a Greek historian living at Rome who wrote about this period from firsthand experience.

144 See Appendix for this term and others designating Roman offices.

tors, consuls, and their wives, was acquiring numerous friends. So that when he crossed the Alps and spent the winter in Luca, a great crowd of men and women came flocking to him, striving to reach him first, including two hundred senators, among whom were Pompey and Crassus;[145] and one hundred twenty fasces of proconsuls and praetors were seen at Caesar's door.[146] Now, all his other visitors he sent away after filling them with hopes and loading them with money; but with Crassus and Pompey he entered into the following compact: that the two of them should run for the consulship; that Caesar should support them by sending large numbers of his soldiers home to vote for them; that as soon as they were elected they should acquire commands of provinces and armies; and that Caesar should have his present provinces confirmed for five more years. When these arrangements came to be generally known, the chief men in Rome were indignant; and Marcellinus, rising in the assembly, asked Pompey and Crassus whether they were going to run for the consulship.[147] And when the majority of the people urged them to answer, Pompey spoke first and said perhaps he would run—and perhaps he would not. Crassus was more tactful, for he said he would take whichever course he judged to be in the best interest of the commonwealth.[148] And when Marcellinus continued to pursue Pompey, and was thought to speak with some vehemence, Pompey remarked that Marcellinus was the most

---

145 See *Caesar* 21. The year is 56 BCE. Caesar, Pompey, and Crassus had by this time entered into an informal power-sharing arrangement later known as the First Triumvirate; the Luca conference was intended to shore it up.

146 On the fasces, see note 43. The number mentioned here implies a dozen or more high officials (proconsuls were preceded by twelve fasces, praetors by six.)

147 Marcellinus was himself consul at this time, but had been elected without the help of the manipulations that Caesar and Pompey were planning.

148 See *Crassus* 15, where Pompey is given an additional reply to the question of whether he would run.

unjust of men, since he was not grateful for Pompey's having made him eloquent instead of mute, and sated to the point of vomiting instead of half-starved.

52. But though the other candidates abandoned their campaigns for the consulship,[149] Cato persuaded and encouraged Lucius Domitius not to desist; for the struggle against the tyrants, he maintained, was not for office but for liberty. Pompey and his partisans, however, fearing this firmness of Cato, and concerned that with the support of the entire Senate he might draw away and infect the more sensible among the citizens, would not let Domitius go down into the Forum, but sent armed men and killed the torchbearer who was leading the way, and put the rest to flight. Cato was the last to retreat, having been wounded in the right arm while defending Domitius.[150]

By such a course did Pompey and Crassus obtain the office;[151] nor did they behave more decently in their other proceedings. In the first place, when the people were choosing Cato praetor and casting their votes, Pompey broke up the assembly, alleging some inauspicious omen; and having corrupted the tribes with money, they proclaimed Vatinius praetor instead of Cato.[152] Then, through Trebonius, they introduced laws that, in keeping with the agreements, continued Caesar in his provincial governorship for a second five-year term, gave Crassus Syria and the command of the expedition against the Parthians, and Pompey himself all of Africa, both Spains,[153] and four legions of soldiers, two of which he lent to Caesar, at Caesar's request,

---

149 Presumably out of fear of the triumvirs, who had already in effect claimed the office.

150 See *Cato* 41.

151 That is, the consulship of 55 BCE.

152 As is clear from *Cato* 42, Cato's bid for the praetorship was intended as a check on the power of Crassus and Pompey, now consuls.

153 The Iberian peninsula was divided by the Romans into two provinces.

for the war in Gaul. But though Crassus went out to his province at the expiration of his consulship, Pompey opened his theater[154] and held gymnastic and musical contests at its dedication, and presented combats of wild beasts in which five hundred lions were slain, and above all, the battle of elephants, a most terrifying spectacle.

53. These entertainments brought him admiration and popularity; but on the other side he incurred no less envy, in that he handed over his armies and provinces to lieutenants who were his friends, while he himself spent his time with his wife in the places of amusement in Italy, either because he loved her, or because she was so fond of him that he could not bear to leave her; for this is also stated. The young woman's devotion to her husband was common knowledge, and though unusual in light of his advanced years, attributable, it would seem, to his fidelity (since he was intimate only with his wife), and to his dignity of manner, which was tempered with grace, and was particularly attractive to women, if one must accept the testimony of Flora the courtesan.[155] It once happened that at an election of aediles people came to blows, and several near Pompey were killed, so that he, finding himself covered with blood, changed his clothes. The servants who brought his clothes home made a great bustle in the house, and the young woman, who was pregnant, catching sight of his bloodstained toga, fainted, and barely regained her senses; and what with her fright and suffering, she went into labor and miscarried. Hence even those who found most fault with Pompey for his friendship with Caesar could not blame him for the love he bore his wife. Afterward, she conceived again and gave birth to a daughter; but she died in labor, and the infant did not outlive her mother many days.[156] Pompey had made preparations to bury her body at

---

154 See note 111.

155 See chapter 2 for Pompey's relations with Flora. Presumably Pompey had already given her to Geminius before marrying Julia.

156 The death of Julia is dated to September 54 BCE.

his house in Alba, but the people seized it by force and brought it down for burial in the Campus Martius, more out of compassion for the young woman than to gratify Pompey and Caesar. Yet of these two, the people seemed to pay Caesar a greater share of honor in his absence than to Pompey, though he was present. For the city at once began to seethe and swell. Things everywhere were in a state of agitation, and all discussion was divisive, since the relationship that had previously disguised rather than restrained the ambition of these two men was now at an end. And before long, news came that Crassus had perished in Parthia,[157] so that yet another great safeguard against civil war was removed; for in fear of Crassus, both Pompey and Caesar had in some way or other continued to treat each other fairly. But as soon as fortune had removed the competitor who sits by to fight the winner, one might have said with the comic poet,[158]

> *. . . each combatant against the other*
> *anoints himself with oil and sprinkles his hands with dust.*

So negligible a thing is good fortune as compared with human nature; for she cannot satisfy its desires, since a domain of that magnitude and breadth could not satisfy the ambition of two men. And though they had heard and read that the gods "divided the universe into three parts, and each obtained his share of honor,"[159] they thought the Roman realm not sufficient to contain them, though they were only two.

---

157 The tale of Crassus' disastrous Parthian campaign is told by Plutarch at *Crassus* 17–31. The death of Crassus came in early June 53 BCE, and news of it reached Rome a few weeks later.

158 Plutarch does not name the comic playwright he quotes here, and the passage is otherwise unknown. It depicts the rituals wrestlers went through before a match.

159 From *Iliad* 15.189, describing the division of the universe among Zeus, Poseidon, and Hades.

54. Yet Pompey once said in an oration to the people that he had received every office sooner than he had expected, and that he had always resigned it sooner than had been expected. And indeed the frequent disbanding of his armies confirmed the truth of this. At present, however, thinking that Caesar would not dismiss his forces, he tried to strengthen himself against him by offices in the city;[160] beyond this he sought no changes, nor did he wish to be thought to distrust Caesar, but rather to disregard and despise him. Yet when he saw that the offices were not bestowed according to his wishes because the citizens were bribed, he allowed anarchy to arise in the city; and at once there was much talk in favor of a dictator,[161] which Lucillius the tribune first dared to make public, advising the people to elect Pompey dictator. But when Cato attacked the proposal, Lucillius was in danger of losing his office. As for Pompey, many of his friends came forward to defend him, alleging that he neither asked for that office nor desired it. When Cato therefore praised Pompey and urged him to support the cause of good order,[162] Pompey acquiesced for a time, out of shame, and Domitius and Messala were elected consuls. But afterward, when there was another anarchy, and more people raised the question of a dictator more vehemently, Cato and his party, fearing that they would be overruled, decided to keep Pompey from that absolute and tyrannical power by giving him an office of more legal authority.

Accordingly, Bibulus, who was an enemy of Pompey, was the first to propose to the Senate that Pompey should be elected sole consul, alleging that the city would either be freed from its present confusion or would become the slave of its strongest citizen. The proposal

---

160 That is, by packing various magistracies with his own supporters.

161 The Roman constitution provided for the appointment of a dictator in times of crisis.

162 Cato's sudden reversal of attitude in regard to Pompey is better explained at *Cato* 47: constitutional government had almost totally collapsed by this point, and Caesar's growing power seemed more threatening than that of Pompey.

seemed strange, considering who voiced it; and when Cato rose, everyone expected that he would oppose it. Yet when silence fell, he said that he himself would never have made such a proposal, but since it was made by another he urged them to adopt it, saying that any form of government was better than none at all, and that no man would govern better than Pompey in a time of such disorder. The Senate approved the measure, and decreed that Pompey, if elected consul, should govern alone, but that if he himself desired a colleague, he should choose whom he pleased once two months had elapsed. Having in this way been elected and proclaimed consul by Sulpicius, the interrex,[163] Pompey addressed himself warmly to Cato, acknowledged that he was greatly indebted to him, and asked him to advise him privately on the conduct of the government. To this Cato replied that Pompey had no reason to thank him; for nothing he had said was spoken for Pompey's benefit, but for the benefit of the city; and that he would give his advice privately if he were asked for it, but if he were *not* asked, he would say what he thought in public. Such was Cato's conduct on all occasions.[164]

55. On returning to the city, Pompey married Cornelia, a daughter of Metellus Scipio. She was not a virgin, but had lately been left a widow by Publius (a son of Crassus), her first husband, who had been killed in Parthia. The girl had many charms besides her youthful beauty. For she had been highly educated in literature, played the lyre, understood geometry, and had been accustomed to listening with profit to lectures on philosophy. In addition she had a character free from the unpleasant pretentiousness that sometimes characterizes young women who engage in such studies; and her father, in family and reputation, was above reproach. Nevertheless, the mar-

---

163 An interrex wielded executive power in place of the regularly elected consuls. The consular elections of 52 BCE had not taken place due to extreme public disorder.

164 See *Cato* 48, where examples are given.

riage was displeasing to some in view of the disparity of their ages, Cornelia being in this respect a more eligible match for Pompey's son.[165] And those who were more fastidious felt that Pompey was disregarding the wretched plight of the city, which had selected him as her physician and committed her care solely to him; meanwhile he was donning garlands and celebrating his nuptials, never considering that his consulship was a public misfortune, since it would never have been given to him so lawlessly had the city been prospering.

Furthermore, though he presided over the cases of those charged with corruption and bribery, and proposed laws regulating the procedure at trials, and in other instances judged with integrity and fairness, making the courtroom safe, orderly, and quiet by his attendance there with an armed force, yet when Scipio, his father-in-law, was on trial, he summoned the three hundred sixty jurors to his house and asked for their support, and the prosecutor dropped the case when he saw Scipio escorted from the Forum by the jurors. At this, Pompey was again maligned, and much more so in the case of Plancus; for though Pompey himself had made a law banning the practice of making speeches in praise of persons on trial, he came into court to speak in praise of Plancus.[166] And Cato, who happened to be one of the jurors, stopped his ears with his hands, and said it was not right for him, in violation of the law, to listen to such praises. Cato was therefore excluded before he could cast his vote, but Plancus was condemned by the other votes, to Pompey's dishonor. A few days later, Hypsaeus, a man of consular rank, who was under accusation, waited for Pompey's return from his bath to his supper, and clasping his knees, begged for his support. Pompey passed him by contemptuously, saying that Hypsaeus had merely spoiled his supper. Accordingly, Pompey was faulted for being partial. But he brought everything else into good order, and chose his

---

165 Cornelia may at this point have been younger than twenty.

166 Plancus, a tribune in 52, was on trial for fomenting violence.

father-in-law as his colleague for the last five months of his term. It was also decreed that he should keep his provinces for another four years, and receive a thousand talents annually for the support and maintenance of his army.

56. But Caesar's friends took this as an occasion to demand that some consideration be shown for Caesar as well, who was fighting so many battles for the empire; they said he deserved either another consulship or an extension of his command, so that no successor might come in to rob him of the glory of his labors, but that he might command and enjoy in peace the honors he had won. When a debate arose about this matter, Pompey, as if moved by affection for Caesar to allay whatever resentment he had incurred, said he had letters from Caesar in which he expressed his desire for a successor and his own discharge from command, though he thought it right that they should allow him to run for the consulship even in his absence. But Cato and his party opposed this, and said that before seeking any favor from his fellow citizens Caesar ought to lay down his arms and become a private citizen. And when Pompey made no protest, but let it pass as if it were a matter in which he had been overruled, suspicion about his true feelings for Caesar only increased. He also sent word to Caesar asking back the legions that he had lent him, making the Parthian War his pretext for doing so.[167] And Caesar, though he knew very well why they were requested, sent them home very generously rewarded.

57. After this, Pompey recovered from a dangerous illness at Naples, and the Neapolitans, on the advice of Praxagoras, offered sacrifices of thanksgiving for his deliverance. The neighboring cities followed their example, and so the thing went its course throughout Italy, each city, small and great, holding festivals for many days. No place could contain those who came from all sides to meet him, but

---

167 See chapter 52 above and *Caesar* 25. Plutarch says that Pompey lent Caesar two of his legions for use in Gaul, but Caesar's own account of the Gallic Wars mentions only one.

roads and villages and ports were filled with people feasting and sacrificing to the gods. Many went to welcome him with garlands on their heads and torches in their hands, and cast flowers upon him as they escorted him on his way, so that his progress and return to Rome was a most beautiful and glorious sight. And yet it is said that this very thing did more than anything to kindle the civil war. For a feeling of arrogance, coming over Pompey in the course of the great public rejoicing, overrode calculations grounded upon facts. Abandoning that prudence that had so far ensured the safe enjoyment of his good fortune and his successes, he gave himself up to an intemperate confidence and contempt for Caesar's power, certain that he needed neither an armed force to oppose him, nor any laborious preparation, but that he could pull Caesar down much more easily than he had set him up. Furthermore, Appius arrived, bringing from Gaul the troops that Pompey had lent to Caesar. And he spoke slightingly of Caesar's actions there, and spread scandalous reports about him. He also told Pompey that he was unaware of his own power and reputation if he made use of any other forces against Caesar than Caesar's own; for such was the soldiers' hatred of Caesar, and so great their love of Pompey, that they would all come over to him the moment he appeared.[168] In this way, then, Pompey was so puffed up, and his confidence filled him with so great a contempt for his adversary, that he laughed at those who feared the war; and when some were saying that if Caesar should march against the city they did not see what forces they had to resist him, he smiled and calmly told them not to worry, saying, "Wherever in Italy I stamp on the ground, there will rise up forces of infantry and cavalry."[169]

58. Caesar, for his part, engaged more vigorously in public affairs. He no longer traveled far from Italy, and was always sending his

---

168 See *Caesar* 29, where it is clearer that the false reports of Caesar's weakness were part of a deliberate effort to make Pompey overconfident.

169 At chapter 60 below and at *Caesar* 33, Plutarch tells of an impatient senator who turned this remark against Pompey.

soldiers back to the city to vote in the elections, and with his money was working secretly upon the magistrates and corrupting many of them. One of these was Paulus the consul, whom he brought over by a bribe of fifteen hundred talents; and Curio, a tribune of the people, by discharging the multitude of debts with which he was overwhelmed; and Mark Antony, who, out of friendship to Curio, had involved himself in Curio's obligations.[170] Indeed, it was said that one of Caesar's centurions who had returned to Rome and was standing near the Senate house, when he heard that the Senate would not give Caesar an extension of his term of office, clapped his hand upon his sword, and said, "Well, *this* will give it." And Caesar's activities and preparations conveyed this intention.

Yet Curio's demands and requests in favor of Caesar seemed quite democratic in spirit. For he demanded one of two things: either that Pompey should give up his army, or that Caesar's should not be taken away from him; for whether they became private citizens on fair terms or remained rivals with their present forces, they would give no trouble; but that senator who made one of them weak would double the power he feared. To this Marcellus the consul replied by calling Caesar a robber, and said he should be proclaimed a public enemy if he did not disband his army.[171] Nevertheless, Curio, supported by Antony and Piso, got the Senate to debate the question. He moved that those should withdraw who felt that Caesar only should lay down his arms, and Pompey command; and the majority withdrew. But then he moved that those should withdraw who thought both men should lay down their arms, and neither com-

---

170 In *Antony* 2 and 5, Plutarch gives more details about the friendship between Curio and Mark Antony and how it led the latter to become a partisan of Caesar.

171 See *Caesar* 30, where it is Lentulus, the consul for 49 BCE, who calls Caesar a robber, not Marcellus, the consul of 50. Plutarch seems to have conflated two different Senate sessions that attempted to neutralize Caesar's power, one late in 50 and the other at the very start of 49.

mand; now only twenty-two favored Pompey, and all the rest supported Curio. And Curio, aglow with his success, dashed out to the people, who welcomed him with applause and pelted him with garlands and flowers. Pompey was not present in the Senate, for commanders of armies do not enter the city. Marcellus, however, rose and said that he would not sit there listening to speeches when he saw ten legions crossing the Alps,[172] but would himself send someone to oppose them in defense of the country.

59. After this the city went into mourning, as in a public calamity, and Marcellus, accompanied by the Senate, proceeded through the Forum to meet Pompey. Standing before him, he said, "I command you, Pompey, to defend your country, to employ the forces that are ready, and to levy others." Lentulus, consul-elect for the following year, said the same. But when Pompey sought to levy troops, some would not answer the summons, a few came together reluctantly and without enthusiasm, and the majority cried out for a settlement. For Antony, contrary to the will of the Senate, had read in a public assembly a letter of Caesar's containing overtures likely to appeal to the common people. He proposed, namely, that both Pompey and he should quit their provinces and dismiss their armies, come before the people, and give an account of their actions. Lentulus, however, who had now become consul, would not convene the Senate; but Cicero, who had just returned from Cilicia, tried to effect a reconciliation, proposing that Caesar should give up Gaul and disband the rest of his forces, keeping only two legions and Illyricum, and wait for his second consulship. As the proposal did not satisfy Pompey, the friends of Caesar agreed that he should give up one of the two legions. But Lentulus continued to oppose this, and when Cato cried out that Pompey was erring again in letting himself be deceived, the reconciliation came to nothing.

60. At that point, news was brought that Caesar had occupied Ariminum, a large city of Italy, and was marching directly toward

---

172 That is, Caesar's Gallic legions, crossing into Italy.

Rome with all his forces. But this was false. For he had with him no more than three hundred horsemen and five thousand men-at-arms. The rest of his forces were beyond the Alps, and he did not intend to wait for them, since he wanted to fall suddenly upon his enemies while they were in disarray and did not expect him, rather than give them time to prepare for battle. And when he had reached the banks of the Rubicon, a river that was the boundary of his allotted province, he stood in silence and hesitated a little, reflecting on the magnitude of the adventure he was undertaking.[173] Then, like men who hurl themselves from some cliff into a vast abyss, he shut the eyes of reason, averting them from the thought of danger; and merely calling out in Greek[174] to those near him, "Let the die be cast," he led his army across the river.

As soon as the news reached Rome, the city was filled with confusion and a fear that had never been known before; all the Senate ran at once to Pompey, and the magistrates followed. And when Tullus[175] asked about an army and a force, and Pompey, after a pause, said glumly that he had the soldiers ready who had come from Caesar, and that he thought he could quickly assemble the thirty thousand that had been previously enrolled, Tullus cried out, "You have deceived us, Pompey,"[176] and advised that they send envoys to Caesar. Favonius, a man not otherwise of bad character, except that he often thought his own audacious insolence was a copy of Cato's outspokenness, ordered Pompey to stamp upon the ground, and summon the forces that he used to promise. Pompey bore patiently with

---

173 Caesar's mandate as commander of the Gallic legions did not allow him to cross the Rubicon with an army; by doing so, therefore, he was declaring war. See *Caesar* 32.

174 Most educated Romans learned Greek as a second language and often used it for especially important pronouncements.

175 Lucius Tullus, a former consul.

176 The "deceit" consisted in Pompey's overly optimistic assessment of how quickly his forces could be marshaled.

this ill-timed mockery; and when Cato reminded him of what he had foretold from the beginning about Caesar, Pompey replied that Cato had indeed spoken more like a prophet, while he himself had acted more like a friend.

61. Cato now advised them to elect Pompey general with absolute power, saying that the same men who cause great evils must bring them to an end.[177] He himself went at once to Sicily, the province that was allotted to him, and all the other senators likewise departed, each to his allotted province. But since nearly all Italy was in an uproar, it was hard to grasp what was happening. For those who lived outside the city came flocking from all sides into Rome, while those who lived in Rome were hurrying away and abandoning the city. In such confusion and disorder the decent element was weak, and the disobedient element strong and not easy for the magistrates to control. For it was not possible to allay the public panic, nor would anyone permit Pompey to exercise his own judgment; every man sought to infect Pompey with the emotion of the moment, whether fear, grief, or helplessness. Opposing views prevailed on the same day, and it was not possible for Pompey to obtain accurate information about the enemy, since many reported to him whatever they happened to hear, and then were annoyed if he did not believe them. He therefore issued a decree acknowledging civil chaos.[178] Ordering all the senators to follow him, and declaring he would regard as a partisan of Caesar anyone who remained behind, he left the city late that evening. The consuls also fled, without even offering the sacrifices usual before a war. But even in the midst of such terrors Pompey was a man to be envied for the goodwill people felt for him; for though many found fault with his generalship, no man hated the general; and among those who left the city, there

---

177 The outcome of this initiative is made clear at *Cato* 52: Pompey declined to serve on the grounds he had too few willing troops.

178 The decree, called *tumultus,* enabled the government to take emergency measures and suspend certain kinds of civil liberties.

were more who did so because they could not forsake Pompey than for love of liberty.[179]

62. A few days later, Caesar entered and took control of Rome, treating everyone fairly and soothing their fears; but when Metellus, one of the tribunes, tried to prevent him from taking money from the treasury, Caesar threatened him with death, and added words even harsher than the threat itself; for he said that it was easier for him to carry it out than to utter it. After removing Metellus and taking what he wanted, he went in pursuit of Pompey, being eager to drive him out of Italy before his forces arrived from Spain. But Pompey, having occupied Brundisium, where he found plenty of ships, immediately embarked the consuls, and with them thirty cohorts of foot soldiers, and sent them ahead to Dyrrachium.[180] He also sent Scipio, his father-in-law, and Gnaeus, his son, to Syria to fit out a fleet. He himself, after barricading the gates and posting his lightest-armed soldiers upon on the walls, ordered the Brundisians to remain quietly in their houses, and then dug up all the ground inside the city, cutting trenches and filling with stakes all the streets except two, by which he himself went down to the sea. On the third day, when he had at leisure put all the rest of his host on shipboard, he suddenly gave the signal for those who were guarding the wall to run swiftly down to the sea, where he took them on board and carried them across to Dyrrachium.[181] Caesar, meanwhile, when he saw the walls deserted, and understood that Pompey had fled, hastened after him and barely avoided getting entangled among the stakes and trenches. But since the Brundisians informed him of the danger, he avoided the city, making a circuit

---

179 Plutarch paints a different picture here than at *Caesar* 34, though there too he remarks on the sense of loyalty that Pompey inspired.

180 Across the Adriatic, in what is now Albania.

181 The stratagem was meant to evacuate all troops possible without allowing the rear guard to be captured by Caesar. See *Caesar* 39 for a very different account.

around it, and found that all the ships had sailed except two, which had only a few soldiers aboard.

63. Others consider this sailing away of Pompey to be one of his finest stratagems, but Caesar himself was amazed that when Pompey had a strong city,[182] and was expecting forces from Spain, and held sway at sea, he gave up and abandoned Italy. Cicero accuses him of imitating the generalship of Themistocles rather than that of Pericles, though his situation was more like that of Pericles than that of Themistocles.[183] Yet Caesar made clear by his actions that he dreaded the passage of time. For when he had captured Numerius, a friend of Pompey, he sent him to Brundisium to solicit a reconciliation on equal terms; but Numerius sailed away with Pompey.[184] Then Caesar, who in sixty days and without bloodshed had become master of all Italy, wished to pursue Pompey at once; but as he had no ships, he turned back and marched into Spain, hoping to join the forces there to his own.

64. In the meantime Pompey assembled a mighty force. His navy was utterly invincible, since he had five hundred warships and an enormous number of light vessels and look-out boats; his cavalry, the flower of Rome and Italy, numbered seven thousand—men of preeminent birth, wealth, and high spirit; but his infantry was a mixed multitude and in need of training, and these he exercised at Beroea,[185] not sitting idly himself but performing in their drills as if

---

182 Meaning Brundisium.

183 The comparison refers back to two famous moments of Greek military history. Themistocles, leader of Athens during a massive Persian invasion of 480–79 BCE, led an evacuation of the city and chose to fight far from its walls; Pericles, faced with the Spartan invasions of 431 BCE and the years following, chose instead to draw the rural population inside Athens and endure a siege without striking a blow.

184 Plutarch's point is that Caesar, seeing that Pompey was about to escape Italy and prolong the war, was anxious to negotiate a settlement even on equal terms; he thought that "the passage of time" would strengthen Pompey's hand.

185 A part of the region then termed Macedonia.

he were in his prime. And it was a great encouragement for them to see Pompey the Great, who was then fifty-eight years old, competing in armor as a foot soldier, and then as a horseman, drawing his sword with ease with his horse at full gallop, and replacing it in its sheath just as easily; and in throwing the javelin, showing not only accuracy but also strength in hurling it distances many of the young men could not surpass. Several kings and princes of nations came to visit him, and an assemblage of high-ranking Romans so numerous that they formed a complete senate. Labienus also came, having forsaken his old friend Caesar, whom he had served in his wars in Gaul;[186] and Brutus, a son of that Brutus who was put to death in Gaul,[187] a man of high spirit who had previously never spoken to Pompey or even saluted him, regarding him as the murderer of his father, but who now put himself under his command in the belief he was liberating Rome. Cicero too, though he had written and advised otherwise, nevertheless was ashamed not to be of the number of those who were risking their lives for their country.[188] There came to Pompey also in Macedonia Tidius Sextius, a man extremely old and lame in one leg. Others mocked and laughed at the sight of him, but Pompey, as soon as he saw him, rose and ran to meet him, considering it a great testimony that men too old and weak to serve should prefer to be with him in danger than in safety at home.

65. When the Senate met,[189] and on Cato's motion decreed that no Roman should be put to death except in battle, and that no city subject

---

186 The defection of Titus Labienus, a high-ranked and revered officer in Caesar's army, was a coup for the Pompeian side.

187 See chapter 16 and note 38. This younger Brutus is the conspirator who helped kill Caesar.

188 See *Cicero* 37–38, where Plutarch makes clear that Cicero was quite torn about the decision and kept aloof from Pompey's cause even after joining it.

189 The senators in exile continued to hold sessions as though constituting Rome's government, even while Caesar convened other Senate meetings in Rome.

to Rome should be plundered, the party of Pompey was even more admired. For even those who took no part in the war, because they either lived too far away or were thought too weak to give aid, were nevertheless, in their wishes at least, on his side, and, in their words, as far as that went, fought on behalf of the right, regarding as an enemy to gods and men anyone who did not wish Pompey to be victorious.

Yet Caesar too showed himself merciful in victory. For when he had defeated and captured Pompey's forces in Iberia he let the commanders go, and took the soldiers into his service. Then he recrossed the Alps, marched hurriedly through Italy, and reached Brundisium at the time of the winter solstice.[190] Crossing the sea there he landed at Oricum, but sent Vibullius, Pompey's friend, who was his own prisoner of war, to Pompey, with a proposal that they hold a conference, disband both their armies within three days, renew their friendship under oath, and return to Italy. Pompey regarded this as another ruse, and therefore marched down swiftly to the sea and occupied all the forts and places that provided strong positions for land forces, as well as havens and landing places to accommodate those who arrived by sea, so that every wind brought Pompey grain, troops, or money. Caesar, on the other hand, was so hemmed in both by sea and land that he was forced to seek a battle, daily assaulting Pompey's fortifications and challenging him to fight. In these skirmishes Caesar was for the most part victorious and carried the day; but one time he came close to being crushed and losing his army, Pompey having fought splendidly until he routed Caesar's whole force and killed two thousand of them. But then, because he either was not able or was afraid,[191] he did not press his advantage and pursue the fugitives into their camp, and Caesar accordingly

---

190 Winter crossings of the Adriatic were perilous and Caesar could not get the main body of his army across until spring.

191 Plutarch shows the same lack of comprehension of Pompey's timidity at *Caesar* 39, where he says the general's failure to follow up his advantage came "either from a certain caution or by some chance."

remarked to his friends, "Today the victory would have been with the enemy, if they had had a victor to gain it."

66. Pompey's men were so emboldened by this victory that they were eager to have the outcome determined by a battle. Pompey, on the other hand, though he wrote to far off kings and generals and cities as if he had been victorious, dreaded the danger of such a battle, believing that by delays and shortages he would wear out men who were undefeated in arms and had long been accustomed to conquer together, but whom old age rendered unfit for the other hardships of war—long marches, shifts of position, the digging of trenches, and the building of fortifications, with the result that they were eager to join battle as soon as possible and fight hand to hand. Thus far Pompey had somehow managed to persuade his soldiers not to take action; but after this latest engagement, when Caesar was forced by lack of provisions to break camp and advance through Athamania into Thessaly, the boldness of his men could no longer be curbed. Crying out that Caesar had fled, some were for going in pursuit of him, others for crossing into Italy, while others were sending their friends and servants ahead to Rome to occupy houses near the forum, planning to campaign straightaway for offices. Several also, of their own accord, sailed to Lesbos to carry the good news to Cornelia that the war was over; for Pompey had sent her there for safety's sake.

A council being assembled, Afranius was of the opinion that Italy should be secured, since it was the greatest prize of the war, and its masters would immediately gain possession of Sicily, Sardinia, Corsica, Spain, and all Gaul; and what meant most to Pompey was that it was his own native land that lay near, reaching out her hands for his help, and it would not be right to let her be insulted and enslaved by servants and flatterers of tyrants. But Pompey himself thought it neither creditable on his part to run away a second time from Caesar[192] and be pursued, when fortune was offering him the

---

192 That is, by sailing back to Italy in advance of Caesar's forces, just as he had sailed away the previous year.

role of pursuer, nor lawful before the gods to forsake Scipio and the men of consular rank throughout Greece and Thessaly, who would at once fall into Caesar's hands, together with their large sums of money and numerous forces;[193] and that he would best show his care for Rome by fighting for her at the greatest distance, so that she might neither suffer any evil nor even hear of any while she awaited her master.

67. With this determination, Pompey marched out in pursuit of Caesar, firmly resolved not to give battle, but rather to besiege and distress him by following him closely and cutting off his supply line. There were other reasons he thought this the best course; but a view that was current among the cavalry came to his ear, to the effect that as soon as they had routed Caesar, they should demote Pompey as well. And some say it was for this reason that Pompey never employed Cato in any matter of importance, but even now, when marching against Caesar, left him at the coast to guard the baggage, fearing that if Caesar were slain, he might at once be forced by Cato to lay down his command.[194] While he was thus slowly following the enemy, he was faulted and denounced for using his generalship not against Caesar, but against his country and the Senate, that he might always continue in office and never cease to have as his guards and servants men who claimed to govern the world. Domitius Ahenobarbus, by calling him Agamemnon,[195] and king of kings, excited jealousy against him. And Favonius was no less displeasing to him than those who spoke out boldly, when he shouted his untimely taunt, "Men, will we have to go another year without gathering

193 The senators and nonmilitary men in Pompey's train would have had more difficulty than the army in making a quick escape from Greece.

194 Relations between Cato and Pompey had been deeply mistrustful and antagonistic before the civil war broke out (see chapters 44, 52, 54, and 55).

195 The mythical leader of the Greek expedition against Troy was often depicted in Greco-Roman literature as vainglorious and overambitious.

figs in Tusculum?"[196] And Lucius Afranius, who had been charged with treachery for the loss of the army in Spain,[197] when he saw Pompey now avoiding a battle, said he was surprised that his accusers did not go themselves and fight the buyer and seller of their provinces.

With these and many such speeches they worked on Pompey, who could never bear to lose face or disappoint his friends, and forced him to alter his plans, so that he compromised his own best resolutions to follow their hopes and impulses—conduct that would have been unbecoming in the pilot of a ship, to say nothing of a sovereign commander of so many nations and armies. Pompey himself commended those physicians who never indulge the appetites of their patients, and yet he yielded to the distemper of his men, afraid to offend, even for the sake of curing them. For how could anyone say these men were healthy, some of whom were already going about the army campaigning for consulships and praetorships, while Spinther, Domitius, and Scipio were quarreling, competing, and conspiring to succeed Caesar as pontifex maximus,[198] as if they were about to engage merely with Tigranes the Armenian or the king of the Nabataeans,[199] and not with that Caesar, and his army, that had taken a thousand cities by storm, subdued more than three hundred nations, and fought undefeated with Germans and Gauls in more battles than one could count, taking a million prisoners and slaying as many on the spot in pitched battles.[200]

---

196 Tusculum was a country seat near Rome, where many elite Romans owned rural estates.

197 See *Caesar* 41. Lucius Afranius is referred to in the previous chapter as Afranius.

198 The Roman pontifex maximus was head of a board of state priests who supervised religious rites and maintained the calendar.

199 See chapters 33 and 41 for these two earlier opponents of Pompey's army; in the latter, the Nabataeans are referred to as "the Arabs around Petra."

200 The references are to the campaigns in Gaul.

68. But they went on entreating and clamoring, and after they had descended to the plain of Pharsalus[201] they forced Pompey to hold a council of war, where Labienus, the commander of the cavalry, stood up first and swore that he would not return from the battle unless he routed the enemy; and all the rest swore the same oath. That night Pompey dreamt that as he entered his theater the people applauded, and that he decorated the Temple of Venus the Victorious with many spoils.[202] This dream partly encouraged but partly also troubled him, since he feared that the family of Caesar, which traced its descent to Venus, would win glory and splendor through him. Furthermore, there were certain panicked uproars that ran through the camp and woke him out of his sleep. And during the morning watch a great light shone over Caesar's camp, where all was quiet, and from there a blazing torch rose up and plunged down upon Pompey's camp, which Caesar himself says he saw as he was making his rounds. At daybreak, when Caesar was about to break camp and move to Scotussa, and his soldiers were pulling down their tents and sending their servants and pack animals on ahead, the scouts arrived and reported that they saw many arms being carried here and there in the enemy's camp, and that there was movement and noise as of men coming out to battle. Not long after, others came in to report that the first ranks were already posted in battle array. Caesar, therefore, after telling them that the expected day had come when they would fight with men, not with hunger and need, quickly gave orders for the crimson tunic to be set up before his tent—that being the signal of battle among the Romans. As soon as his soldiers saw it they left their tents, and with shouts of joy ran to their arms. And when their officers led them to their stations, every man fell into his proper rank without any hubbub, but with the quiet and ease of a trained chorus.

---

201 A town in Thessaly, in what is now northern Greece.

202 In Rome, the new Theater of Pompey adjoined the temple dedicated to Venus *Victrix*. The family of Julius Caesar traced its descent to the legendary Iulus, the son born to Aeneas by Venus.

69. Pompey himself intended to oppose Antony with his right wing, and stationed his father-in-law, Scipio, in the center against Lucius Calvinus. The left wing was commanded by Lucius Domitius, and supported by the great mass of the cavalry. For almost all the horsemen had streamed to that point in the hope of overpowering Caesar and cutting to pieces the tenth legion, which was reputed to be the most warlike in the army, and in which Caesar himself usually fought in person. But Caesar, seeing that the left wing of the enemy was fortified with such a large body of horsemen, and growing alarmed at their splendid appearance, sent for six cohorts from the reserves and placed them behind the tenth legion, commanding them to keep still lest they be seen by the enemy; but whenever the enemy cavalry charged, they were to run up through the foremost ranks, and not hurl their javelins, as the bravest soldiers usually do in their eagerness to fight with their swords, but to strike upward with them and wound the eyes and faces of the enemy; for these handsome and blooming war-dancers,[203] he said, would not stand their ground and risk harming their youthful beauty, nor would they face the steel shining in their eyes. These were Caesar's actions at the time.

Meanwhile Pompey, on horseback, was viewing the array of both armies, and when he saw that his antagonists were maintaining their ranks and quietly awaiting the signal of battle, whereas the greater part of his own army did not keep still but was agitated and wavering for lack of experience, he feared that his array would be utterly broken up at the start of the battle, and therefore gave orders that his front ranks should stand with their spears lowered for attack and remain stationary as they received the enemy's charge. Caesar finds fault with this tactic,[204] for he says that Pompey, by forgoing the momentum his men would have had in a

203 Plutarch quotes a similar speech in *Alexander* 71, in which inexperienced troops are referred to as *purrichistai*, "dancers of the war-dance."

204 The critique that follows comes from Caesar's *Civil War* 3.92, with Plutarch evidently in agreement.

charge, blunted the impact of their blows. And as for the counter-thrust, which more than anything fills most soldiers with enthusiasm and drive as they join battle with the enemy, and along with their shouts and rapid pace increases their fury, Caesar says that Pompey deprived his men of this by arresting them and cooling their spirits. Yet Caesar's army consisted of twenty-two thousand, and Pompey's somewhat more than twice as many.

70. When the signal was given on both sides, and the trumpets began to summon the fighters into battle, most men looked to do their part. But a few of the noblest Romans, and some Greeks who were present without taking part in the battle, seeing that the crisis was imminent, considered to what a pass greed and contentiousness had brought the empire. Kindred arms and fraternal ranks drawn up under the same standards, the great manliness and strength of a single city now turning against itself, showed how blind and how mad a thing human nature is when possessed by any passion. For if they had been content only to rule, and enjoy in peace what they had conquered in war, the greatest part of the world was subject to them both by sea and land; and had they still wished to gratify their thirst for trophies and triumphs they might have had their fill of wars with Parthians or Germans. For a considerable task still remained in the conquest of Scythia and India,[205] and their greed would have had no inglorious pretext in the civilizing of barbarian peoples. And what Scythian cavalry, or Parthian bowmanship, or Indian wealth could have resisted seventy thousand Romans approaching in arms under Pompey and Caesar, whose names they had heard of long before that of Rome? So unsociable and diverse and savage were the tribes these men had attacked and conquered. But now they were joining battle with each other; nor were they even moved by pity for their own glory to spare their country—men who until that day had been proclaimed invincible. As

---

205 Plutarch seems here to be thinking more of the empire of Alexander the Great, which bordered Scythian and Indian lands, than of Rome, which was farther from these regions and never had any interest in acquiring them.

for their family connection, and the charms of Julia, and her marriage to Pompey, these were now seen to have been deceptive and dubious pledges of an alliance based on expediency, not on true friendship.

71. Now, therefore, as soon as the Pharsalian plain was covered with men, horses, and armor, and the signal for battle had been raised on both sides, the first to run out from Caesar's ranks was Caius Crassianus,[206] a centurion who commanded one hundred twenty men, and was now fulfilling a great promise he had made to Caesar. For he had been the first man whom Caesar had seen going out of the camp, and Caesar, after saluting him, had asked what he thought about the battle. The centurion, stretching out his right hand, cried, "You will win a glorious victory, O Caesar! And today you will praise me, whether I live or die." Recalling these words now, he rushed forward, followed by many more, and charged into the midst of the enemy. A fight with swords immediately ensued, and many were slain, and as Crassianus was still pressing forward and cutting down the men of the front ranks, one of them stood opposite him and drove his sword through the centurion's mouth, so that its point came through the back of his skull.

Once Crassianus had fallen, the battle became equal at that part of the field. Pompey did not lead up his right wing swiftly, but looked about and lost time as he waited to see what his horsemen would do on the left. These had already drawn up their squadrons, intending to encircle Caesar and force the few horsemen whom he had posted in front to fall back upon their infantry. But Caesar gave a signal, his horsemen retreated, and the cohorts stationed to resist the encircling movement ran out, three thousand in number, and met the enemy. Coming right up to the horses, as they had been instructed to do, they thrust their javelins upward, aiming at the faces of the riders. These men, since they were inexperienced in any sort of fighting, and neither expected nor understood anything of the kind, had neither the courage nor endurance to resist blows

---

206 In Caesar's *Civil War* (91 and 99), the man's name is Crastinus.

aimed at their eyes and faces, but wheeled about, shielding their eyes with their hands, and shamefully took to flight. Then Caesar's men, disregarding the fugitives, marched against the enemy's infantry and attacked precisely where the left wing, exposed by the flight of the cavalry, could be surrounded and encircled. And when these cohorts attacked them on the flank, and at the same time the tenth legion fell upon their front, the enemy made no further resistance, nor did they even hold together, seeing that whereas they had hoped to surround their enemy, they were themselves being surrounded.

72. These men were likewise routed and put to flight, and when Pompey, noticing the cloud of dust, guessed the fate of his cavalry, it would be hard to say what thoughts or intentions passed through his mind; but he looked most like a man distracted and beside himself—one who had no recollection that he was Pompey the Great. Without a word to anyone, he walked slowly away to his camp, the very image of Ajax in these verses:[207]

But father Zeus, enthroned on high, struck fear in Ajax;
The man stood dazed, and flung his sevenfold shield behind him,
Trembling as he gazed upon the throng.

In such a state he entered his tent and sat down speechless, until many enemy pursuers burst into the camp with the fugitives. Then he said only, "What, even into my quarters?" Without another word, he rose up, took clothes suitable to his present fortune, and stole away. The rest of his legions also fled, and there was a great slaughter in the camp of tent guards and servants; but only six hundred soldiers fell, according to Asinius Pollio, who fought in this battle on Caesar's side.[208]

---

207 *Iliad* 11.544. The point of the comparison is the uncharacteristic passivity and withdrawal of a great warrior.

208 Pollio was a general and politician who published an account of his times, beginning in 60 BCE. Plutarch made extensive use of this work, consulting it either in the Latin original or some Greek translation or summary.

When Caesar's soldiers took the camp, they beheld the folly and vanity of the enemy. For every tent was decked with garlands of myrtle and adorned with brightly colored couches and tables covered with goblets; there were bowls of wine set out, and everything prepared and arrayed in the manner of people who had sacrificed and were holding a festival, rather than of soldiers who were arming themselves for battle. With such deluded hopes and so full of foolish confidence had they gone forth to war.[209]

73. But Pompey, when he had gone a little way from the camp, let his horse go, and with only a small party, since no one pursued him, went quietly on his way, taken up altogether with such thoughts as might naturally occupy a man who for thirty-four years had been accustomed to victory and conquest, and who now in his old age was for the first time getting a taste of defeat and flight. He was reflecting that in a single hour he had lost all the power and glory he had gained in so many wars and conflicts; and that he who only a little while before was guarded by so vast an army of infantry and cavalry, was now departing in so poor and humble a condition as to escape the notice of the enemies who were searching for him. After passing by Larissa, and coming to the Vale of Tempe, being very thirsty, he threw himself down on his face and drank of the river; then rising up again, he passed through Tempe, and at last came down to the sea. There he rested for the remainder of the night in a fisherman's hut. At daybreak he boarded a riverboat, taking with him the free men who accompanied him, and telling his servants to go back to Caesar and have no fear.[210] As he was being conveyed along the coast, he noticed a large merchant ship about to set sail, the master of which was a Roman citizen, who, though he was not acquainted with Pompey, nevertheless knew him by sight; the

---

209 Compare *Caesar* 46, where Plutarch omits mention of the luxuries in Pompey's camp. At *Caesar* 45, Plutarch cross-references *Pompey* for Pompey's life after Pharsalia.

210 Caesar made a point of granting amnesty to those members of Pompey's faction who surrendered to him (*Caesar* 46).

man's name was Peticius. Now it happened that this man had dreamt the night before that Pompey, not as he had often seen him, but humble and dejected, was conversing with him. He was then telling his dream to his shipmates, since men who are at leisure tend to spin out such stories, when suddenly one of the sailors told him he saw a riverboat rowing out from shore, and that some of the men in it were waving their outerwear and stretching out their hands toward them. Peticius, therefore, looking attentively, at once recognized Pompey, just as he had seen him in his dream; and smacking his head, he ordered the sailors to let down their towboat, he himself waving and calling Pompey by name, already aware by the man's dress of the change in his fortune. So without waiting for an entreaty or speech, he took him onto his ship, together with as many companions as Pompey wished to have with him (these were the two Lentuli[211] and Favonius), and set sail. Shortly thereafter, seeing Deiotarus the king[212] hastening toward them from the shore, they took him on board as well. When it was time for supper, and the master of the ship had made ready such provisions as he had aboard, Favonius, seeing that Pompey, for lack of servants, was beginning to undo his shoes himself, ran to him and undid them, and helped him to anoint himself. And from then on he continued to wait upon and attend him in all things, as slaves do their masters, even to the washing of his feet and the preparation of his supper, so that anyone who observed the free and simple courtesy of that service might well have exclaimed,

All hail generous souls, whose every act is noble![213]

74. Pompey, after sailing along the coast to Amphipolis, crossed over from there to Mitylene, hoping to pick up Cornelia and his

---

211 Referring to Publius Lentulus and his son, Lucius (seen in chapter 59).

212 King of Galatia and an ally of Pompey in the recent battle.

213 Plutarch quotes this line again in his *Moralia* and attributes it to Euripides, but it is otherwise unknown.

son. And as soon as he came ashore, he sent a messenger to the city, not of the sort that Cornelia was expecting in light of the joyful messages and letters she had received, since she was hoping that the war at Dyrrachium had ended and that Pompey's only remaining task was the pursuit of Caesar. The messenger, finding her in this state of mind, was unable to greet her, but declaring the greatest of her troubles by his tears rather than by his speech, urged her to hurry if she would see Pompey with one ship only, and that not his own. On hearing this she fainted, and lay for a long time senseless and speechless; and when with some difficulty she came to her senses, and understood that this was no time for lamentation and tears, she ran out through the city to the sea. Pompey met her and caught her in his arms as she tottered and sank down. "It is through *my* fortune, husband," she said, "not yours, that I see you reduced to one small vessel—you, who before your marriage with Cornelia sailed this sea with a fleet of five hundred ships. Why did you come to see me, and why did you not abandon to her wretched fate one who has afflicted you with her own ill fortune? What *good* fortune I would have had, had I died before hearing that Publius, whose virgin bride I was, lay dead among the Parthians! And how prudent if, even after his death, as I tried to do, I had succeeded in ending my life! But I was reserved, as it seems, to be the ruin of Pompey the Great."

75. So spoke Cornelia, we are told, and Pompey replied, "Well, Cornelia, you have, after all, known only one phase of fortune, namely the better one, and this has perhaps deceived you as well as me, by lasting with me longer than is usual. But we are obliged, being mortal, to endure these things, and to try fortune yet again. For I am as likely to regain my former state as I was to fall from that into this."

His wife, accordingly, sent for her goods and servants from the city. And though the Mitylenaeans welcomed Pompey and invited him to enter their city, he declined to do so, and advised them to obey the conqueror and take courage, for Caesar was reasonable and humane. Then he himself, turning to Cratippus the philosopher,[214] who had come from the city to see him, raised some objection and argued with him briefly about Providence; but Cratippus gave in, and tried to lead him toward better hopes, lest he cause him pain by opposing him at such a moment. For when Pompey raised questions about Providence, Cratippus might have demonstrated that the commonwealth now needed a monarchy because it had been so badly governed; he could have asked, "How, Pompey, and by what evidence are we to be persuaded that if you had been victorious you would have used your fortune better than Caesar?"[215] But we must forgo further discussion of the role played by divinity in these events.

76. After taking aboard his wife and friends, Pompey sailed onward, putting ashore only when he was forced to take in provisions or freshwater. The first city he entered was Attaleia in Pamphylia. There some triremes met him from Cilicia, together with a body of soldiers, and he was again surrounded by sixty senators. Hearing, also, that his fleet still held together, and that Cato had rallied many soldiers and was crossing with them to Africa, he complained to his friends, blaming himself for having been driven into engaging by land, without making use of his navy, in which he was indisputably superior, and for not even anchoring it at a place where, if he were defeated on land, he might have reinforced himself by sea, and would then have been able to meet the enemy on equal terms. For in fact Pompey made no greater error, and Caesar devised no cleverer stratagem, than in drawing the battle so far from naval assistance. But since Pompey had to come to some decision and do his best under the circumstances, he sent messengers to the neighboring cities; he also sailed round in person, asking for money

---

214 A leading Aristotelian (or "Peripatetic;" Plutarch gives him that epithet at *Cicero* 24) of the first century BCE, who taught both at Athens and Mitylene.

215 That is, given that divinity had seen fit to provide Rome with an autocrat, Pompey has no reason to assume that his defeat was not part of that plan. Many editors assign the following sentence to the imagined speech of Cratippus rather than to Plutarch's authorial voice.

and manning ships. But fearing the speed and quickness of the enemy, who might attack and seize him before he was prepared, he began to consider what place would afford him a refuge and retreat at present. A conference was held, and it was agreed that no Roman province was secure enough; as for the kingdoms, Pompey himself was of the opinion that Parthia was the fittest to receive them in their present weakness, and afterward to strengthen them and send them off with a large force. Others were for going to Africa and Juba.[216] But Theophanes of Lesbos thought it madness to rule out Egypt, which was a three days' sail away, and make no use of Ptolemy, who was a boy, and was indebted to Pompey for the friendship and kindness he had shown to his father,[217] only to put himself in the hands of the Parthians, a most treacherous nation; and to refuse to accept second place under a Roman who had been connected to him by marriage, and to be chief over all the rest, and not even to make trial of that Roman's moderation, but instead to make Arsaces his master, which even Crassus could not be forced to do while he lived;[218] and to take a young wife, of the family of Scipio, to barbarians who measure their power by their insolence and licentiousness, and where, even if she suffered no dishonor but were only thought to have suffered it, her fate would be terrible, since she would be at the mercy of those who were able to harm her. This argument alone, they say, dissuaded Pompey from sailing to the Euphrates, if in fact any calculation of Pompey's, rather than some divine power, was guiding him on that journey.

---

216 Juba I, king of Numidia, had been Pompey's ally during the civil war.

217 The young Ptolemy XIII, along with his sister (and wife) Cleopatra, had by this time succeeded Ptolemy XII, the once exiled ruler whom Ptolemy had helped restore (see chapter 49 and note 142). On Theophanes, see note 102.

218 Arsaces was the name of several Parthian kings, but it was in fact Orodes II who was on the Parthian throne at the time that Crassus led an ill-fated invasion. The question of whether Crassus was willing to submit to the Parthian king is moot, since, by Plutarch's own account, Crassus was killed in an accidental skirmish when he was negotiating terms of surrender (*Crassus* 30–31).

77. Accordingly, when it was decided that he should flee to Egypt, he set sail from Cyprus on a Seleucian trireme with his wife (the rest of his company sailing along near him, some in warships like his own, others in merchant vessels), and crossed the sea in safety. But on learning that Ptolemy was posted with an army at Pelusium, making war against his sister,[219] he put in there, and sent a messenger ahead to notify the king of his arrival and to request his aid. Ptolemy himself was quite young; and therefore Potheinus, who managed all his affairs,[220] assembled a council of the most influential men (these being the most influential because he wished to make them so), and commanded each one to give his opinion. It was, indeed, a dreadful thing that the fate of Pompey the Great should be decided by Potheinus the eunuch, Theodotus of Chios, a hired teacher of rhetoric, and Achillas the Egyptian. For these, among the chamberlains and tutors who made up the rest of the council, were its chief members. And it was the verdict of such a tribunal that Pompey, riding at anchor a distance from shore, was forced to await, since he did not think it honorable to owe his safety to Caesar.

The councilors were so far different in their opinions that some were for driving the man away, others for inviting and receiving him. But Theodotus, displaying his cleverness and the cogency of his rhetoric, demonstrated that neither course was safe. For if they received him, they would make Caesar their enemy and Pompey their master; or if they dismissed him, they would be blamed by Pompey for expelling him, and by Caesar for prolonging his pursuit; so the most expedient course would be to send for the man and take his life; for by doing so they would gratify Caesar and have no reason to fear Pompey. So saying, he is reported to have smiled and added, "A dead man does not bite."

78. When this advice was approved, they entrusted the execution of

---

219 Cleopatra had raised an army to support her bid for sole power. Her brother, husband, and co-ruler, Ptolemy XIII, was only twelve at this time.

220 For more on the grasping eunuch Potheinus and his fate, see *Caesar* 48–49.

it to Achillas. He, therefore, taking with him a certain Septimius, who had once been a tribune under Pompey, and Salvius, another centurion, and three or four servants, put out toward Pompey's ship. Meanwhile all the most notable of those who accompanied Pompey in this voyage had come aboard his ship to see what was happening. But when they saw that their reception by the Egyptians was neither royal nor honorable, nor consistent with the hopes of Theophanes, since only a few men came in a fishing boat to meet them, they began to think there was something suspicious about this meager welcome, and advised Pompey to row his ship back to the open sea, outside the range of arrows. But by that time the Egyptian boat had drawn near, and Septimius, standing up first, hailed Pompey in the Roman language as *imperator.* Then Achillas, hailing him in Greek, invited him to come aboard his vessel, telling him that the shallows were broad, and that the sea, which had a sandy bottom, could not keep a trireme afloat. At the same time some of the king's ships were taking their crews on board,[221] and the shore was covered with men-at-arms, so that no escape seemed possible even if Pompey and his party changed their minds; and besides, their distrust might have given the assassins a pretext for their crime. Pompey, therefore, embracing Cornelia, who was already lamenting his death before it came, ordered two centurions, with Philip, one of his freedmen, and a servant called Scythes, to board the boat before him. And as Achillas was already reaching out his hand to help him from the boat, he turned toward his wife and son and repeated the iambic verses of Sophocles,[222]

He who traffics with a tyrant becomes his slave,
Though he goes to him a free man.

79. With these last words to his friends, he boarded the boat. And as there was a considerable distance between his trireme and the shore,

---

221 That is, they were preparing to put to sea.

222 From an unknown play.

but none of the company spoke any friendly word to him, he gazed steadfastly at Septimius and said, "Am I mistaken, or were you not once my fellow soldier?" But Septimius merely nodded his head, making no reply, nor showing any friendliness. Since there was again a prolonged silence, Pompey took out a little roll containing a speech he had written in Greek, which he had prepared for his address to Ptolemy, and began to read it. When they drew near the shore, Cornelia, together with his friends on the trireme, was in a state of anxiety as she watched for the outcome, and began to take courage when she saw several of the king's people gathering at the landing as if to give him an honorable welcome. But at that moment, as Pompey was taking Philip by the hand to rise up more easily, Septimius stabbed him from behind, and then Salvius and Achillas also drew their swords. Pompey, therefore, drawing his toga over his face with both hands, and neither saying nor doing anything unworthy of himself, but only groaning, endured their blows, having lived for fifty-nine years,[223] and ending his life one day after his birthday.

80. When the people on the ships saw the murder, they gave out a wail that was heard on the shore, and weighing anchor with all speed, they fled. A strong breeze assisted their flight into the open sea, so that the Egyptians, though eager to pursue them, returned to shore. But they cut off Pompey's head, and threw the rest of his body naked out of the boat, and left it for those who longed for such a sight. Philip stayed by the body until they had had their fill of gazing at it; then he washed it with seawater, wrapped it in his own tunic, and since he had nothing else, sought up and down the coast until he found some remnants of a small fishing boat—old planks, but enough to furnish a funeral pyre for a naked body, though not quite a whole one. As he was gathering the planks and building a pyre, an old Roman citizen, who in his youth had served in his first campaigns with Pompey, came up and said, "Who are you, sir, that you think to prepare a funeral for Pompey the Great?" And when

223 Plutarch's math is slightly off; Pompey died just after turning fifty-eight.

Philip replied that he was his freedman, the man said, "But you will not have this honor all to yourself. Let me too have my share in such a sacred windfall, that I may not altogether repent my living abroad, but in compensation of my many misfortunes may obtain this happiness at least, to touch with my hands and lay out for burial the greatest of Roman generals." In this way were Pompey's funeral rites performed. The next day Lucius Lentulus, not knowing what had happened, came sailing from Cyprus along the shore of that coast, and seeing a funeral pyre, and Philip standing by, exclaimed, before he was seen by anyone, "Who rests here at the end of his allotted time?" Then, after a brief pause, he groaned and said, "Perhaps it is you, Pompey the Great." And after a little while he went ashore, where he was seized and slain.

This was the end of Pompey. Not long after, Caesar arrived in Egypt and found it filled with this abominable deed. From the man who brought him Pompey's head he turned away as from a murderer; and when he received Pompey's seal ring, on which was carved a lion holding a sword, he burst into tears. Achillas and Potheinus he put to death; and the king himself, being defeated in battle beside the river,[224] disappeared. Theodotus the sophist, however, escaped Caesar's justice; for he fled from Egypt and wandered about in misery, a hated man. But Marcus Brutus, after he had killed Caesar, found him in Asia, subjected him to every form of torture, and put him to death.[225] The ashes of Pompey were carried to Cornelia, who deposited them near Alba.

---

224 Ptolemy XIII was defeated by his sister, Cleopatra, aided by Caesar, in a battle by the Nile.

225 See *Brutus* 33.

CAESAR

When Sulla became master of Rome,[1] he tried to make Caesar divorce his wife Cornelia, the daughter of Cinna, who had once held sole rule in the city;[2] but as he was unable to effect this either by promises or threats, he confiscated the woman's dowry. The reason for Sulla's hostility to Caesar was Caesar's relationship to Marius.[3] For Marius the Elder married Julia, the sister of Caesar's father, and had by her the younger Marius, who was therefore Caesar's first cousin. Now at first, Caesar was overlooked (Sulla being busy with a great many murders[4]); he did not take this well, but presented himself to the people as a candidate for a priesthood, though he was still a mere boy. Sulla, who secretly opposed this candidacy, took steps to have Caesar rejected, and when he was considering whether he should put him to death, and some said there was no reason to kill a boy like him, Sulla replied

---

1 Sulla became dictator in 82 BCE, when Caesar was already eighteen. The first few chapters of *Caesar*, which must have contained accounts of its subject's parentage, birth, and childhood, have been lost.

2 Lucius Cornelius Cinna served as consul for four consecutive years, 87–84 BCE, and from that office exercised an almost unchallenged power.

3 Marius (referred to just below as Marius the Elder), Sulla's bitter enemy in a long power struggle in the 80s BCE, is the subject of another Plutarchan Life.

4 After assuming dictatorial power in 82 BCE, Sulla embarked on a series of proscriptions, whereby names of his enemies were posted and rewards were offered for their arrest or execution.

that they were foolish not to see in this boy many Mariuses. When this remark was reported to Caesar, he hid himself, wandering about for some time in the country of the Sabines.[5] Then one night, as he was moving from one house to another to avoid illness, he fell into the hands of Sulla's soldiers, who were searching those regions in order to arrest any who were in hiding there. Bribing Cornelius their captain with two talents to let him go, he at once went down to the sea and sailed to King Nicomedes in Bithynia.[6] After a short visit, he was captured on his return voyage near the island of Pharmacusa[7] by pirates, who at that time controlled the sea with large ships and innumerable small vessels.

2. At first, when the pirates demanded twenty talents for his ransom, he laughed at them for not knowing whom they had captured, and agreed to give them fifty.[8] Then, when he had sent several of his followers here and there to raise the money, he was left among the Cilicians,[9] the most bloodthirsty of men, with one friend and two attendants. He showed such contempt for the Cilicians that whenever he lay down to sleep he would send word to them, ordering them to keep quiet. For thirty-eight days, without a care in the world, he would join in their games and exercises as if they were not his captors but his bodyguard. Writing poems and speeches, he treated them as his audience, and those who did not admire them he called to their faces illiterate barbarians, and would often, as a joke, threaten to hang them. They were amused, and attributed his

---

5 A mountainous region of Italy, north and east of Rome.

6 An independent monarch ruling northern Anatolia. His kingdom became a Roman vassal state shortly after this time.

7 In the eastern Aegean.

8 Fifty talents (over one million sesterces) represented a considerable fortune; as related above, Caesar had earlier "ransomed" himself from an arresting Roman officer for only two talents.

9 That is, the pirates.

outspokenness to simplicity and playfulness. When his ransom came from Miletus, and he had paid it and was set free, he immediately manned some ships and set out against the pirates from the harbor of Miletus. Catching them still lying at anchor, he got most of them into his clutches. Their money he made his booty, but he had the men themselves locked up in the prison at Pergamum, and went in person to Juncus, who was then governor of Asia,[10] thinking that it was for him as praetor to punish the captives. But Juncus, who had his eye on their money (a veritable fortune), said he would consider at his leisure what to do with the prisoners, whereupon Caesar took leave of him, went off to Pergamum, and had all the prisoners brought out and crucified, inflicting the very punishment he had threatened them with on the island when they thought he was joking.

3. After this, Sulla's power being in decline, and Caesar's friends having invited him to return to Rome, Caesar sailed to Rhodes, where he entered the school of Apollonius, son of Molon, a famous rhetorician and a man renowned for his good character, who also had Cicero as a student. Caesar is also said to have had a great natural talent for political oratory, and to have cultivated that talent ambitiously, so that no one might challenge him for second place. First place, however, he renounced, preferring to devote his efforts to being first as a statesman and commander; he therefore never attained the height of eloquence to which his natural talent might have carried him, his energies being devoted to the campaigns and political activities that gained him sovereignty. And he himself, at a later time, in his answer to Cicero's *Cato*,[11] asks the reader not to compare the discourse of a soldier with the eloquence of an orator

10 "Asia" here (as often in Plutarch) refers to the Roman province of Asia, roughly the western portion of modern Turkey. Marcus Juncus was praetor there in 76 BCE and proconsul in 75.

11 See chapter 54 below.

who was naturally gifted and enjoyed plenty of leisure to pursue this study.[12]

4. On his return to Rome he accused Dolabella of maladministration,[13] and many cities of Greece supplied him with testimony. Dolabella was acquitted, but Caesar, in return for the support he had received from the Greeks, assisted them in their prosecution of Publius Antonius for corruption when the man appeared before Marcus Lucullus, the praetor of Macedonia. And he succeeded so well that Antonius appealed to the tribunes at Rome, alleging that he could not have a fair trial against Greeks in Greece. In Rome, Caesar's eloquence as an advocate won him great favor and prestige, and his affability and amiable manners great goodwill among the common people, since he showed a tact and courtesy unusual in a man of his age; and his generous hospitality and the splendor of his way of life served little by little to increase his political influence. At first his detractors thought this influence would vanish as soon as his funds were exhausted, and therefore allowed it to flourish among the common people. But when his power had become great and hard to overthrow, and tended openly toward a complete revolution in the state, they perceived too late that there is no beginning so small that continuance will not make it large, if a danger becomes impossible to reverse because it has been disregarded. The man thought to have been the first to suspect Caesar's policy and to fear it, as a pilot might fear a smiling sea, and who detected the formidable character concealed beneath his kindliness and affability—Cicero—said that he saw in all of Caesar's schemes and political ventures a tyrannical intention, "though when I see his hair so carefully arranged, and watch him scratching his head with one finger,[14] I find it hard to suppose that this

12 That is, not to hold Caesar to the same high standard as Cicero.

13 Dolabella had been one of Sulla's former commanders and had served as governor of the Roman province of Macedonia. Sulla was dead by this time.

14 Several Roman writers attest that this gesture was considered a mark of effeminacy or lasciviousness.

man would ever conceive of so great a crime as the overthrow of the Roman constitution." But this belongs to a later period.

5. The first proof he had of the people's goodwill toward him was when he competed with Gaius Popilius for a military tribuneship and was elected in preference to him; he received a second and clearer proof when, as the nephew of Julia, the deceased wife of Marius, he delivered a splendid encomium in the Forum, and in the funeral procession dared to bring forth the images of Marius,[15] which were then seen for the first time since the regime of Sulla; for Marius and his party had been declared enemies of the state. When some denounced Caesar for this, the people answered with a resounding cry, greeted Caesar with applause, and admired him for bringing back the honors of Marius, as if from Hades, after so long a time. It had always been the custom in Rome to deliver funeral orations in praise of elderly women; but this had never been done for young women, and it was Caesar who initiated the practice when his own wife died. This made him popular, and so touched the hearts of his fellow citizens that they adored him as a man of great gentleness and sensibility.

After burying his wife, he went out to Spain as quaestor under Vetus, one of the praetors, whom he never failed to honor; and later, when he himself was praetor, he made Vetus' son his quaestor. After serving in that office, he married his third wife,[16] Pompeia, having already by Cornelia a daughter who was later married to Pompey the Great.

He spent lavishly and was thought to be purchasing an ephemeral and short-lived renown at great cost, though he was actually buying things of the greatest value at a small cost.[17] It is said, at any rate,

---

15 Masks of ancestors were worn by actors in Roman funeral processions.

16 Plutarch has mentioned only one other before Pompeia, but apparently thought that Caesar had also been briefly married in his teens.

17 Roman magistrates spent not only from public funds but from their own

that before he assumed public office he was thirteen hundred talents in debt. When he was made a caretaker of the Appian Way,[18] he expended on it considerable sums of his own money; and when he was aedile[19] he furnished three hundred twenty pairs of gladiators, and by producing spectacles, processions, and public banquets, he washed away the ambitious efforts of his predecessors. He thereby gained such favor with the people that everyone was eager to find new offices and new honors with which to requite him.

6. There were two factions in the city—that of Sulla, which was powerful, and that of Marius, which was then in a fractured and lowly state. This party Caesar wished to revive and make his own. Accordingly, while he was at the height of his popularity as aedile, he had images of Marius made in secret, and trophy-bearing Victories,[20] which he had conveyed by night and set up in the Capitol. In the morning, those who saw them gleaming with gold and exquisitely sculpted, with inscriptions linking them to Marius' successful exploits against the Cimbri, were astounded at the boldness of the man who had set them up (for it was clear who it was), and word soon spread and brought everyone together to view them. Some cried out that Caesar, by reviving honors that had been buried by the laws and decrees of the Senate,[21] was seeking a tyranny, and that this had been done to test the people, whom he had mollified earlier, and to find out whether they had been tamed by his ambitious spectacles, and would indulge his taste for such innovations.

---

as well, as a way to gain popularity. Plutarch's point here is that the public acclaim Caesar won with his generosity was well worth the expense.

18 The Appian Way, a road leading south out of Rome, was lined with elegant monuments that needed upkeep and repair.

19 See Appendix for this term and others designating Roman offices.

20 Statues of the goddess Victory were apparently used to rally political support at this time; Plutarch also mentions them in his *Marius* (ch. 32) and *Sulla* (ch. 6).

21 Under Sulla's dictatorship, such Marian displays had been outlawed.

But Marius' partisans, taking heart, suddenly appeared in amazing numbers and filled the Capitol with their applause. Many, at the sight of Marius' likeness, were moved to tears of joy, and Caesar was highly exalted as the one man who was worthy beyond all others of his kinship with Marius. When the Senate met to debate these matters, Lutatius Catulus, one of the most eminent Romans of his day, rose up and denounced Caesar, making the memorable remark, "Caesar is no longer using underground passages but siege engines to usurp the government." But when Caesar had defended himself against these charges, and persuaded the Senate, his admirers were even more elated, and advised him not to lower his aspirations for any man, since with the people's support he would triumph and be the foremost man in the state.

7. At this time, Metellus, the pontifex maximus,[22] died, and Catulus and Isauricus, men of distinction who exercised great influence in the Senate, competed for the office. Caesar would not give way to them, however, but presented himself to the people as a rival candidate. Their chances seemed nearly equal, and therefore Catulus, who, owing to his greater prestige, was more afraid of the uncertainty, sent to Caesar to persuade him to forgo his ambitious candidacy, offering him a large sum of money. But Caesar replied that he was ready to borrow an even larger sum to carry the campaign through.

On the day of the election, as his mother walked him to the door in tears, Caesar kissed her and said, "Mother, today you will see your son either pontifex maximus or an exile." The contest was heated, but when the vote was taken Caesar prevailed, and made the Senate and the nobles apprehensive that he would lead the people on to every kind of recklessness. Hence Piso and Catulus reproached Cicero for having spared Caesar when, in the conspiracy of Catiline, Caesar had made himself so vulnerable.[23] For Catiline, who

---

22 The Roman pontifex maximus was head of a board of state priests who supervised religious rites and maintained the calendar.

23 Catiline's conspiracy, in the early 60s BCE, had aimed at a takeover of

had planned not only to change the constitution, but to subvert the entire empire and throw everything into confusion, had fled the city after being confronted with proofs of lesser transgressions before his ultimate intentions were discovered; but he had left Lentulus and Cethegus behind as his successors in the conspiracy, and whether Caesar gave them any secret encouragement or help is uncertain.[24] They were decisively convicted in the Senate; and when Cicero the consul asked each senator for his opinion as to how they should be punished, all who spoke before Caesar urged that they be put to death; but Caesar stood up and made a carefully reasoned speech in which he argued that to put to death men of their high rank and birth without a fair trial was neither traditional nor just, unless there was an absolute necessity for it; but if they were bound and kept in custody in any towns in Italy that Cicero himself should choose, until Catiline had been defeated, then the Senate might in time of peace, and at their leisure, determine what should be done with them.

8. This proposal of his seemed so humane, and the eloquence with which it was urged gave it such power, that not only those who spoke after him supported it but many who had before given contrary views now came over to his, until the question came round to Cato and Catulus. They vehemently opposed it, and Cato even raised a suspicion against Caesar himself, and made so strong an argument that the men were handed over for execution.[25] Then, as Caesar was leaving the Senate house, many of the young men of Cicero's bodyguard ran up to assault him. But Curio, it is said, threw his toga over Caesar and spirited him away, and Cicero himself, when the young men looked to see what he wished, shook his

---

the state; Caesar's part in it was ambiguous, as Plutarch goes on to describe. A detailed account can be found at *Cicero* 10–24.

24 See *Cicero* 20, where Plutarch seems more convinced that Caesar had played some part in the conspiracy.

25 See *Cicero* 21 and *Cato* 22–23.

head, either through fear of the people or because he felt that murder would be wholly unjust and illegal.

But if this is true, I do not see why Cicero never mentioned it in his account of his consulship.[26] He was blamed afterward, however, for not having taken advantage of the best opportunity against Caesar, as if he feared the people, who were extraordinarily devoted to the man. A few days later, at any rate, when Caesar went to the Senate to clear himself of the suspicions that had been raised against him, and met with a disapproving uproar, the people, when the Senate's session ran longer than usual, approached with loud cries, surrounded the Senate house, demanded Caesar, and ordered the Senate to let him go. It was for this reason that Cato, terrified at the prospect of a revolution instigated by the poor citizens, who were inflaming the whole multitude with the hopes they placed in Caesar, persuaded the Senate to distribute a monthly allowance of grain, which added an outlay of 7,500,000 drachmas to the state's annual expenditures.[27] But this measure quite obviously allayed the great fear that then prevailed, and substantially weakened and dissipated Caesar's power at a critical moment, since he was about to be made praetor and would have been more formidable because of his office.

9. But no disturbance resulted from Caesar's praetorship, though an unpleasant incident occurred in his family.[28] Publius Clodius was a patrician by birth, distinguished for his wealth and eloquence, but in insolence and audacity second to none of the most notorious libertines of the day. This man was in love with Pompeia, Caesar's wife, and she was not unwilling. But a strict watch was kept on the

---

26 A treatise now lost.

27 See *Cato* 26 for another version of the story. As often, Plutarch uses Greek drachmas as a rough equivalent for Roman denarii.

28 See *Cicero* 28–29 for another version of this story.

women's quarters,[29] and Aurelia, Caesar's mother, who was a sensible woman and always accompanied her daughter-in-law, made it difficult and dangerous for the lovers to meet.

The Romans have a goddess whom they call Bona, corresponding to the Greek Gynaeceia. The Phrygians claim her as their own and maintain that she was the mother of King Midas; the Romans, on the other hand, say she was a dryad nymph, and married to Faunus; and the Greeks that she was one of the mothers of Dionysus—the goddess whose name must not be uttered.[30] Hence when the women celebrate her festival they cover their tents with vine branches, and a sacred serpent is enthroned beside the goddess in accordance with the myth. It is not lawful for a man to be present, or even to be in the house, while the ceremonies are held; but the women by themselves perform the rites, many of which are said to resemble those used in the Orphic observances. When the time for the festival has come, the consul or praetor at whose house the rites are performed goes away, and every male with him, and the wife takes charge and arranges the house. The principal rites are performed at night; the women play and amuse themselves throughout the vigil, and plenty of music is heard.

10. Pompeia was at that time celebrating this festival, and Clodius, who still had no beard and for that reason thought he would likely escape detection, donned the dress and ornaments of a lute girl and went to the house, looking like a young woman. He found the doors open and was brought in safely by the maid, who was privy

---

29 Plutarch transposes to a Roman house the *gunaikeion* he knew from the Greek world.

30 The deities listed are all connected with fertility, sexuality, and agriculture. The Phrygian goddess can be identified as Cybele, while the unnameable mother of Dionysus is Persephone, often called simply Kore ("the Maiden"). These Aegean figures were the focus of secret and ecstatic rites, making them seem to Plutarch the equivalent of the Roman Bona Dea ("Good Goddess"). The ritual Plutarch goes on to describe is that of the Bona Dea.

to the intrigue; but after she had run to tell Pompeia, and some time had passed, Clodius could not bear to remain where he had been left; he wandered through the large house, avoiding the light, until an attendant of Aurelia met him and asked him, as one woman to another, to play a game with her. When he refused, she dragged him forward and asked him who he was and where he came from. When Clodius said he was waiting for Pompeia's Abra (that was the maid's name) and his voice gave him away, the attendant immediately leapt up shrieking, and ran to the lights and the throng, shouting that she had caught a man. The women were panic-stricken; Aurelia stopped the goddess's rites and covered up the sacred objects.[31] Then she ordered the doors to be shut and went about the house with torches, searching for Clodius. He was found in the room of the maid who had let him in. And when he was recognized the women drove him out of doors, and at once, that night, went off and told the story to their husbands. In the morning a rumor spread through the city that Clodius had committed a sacrilege and ought to pay a penalty not only to those whom he had insulted, but also to the city and to the gods. Accordingly, one of the tribunes of the people indicted Clodius for impiety, and the most influential senators leagued against him, bearing witness that, in addition to his other horrible crimes, he had committed adultery with his sister, who was married to Lucullus. But against the zealous efforts of these men the people arrayed themselves and defended Clodius, and were of great benefit to him with the jurors, who were terrified of the multitude. Caesar at once divorced Pompeia; but when he was summoned to testify at the trial, he said he knew nothing about the allegations against Clodius. As his statement seemed odd, the prosecutor asked, "Then why did you divorce your wife?" "Because," Caesar replied, "I thought that my wife should be above suspicion."

Some say that Caesar made this statement sincerely, others, that he

---

31 As in other mystery cults, the worship of Bona Dea seems to have involved the uncovering of potent symbolic objects.

made it to gratify the people, who were determined to save Clodius. Clodius, at any rate, was acquitted of the charge, the majority of the jurors defacing the letters on their ballots[32] lest they risk their lives with the people by condemning him, or, by acquitting him, forfeit the good opinion of the nobility.

11. Caesar, immediately after his praetorship, obtained the province of Spain, but found it hard to manage his creditors, who, as he was departing, barred his way and raised an uproar. He therefore fled to Crassus, the richest man in Rome,[33] who needed Caesar's youthful vigor and heat to support the political opposition to Pompey. Crassus agreed to satisfy the most difficult and implacable of these creditors, and committed himself to the amount of eight hundred thirty talents, whereupon Caesar departed for his province.

It is said that as he was crossing the Alps and passing by a miserable barbarian village that had few inhabitants, his companions, joking among themselves, said, "Do you suppose that here, too, there are ambitious struggles for office, and competitions for supremacy, and jealousies among the great and powerful?" At this Caesar grew serious and replied: "I would rather be first among these men than second in Rome." It is said that at another time, in Spain, when he was at leisure and reading something from a history of Alexander, he sat for a long time, deep in thought, and then burst into tears. His friends were surprised, and asked what was wrong. "Don't you think I have reason to lament," he replied, "that while Alexander at my age already ruled so many nations, I have not yet achieved any splendid success?"

---

32 Plutarch apparently misunderstood Roman juridical balloting. The scratching out of both the letters on a ballot ("A" for *absolvo* to acquit, "C" for *condemno* to convict) was a legitimate way for jurors to indicate abstention. According to a modern reconstruction of the vote in this case, about a quarter of the jury abstained.

33 Marcus Licinius Crassus is the subject of another Plutarchan Life; see *Crassus* 7 for the episode related here.

12. As soon as he reached Spain he went to work, and in a few days had levied ten cohorts in addition to the twenty that were there before. He then marched against the Callaici and Lusitanians, overpowered them, and advanced as far as the Outer Sea,[34] subduing the tribes that had never before been subject to Rome. Having prosecuted the war successfully, he was equally fortunate in administering affairs in peacetime, both by establishing concord between the cities, and especially by healing the differences between debtors and creditors. For he prescribed that the creditor should take two-thirds of his debtor's annual income, and that the rest should be managed by the debtor himself until by this schedule the debt was cleared. Highly esteemed for these measures, he retired from the province. He had himself become rich, had enriched the soldiers from his campaigns, and had been hailed by them as *imperator.*[35]

13. Since those who sought to be awarded a triumph[36] had to remain outside the city, while those who stood for a consulship had to appear there in person, Caesar found himself in a strait between two laws. As he had arrived at the very time of the elections, he sent to the Senate, requesting that he be permitted to present himself for the consulship *in absentia*, through his friends. Cato began by enforcing the law in opposition to Caesar's request; but then, when he saw that many of the senators had been won over by Caesar, he postponed the issue by using up the day delivering a speech.[37] Caesar decided to give up the triumph and go after the consulship. And as

---

34 That is, the Atlantic.

35 The honorific *imperator* (roughly meaning "commander") could be awarded to a victorious general by his troops or by an official act of the Senate. Later the term was used by the Praetorian Guard to acclaim newly installed emperors.

36 The triumphal procession, in which a conquering general displayed his captives and plunder to cheering throngs of Romans, was awarded by an act of the Senate.

37 Senate decrees had to be passed before sundown on the day of debate.

soon as he arrived he adopted a policy that deceived everyone but Cato. This was to reconcile Pompey and Crassus, the most influential men in the city.[38] Uniting these men in friendship after their quarrel, and combining both men's strengths for his own purposes, he managed, without being detected, and by an act that would be considered kind and generous, to change the form of government. For it was not, as most believe, the quarrel between Caesar and Pompey that caused the civil wars, but rather their friendship; for they banded together in the first place to overthrow the aristocracy, and only afterward quarreled with each other.[39] And Cato, who often foretold the consequences of this alliance, earned then the reputation of a bitter and meddlesome fellow, but later that of a wise, but unfortunate, adviser.

14. Thus Caesar, with the friendship of Crassus and Pompey as his bodyguard, stood for the consulship; and as soon as he had been triumphantly proclaimed, with co-consul Calpurnius Bibulus, and had assumed his office, he proposed laws that were suitable not for a consul but for an exceptionally audacious tribune,[40] introducing various allotments and distributions of land to gratify the multitude. In the Senate, the opposition of the nobility furnished him with a pretext he had long desired. Loudly protesting, and bearing witness that he was driven against his will to the popular assembly, and compelled to court it by the insolence and harshness of the Senate, he hastened to appear before it. And placing Crassus and Pompey on either side of him, he asked them whether they approved of his laws. They declared they did approve of them, at which point he urged them to aid him against those who threatened to oppose him with swords. They promised to do so, and Pompey even added that he would

38 See *Crassus* 14 and *Pompey* 47. The resulting arrangement has been termed the First Triumvirate.

39 Plutarch looks ahead to the events of chapters 28–47 below.

40 Rome's ten tribunes were elected to represent the interests of the masses against those of the aristocrats who filled the Senate and the consulship.

meet their swords with both a sword and a shield. With this mad and impetuous speech he vexed the nobles, who found it unworthy of Pompey's dignity and unbecoming to the reverence due to the Senate; but the people were delighted with it.

Caesar now tried to get a better hold on Pompey's influence. He had a daughter, Julia, who was betrothed to Servilius Caepio. This daughter he betrothed to Pompey, and said he would give Pompey's daughter in marriage to Servilius, though this young woman was also not unbetrothed, but had been promised to Faustus, son of Sulla. And shortly thereafter Caesar married Calpurnia, the daughter of Piso, and got Piso made consul for the following year, though here too Cato strenuously objected, and loudly protested that it was insufferable to have the supreme authority prostituted by marriages, and to witness men advancing one another to provinces, armies, and powers by means of women.

As for Bibulus, Caesar's colleague, since he found it impossible to hinder Caesar's laws, and often ran the risk, with Cato, of being killed in the Forum, he confined himself to his house for the remainder of his consulship. Pompey, on the other hand, as soon as he had married, filled the Forum with armed men, helped the people to enact the laws that gave Caesar control of Gaul on both sides of the Alps, and Illyricum, together with four legions, for five years. When Cato tried to argue against these measures, Caesar had him led off to prison, thinking the man would appeal to the tribunes. But when Cato went along without a word, and Caesar saw not only that the nobility were unhappy, but that the common people too, out of respect for Cato's virtue, followed him in sorrowful silence, he himself secretly asked one of the tribunes to let Cato go.

Of the other senators, a few went with him to the Senate house; the rest, disgusted, stayed away. When Considius, a very old senator, once told Caesar that his colleagues did not meet because they feared his weapons and soldiers, Caesar asked, "Why, then, don't *you*, out of the same fear, stay at home?" To this Considius replied, "Because old age makes me fearless. One with only a few years left need not take much thought for the future." But the most disgraceful political measure at the time was thought to be the election, during Caesar's consulship, of the infamous Clodius, who had trespassed upon Caesar's marriage and the secret nocturnal rites. He was elected, however, for the overthrow of Cicero; and Caesar did not embark on his campaign until, with Clodius' help, he had established a faction against Cicero and driven him out of Italy.

15. Such, then, is said to have been Caesar's career before the Gallic campaigns. But after this it seems as if he made a fresh start and entered upon a new path of life and of novel achievements. And the period of the wars that he now fought, and those campaigns in which he subdued Gaul,[41] showed him to be a soldier and general not in the least inferior to any of the greatest and most admired commanders. For if one compares him with the Fabii, the Scipios, the Metelli, and with those who were his contemporaries, or a little before him—Sulla, Marius, the two Luculli, or even Pompey himself, whose renown for every sort of excellence in war was at that time flourishing and soaring to the heavens[42]—Caesar's achievements will be found to have surpassed them all. One he outshone in the difficulty of the terrain in which he fought, another in the extent of territory that he acquired; another in the number and strength of the enemy whom he defeated; another in the wildness and duplicity of the tribes whom he conciliated; another in his humanity and gentleness toward his captives; another in the gifts and favors he bestowed on his soldiers; and every one in the number

41 Plutarch here and elsewhere identifies Gaul as "the land of the Celts," though this loosely connected amalgamation of tribes in fact spread far more widely across Europe.

42 From this honor roll of great Roman commanders, Plutarch has made nearly all the more recent ones subjects of his *Lives*: Sulla, Marius, Pompey, and one of the Lucullus brothers (Lucius Licinius Lucullus). From among the earlier group, Fabius Maximus, the adversary of Hannibal, is also the subject of a surviving Life, while the Life of Scipio Africanus, originally part of the opening pair in Plutarch's collection, has been lost.

of battles he fought and the enemies he killed. For he had not been waging war for ten years in Gaul before he had taken by storm more than eight hundred cities and subdued three hundred nations; and of the three million men with whom, at various times, he had fought pitched battles, he had killed one million, and taken another million prisoner.

16. He could so count on the goodwill and zeal of his soldiers, that those who in other campaigns had been in no way superior to the rest were invincible and irresistible when facing any danger on behalf of Caesar's glory. Such a man, for example, was Acilius, who in the sea battle off Massilia, after boarding an enemy ship, had his right hand cut off with a sword, but kept hold of his shield with the other, and with it struck his enemies in the face, routed them all, and got possession of the vessel. Such a man too was Cassius Scaeva, who, in the battle near Dyrrachium, had an eye shot out with an arrow, his shoulder pierced with one javelin, and his thigh with another; and having received on his shield the blows of one hundred thirty darts, called out to the enemy, as if he meant to surrender. But when two of them approached, he cut off the shoulder of one with his sword, and with a blow to the face of the other put him to flight, whereupon his friends came to his aid and he got safely away. Again, in Britain, when the foremost centurions had fallen into a watery marsh and were attacked by the enemy, a soldier, while Caesar was watching the battle, thrust himself into the fray, performed many outstanding deeds of valor, rescued the centurions, and routed the barbarians. Then the man himself, making his way with difficulty after all the others, plunged into the muddy current, and finally, without his shield, partly by swimming and partly by wading, got across. Caesar and his officers were amazed, and went to meet him with joyful cries; but the man, despondent and tearful, threw himself down at Caesar's feet, begging his pardon for having lost his shield. And again, in Africa, when Scipio had seized a ship of Caesar's in which Granius Petro, who had been appointed quaestor, was sailing, he treated the other passengers as booty, but told the

quaestor that he would offer him mercy. But Granius, saying it was customary for Caesar's soldiers not to receive mercy but to offer it, struck and killed himself with his sword.

17. Such spirit and ambition were created and fostered in his men by Caesar himself, who, by his unsparing distribution of rewards and honors, showed them he did not amass wealth from his wars for his own comfort, or for luxurious living, but preserved it as a common reward for deeds of valor, and took no greater share than that which he offered to the deserving among his soldiers; in addition, he willingly exposed himself to every danger and declined no toil. Now his love of danger did not surprise his men, since they knew his ambition. But his willingness to endure toils beyond his natural strength very much astonished them. For he was a lean man, had a soft and white skin, suffered a malady in the head, and was subject to epilepsy, which is said to have first afflicted him in Corduba. Yet he did not make his weak health an excuse for soft living, but rather made military service a remedy for his weak health, since by exhausting journeys, simple fare, frequent sleeping out of doors, and constant toil, he fought off his illness and fortified his body against its attacks. He slept mainly in chariots or litters, devoting even his rest to the pursuit of action, and in the daytime was carried in such vehicles to forts, cities, and camps, one servant sitting with him, who used to write from dictation as he traveled, and one soldier standing behind him with a sword. And he drove so rapidly that on his first journey from Rome he reached the Rhone in seven days.

Riding had been easy for him from his childhood; he was accustomed to clasp his hands behind his back and ride his horse at full speed. And in the Gallic campaigns he trained himself to dictate letters on horseback and to keep two scribes busy at the same time, as Hippius says, or even more. It is also said that Caesar was the first to contrive to communicate with his friends by letter,[43] since he could not wait for

---

43 Plutarch writes as though Caesar was the first to use written communiqués, but of course this was long established practice. He seems to have misunderstood

interviews about pressing matters, given the multitude of his occupations and the size of the city. His indifference to his diet is proved in the following instance: when Valerius Leo, the host who entertained him in Mediolanum, served asparagus dressed with scented oil instead of olive oil,[44] Caesar simply ate it, and chided his friends when they complained. "It's enough," he said, "not to eat what you don't like; but he who finds fault with such boorish fare is boorish himself." And once on a journey, when he was driven with his party into the hut of a poor man, and found that the hut had only one room, and that it could barely accommodate one person, he told his friends that honors must be provided to the strongest, but necessities to the weakest, and ordered Oppius to rest there, while he and the others slept on the porch.

18. The first of his Gallic wars[45] was against the Helvetii and Tigurini, who had burned their twelve cities and four hundred villages and were marching through that part of Gaul that was subject to the Romans, as the Cimbri and Teutones had done long ago.[46] To these they were thought to be not inferior in courage; and in numbers they were equal, being 300,000 in all, of whom 190,000 were fighting men. Caesar did not engage the Tigurini in person; instead his deputy Labienus crushed them near the river Arar. The Helvetii, on the other hand, unexpectedly attacked Caesar himself as he was leading his army toward a friendly city; he succeeded, how-

---

a sentence in his sources that credited Caesar with being first to write in *coded* form, by substituting different letters of the alphabet.

44 The oil that was meant for washing and anointing was instead used for cooking.

45 The Gallic Wars, here referred to in the plural even though Ceasar's own account of them (*Bellum Gallicum*) used a singular label, occupied Caesar during most of the 50s BCE and resulted in the Roman conquest of vast new territories stretching from the Alps to the river Rhine.

46 These two tribes had invaded Roman Gaul about fifty years before this time and had been defeated by Marius; see *Marius* 11–12.

ever, in escaping to a stronghold. There, when he had mustered and marshaled his forces, a horse was brought to him. "When I have won the battle," he said, "I will use this horse for the pursuit," and accordingly charged the enemy on foot.[47] After a long and difficult struggle he had pushed the enemy back, but had the greatest trouble at their wagons and ramparts, where not only the men stood and fought, but the women and children also defended themselves to the death until they were cut to pieces. The battle was scarcely over by midnight. To this glorious action Caesar added another even nobler, by settling those barbarians who had escaped alive from the battle (more than one hundred thousand in number) and forcing them to reoccupy the territory they had deserted and the cities they had destroyed. He did this for fear that if the land remained uninhabited the Germans might cross the Rhine and take possession of it.

19. Next he made war in defense of the Gauls against the Germans, though earlier, in Rome, he had made the German king Ariovistus his ally. But the Germans were insufferable as neighbors of those under Caesar's protection,[48] and it was thought that if the opportunity presented itself they would not remain quietly in their present homes, but would encroach and take possession of Gaul. Seeing that his own officers were fearful, and especially the highborn youths who had come out with him, and who hoped to make the campaign an opportunity for luxurious living and moneymaking, Caesar called them together and advised them to depart, and not be so foolish as to risk their lives, since they were so unmanly and effeminate. He said he would himself take only the tenth legion and march against the barbarians, who would be no more formidable than the Cimbri, nor was he a worse general than

---

47 Fighting from horseback, Caesar would have had good hopes of getting away safely in the event of a defeat; on foot, his situation was more "do or die."

48 That is, those Gauls who were subjects of Rome.

Marius.[49] After this the tenth legion sent representatives to him to express their thanks, and the other legions rebuked their own officers, whereupon the entire army, with great earnestness and zeal, followed Caesar on a march of many days. Finally they encamped two hundred stades from the enemy.[50]

The mere approach of Caesar somewhat undermined Ariovistus' resolve. Not having expected that the Romans would attack the Germans, whose assault he thought they could not withstand, he was amazed at Caesar's daring and observed that his own army was disconcerted. The Germans' zeal was even more blunted by the prophecies of their holy women, who foretell the future by observing the eddies of rivers and taking signs from the whirlpools and splashings of streams, and who now forbade them to join battle until the new moon appeared. When Caesar was informed of this and saw the Germans refraining from attack, he thought it would be wise to engage them while they were disheartened, rather than sit still while they awaited their opportunity. Attacking their strongholds and the hills on which they were encamped, he exasperated them and provoked them to come down in their fury and fight it out. They were decisively routed, and Caesar, pursuing them for four hundred stades, all the way to the Rhine, filled the entire intervening plain with corpses and spoils. Ariovistus, with a small party, got to the Rhine before Caesar and managed to cross. His dead are said to have numbered eighty thousand.

20. After this action, Caesar left his forces at their winter quarters among the Sequani, and he himself, wishing to attend to affairs at Rome,[51] came down to the part of Gaul that lies along the Po, which

---

49 See note 46.

50 Caesar himself gives the distance at twenty-four miles; Plutarch uses a rough conversion formula of eight stades to the mile.

51 These affairs included the showdown between Clodius and Cicero; see *Cicero* 30–33.

was part of his province; for the river called Rubicon separates Cisalpine Gaul from the rest of Italy.[52] There he settled and occupied himself with courting the people. Many came to him,[53] and he gave each man what he requested, and sent everyone away in possession of some of his favors, and hoping for more. And during all the rest of this campaign in Gaul, Pompey never noticed that Caesar was on the one hand subduing the enemy with the arms of the citizens, and, on the other, winning over and pacifying the citizens with the money he took from the enemy.

But when Caesar heard that the Belgae, who were the most powerful of the Gauls, and inhabited a third of their entire country, had revolted and had assembled a great many thousands of armed men, he immediately turned back and hastened to meet them. He fell upon the enemy as they were ravaging the Gauls who were his allies, and so routed and destroyed the most numerous and least scattered of their divisions (these had fought disgracefully), that the lakes and deep rivers became passable for the Romans by the multitude of corpses in them. All the peoples who lived near the ocean[54] came over to him without a battle, whereupon he led his army against the Nervii, the fiercest and most warlike people in those parts. The Nervii live in a densely wooded country; and after placing their children and property in the farthest depths of the forest, they fell upon Caesar suddenly with a body of sixty thousand men when he was not expecting them, as he was building a palisade around his camp. They routed his cavalry, and having surrounded the twelfth and seventh legions, killed all their centurions. And had Caesar not snatched up a shield and forced his way through his own ranks to

---

52 Cisalpine Gaul was a region that mostly comprised the northern portion of modern Italy, as compared with Transalpine Gaul, or "Gaul across the Alps."

53 Plutarch refers to the politicians and businessmen who came to Caesar from Rome seeking support.

54 The English Channel is meant.

attack the barbarians, and had the tenth legion,[55] when they saw him in danger, not run down from the heights and cut through the ranks of their enemies, no Roman, it is thought, would have survived. But as it was, because of Caesar's daring, they fought beyond their power, as the saying goes, and not even then did they rout the Nervii, but cut them down as they defended themselves;[56] for out of sixty thousand men, it is said that only five hundred survived the battle, and only three of their four hundred senators.

21. When the Senate learned of this, they voted sacrifices to the gods and a festal holiday to be held for fifteen days—longer than any previous victory celebration. For their danger, when so many nations broke out in revolt at the same time, was seen to have been grave; and because Caesar was the victor, the people's fondness for him made his victory more splendid. Caesar himself, after settling matters in Gaul, returned and spent the winter in the region near the Po, carrying out his projects at Rome. For not only did all who were candidates for office there obtain his assistance, and use money from him to corrupt the people, and do everything they could to increase his power, but what was more, the most eminent and powerful men came to visit him at Luca:[57] Pompey, Crassus, Appius (the governor of Sardinia), and Nepos (the proconsul of Spain), so that there were one hundred twenty lictors[58] in the place at one time, and more than two hundred senators.

Taking counsel there, they decided that Pompey and Crassus should be made consuls for the following year, that Caesar should be

---

55 Caesar's favorite and most trusted corps.

56 That is, the Romans did not succeed in forcing the Nervii to turn and flee (a "rout"), but rather killed them still standing in their battle formation and resisting.

57 A town in the south of the region under Caesar's control, more than two hundred miles from Rome.

58 These honorary bodyguards accompanied the holders of high offices, in varying numbers.

voted additional funds, and that his command should be extended for five more years. This seemed very strange to sensible men. For those who had received so much money from Caesar were trying to persuade the Senate to give him more, as if he had none. In fact they forced the Senate to pass these measures, though its members groaned about them. Cato was not present, for they had purposely sent him on a mission to Cyprus;[59] and Favonius, who was a zealous follower of Cato, when he found he could do nothing to oppose it, burst through the doors and denounced its proceedings to the people. But no one listened to him; some felt respect for Pompey and Crassus, but most held their peace because they wished to gratify Caesar and lived in hope of his favors.

22. Returning to his forces in Gaul, Caesar found the country embroiled in a serious war, two strong German nations having just crossed the Rhine to seize the territory, one of them called the Usipes, the other the Tenteritae. Writing in his journal of the battle that was fought with them,[60] Caesar says that the barbarians, while negotiating with him under a truce, attacked him on his march, and thereby with their eight hundred men routed his five thousand horsemen, who were taken by surprise; and that they then sent other ambassadors to him who again sought to deceive him. These he detained, and led his army against the barbarians, regarding it as naive to keep faith with those who had so faithlessly broken their word. But Tanusius says that when the Senate decreed festivals and sacrifices for the victory, Cato said that in his opinion Caesar ought to be handed over to the barbarians so that the guilt this breach of faith might bring upon the state could be expiated by transferring the curse to him who was responsible for it.[61]

---

59 See *Cato* 34–40 for Plutarch's account of the Cyprus mission.

60 The "journal" referred to is Caesar's extant *Gallic War*, which records the ambush discussed here in Book 4.

61 Such punishments were dealt out by the Roman Senate if it was felt that a representative of Rome had violated the norms of international relations.

Of those Germans who had crossed the Rhine, four hundred thousand were cut down, and the few who escaped back across the river were received by the Sugambri, a German nation. Caesar took this as a provocation by the Sugambri, especially as he coveted the glory of being the first man to cross the Rhine with an army. He then set about bridging the river, though it was very wide and at that point very swollen and turbulent, bringing down with its current trunks and branches of trees, which kept striking and weakening the supports of his bridge. But he caught the trunks and branches by spanning the stream with great timbers, and thereby bridled and yoked the rushing current and completed his bridge in ten days, a marvel that defied belief.

23. The army crossed the river and met with no opposition. Even the Suevi, the most commanding nation in Germany, fled with their belongings into deep and densely wooded valleys. Caesar wasted the enemy's country with fire, heartened those who embraced the Romans' cause, and returned into Gaul, having spent eighteen days in Germany.

His expedition against the Britanni was renowned for its daring. For he was the first to bring a fleet into the western part of Ocean[62] and to sail through the Atlantic sea with an army to prosecute a war. The island was of an incredible size, and had furnished considerable controversy to writers, many of whom maintained that its name and legend had been invented, since it existed neither now nor in the past; and in his attempt to occupy it he carried the Roman empire beyond the limits of the known world. After crossing twice to the island from the opposite coast of Gaul, and in several battles doing more to harm the enemy than to benefit his own men (since the islanders lived in such miserable poverty they had nothing worth plundering),

---

62 "Ocean" was considered by most Greeks to be a continuous band of water surrounding on all sides the group of three continents they knew. Thus Caesar's first penetration of Ocean in the West mirrors the voyage of Alexander, the figure with whom Plutarch paired him, in the Indian Ocean (*Alexander* 66).

and finding himself unable to bring the war to the end he desired, he took hostages from the king, imposed tributes, and sailed away.

In Gaul he found letters that were about to be sent across to him from his friends in Rome, informing him of his daughter's death; she had died in childbirth at Pompey's house. Great was Pompey's grief, and great was that of Caesar, and their friends were also troubled, thinking that the alliance that had kept the ailing state in peace and harmony was now broken;[63] for the baby also died, only a few days after the mother. In spite of the tribunes' opposition, the people carried Julia to the Campus Martius, where her funeral was held and where she lies buried.[64]

24. Caesar's forces were now so large that he was forced to distribute them into several winter quarters, while he himself went to Italy as usual. Then all of Gaul again broke out in rebellion, and large armies marched about attacking and trying to cut down the Romans' winter quarters and their entrenchments. The largest and strongest party of rebels, under the command of Abriorix, utterly destroyed Cotta and Titurius with all their men, while a force of sixty thousand surrounded and besieged the legion under Quintus Cicero,[65] which barely escaped being taken by storm, since all the Romans were wounded, though they surpassed their own strength in the zeal of their self-defense.

When word of this reached Caesar, who was far away, he quickly turned back, gathered seven thousand men, and hastened to extricate Quintus Cicero from the siege. The besiegers were aware of this and went to meet him, despising his small numbers and intending to intercept them. To deceive them, Caesar constantly avoided battle; and when he found a place suitable for one

---

63 See chapter 14, where Julia was betrothed to Pompey to seal the alliance between Pompey and her father. See also *Pompey* 53.

64 The open "Field of Mars" had been used for burials of national heroes and later would become the site of Augustus' mausoleum.

65 The brother of the famous orator.

with few men to fight against many, he fortified a camp, where he kept his men from all combat and made them raise the ramparts higher and barricade the gates, as if they were afraid. He thus increased the enemy's contempt until at last, when the besiegers were emboldened to attack here and there, he sallied forth, routed them, and slaughtered many.

25. This quieted the numerous revolts in these parts of Gaul, and Caesar, during the winter, traveled about in all directions and kept a sharp eye on the agitators. For three legions had come from Italy to replace the men he had lost, Pompey furnishing him with two of the legions formerly under his command; the other was newly raised in the part of Gaul near the Po. But far away the seeds of the greatest and most dangerous war in those regions were clearly sprouting; they had long since been secretly sown and scattered by the most powerful men among the most warlike tribes, and nurtured by large numbers of men in their prime who were assembled and armed from all sides, by vast sums of money that were collected in one place, by strong cities, and by countries that were hard to enter. It being winter, the rivers were frozen, the forests covered with snow, and the plains transformed into lakes by winter torrents, so that in some places the roads were lost through the depth of the snow, and in others the overflowing of marshes and streams made all marches uncertain. All of these difficulties seemed to make it impracticable for Caesar to oppose the rebels. Accordingly many tribes revolted, and at their head were the Arverni and Carnutini. Vercingetorix[66] was chosen to hold supreme command in the war. His father had been put to death by the Gauls, who suspected him of aiming at a tyranny.

26. This man, after dividing his forces into several parts and setting many officers over them, won over all the surrounding country as far as the Arar, intending, now that there was united opposition against

---

66 The name of this famous chieftain has been restored to its familiar form; the manuscripts of Plutarch have "Vergentorix."

Caesar at Rome,[67] to engage all Gaul in the war. And had he done this a little later, when Caesar was preoccupied with the civil war, Italy would have been overwhelmed by fears no less daunting than those awakened in times past by the Cimbri.[68] But Caesar (the man best suited by nature to make use of every aspect of war, and particularly its golden opportunities), as soon as he heard of the revolt, returned the same way he went earlier; and by the strength and quickness of his march in so severe a winter showed the barbarians that an army impossible to fight or defeat was advancing against them. For in an interval of time one could not have imagined one of Caesar's couriers or letter carriers reaching the place after a long journey, Caesar himself was seen, with his entire army, ravaging their lands, destroying their estates, subduing their cities, and receiving those who deserted to him, until the nation of the Aedui joined the war against him. Up to this time the Aedui had called themselves brothers of the Romans and had been splendidly honored by them; but now they joined the rebels, to the great discouragement of Caesar's army. Accordingly he withdrew from there and crossed the territory of the Lingones, wishing to reach the country of the Sequani, who were his friends, and stood like a bulwark between Italy and the rest of Gaul. There the enemy came upon him and surrounded him with many tens of thousands, whom he hastened to engage. For the most part he prevailed, and after a long time and much slaughter gained a complete victory; but it seems that at first he suffered a setback, and nowadays the Arverni display a short sword hanging in a temple, which they say was taken from Caesar.[69] He saw it himself some time later, and smiled, and when his friends urged him to have it taken down, he would not allow it, since he regarded it as sacred.

---

67 This looks ahead to chapters 28–29.

68 See chapter 18 for the earlier invasion of Italy by the Cimbri.

69 Spoils of war were often thus displayed in shrines as dedicatory offerings to the gods and as national trophies.

27. But most of those who had escaped took refuge with their king in the city of Alesia.[70] And while Caesar was besieging that city, which was thought to be impregnable on account of the height of its walls and the number of their defenders, he was assailed by danger, greater than could be described, arriving from outside. For the mightiest force, drawn from all the nations of Gaul, and numbering 300,000, had assembled and come in arms to Alesia. And the number of men fighting inside the city was not less than 170,000. Thus Caesar, hemmed in and besieged between two such forces, was forced to build two defensive walls, one toward the city, the other against the relieving force, aware as he was that if these forces should unite, his cause would be utterly lost.

Caesar's danger at Alesia was justly famous, and for many reasons, since none of his other struggles produced such brave and clever exploits. One might marvel that he was able to engage and prevail over so many tens of thousands outside the city without the knowledge of those inside, and what is more, without the knowledge of the Romans who were guarding the wall that faced the city.[71] For these remained unaware of the victory until the cries of the men and the wailing of the women were heard, as they saw many shields adorned with silver and gold, and many breastplates smeared with blood, and cups and Gallic tents being carried by the Romans to their camp. So quickly did so large a force dissolve and vanish like a phantom or a dream, the greatest part of them having fallen in the battle. Those who held Alesia, after causing themselves and Caesar great trouble, finally surrendered. And the leader of the whole war, Vercingetorix, donning his finest armor and adorning his horse, rode out through the gates. After making a circuit around where Caesar was sitting, he dismounted, threw off his

---

70 Probably the modern Mont Auxois in central eastern France.

71 The implied danger for Caesar was that if the Gauls inside Alesia learned, from the anxiety of the Romans stationed nearest the walls, that a battle was taking place outside the fortress, they might have sallied out so as to force the Romans to fight on two fronts at once.

armor, seated himself at Caesar's feet, and remained there quietly until he was handed over to be kept under guard for the triumph.[72]

28. Caesar had long ago decided to overthrow Pompey, just as Pompey, for his part, had decided to overthrow Caesar. For now that Crassus, who had been lying in wait for the victor in that rivalry,[73] had been killed in Parthia,[74] it remained for the man who wished to be the greatest—Caesar—to overthrow the other; and for the greatest man—Pompey—in order to prevent his own overthrow, to lose no time in eliminating the man he feared. Pompey had only lately come to fear Caesar, whom until now he had disdained, thinking it would be no trouble to put down the man whom he himself had advanced.[75] But Caesar had entertained this design from the beginning and had put himself out in front of his rivals, like an athlete, and by exercising himself in the Gallic Wars had trained his troops and enhanced his renown, raising himself by his exploits to a position where he might compete with the successes of Pompey. He exploited advantages given to him both by Pompey himself and by the times and the sorry state of government at Rome, where candidates for office, setting up counting tables in public, shamelessly bribed the people, who, upon receiving their pay, went down to the Forum to contend for their benefactors not with votes, but with bows, swords, and slings. On many occasions the combatants separated only after

---

72 Triumphal processions, awarded by the Roman Senate to victorious generals, often included the display of an enemy leader, bound and subdued.

73 The untranslatable Greek term *ephedros* casts Crassus as an athletic contestant who receives a bye in the first round and waits to take on the victor between his two rivals. The aptness of the metaphor appealed to Plutarch, who also used it of Crassus at *Pompey* 53.

74 See *Crassus* 16–33 for Plutarch's account of this disastrous campaign.

75 See *Pompey* 57 for Pompey's state of mind at this juncture. From the point reached here to chapter 45 below, the events of *Caesar* closely track those of *Pompey* 57–72, and indeed Plutarch himself cross-references *Pompey*—a Life he had planned out but not yet written—in chapters 35 and 45.

defiling the rostrum[76] with blood and corpses, leaving the city to anarchy, like a ship swept along without a helmsman, so that men of intelligence could only be grateful if such tempestuous madness ended in nothing worse for them than a monarchy. There were many who also dared to declare openly that the government was curable only by a monarchy, and that they ought to take that remedy from the gentlest of physicians, meaning Pompey. And even Pompey, though in words he pretended to decline it, in fact did his utmost to be appointed dictator.[77] But Cato, detecting his design, persuaded the Senate to make Pompey sole consul,[78] placating him with a more legal sort of monarchy so that the man might not force his way to the dictatorship. They also voted to extend his term in the provinces; for he had two, Spain and all Africa, which he administered by sending legates there and maintaining armies, for which he received a thousand talents annually from the public treasury.

29. After this, Caesar sent to petition for a consulship and an extension of his provincial governorships. At first Pompey remained quiet, whereas Marcellus and Lentulus opposed these petitions; they resented Caesar on other grounds, and exerted themselves beyond what was necessary to dishonor and disgrace him. For instance, they deprived of their civic rights the inhabitants of Novum Comum, a colony recently founded by Caesar in Gaul; and Marcellus, who was then consul, beat with rods one of the senators of Novum Comum who had come to Rome, and told him that he put these marks on him to signify that he was not a Roman citizen,[79] urging him to go

---

76 The speaker's platform in the Forum, called either *rostrum* or *rostra* because it was adorned with the beaks (*rostra*) of captured enemy warships.

77 The Roman constitution provided for the appointment of a short-term dictator to manage crises.

78 An extraordinary measure; Rome normally had two consuls (serving for one-year terms), each providing a check on the other's power.

79 A Roman citizen could not be thus beaten indiscriminately. Marcellus served as consul in the year after Pompey's sole consulship, 51 BCE.

home and show them to Caesar. After Marcellus' consulship, Caesar began to lavish gifts on all the public men from the riches he had taken from the Gauls, and cleared the many debts of Curio the tribune, and gave Paulus the consul fifteen hundred talents from which he ornamented the basilica in the Forum, a famous offering, built to replace the Fulvian one. Pompey, alarmed at the coalition, now openly took steps, both on his own and with his friends, to have a successor appointed in Caesar's place,[80] and sent to demand back the soldiers whom he had lent him to prosecute his Gallic wars.[81] Caesar sent them back, having made each soldier a present of two hundred fifty drachmas.[82] But the officers who brought these men to Pompey spread among the people stories about Caesar that were neither reasonable nor true, and corrupted Pompey himself with vain hopes that he was longed for by Caesar's army, and that whereas he was having trouble managing affairs in the city by reason of the envy that festered in the government, the army in Gaul were prepared to obey him, and Pompey had only to cross into Italy and they would at once be on his side; so weary had they become of Caesar's endless campaigns, and so suspicious of his designs for a monarchy. As a result, Pompey grew vain; he neglected to provide himself with soldiers, in the belief that he had nothing to fear, and worked against Caesar only by speeches and resolutions for which Caesar cared nothing. And it is said that one of the centurions sent by Caesar to Rome, standing before the Senate house and learning that the Senate would not give Caesar an extension of his term of office, tapped the hilt of his sword and said, "But *this* will give it."

30. Yet the demands Caesar made gave a brilliant impression of fairness. For he proposed to lay down his arms, and that Pompey should do the same, and that both, on becoming private men, should

---

80 That is, as commander of the Gallic legions.

81 See chapter 25.

82 More than a full year's pay.

expect some small reward from their fellow citizens. For those who proposed to take away Caesar's forces, and at the same time confirmed Pompey in the possession of his, were simply accusing one of aiming at a tyranny and making the other a tyrant. When Curio made these proposals to the people on Caesar's behalf, he was loudly applauded; some even threw garlands at him as if he were a victorious athlete. Antony, being a tribune, brought to the people a letter from Caesar about these matters, and read it in spite of the consuls' opposition.[83] But Scipio, Pompey's father-in-law,[84] proposed in the Senate that if by an appointed day Caesar did not lay down his arms he should be proclaimed an enemy. And when the consuls put the question whether Pompey should dismiss his soldiers, and again, whether Caesar should do so, very few voted for the first, but almost all for the second. But when Antony's faction again proposed that both should resign their commands, the people agreed to it unanimously. Scipio, however, was violently opposed, and Lentulus the consul cried out that they needed arms, not votes, against a robber. The senators then adjourned and donned mourning[85] in their sorrow at the dissension.

31. But soon other letters came from Caesar that seemed more moderate; for he agreed to yield everything else, but demanded that Cisalpine Gaul, Illyricum, and two legions be given to him until he stood for his second consulship. Cicero the orator, who had recently returned from Cilicia and was trying to reconcile their differences,[86] softened Pompey, who gave way in everything else, but insisted on taking the soldiers. Cicero even tried to persuade Caesar's friends to

---

83 See *Antony* 5, where Plutarch clarifies that the reading was opposed by Pompey's faction because the letter proposed such reasonable terms.

84 Pompey had married Metullus Scipio's daughter after the death in childbirth of Caesar's (see *Pompey* 55).

85 A strong gesture of political dissent or disaffection; see *Cicero* 30.

86 See *Cicero* 37.

resolve the quarrel by agreeing to accept the provinces and six thousand soldiers only, and Pompey was willing to be satisfied with this, but Lentulus the consul would not permit it, and even insulted Antony and Curio and drove them out of the Senate house,[87] thereby contriving for Caesar the most plausible of pretexts, and the one with which he particularly provoked his soldiers, showing them men of repute and authority who had fled in hired carriages in the clothes of slaves.[88] For that is how they had disguised themselves in their fear when they slipped out of Rome.

32. Caesar had with him not more than three hundred horsemen and five thousand foot soldiers; for the rest of the army, which had been left on the other side of the Alps, was to be brought to him by officers he had sent for that purpose. But he saw that the beginning of his enterprise[89] and its opening gambit did not require a large force at present, and that he should seize a perfect opportunity to shock the enemy with his boldness and speed, since he could more easily terrify them with an unexpected offensive than overpower them with his present preparations. He therefore ordered his centurions and other officers to go only with their swords, taking no other weapons, and occupy Ariminum, a large city of Gaul,[90] with as little bloodshed and turmoil as possible. He entrusted this force to Hortensius.

He himself spent the day in public, attending and watching the gladiatorial exercises; but a little before evening he bathed and

---

87 See *Antony* 5, where the name of Antony's companion in flight is given as Quintus Cassius, not Curio.

88 That is, Antony and his fellow tribune, having fled in disguise to Caesar's camp (probably at Ravenna), were displayed to the troops as examples of how elected officials were being humiliated by opponents of Caesar's cause.

89 "Enterprise" is Plutarch's euphemistic way of referring to Caesar's armed invasion of Rome.

90 Modern Rimini, a town some thirty miles to the south of Caesar's present position. "Gaul" in this case means Cisalpine Gaul.

dressed and went into the hall to converse briefly with those he had invited to supper. When it began to grow dark, he rose from the table, addressed some friendly remarks to the company, and urged them to stay until he came back. But he had already instructed a few of his friends to follow him, not all by the same route, but some one way, some another. He himself entered one of the hired carriages and drove at first yet another way, but then turned toward Ariminum. When he came to the river that separates Cisalpine Gaul from the rest of Italy (it is called the Rubicon), he had second thoughts, since he was now nearing the moment of danger, and he wavered as he considered the magnitude of what he was attempting. Checking his speed and then calling a halt, he reflected in silence, his resolution fluctuating, and his plan undergoing change after change. He also spoke at length with the friends who were with him, included Asinius Pollio, calculating the calamities his crossing of the river would visit upon mankind,[91] and imagining what an account of it they would leave to posterity. Finally, in a kind of passion, as if throwing aside calculation and abandoning himself to what might come, and uttering the phrase with which men commonly preface their plunge into reckless and daring exploits, "Let the die be cast," he hastened to cross the river. He then advanced on the run, and before it was day he entered Ariminum and took it. It is said that on the night before the crossing he had a monstrous dream; for he dreamt he was having intercourse with his mother, an unspeakable act.

33. As soon as Ariminum was taken, it was as if wide gates were thrown open to let war in upon every land and sea, and the laws of the city were transgressed along with the boundaries of the province. One would not have thought, as at other times, that mere men and women were fleeing in their panic from one town of Italy to another, but that the very towns themselves had risen up and were

---

91 Caesar's mandate as commander of the Gallic legions did not allow him to cross the Rubicon with an army; therefore, by doing so, he was declaring war. See *Pompey* 60.

fleeing for refuge to one another. Rome herself was deluged, as it were, by people pouring in from neighboring towns; and by refusing to obey its magistrates or listen to reason it nearly suffered shipwreck by the violence of its own agitations. For conflicting passions and violent impulses were at work everywhere. Those who rejoiced did not keep quiet, but when they met the alarmed and aggrieved, as was likely to happen in a large city, they provoked quarrels by their confidence in the outcome. Pompey himself was panic-stricken, finding himself attacked on all sides—some reproaching him for having strengthened Caesar against himself and the government, others blaming him for having allowed Lentulus to insult Caesar when he had made concessions and offered reasonable terms for a settlement. Favonius now told him to stamp on the ground; for on an earlier occasion, talking boastfully in the Senate, Pompey had told them not to worry about preparing for the war, since he himself, with a stamp of his foot, would fill Italy with soldiers.[92]

Yet Pompey at that time had more forces than Caesar; but no one would let him exercise his own judgment; and so, harassed by false reports and alarms, thinking that the war was already upon him and prevailing everywhere, he gave way and was swept along by the universal feeling. He issued an edict declaring that civic order had broken down, and departed, having told the Senate to follow him and forbidding anyone to stay behind who preferred homeland and freedom to tyranny.

34. The consuls soon fled, without even making the usual sacrifices before departure; most of the senators were also fleeing, carrying off their own goods as fast as if they were robbing others. And some who before had warmly embraced Caesar's cause were now senseless with fright and were needlessly carried along by the force of that current. Most pitiful of all was the sight of the city tossed in such a storm, like a ship abandoned by her pilots and left to plunge against anything in her path. Yet though their removal

---

92 See *Pompey* 57.

was so melancholy, for Pompey's sake they considered exile to be their homeland, and abandoned Rome as if it were Caesar's camp. Even Labienus, who had been one of Caesar's closest friends, and his ambassador, and who had fought alongside him with great zeal in all his Gallic wars,[93] now deserted him and went over to Pompey.

But Caesar sent Labienus all his money and baggage,[94] and then encamped near Corfinium, which was garrisoned with thirty cohorts under the command of Domitius. This man, despairing of his chances, asked his doctor, a slave, for a poison; and taking what was given, he drank it, hoping he would die. But a little later, when he heard that Caesar showed a wonderful generosity toward his prisoners, he mourned over himself and blamed the hastiness of his resolution. Then his physician comforted him, explaining that he had taken a sleeping potion, not a deadly poison, whereupon Domitius rose up overjoyed, went to Caesar, and received the pledge of his right hand (but then ran off and went back to Pompey). When word of these actions reached Rome, people were more cheerful, and some of the fugitives returned.

35. Caesar took over Domitius' soldiers, as he did all those he surprised in various cities who were enlisted to serve under Pompey. Now that his force was strong and formidable, he advanced against Pompey himself, who did not await his coming but fled to Brundisium, having sent the consuls ahead of him with a force to Dyrrachium,[95] and shortly thereafter, when Caesar approached, sailed away, as will be related in detail in his *Life*.[96] Though Caesar wished to pursue him at once he lacked ships; he

---

93 See chapter 18.

94 A gesture of clemency, the quality Caesar was seeking to demonstrate in order to win back the support of important senators.

95 Across the Adriatic, in modern-day Albania.

96 Plutarch's cross-reference here is framed in the future tense, showing that he had not yet written *Pompey*, even if he knew more or less what it would contain. The episode of the flight by sea from Brundisium is at *Pompey* 62.

therefore returned to Rome, having in sixty days, and without bloodshed, made himself master of Italy.

He found the city more quiet than he expected and many senators still in it. With these he conferred in a courteous and respectful manner; he even encouraged them to send a deputation to Pompey to negotiate the terms of a peace. But no one would listen to him, either because they were afraid of Pompey, or because they thought Caesar did not mean what he said, but was merely using fine words. When the tribune Metellus tried to prevent him from taking money from the public treasury and cited certain laws against it, Caesar replied that arms and laws had not the same season; "but if you are unhappy with what is being done, leave the city for the time being, since war has no use for free speech. When I have laid down my arms and peace has been made, come back then and play the demagogue. And in saying this," he added, "I waive my own rights; for you are mine, as are all of the opposition party whom I have caught." Having said this to Metellus, he went to the doors of the treasury, and when the keys were not to be found, he sent for smiths to break them open. Metellus again opposed him, and was encouraged by some for doing so, whereupon Caesar, raising his voice, threatened to kill him if he did not stop interfering. "And this," he said, "you must know, young man, is more unpleasant for me to say than to do." These words made Metellus withdraw in fear, and ensured that everything was readily and speedily furnished to Caesar for the war.

36. He was now marching to Spain, having decided first to cast out Afranius and Varro, Pompey's envoys, and assume control of their armies and provinces so that he might then advance against Pompey, leaving no enemy behind him. And though he himself was often in danger from ambushes, and his army from famine, he did not cease pursuing, challenging, and besieging the enemy until by main force he made himself master of their camps and forces. Their generals, however, escaped and fled to Pompey.

37. When Caesar returned to Rome, Piso, his father-in-law,

advised him to send a deputation to Pompey to negotiate a settlement; but Isauricus, to gratify Caesar, opposed it. Thereafter, made dictator by the Senate, he brought the exiles home, restored civic rights to the children of those who had suffered under Sulla,[97] lightened the burdens[98] of debtors by remitting some of the interest they owed, and passed a few other measures of the same kind. Within eleven days he resigned his dictatorship, proclaimed himself and Servilius Isauricus consuls,[99] and embarked on his campaign.

He marched past the rest of his forces, and with six hundred chosen horsemen and five legions he put out to sea at the time of the winter solstice in early January (this would be the month of Poseideon in Athens);[100] and having crossed the Ionian Sea, he took Oricum and Apollonia, and then sent his vessels back to Brundisium to bring over the soldiers who had arrived there later. These, while they were on the march, since they were now past their prime and worn out by their many wars, fell to grumbling about Caesar. "Where and to what end will this man bring us, rushing us here and there and treating us like untiring, soulless things? Even a sword is blunted by blows, and should we not spare our shields and breastplates after so long a time? Does Caesar not see from our wounds that the men he rules are mortal, and subject to the same suffering and pain as other human beings? Not even a god can temper the

---

97 See *Sulla* 31. Sulla, dictator some thirty-five years before this, had proscribed many of his enemies and deprived their sons and grandsons of political rights.

98 Plutarch uses a Greek word here associated with Solon's measures in early Athens (see *Solon* 15–16), thus giving a positive tone to Caesar's debt-relief measures.

99 The elected consuls had fled the city with Pompey.

100 A sea crossing to Greece was considered dangerous at this time of year. Greek calendar months do not in fact match up so neatly with Roman ones as Plutarch here implies.

winter season, or prevent a storm at sea; but this man runs risks[101] as if he were not pursuing enemies but fleeing from them." Such was their talk as they proceeded at a leisurely pace to Brundisium. When they got there, and found that Caesar had sailed ahead of them, they changed their tune and reproached themselves as traitors to their commander; they also berated their officers for not having hastened the march, and planted themselves on the heights, surveying the open sea toward Epirus and keeping watch for the ships that were to carry them across to Caesar.

38. At Apollonia, since the army Caesar had with him would not be a match for the enemy, and the force from the other side[102] was slow to arrive, he was worried and perplexed, and conceived a dangerous plan—that of embarking on a twelve-oared boat without anyone's knowledge, and crossing over to Brundisium, though the sea was covered with a vast enemy fleet. He went on board at night, disguised in the dress of a slave, threw himself down like a person of no consequence, and kept still. The river Aous[103] was carrying the vessel down to the sea, and the early morning breeze, which usually blew from the land and made the river calm at its mouth, was overpowered during the night by a strong wind from the sea. And consequently the river, meeting the influx of seawater and the opposition of its waves, grew rough, being beaten back with such thunderous and violent swells that the helmsman could not advance and ordered his sailors to reverse course and head back. Noticing this, Caesar revealed himself, and taking the hand of the man, who was astonished at the sight of him, said, "Go on, my good fellow, be brave and fear nothing; you carry Caesar, and Caesar's fortune sails with you." The sailors now forgot the storm, fell to their oars, and with all their

---

101 Referring to the danger of winter sailing.

102 That is, from Italy.

103 The text has been changed here to the correct Latin from Plutarch's "Anius"; today the river is known as the Aóös or Vijosë.

might tried to force their way down the river. But when no progress was made, and the boat took on considerable water and found itself in danger at the mouth of the river, Caesar reluctantly allowed the helmsman to turn around. When he returned, his soldiers met him in a throng, reproaching him for what he had done, and indignant that he believed himself not strong enough to gain a victory with them alone, but was worried, and risked his life for those who were absent, as if he could not rely on those who were present.

39. After this, Antony sailed over with the forces from Brundisium,[104] and Caesar, taking heart, challenged Pompey to a battle. Pompey was encamped advantageously, and well furnished with provisions both from land and sea, whereas Caesar was meagerly supplied at first, and afterward was hard pressed for lack of necessities. But his soldiers cut down a certain stalk, mixed it with milk, and fed on it. And one time they even made bread from it, and running up to the enemy's outposts, threw in the loaves and tossed them to one another, declaring that as long as the earth produced such stalks they would not stop besieging Pompey. But Pompey would not allow either the loaves or these words to reach the main body of his army. For his men were disheartened, dreading the ferocity and toughness of their enemies, whom they regarded as wild beasts.

There were constant skirmishes around Pompey's fortifications, in all of which Caesar came off better except one, in which there was a great rout of his men and he was in danger of losing the camp. For when Pompey attacked, not one of Caesar's men stood his ground. The trenches were filled with the dead, and many were falling at their own ramparts and barricades, to which they had been driven headlong. Caesar met the fugitives and tried to turn them back, but could do nothing; and when he tried to lay hold of the standards, the men who carried them threw them down, so that the enemy seized

---

104 See *Antony* 7.

thirty-two of them.[105] Caesar himself narrowly escaped; for he took hold of one of his soldiers, a tall, sturdy fellow who was running past him, and ordered him to stand and face the enemy; and the soldier, filled with terror at the danger he was in, raised his sword as if to strike Caesar, whereupon Caesar's shield bearer, anticipating the blow, cut off the man's arm at the shoulder. Caesar had now so despaired of his cause that when Pompey, either from a certain caution or by some chance, did not give the finishing touch to his great success, but retreated after confining the fugitives inside their camp, Caesar, as he was departing, said to his friends, "Today victory would have been with the enemy, had they had a victor in command." Retiring to his tent and lying down, he passed the most wretched of nights in vain reflections, thinking that he had mismanaged the war. For when he had a fertile country before him, and all the wealthy cities of Macedonia and Thessaly, he had neglected to carry the war *there*, and had sat down here by the seaside, which his enemies controlled with their fleets, so that he was besieged by lack of necessities rather than besieging with his arms. Being thus distracted and anguished by the difficulty and perplexity of his situation, he broke camp, having decided to lead his army into Macedonia against Scipio. There he would either draw Pompey into a place where he would fight without the advantage he now enjoyed of getting his supplies by sea, or overpower Scipio, who would be left on his own.

40. This incited Pompey's soldiers and officers to keep after Caesar, whom they thought defeated and in flight. For Pompey himself was cautious about hazarding a battle on which so much depended; and as he was excellently provided with all that was needed for a long war, he thought it best to wear down and waste the enemy's vigor, which could not last long. For Caesar's best fighting men, though they had great experience and an irresistible daring in all engagements, yet by their frequent marches, encampments, siege

---

105 Loss of these "eagles" was considered a grave injury to a legion's honor.

warfare, and night watches, were flagging with age; their bodies were too heavy for labor, and their loss of strength was sapping their ardor. Furthermore, at that time a pestilential illness, caused by the strangeness of their diet,[106] was said to be prevailing in Caesar's army. And what was of most importance, since Caesar was furnished with neither funds nor provisions, it was thought that his army would soon break up.

41. For these reasons Pompey was unwilling to fight, and Cato, desiring to spare his fellow citizens, was the only person who commended him. Indeed when Cato saw the bodies of those on Caesar's side who had fallen in battle[107] (up to a thousand in number), he covered his face, burst into tears, and departed. But everyone else reproached Pompey for avoiding battle, and tried to provoke him, calling him Agamemnon[108] and king of kings, as if he were unwilling to lay down his sovereign authority, but enjoyed having so many commanders dependent on him and visiting his tent. And Favonius, affecting Cato's outspokenness, railed madly that they would enjoy no figs again this year at Tusculum[109] thanks to Pompey's love of command. Afranius, who had just arrived from Spain, where he had acquitted himself poorly in his command, when accused of having betrayed his army for a bribe, asked why they did not fight with the merchant who had bought the provinces from him.[110] Driven by all these attacks, Pompey reluctantly marched out to pursue Caesar and offer battle.

---

106 The consumption of "stalks" just described.

107 Plutarch briefly looks forward to the aftermath of the coming battle (Pharsalus). The time frame reverts to the prebattle period in the next sentence.

108 According to Greek myth, the leader of the Trojan War expedition, portrayed in Homer's *Iliad* as an imperious and pompous leader.

109 That is, the army would not get home to Italy in time to enjoy the celebrated Tusculan figs.

110 See *Pompey* 67. The point of the comment is that Caesar, who paid bribes for the surrender of Spain, is more blameworthy than Afranius, who accepted them.

Caesar met with great difficulties on his march, as no country would allow his men to buy food, and everyone despised him for his recent defeat. But when he had taken Gomphi, a town of Thessaly, he not only found provisions for his soldiers but an unexpected relief for their illness. For there they met with plenty of wine, which they drank freely; and fortified with this, carousing and reveling on their march, they shook off the disease and regained their health and strength.

42. When both armies entered the region of Pharsalus and encamped there, Pompey reverted to his earlier view,[111] and all the more because of some unlucky apparitions and a vision he had in his sleep. For he dreamt that he saw himself applauded by the Romans in his theater.[112] But those in his circle were so confident of victory that Domitius and Spinther and Scipio vied with one another over Caesar's office of pontifex maximus,[113] and many sent agents to Rome to lease and take possession of houses suitable for consuls and praetors, believing they would assume those offices as soon as the war was over. The cavalrymen were especially impatient for the battle, since they had splendid armor, well-fed horses, and good looks, and drew confidence from their numbers, being seven thousand against Caesar's thousand. The numbers of the infantry were also unequal, forty-five thousand being arrayed against twenty-two thousand.

43. Gathering his soldiers together, Caesar told them that Cornificius[114] was approaching with two legions, and that fifteen cohorts more under Calenus were posted at Megara and Athens; he then asked them whether they preferred to wait for these troops or to risk

---

111 That is, not to give battle.

112 The dream as described here does not seem ill-omened. At *Pompey* 68, Plutarch narrates a further stage of the dream, in which Pompey saw himself placing offerings at the Temple of Venus, the goddess considered the ancestress of Julius Caesar's line. Some editors believe that the version given here is incomplete due to a sentence having been lost in the transmission of the text.

113 See note 22.

114 The text has been emended from "Corfinius."

the battle by themselves. They all cried out to him not to wait, but to do all he could to bring about an engagement as soon as possible. He sacrificed to the gods for the purification of his army, and at the death of the first victim the augur told him that within three days there would be a decisive battle. When Caesar asked him whether he saw in the entrails any favorable signs, the priest replied, "You can better answer that yourself; for the gods signal a great alteration from the present state of affairs to its opposite. So if you think yourself well off now, expect a worse fortune; if you are badly off, hope for something better." The night before the battle, as he made the rounds of the watch about midnight, a fiery light was seen in the heavens, which seemed to pass over Caesar's camp and fall into Pompey's. And during the morning watch they noticed a panicked confusion among their enemies. But Caesar did not expect to fight that day; instead he broke camp with the intention of marching to Scotussa.

44. When their tents had already been taken down, his scouts rode up to him to report that the enemy were coming down for battle. He was overjoyed at the news, and after praying to the gods, arrayed his forces, dividing them into three. Over the middle division he placed Domitius Calvinus, while Antony commanded the left wing and he himself the right, where he intended to fight with the tenth legion. But when he saw the enemy's cavalry drawing up opposite him, he dreaded their splendid appearance and their numbers, and ordered six cohorts from the rear to come round to him unseen;[115] posting these behind his right wing, he taught them what to do when the enemy cavalry charged. On the other side, Pompey commanded one of the wings himself, Domitius the left, and Scipio, Pompey's father-in-law, the center. But all his horsemen were crowded toward the left wing, intending to surround the enemy's right and decisively rout the body of men around the commander

115 Last-minute movements of forces could be concealed behind the screen of the front-line troops. In this way the enemy could be thrown off guard by the unexpected strength of a particular position.

himself. For they thought that no phalanx of infantry could be deep enough to resist them, and that the enemy would be utterly broken and shattered by the onset of so large a cavalry force.

When both sides were about to signal the charge, Pompey ordered his foot soldiers to stand their ground, maintain their array, and await the attack of the enemy until they came within a javelin's cast. But Caesar says that here too Pompey made a mistake, not grasping that the first clash, when made with an impetus and on the run, adds force to the blows and fires the men's courage, which everything then fans to full heat. Caesar himself was about to move his men forward and advance to the action when he saw one of his centurions, a faithful and experienced soldier, encouraging his men and challenging them to vie with him in valor. Addressing him by name, Caesar said, "What can we hope for, Gaius Crassinius, and how stands our confidence?" Crassinius then stretched out his right hand, and cried in a loud voice, "We shall conquer gloriously, Caesar; and you will praise me today, whether I am alive or dead." So saying, he was the first man to run toward the enemy, followed by the one hundred twenty soldiers under his command. And after cutting through the first rank, he pressed forward with much slaughter of the enemy, until he was beaten back by the blow of a sword, which went through his mouth with such force that it came out at the back of his neck.

45. When the infantry had thus engaged in the center and were fighting, Pompey's cavalry rode up confidently and opened their ranks to surround Caesar's right wing. But before they attacked, Caesar's cohorts rushed out, not hurling their javelins, as they usually did, nor striking at the enemy's thighs and legs, but aiming at their eyes and faces. Caesar had instructed them to do this, in the hope that men who had not known many wars or wounds,[116] but were young and in the flower of their beauty and youth, would especially dread such wounds and not stand their ground, fearing both their present danger and future disfigurement. And so it turned out;

---

116 Unlike Caesar's forces, who had been through the Gallic campaign.

for they could not abide the upward thrusts of the javelins, nor even dare to look at them directly, but turned away and covered their heads to spare their faces. And finally, having thrown themselves into such confusion, they fled most shamefully and ruined everything. For their conquerors immediately encircled the infantry, fell upon their rear, and cut them to pieces.

When Pompey, who commanded the other wing, saw his horsemen scattered and fleeing, he was no longer himself, nor did he remember that he was Pompey the Great; but like one whom the gods have deprived of his senses, he retired to his tent without saying a word, and sat there to await what was to come, until his whole army was routed and the enemy were assaulting his fortifications and fighting their defenders. Then he seemed to have recovered his senses; and reportedly saying only, "What, in our camp too?" he took off his general's dress, put on clothes suitable for a fugitive, and stole away. The fortunes he met with thereafter, and how, after surrendering himself to the Egyptians, he was murdered, I shall relate in his *Life*.[117]

46. Caesar, when he reached Pompey's camp, and saw some of his enemies lying dead and others dying, groaned and said, "This is what they wanted; it was to this necessity that they brought me, that I, Gaius Caesar, after succeeding in so many great wars, would have been tried and convicted had I dismissed my forces." Asinius Pollio says that Caesar uttered these words in Latin at the time, and that he himself wrote them down in Greek;[118] he adds that most of those who were slain at the taking of the camp were servants, and that no more than six thousand soldiers fell. Caesar incorporated in his own legions most of those who were taken alive, and gave immunity to

117 See note 75. At chapter 72, *Pompey* diverges from *Caesar* in order to follow the retreat of its subject from Pharsalus.

118 If the text is sound, it appears that Pollio, the author of a Latin account of Caesar's wars, translated this remark into Greek for some unknown reason. Other, emended versions of the text have Caesar speaking in Greek, again for unknown reasons, and Pollio translating the remark into Latin.

many men of distinction, including Brutus, who later killed him. Caesar was anxious when Brutus did not appear after the battle, and immensely pleased when he presented himself safe and sound.[119]

47. There were many signs that foreshadowed the victory, but the most remarkable we are told of was the one seen at Tralles. In the Temple of Nike[120] stood a statue of Caesar, and the ground around it was naturally hard and paved with hard stone, yet it is said that a palm tree[121] shot up near the statue's pedestal. In the city of Patavium, a renowned augur, Caesar Cornelius, a fellow citizen and acquaintance of Livy the historian, happened to be sitting and taking auguries[122] on the day the battle was fought. And first, as Livy maintains,[123] he indicated the time of the battle, and said to those who were with him that the fight had just begun and the men were engaging. And when he looked again and observed the signs, he leapt up as if inspired, crying, "You are victorious, Caesar." The bystanders were amazed, but he took the garland from his head and swore that he would never wear it again until the event bore witness to his art. Livy affirms that this was so.

48. In honor of his victory Caesar granted the Thessalians their freedom[124] and then went in pursuit of Pompey.[125] On reaching Asia

---

119 See *Brutus* 5–6, where Plutarch adds the complexity that Caesar suspected Brutus might be his own son.

120 The winged goddess whose name translates to "Victory."

121 The palm was frequently a signifier of military victory in the ancient world.

122 That is, he was observing the flight paths of birds.

123 Livy's colossal history of Rome is preserved only in part, and the books on Julius Caesar, containing the passage Plutarch cites here, have been lost.

124 Thessaly had formerly been subject to taxation and to military levies, but now these obligations to Rome were apparently removed in honor of the Thessalian location of the victory.

125 Pompey had fled to Egypt, relying on his former friendship with the king there, Ptolemy XII Auletes.

he also freed the Cnidians as a favor to Theopompus, the collector of myths,[126] and reduced by a third the taxes of all the inhabitants of Asia.[127] Arriving in Alexandria after Pompey's death,[128] he averted himself from Theodotus,[129] who presented him with Pompey's head; and on receiving Pompey's seal ring, shed tears. He treated well and won over to his side all Pompey's friends and intimates who had been arrested by the king as they wandered over the country. And to his friends in Rome he wrote that this was the greatest and sweetest pleasure he derived from his victory, namely to save the lives of fellow citizens who had fought against him.

As for the war in Egypt, some say it was not at all necessary, that it came about because of Caesar's passion for Cleopatra, and that it was inglorious and dangerous for him. Others blame the king's party, and especially the eunuch Potheinus, who wielded the most influence and had recently killed Pompey; he had also driven Cleopatra from the country, and was secretly plotting against Caesar.[130] They say this is why, from then on, to protect himself, Caesar would spend whole nights at drinking parties. Potheinus was also patently insufferable, saying and doing many things that were invidious and insulting to Caesar. For example, when the soldiers had the worst

---

126 Not the more famous historian Theopompus, but a mythographer from whom Caesar apparently had derived favorable treatment, or hoped to.

127 "Asia" here refers to the Roman province (roughly, the western portion of modern Turkey), not to the continent.

128 See *Pompey* 77–79. Pompey had been beheaded by the new ruler of Egypt, who hoped to gratify Caesar by this means.

129 A Greek rhetorician advising the newly installed teenage king, Ptolemy XIII (brother of Cleopatra).

130 Potheinus exercised regentlike power over the very young Ptolemy XIII, who was engaged in a struggle for the throne with his sister, Cleopatra. Potheinus had not himself killed Ptolemy but had presided over the decision to kill him, and was now also directing other policy efforts with an eye to retaining Egyptian independence from Rome.

and oldest grain measured out to them, he told them to bear with it and be content, since they were eating what belonged to others; and at suppers he used wooden and earthenware dishes, claiming that Caesar had appropriated all the gold and silver to pay a debt. For the father of the present king owed Caesar 17,500,000 drachmas;[131] Caesar had previously sent a part to his own children, but now demanded 10 million for the maintenance of his army. And when Potheinus told him to go now and "attend to his affairs, since they were so important," promising that he would receive his money later with thanks, Caesar replied that he had no need for Egyptian advisers, and secretly sent for Cleopatra from the country.[132]

49. And she, taking only one of her friends, Apollodorus the Sicilian, embarked on a small boat and landed near the palace at dusk. It being impossible to escape notice otherwise, she placed herself in a bedding sack[133] and lay at full length, whereupon Apollodorus tied up the sack with a cord and carried it inside to Caesar. We are told that it was by this ingenuity of Cleopatra's that Caesar was first captivated by her, as she showed herself to be a charmer;[134] and so overcome was he by her graciousness and her company that he reconciled her to her brother, Ptolemy, on condition that she rule as Ptolemy's colleague in the kingdom. Then, when a banquet was held to celebrate the reconciliation, Caesar's barber—an excessively timid fellow, who left nothing uninvestigated, but liked to eavesdrop and meddle—discovered that Achillas the general and Potheinus the eunuch were plotting against Caesar. On being informed,

---

131 Ptolemy XII had incurred huge debts at Rome when attempting to firm up his claim on the throne.

132 Cleopatra had been exiled and was gathering an army in Syria in hopes of ousting her brother.

133 A kind of bag used for carrying bedclothes. The idea of Cleopatra's being rolled up in a carpet arose through a now outdated eighteenth-century translation of the Greek word.

134 Cleopatra's charms are discussed in more depth at *Antony* 27.

Caesar set a guard around the hall and had Potheinus put to death. Achillas, however, escaped to his camp and raised a difficult, impracticable war against Caesar, who had to defend himself with a small band of soldiers against so powerful a city and army. The first danger he faced was lack of water; for the canals were dammed up by the enemy; the second emerged when the enemy tried to cut off his fleet and he was forced to ward off the danger by using fire, which spread from the docks and destroyed the great library.[135] The third arose in an engagement near Pharos,[136] when he leapt from the mole into a small boat to aid his men who were in danger; but the Egyptians sailed against him from all sides, so he threw himself into the sea and with difficulty swam away. It was then, according to the story, that he was holding a number of manuscripts, and would not let them go, though he was assailed by missiles and had to keep his head under water, but held them up safe and dry with one hand while he swam with the other; his skiff had been sunk at the start. At last, after the king had gone off to the enemy,[137] Caesar engaged and conquered him. Many fell in that battle and the king himself disappeared. Leaving Cleopatra reigning in Egypt—she soon bore him a son, whom the Alexandrians called Caesarion—he departed for Syria.

50. From there he traversed Asia,[138] where he learned that Domitius had been defeated by Pharnaces, son of Mithridates, and had fled from Pontus with a few men; and that Pharnaces was exploiting

---

135 Alexandria had long maintained the ancient world's largest collection of papyrus scrolls. Plutarch gives only a vague account of the library's destruction in this accident. In *Antony* 58 he records that Antony promised to move a huge number of scrolls from Pergamum to Alexandria, perhaps to compensate for the losses there.

136 A small island controlling the harbor of Alexandria.

137 Ptolemy XIII had up to this point stayed out of the war waged by his generals.

138 See note 127.

his victory to the utmost, occupying Bithynia and Cappadocia, aiming to subdue so-called Lesser Armenia, and inciting all the kings and tetrarchs there to revolt. Caesar, accordingly, marched against him at once with three legions, fought a great battle with him near Zela, drove him out of Pontus, and utterly destroyed his army. In reporting the sharpness and speed of this battle to Matius,[139] a friend of his at Rome, Caesar wrote three words: "I came, I saw, I conquered." The words in Latin, however, having all the same cadence, have an impressive brevity.[140]

51. Then he crossed into Italy and reached Rome at the end of the year for which he had been chosen dictator for a second time (though that office had never before been held for a year's term),[141] and was elected consul for the next. He was disparaged because, after a mutiny of some of his soldiers, who had killed two praetors (Cosconius and Galba), he reprimanded them only to the extent of calling them "citizens" instead of "soldiers," and gave each man a thousand drachmas and a large allotment of land in Italy. He was also denounced for the madness of Dolabella, the greed of Matius, and the drunkenness and extravagance of Antony, who razed and rebuilt Pompey's house, claiming it was not good enough for him.[142] For the Romans were displeased with these excesses. But Caesar, in

---

139 The name "Amantius" found in the manuscripts has been emended, here and in the next chapter.

140 Plutarch regretted having to give up the economy of *veni, vidi, vici* when translating to three Greek verb forms that do not have the same number of syllables. The modern English translator has to make even greater compromises by adding "I" three times, where Greek and Latin both express the first-person subject as part of the verb.

141 The dictatorship had been established to meet crises, and was either six months in length or had no definite term. The one-year term made it seem a more regular office, like the consulship.

142 See *Antony* 21. The manuscript text, which makes a certain "Corfinius" the rebuilder of the house, has been emended.

view of his political program, though he was aware of these things and disliked them, was forced to make use of those who served him.

52. After the battle at Pharsalus, those following Cato and Scipio fled to Africa, and there, with the aid of King Juba,[143] collected a sizable force.[144] Caesar decided to march against them. He crossed into Sicily at about the time of the winter solstice, and to dispel from his officers' minds all hope of delay he pitched his own tent on the beach.[145] Embarking for Africa as soon as he had a favorable wind, he put to sea with three thousand foot soldiers and a few horsemen. After landing these men without attracting attention, he put to sea again, in some fear for the larger part of his force, but met them when they were already at sea, and brought them all to the camp.

On learning that the enemy were heartened by an ancient oracle to the effect that the family of the Scipios would always be victorious in Africa,[146] he either sought to ridicule Scipio, who commanded the opposing army, or seriously hoped to turn the omen to his own advantage. (It is hard to say which.) He had in his army a man who was otherwise mean and contemptible, but belonged to the family of the Africani, and was called Scipio Sallustio. This man Caesar put at the head of his troops, as if he were general, in all the battles he was forced to fight. For there was neither abundant food for his men nor fodder for his pack animals; they were even forced to feed their horses seaweed, which they washed to get rid of the salt and mixed with a little grass to give it a sweeter taste. For the Numidians appeared everywhere, swiftly and in great numbers,

---

143 King of Numidia.

144 The events of this chapter and the next two are told at greater length, and from the perspective of the other side, in *Cato* 56–72.

145 Since sea travel was dangerous in this period and campaigning uncomfortable, Caesar's officers were hoping he would wait for spring before crossing to Africa.

146 Scipio Africanus, the subject of a now lost Plutarchan Life, had defeated the Carthaginians in North Africa, thereby earning his honorific surname.

and held sway over the country.[147] On one occasion, when Caesar's horsemen were at leisure (an African was showing them how he could dance and play the flute at the same time in a marvelous way, and they were sitting on the ground, enjoying the entertainment, having entrusted their horses to some boys), the enemy suddenly surrounded and attacked them, killing some, and pursuing the rest headlong all the way into their camp. And if Caesar himself and Asinius Pollio had not come to their aid from the ramparts and put a stop to their flight, the war would have been at an end. And in another battle, when the enemy had again got the advantage, Caesar is said to have grabbed the fleeing standard-bearer by the neck, turned him around, and said, "*There* is the enemy."

53. Yet Scipio was encouraged by his advantages to engage in a decisive battle. Leaving Afranius and Juba encamped separately, not far from each other, he himself proceeded to fortify a camp above a lake near the city of Thapsus, to serve as a site from which to launch the battle and as a place of refuge. While Scipio was thus occupied, Caesar made his way with incredible speed through densely wooded regions that afforded covert access to the place, intercepted some of the enemy, and attacked the rest head-on. After routing these, he took advantage of his opportunity and the strength of his good fortune; he captured Afranius' camp at the first onset, and sacked that of the Numidians, from which Juba fled. Thus in a small part of a single day he became master of three camps and killed fifty thousand of the enemy, losing not even fifty of his own men.

This is the account some give of that battle; others say Caesar was not in the action, but that his old illness[148] took hold of him as he was marshaling and arraying his army. And as soon as he noticed its onset, before it had disturbed and overpowered his already shaken senses, he was carried to a neighboring tower where he rested

---

147 This made foraging for food impossible for Caesar's army.

148 See chapter 17 for Caesar's epilepsy.

quietly. Of the men of consular and praetorian rank who escaped from the battle, some killed themselves when captured, and many were put to death by Caesar.

54. Eager to take Cato alive, Caesar hastened to Utica; for Cato had undertaken to guard that city, and took no part in the battle. And when he learned that the man had committed suicide,[149] he was clearly stung, though for what reason is not known. At any rate, he said, "Cato, I begrudge you your death, since you begrudged me the saving of your life." Yet the treatise he wrote against Cato after his death gives no great sign of any kindly feeling or willingness to be reconciled to him. For how should he have spared Cato's life when after the man's death he expressed such hostility toward him? But from his clemency to Cicero, Brutus, and countless others who had fought against him, it can be conjectured that this treatise was written not out of animosity, but from political ambition, and for the following reason. Cicero had written an encomium on Cato, the title of which was *Cato*; the work was eagerly read by many, as was natural, since it was composed by the cleverest of orators on the noblest of themes. This vexed Caesar, who regarded Cicero's praise of the dead man as a denunciation of himself. He therefore wrote a treatise in which he collected many charges against Cato. The book is entitled *Anti-Cato*.[150] Both compositions, like Caesar and Cato themselves, have many admirers.

55. In any event, on his return to Rome from Africa, Caesar began by delivering a boastful oration to the people about the victory, claiming that he had subdued a country that would supply the public annually with two hundred thousand Attic bushels of grain and three million cups of olive oil. Then he celebrated triumphs—the Egyptian, the Pontic, and the African, the last not for his victory over Scipio, but purportedly over King Juba. On that

---

149 See *Cato* 69–71. Cato's suicide had by Plutarch's time become enshrined as an act of philosophic courage and resistance to tyranny.

150 Neither this work nor Cicero's *Cato* has survived.

occasion Juba, a son of the king, then a mere infant, was carried in the triumphal procession, the most fortunate of captives, since later, after being a barbarian and a Numidian, he was numbered among the most learned historians of Greece.[151] After the triumphs, Caesar gave his soldiers generous rewards and regaled the people with banquets and spectacles, entertaining them all at one feast on twenty-two thousand triple couches,[152] and providing spectacles of gladiatorial and naval combats[153] in honor of his daughter Julia, who had died years before.

After the spectacles a census was taken, and instead of the 320,000 of the previous census, only 150,000 citizens were enrolled. So great was the disaster the civil wars had wrought, and so large a portion of the population had they consumed, not to mention what the rest of Italy and the provinces had suffered.

56. Caesar was now proclaimed consul for the fourth time, and marched into Spain against Pompey's sons. They were still young but had assembled an army of astonishing size, and showed that they had the courage to lead it; they had accordingly placed Caesar in the utmost danger. The great battle was fought near the city of Munda, in which Caesar, seeing his men pressed hard and mounting a weak resistance, ran through the armed ranks, asking them in a loud voice whether they were not ashamed to deliver him into the hands of those boys. With difficulty, and after putting forth his best efforts, he repelled the enemy, killing thirty thousand of them, though he lost a thousand of his best men. Returning after the battle, he told

---

151 Juba II was raised at Rome and educated in Greek and Latin. He went on to become an accomplished historian and lore collector (whose now lost treatises were consulted by Plutarch), as well as a successful ruler after his restoration to his father's throne.

152 The *triclinia* referred to here were sets of three couches, each couch accommodating three reclining banqueters.

153 A mock naval battle was staged by Julius Caesar in the flooded Campus Martius, the first of many such spectacles.

his friends that he had often fought for victory, but this was the first time he had fought for his life. He won this battle on the day of the festival of Bacchus, the very day on which Pompey the Great, four years earlier, had set out for the war.[154] The younger of Pompey's sons escaped, but a few days later Dedius brought back the head of the elder.

This was the last war Caesar fought; and the triumph he celebrated for it displeased the Romans more than any other. For he had not defeated foreign generals or barbarian kings, but had destroyed the sons and family of one of the greatest men of Rome, who had met with misfortune; and it was not proper for him to lead a procession in celebration of the calamities of his country, rejoicing in things for which no other defense could be made to gods or men than that they had been done out of necessity. Furthermore, in times past he had never sent a messenger or letters to announce a victory in the civil war but had out of reverence pushed glory aside.

57. But the Romans yielded to the man's good fortune and accepted the bridle; and hoping the monarchy would give them a respite from the evils of the civil wars, they appointed him dictator for life. This was an acknowledged tyranny, since to the unaccountability of one-man rule was now added the element of permanence. Cicero proposed the first honors for him in the Senate, and their magnitude, in some way or other, did not exceed what was appropriate for a human being. But others added excessive honors, and competing with one another in proposing them, made Caesar oppressive and obnoxious to even the mildest citizens because of the pomposity and outlandishness of the honors they decreed him.[155] It is also thought that Caesar's enemies, no less than his flatterers, had some share in this, so that they might have as many pretexts as possi-

---

154 The departure from Italy for Greece is meant; see chapter 35 above, as well as *Pompey* 62.

155 These "outlandish" honors included statues set up in sacred places, honorific titles, and a golden throne in the Senate house.

ble against him, and the best justification for attempts on his life. For in other respects, now that the civil wars were over, he furnished no other grounds of accusation; at any rate, it was thought quite appropriate to decree a temple to Clemency[156] as an offering of thanks for his mildness. For he pardoned many of those who fought against him, and to some he even gave honors and offices, as to Brutus and Cassius, both of whom became praetors. And he did not overlook the statues of Pompey that had been thrown down; he set them up again, whereupon Cicero said that by raising Pompey's statues he had firmly fixed his own.[157] When his friends advised him to use a bodyguard, and several volunteered to serve in it, he would not consent, saying that it was better to suffer death once than always to be expecting it. He hoped to surround himself with the goodwill of the people as the finest and surest protection; he entertained them again with banquets and distributions of grain, and presented his soldiers with newly restored colonies, of which the most distinguished were Carthage and Corinth.[158] It turned out that just as these cities had previously been captured at the same time, so they were now, at the same time, restored.

58. As for the powerful men, to some he promised future consulships and praetorships, others he pacified with various other powers and honors, and in everyone he stirred hopes, as he desired to rule over willing subjects. Accordingly, when Marcus the consul died, he appointed Caninius Rebilius consul for the one day that remained of his term.[159] And when many were going to congratulate

---

156 *Clementia*, the quality by which a conqueror or potentate exercised leniency toward those in his power, could be personified as a deity.

157 That is, he had established a glorious reputation, worthy of a statue.

158 Both cities had been destroyed, almost simultaneously, in Roman campaigns, about a century before this. It was common for expansionist states in antiquity to refound destroyed cities and parcel out the land thus gained among allies, veterans, or political dependents.

159 "Suffect" consulships, filling out the yearlong terms of regularly elected

and accompany him, Cicero said, "Let's hurry, or else the man will be out of office before we get there."[160]

Caesar's many successes did not divert his natural industry and ambition to the mere enjoyment of what he had worked to achieve, but served as fuel and incentive, and sparked in him ideas for even greater exploits and a passion for fresh glory, as if what he had attained were already used up. What he felt was nothing other than a desire to emulate himself, as if he were another man, and a sort of competition between what he had done and what he intended to do. For he was planning and preparing to march against the Parthians;[161] and after subduing them, and marching around the Black Sea by way of Hyrcania, the Caspian Sea, and the Caucasus, to invade Scythia;[162] and after overrunning the countries bordering on Germany, and Germany itself, to return through Gaul to Italy, having completed the entire circuit of his empire and bounded it on all sides by the ocean.[163] In the course of this campaign he intended to dig through the Isthmus of Corinth,[164] and had already put Anienus in charge of the work; he also planned to divert the Tiber just south of

---

consuls who had died or could not serve, gave consular rank and stature to those who held them and so were seen (in later periods at least) as a mark of the ruler's favor. To appoint a suffect consul for a single day, rather than leave the office vacant, seemed to Plutarch an obvious political handout.

160 Cicero's reputation for quips is noted by Plutarch at *Cicero* 7.

161 The campaign by Marcus Crassus against the Parthians, about a decade before this, had resulted in a disastrous defeat, as yet unavenged (see *Crassus* 19–31).

162 "Scythia" in Greco-Roman usage denoted the steppe country north and east of the Black Sea, the home of a loose aggregation of nomadic tribes famous for their archery and horsemanship.

163 Plutarch clearly wants to make Caesar's ambitions as large as those of his parallel, Alexander the Great (see, e.g., *Alexander* 58).

164 A canal at this isthmus (finally completed in the nineteenth century) would have replaced the cumbersome dragway by which ships were hauled overland.

the city into a deep channel, and cause it to bend toward Circeium and then empty into the sea at Terracina, thereby giving merchants a safe and easy passage to Rome; and to drain the marshes near Pomentinum and Setia, transforming them into a plain that could supply arable land for many tens of thousands; and to raise moles and breakwaters on the shore closest to Rome; and to clear away all the hidden obstacles along the shore of Ostia and then build harbors and safe anchorages for the large fleets that would visit them. All of these projects were in preparation.

59. The reformation of the calendar and the correction of the irregularity of time were objects of his clever study, and when completed proved of great utility. For not only in very ancient times was the relationship between their months and the solar year a matter of confusion among the Romans, so that their sacrifices and festivals, diverging little by little, eventually fell at seasons contrary to those originally intended,[165] but even at this period the people had no way of computing the solar year; only the priests knew the proper time, and would suddenly, and without giving any notice, insert the intercalary month called Mercedonius. King Numa is said to have been the first to insert this month, having discovered a minor and short-lived remedy for the error in calculating the periodic returns of the annual cycles, as I have mentioned in his *Life*.[166] But Caesar assigned the problem to the best philosophers and mathematicians, and out of the methods already available he devised one of his own that was a more exact method of correcting the calendar. This method the Romans use to this day,[167] and they are thought to be less in error

---

165 The lunar calendar falls quickly out of step with the solar year unless intercalary months are inserted on some regular pattern, and the Romans had never devised such a pattern. Caesar had to lengthen the year 46 BCE by some eighty days in order to bring things into line.

166 See *Numa* 18, where Numa is credited with introducing a very loose system of intercalation.

167 The Julian calendar in fact remained in use until the sixteenth century,

than other nations with regard to the inequality of the cycles. Yet even this gave occasion for censure to those who envied Caesar and were oppressed by his power. It would seem, at any rate, that the orator Cicero, when someone said, "The constellation Lyra will rise tomorrow," replied, "Yes, by decree," implying that mankind had to accept even this as a matter of compulsion.

60. But the most apparent and deadly hatred of him was awakened by his passionate desire for kingship.[168] This gave the common people the first occasion to hate him and proved a most plausible pretext for those who had long been his secret enemies. Yet those who promoted this honor for Caesar made it known that it was foretold in the Sibylline books[169] that Parthia might be taken if the Romans went against it under the command of a king, but not otherwise. And when Caesar was coming down from Alba to the city,[170] some of them dared to hail him as king. But as this disturbed the people, Caesar, in irritation, said that he was called Caesar, not king. Then everyone fell silent, and he passed on, looking neither cheerful nor contented. On another occasion, when various splendid honors had been voted him by the Senate, it happened that he was sitting above the rostrum;[171] and as the praetors and senators approached, accompanied by the entire Senate, he did not stand up, but told them, as if he were dealing with private citizens, that his honors should be curtailed rather than increased. This offended not only the Senate but the people too, who felt that the slight to the Senate reflected on

---

when most western countries adopted the small reforms of the Gregorian calendar.

168 Rome had banished its last king, Tarquin the Proud, almost five centuries before this, and monarchy had been officially reviled ever since.

169 A set of oracles, supposedly deriving from the mantic Sibyl at Cumae, were kept by Roman officials and consulted periodically on matters of state.

170 Caesar had gone up to the Alban Mount in January of 44 BCE to preside over a religious rite.

171 See note 76.

the state; and all who were not obliged to remain there went away at once, looking terribly unhappy. Caesar, perceiving his mistake, went home, and pulling his toga from his neck, cried out to his friends that he was ready to offer his throat to anyone who would administer the fatal blow. But afterward he made his disease the excuse for his behavior, saying that those who are afflicted by it lose their awareness when they address a multitude; that they are soon shaken and whirled about, become dizzy, and lose consciousness. But what he said was not true; on the contrary, they say that he was perfectly willing to stand up to meet the Senate, but that one of his friends, Cornelius Balbus, restrained him, saying, "Will not you remember that you are Caesar, and demand the respect you are owed as their superior?"

61. Added to these causes of offense was Caesar's humiliating affront to the tribunes. For the Lupercalia was in progress, the festival that many writers say was celebrated in ancient times by the shepherds and had some connection with the Arcadian Lycaea.[172] At this festival many wellborn youths and magistrates run naked through the city, and for sport and laughter strike anyone they meet with leather thongs. Many wellborn women also meet them on purpose, and offer their hands, like children in school, to be struck, believing that the pregnant will thereby have an easy labor, and the barren will conceive. Caesar was observing these ceremonies, seated on the rostrum on a golden throne,[173] dressed in triumphal garments. Antony was one of those running the sacred race; for he was a consul. Accordingly, when he entered the forum, and the crowd parted for him, he held out to Caesar a diadem wreathed with laurel.[174] There was applause, but it was light, faint, and prearranged. And when

172 Plutarch here tries to correlate a Roman religious festival with a Greek one, based partly on their names (the roots of both words are connected to "wolf"). At *Romulus* 21 however he rejects the same correlation.

173 See note 155.

174 The simple headband known as the diadem had for centuries signified kingship in the realms ruled by the successors of Alexander the Great. The

Caesar rejected the diadem, everyone applauded. When it was offered a second time a few applauded, but when Caesar declined it a second time, all did. The experiment having thus failed, Caesar stood up and ordered the wreath to be carried to the Capitol.[175] But soon his statues were found with royal diadems on their heads. Two of the tribunes, Flavius and Maryllus, went there and pulled them off; and after apprehending those who first hailed Caesar as king, led them away to prison. The people followed them, applauding and calling the consuls Brutuses, because Brutus was the first man who ended the succession of kings and empowered the Senate and the people instead of a monarch.[176] Incensed at this, Caesar removed Maryllus and Flavius from office; and in denouncing *them*, repeatedly calling them Brutes and Cymaeans,[177] he at the same time insulted the people.

62. The people then turned to Marcus Brutus, who was thought to be descended from that Brutus of old on his father's side, and on his mother's side from the Servilii, another distinguished family, and was also the son-in-law and nephew of Cato. Brutus' own desire to attempt by himself to overthrow the monarchy was blunted by the honors and favors he had received from Caesar. For not only had he been pardoned at Pharsalus after Pompey's flight,[178] and had by his

---

laurel wreath was also a Greek honorific insignia, usually awarded to victorious athletes or poets. Here the two types of headdress seem to be combined.

175 As an offering to Jupiter (as true "king"), whose temple stood atop the Capitoline.

176 The Brutus referred to here is not the current senator but his distant ancestor, Lucius Junius Brutus—called "the Brutus of old" at the start of the next chapter—who had helped expel Rome's last king and had thereafter become its first consul. See *Brutus* 1.

177 The Latin word *brutus* means "fool," so Caesar here puns on the people's praise of the consuls; he uses their own word *Bruti,* "Brutuses," to insult them. Residents of Greek Cyme, in modern Turkey, were frequently the butt of jokes about lack of intelligence.

178 See chapter 46 above, and *Brutus* 6.

entreaties saved the lives of many of his friends, but he was one in whom Caesar placed his trust. He had received the most prestigious praetorship that year, and was to be consul three years hence, having been preferred before Cassius, his rival. For Caesar is said to have remarked that Cassius had fairer claims for the office, but that he himself could not pass Brutus by. And once when some were speaking against Brutus, the conspiracy being already in progress, he would not listen to them, but laid his hand upon his body and said to the informers, "Brutus will wait for this old hide," intimating that Brutus was worthy to rule because of his virtue, and would not, for the sake of ruling, be ungrateful or base.[179] But those who were eager for the change, and looked only to Brutus, or looked to him first, did not venture to speak with him, but at night covered his rostrum and praetorial chair with messages of this sort: "Are you asleep, Brutus?" and "You are no longer Brutus." When Cassius became aware that Brutus' ambition was roused by this, he urged and prodded him more than before, since he himself had some private grudge against Caesar for reasons I have mentioned in the *Life* of Brutus.[180] And in fact Caesar harbored some suspicions of him, and once said to his friends, "What do you suppose Cassius wants? I myself don't care for him, as he is far too pale." It is also reported that when someone told him that Antony and Dolobella were plotting a rebellion he declared, "I have no fear of these fat, long-haired men, but rather of those pale, thin ones," meaning Cassius and Brutus.

63. But fate, it would seem, is not so much unexpected as it is unavoidable, since they say that amazing portents and apparitions were observed. As for the lights in the heavens, the noises heard at night, and the wild birds that alit in the Forum, it may not be worth citing them as harbingers of such a calamity; but Strabo the

---

179 See *Brutus* 8–9, where Plutarch again implies that Caesar considered Brutus some kind of potential successor.

180 See *Brutus* 7.

philosopher[181] says that many men, apparently on fire, were assaulting one another, and that a soldier's slave hurled an enormous flame from his hand and seemed to those who saw him to be burning, but when the flame died away the man was unhurt. He also reports that when Caesar was sacrificing he found the victim's heart was missing—a terrible omen, since without a heart no living creature can exist. Many also relate that a seer told him to guard against a great danger on the day in March that the Romans call the Ides;[182] and when that day had come, and Caesar went to the Senate, he met the seer and remarked by way of a jest, "Well, the Ides of March have come," and the seer calmly replied, "Yes, they have come, but they have not gone." Furthermore, on the day before, when Marcus Lepidus was entertaining him at dinner, Caesar happened to be signing some letters, as was his custom, while reclining at table; and when someone raised the question what sort of death was best, Caesar, before anyone else could answer, cried out, "An unexpected one." After this, when he was sleeping, as was his custom, beside his wife, all the doors and windows of his room flew open at the same moment, and Caesar, startled by the noise and the light of the moon shining down, noticed that Calpurnia was fast asleep, but in her dream was uttering indistinct words and inarticulate groans; and it turned out that she had been dreaming that she was weeping over Caesar and holding him murdered in her arms.

Others say that this was not her dream, but that she dreamt that a pediment, which the Senate, as Livy says,[183] had voted to be raised on Caesar's house as a stately ornament, had fallen down, and this was what prompted her groans and tears. When it was day, she begged Caesar, if this was possible, not to go out, but to postpone the session of the Senate; and if he belittled her dreams, she urged

---

181 Strabo, a Greek writer who preceded Plutarch by some decades, and whose huge *Geographies* has survived, also wrote a now lost work of history.

182 Corresponding to our March 15.

183 On Livy as a source, see note 123. The Greek word here translated as "pediment" suggests an element normally seen on temples.

him to inquire about his fate by other kinds of divination and sacrifices. And he too, as it seems, harbored some suspicion and fear; for he had never before noticed any womanish superstition in Calpurnia, whom he now saw in great distress. And when the seers, after sacrificing many victims, reported that the omens were unfavorable, he decided to send Antony to dismiss the Senate.

64. At this juncture Decimus Brutus, surnamed Albinus, a man so trusted by Caesar that he was included in his will as a second heir,[184] but who was part of the conspiracy with the other Brutus and Cassius, fearing that if Caesar put off the Senate to another day their exploit might become known, poked fun at the seers and reproached Caesar for giving the senators grounds for thinking they were being toyed with; for they had come at his bidding, and were ready to vote unanimously that he should be declared king of all the provinces outside of Italy, and might wear a diadem when he went anywhere else by land or sea.[185] But if anyone should tell them to adjourn for now, and come back when Calpurnia chanced to have better dreams, what would his enemies say? Or who would listen to his friends when they tried to argue that this was not slavery or tyranny? But if he was determined, said Albinus, to consider the day inauspicious, it would be better to go himself to the Senate, and adjourn it in person. So saying, Brutus took Caesar by the hand and led him along. And he had gone only a little way from his door when someone else's servant, eager to have a word with Caesar but unable to do so on account of the crowds that pressed round him, forced his way into the house and entrusted himself to Calpurnia, begging her to keep him safe until Caesar returned, since he had matters of great importance to communicate to him.

65. Artemidorus—a Cnidian by birth, a sophist who taught Greek

---

184 Caesar's primary heir was Octavian, his nephew, adopted in his will as his son. Decimus, not a blood relative, stood to inherit if Octavian declined.

185 See note 174 on the diadem. The proposed monarchy was restricted to nations outside Italy since the Romans abjured kingship.

rhetoric, and was therefore so well acquainted with Brutus and his friends as to know most of what they were doing—brought Caesar a written note in which were listed the disclosures he was about to make. But observing that Caesar, as he received any such paper, would hand it to his attendants, Artemidorus came quite near and said, "Read this, Caesar, by yourself, and quickly; for it contains matters of importance that concern you." Accordingly, Caesar took the note, and tried several times to read it, but was prevented by the crowd of those who came to meet him. Yet this was the only note he kept in his hand until he entered the Senate house. Some, however, say that it was another person who gave Caesar the note, and that Artemidorus could not get to him at all, but was always kept at a distance by the crowd.

66. All these things may have been random occurrences. But it was perfectly clear from the place that was the scene of that struggle and murder, in which the Senate met that day[186] (and which contained the statue of Pompey that Pompey himself had dedicated as an additional ornament of his theater), that some divine power was guiding the action and calling it to that place. It is also said that Cassius turned his eyes toward Pompey's statue just before the attack, and silently invoked it, though he had been an adherent of the doctrines of Epicurus.[187] But his present danger evidently dispelled his earlier ideas and filled him with some sort of inspiration.

As for Antony, who was loyal to Caesar, and a strong man, he was kept outside by Brutus Albinus, who purposely engaged him in a long conversation.[188] When Caesar entered the chamber, the Senate rose out of respect, and some of Brutus' confederates came

---

186 Not the Senate house in the Forum but the Curia Pompeii, a different chamber adjoining the Theater of Pompey in the Campus Martius.

187 Epicureans believed that the gods were remote and detached from human activity, and rejected the idea of an afterlife for the soul.

188 See *Antony* 13 and *Brutus* 17, each giving different accounts of who detained Antony.

and stood behind his chair, while others approached him, as if they meant to support the petition of Tillius Cimber on behalf of his exiled brother, and accompanied him until he reached his chair. But when, after taking his seat, he spurned their petitions, and, as they pressed him more urgently, began to reproach them individually, Tillius grabbed his toga with both hands and pulled it down from his neck, which was the signal for the attack. Casca gave him the first blow with his dagger, in the neck, inflicting a wound that was not mortal, nor even deep, as was likely coming from one who at the beginning of such a momentous exploit was unnerved. Caesar instantly turned about, grabbed hold of the dagger, and held it fast. And both of them at the same time cried out, the stricken man in Latin, "You villain, Casca, what are you doing?" and the assassin, in Greek, to his brother, "Brother, help me!"

Such was the beginning, and those who were unaware of the plot were thunderstruck and so horrified at what was happening that they dared not flee or defend Caesar, or even utter a sound. But each of those who had prepared for the murder bared his dagger and surrounded Caesar. Whichever way he turned he met with blows aimed at his face and eyes, and was driven here and there like a wild beast, trapped in everyone's hands. For all had to begin the sacrifice[189] and taste of the murder, which is why Brutus also stabbed him in the groin. It is said by some that he fought against all the rest, shifting his body this way and that and crying out, but that when he saw Brutus with his drawn sword he covered his head with his toga[190] and let himself fall, either by chance or pushed there by his murderers, at the base of the pedestal on which Pompey's statue stood. The slaughter drenched it with blood, so

---

189 Plutarch's language compares the assassination to the ritual slaughter of a sacrificial animal.

190 Frequently the gesture of a Roman who felt death to be near. The detail immortalized by Shakespeare, in which Caesar addressed his dying words to Brutus, is taken not from Plutarch but Suetonius and Dio.

that Pompey himself seemed to have presided over the vengeance wrought upon his enemy, who lay at his feet, quivering from a multitude of wounds. For he is said to have received twenty-three. And many of the conspirators were wounded by one another as they strove to land their blows in one body.

67. When the man was slain, Brutus came forward as if to speak about what had been done, but the senators would not listen to him. They burst through the doors and fled, filling the people with so much confusion and helpless fear that some closed their houses, while others left their counters and shops and ran, some toward the place to see the sad spectacle, others back again after they had seen it. Antony and Lepidus, Caesar's greatest friends, slipped away and took refuge in the houses of others. But Brutus and his followers, just as they were, still hot from the slaughter and showing their drawn swords, marched in a body from the Senate house to the Capitol, not like fugitives but with an air of good cheer and confidence, summoning the multitude to reclaim their liberty and welcoming the company of the most distinguished people they met. Some joined them and went up with them as if they had been part of the conspiracy, and claimed a share in the honor of what had been done, including Gaius Octavius and Lentulus Spinther. These men later paid the price for their vanity, being put to death by Antony and the young Caesar,[191] and lost the glory for the sake of which they died, since no one believed they had taken part in the action. For even those who punished them exacted a penalty not for what they actually did, but for their willingness to act.

On the next day Brutus came down with his followers and addressed the people, who listened to what was said without expressing either resentment or approval of what had been done, but showed by their great silence that they pitied Caesar and respected

---

191 Following their later victory over the conspirators, Antony and Octavian ("the young Caesar") proscribed many whom they considered complicit; see *Antony* 19.

Brutus. The Senate too, eager to effect an amnesty and the reconciliation of all parties, decreed that Caesar should be worshipped as a god, and that not even the most trifling measure he had planned when in office should be revoked; and to Brutus and his followers they distributed provinces and granted suitable honors, so that everyone thought that things were settled and arranged in the best possible manner.

68. But when Caesar's will was opened, and it was found that he had given a generous bequest to every Roman citizen, and when his body, mutilated with wounds, was seen being carried through the Forum, the multitude could no longer keep within the bounds of order and discipline; heaping benches around the body, and railings and tables from the Forum, they set fire to them and burned it there. Then, taking flaming brands, some ran to burn down the houses of the murderers, while others ranged up and down the city, seeking to arrest the men and tear them to pieces. But not one of these was to be found; they had all taken good care to protect themselves. It is reported that a certain Cinna, one of Caesar's friends, chanced to have had a strange dream the night before; he dreamt that he was invited to dinner by Caesar, and when he declined to go with him, Caesar took him by the hand and led him along, though he resisted. When Cinna heard that Caesar's body was burning in the Forum, he rose up and went there out of respect, though his dream made him apprehensive, and though he was running a fever. And when he was spotted, one of the crowd told his name to another who asked what it was, and that man told another, and word soon spread that he was one of Caesar's murderers. For among the conspirators was another Cinna; and taking this to be the man, they rushed at him and tore him limb from limb on the spot. Brutus and Cassius, terrified at this, left the city within a few days. What they did and suffered before they died has been related in the *Life* of Brutus.[192]

69. Caesar was fully fifty-six years old when he died, not having

192 See *Brutus*, chapter 21 onward.

survived Pompey for much more than four years. The power and empire he had pursued all his life through many dangers and had at last scarcely attained—of these he reaped no other fruit than fame and a glory that aroused the envy of his fellow citizens. But the great divine luck[193] that attended him throughout his life followed him, even after his death, as an avenger of his murder, driving and tracking down his killers over every land and sea until not one was left, reaching even those who in any way whatsoever had taken a hand in the deed or promoted the plot.

The most remarkable of human coincidences was that which befell Cassius, who, after his defeat at Philippi,[194] killed himself with the same dagger he had used against Caesar. Among the divine signs, there was the great comet, which shone brilliantly for seven nights after Caesar's murder and then disappeared, and the dimness of the sun. For during that year the disc rose pale and without brightness, and the heat it gave off was feeble and meager. The air, accordingly, was dark and heavy owing to the weakness of the heat that permeated it, and the fruits, imperfect and half-ripened, withered and shriveled from the cold. But above all, the phantom that appeared to Brutus, which I will now describe, showed that the murder of Caesar was not pleasing to the gods. When Brutus was about to lead his army across from Abydos to the other continent,[195] he was resting at night, as he used to do, in his tent, and was not asleep, but thinking of the future. For Brutus was the least inclined to sleep of all generals, and had the greatest natural capacity to keep awake. He thought he heard a noise at the door, and looking toward it by the light of the lamp, which was almost out, he saw a terrible vision of

---

193 The Greek word translated as "divine luck" is *daimōn*, a term that, in Plutarch's usage, can refer variously to a demigod mediating between heaven and earth, a guardian spirit, or a divinized embodiment of personal destiny.

194 A town in Thrace, named for its founder, Philip of Macedon.

195 The conspirators had gone to Asia to rally troops, and were now crossing the Dardanelles to return to Europe (see *Brutus* 36).

a man of unusual size and severe countenance. He was stunned at first, but when he saw that the apparition neither did nor said anything, but merely stood silently by his couch, he asked who he was. The phantom replied, "Your evil spirit,[196] Brutus, and you will see me at Philippi." Brutus answered bravely, "Then I will see you," and the vision immediately departed. When the time had come, Brutus arrayed his army against Antony and Caesar[197] at Philippi, and in the first battle defeated the enemy, routed and dispersed them, and sacked Caesar's camp.[198] But when he was about to fight the second battle, the same phantom visited him again at night, and though it spoke not a word, Brutus understood his fate, and threw himself headlong into danger. He did not fall in the fight; but when his men were routed he retreated to the top of a crest, put his naked sword to his chest (while a friend, we are told, helped him to give the thrust), and met his death.

---

196 The word rendered as "spirit" is again *daimōn*.

197 "Caesar" here refers to Octavian, Julius Caesar's grandnephew and heir. Plutarch never calls him either Octavian or his later name, Augustus, but simply "Caesar" or "the young Caesar"; the name Octavian has occasionally been used in this translation for clarity.

198 See *Brutus* 40–42 and *Antony* 22.

CICERO

It is said that Helvia, the mother of Cicero, was of noble birth and lived an honorable life; but of his father nothing is reported except in extreme terms. For some say that he was born and raised in a fuller's shop, while others trace the origin of his family to Tullus Attius, a distinguished king of the Volscians, who waged war very capably against the Romans.[1] Yet the first of that family who was surnamed Cicero seems to have been worthy of note, and therefore his descendants did not reject the name but were fond of it, though it was ridiculed by many. For *cicer* is the Latin word for "chickpea," and that first Cicero had a nick at the end of his nose that resembled the cleft of a chickpea, from which he acquired his surname. Now when Cicero himself, whose *Life* I am writing, first ran for office and engaged in politics, and his friends thought he should drop or change the name, he is said to have replied with youthful spirit that he would strive to make the name of Cicero more glorious than that of the Scauri and Catuli.[2] And when he was quaestor in Sicily,[3] and was making an offering

1 Tullus Attius, sometimes known as Tullus Aufidius (so called by Shakespeare in *Coriolanus*), led the Volscians against Rome in the early fifth century BCE.

2 Two noble families who played prominent roles in Republican politics in the late second and first centuries BCE.

3 In 75 BCE. The office of quaestor, an elected post in Cicero's day, was the first step on the *cursus honorum*, the progression of offices followed by ambitious Romans. See the Appendix on Roman constitutional structure.

of silver plate to the gods, he had his first two names engraved upon it, Marcus and Tullius, but in place of the third he humorously told the artisan to engrave a chickpea next to them. This is what we are told about his name.

2. It is reported of Cicero that his mother gave birth to him without pain or labor on the third day of the new calends,[4] the day on which at the present time the magistrates pray and make sacrifice on behalf of the emperor.[5] It is also said that a phantom appeared to his nurse, and foretold that the child she was nourishing would become a great blessing to all the Romans. And though these predictions might be thought mere dreams and fancies, he himself soon showed them to be genuine prophecy. For when he reached the age for taking lessons, he became so distinguished for his natural gifts, and got such a name and renown among the boys, that their fathers would often visit the school in order to set eyes on him and observe the quickness and understanding in his studies, for which he was praised, though the ruder among them would be angry with their sons when they saw them walking together and placing Cicero in their midst as a mark of respect. And though capable of embracing every branch of learning, as Plato thought a scholarly and philosophic nature should be, and averse to no kind of literature or training,[6] he devoted himself with somewhat greater zeal to poetry. (A little poem in tetrameter verse, composed by him when a boy—"Glaucus of the Sea"[7]—has survived.) As he grew older and applied himself more ingeniously to these creations, he got the reputation of being not only the best orator, but also

---

4 January 3, of the year 106 BCE.

5 Plutarch here refers to the customs of his own time. The yearly sacrifice to ensure the health of the princeps was begun under Augustus in 30 BCE.

6 See *Republic* 475b for Plato's clearest statement of this idea.

7 The poem, which concerned a Greek fisherman transformed into a sea creature with divinatory powers, has not survived.

the best poet among the Romans.[8] His renown for rhetoric abides, though there have been many innovations since his time;[9] but his verses, since so many gifted poets have followed him, are today altogether forgotten and unappreciated.

3. Leaving his boyhood studies, he attended the lectures of Philo the Academic,[10] whom the Romans admired above all the other disciples of Clitomachus[11] for his eloquence and loved for his character. He also associated with the followers of Mucius,[12] who were statesmen and leaders in the Senate, and was helped by them to an understanding of the laws; and for a short time he served under Sulla in the Marsic War.[13] Then, seeing the commonwealth falling into factions, and from factions into an absolute monarchy, he devoted himself to a retired and contemplative life, associated with Greek scholars, and applied himself to his studies until Sulla took power and the city seemed to be somewhat settled.[14]

At this time Chrysogonus, a freedman of Sulla's, having announced

---

8 There is no surviving evidence that bears out Plutarch on this point; in fact, most Roman writers were disparaging of Cicero's verse.

9 Though no student of Latin oratory, Plutarch was aware of the evolution in Roman rhetoric—the movement toward shorter, more epigrammatic clauses—during the 150 years or more that separated him from Cicero.

10 Philo of Larissa came to Rome from Greece in 88 BCE. "Academic" here refers to the Academy of Plato.

11 Clitomachus of Carthage was also an Academic philosopher.

12 Quintus Mucius Scaevola, an old man in Cicero's youth, was an influential jurist, politician, and teacher. Cicero used him as a mask in some of his later dialogues, including *De Amicitia* and *De Re Publica*.

13 The Marsic War (90–88 BCE) is usually referred to today as the Social War, in that it was fought between Rome and its Italian allies (or *socii*). Cicero served under Sulla, a general on the Roman side (and the subject of a Plutarchan Life), in the position of *legatus*, or subcommander.

14 In 82 BCE, after six years of turmoil, Sulla was appointed dictator and granted special powers to restore order (see *Sulla* 33).

the sale of an estate belonging to a man who was said to have been put to death by proscription,[15] bought it himself for two thousand drachmas. And when Roscius, the son and heir of the deceased, complained, and proved that the estate was worth two hundred fifty talents,[16] Sulla was incensed to have his actions questioned, and indicted Roscius for the murder of his father, Chrysogonus having manufactured the evidence. None of the advocates would assist Roscius; fearing Sulla's cruelty, they avoided the case. The young man, thus deserted, came for refuge to Cicero. Cicero's friends encouraged him to take the case, saying he would never again have a fairer and more honorable occasion to win renown. Accordingly, he undertook the defense, won the case, and was admired for it.[17] But fearing Sulla, he went abroad to Greece after spreading it about that he had to attend to his health. For he was indeed thin and lean, and because of a weakness in his stomach could take nothing but a meager amount of light food, and that not until late in the day. His voice, however, was loud and good, but so harsh and untrained that, owing to the vehemence and emotion of his oratory, it was always raised to so high a pitch as to make people fear for his health.

4. When he came to Athens he attended the lectures of Antiochus of Ascalon, and was captivated by the fluency and elegance of his diction, though he did not approve of his innovations in doctrine. For Antiochus had already fallen away from the so-called New Academy, and abandoned the sect of Carneades, either because he was moved by the argument of self-evidence and the sense perceptions

---

15 Proscription, the public listing of political enemies who were then subject to execution and loss of estate, was widely practiced by Sulla after 82 BCE and was often used as a means of raising revenue.

16 A sum hundreds of times larger than the purchase price. Roscius' complaint was a direct challenge to Sulla's provision that the heirs of those proscribed no longer had any claim on their fathers' property.

17 The speech delivered by Cicero on this occasion, *Pro Roscio Amerino*, survives.

or, as some say, had been prompted by feelings of rivalry and opposition to the disciples of Clitomachus and Philo to change his opinions and to foster in most instances the doctrine of the Stoics.[18] But Cicero adored and adhered to the doctrines of the New Academy, and intended, if he should be altogether deprived of employment in public life, to retire to Athens from the Forum and political affairs, and pass his life in the quiet study of philosophy.

But when word was brought to him that Sulla was dead, and Cicero's body, strengthened again by exercise, had attained a vigorous condition, while his voice, through training, had become pleasant to the ear and had been brought into harmony with his physical condition, his friends at Rome wrote to him earnestly, and Antiochus strongly encouraged him to take part in public affairs. Accordingly, he again cultivated his rhetorical style—his instrument, as it were—and exercised his political gifts, diligently laboring over declamations and studying the most admired rhetoricians of his day. For this purpose he sailed to Asia and Rhodes.[19] Among the Asian orators, he studied with Xenocles of Adramyttium, Dionysius of Magnesia, and Menippus the Carian; in Rhodes he studied oratory with Apollonius, son of Molon, and philosophy with Poseidonius. It is reported that Apollonius, not understanding Latin, asked Cicero to declaim in Greek. He complied willingly, thinking that in this way his faults would be better corrected. After he had finished, his other hearers were astonished, and vied with one another in their praises,

---

18 The New Academy, led by Carneades and later Philo, was characterized by a belief that true knowledge was not attainable by the human intellect (skepticism). Antiochus subscribed to this belief for a time but then broke with his fellow skeptics and proclaimed a return to the so-called Old Academy, in which knowledge was held to be attainable.

19 The great cities of western Turkey (here referred to as "Asia") and the island of Rhodes, all wealthy trade hubs in the Hellenistic world, had important schools of rhetoric. The term "Asian" refers not just to a location in the eastern Greek world but a florid, ornate style of rhetoric, as opposed to the more sober Attic style.

but Apollonius had not been moved while hearing him, and when the speech had ended, sat thinking for a long time. And when Cicero was disconcerted by this, Apollonius said, "*You* have my praise and admiration, Cicero, but Greece has my pity for her misfortune, since I see that the only glories that were left to us will now, through you, belong also to the Romans—culture and eloquence."

5. But when Cicero, full of hope, was being swept along into a public career, a certain oracle blunted the edge of his desire. For when he asked the god at Delphi[20] how he might become most celebrated, the Pythian priestess advised him to regard his own nature, and not the opinion of the multitude, as the guide of his life. And therefore at first he passed his time in Rome cautiously, hesitated to seek public offices, and as a result was overlooked and got the names "Greek" and "Scholar," which are readily given by the vulgar and ignorant classes in Rome. But when, ambitious by nature, he was urged on by his father and his friends, and devoted himself in earnest to pleading in court, he was not slow to attain the highest prestige, but right away shone out in full glory, and far surpassed his fellow advocates in the Forum.

It is said that he, no less than Demosthenes, was deficient in his delivery, and therefore paid close attention both to Roscius the comedian[21] and Aesop the tragedian.[22] (This Aesop, they say, was once playing the role of Atreus planning to take revenge on Thyestes,[23] and when one of the servants suddenly ran across the stage, Aesop was so carried away by emotion that he struck the man with

---

20 That is, the oracle of Apollo at Delphi, in western Greece.

21 Not the same Roscius as the man mentioned in chapter 3, although related to him. The speech Cicero wrote on behalf of this second Roscius, *Pro Roscio Comoedo*, has survived.

22 Claudius Aesopus, not connected to the legendary Aesop whose name has become attached to the famous fables.

23 The myth concerns the sons of Pelops, who fell out with each other; Atreus dealt his brother Thyestes a lethal blow by feeding him a stew made from his

his scepter and killed him.) And in time Cicero's power to persuade owed much to his delivery. He used to make fun of orators who shouted, saying that because of their weakness they resorted to shouting, just as the lame resort to horses. His ready and sarcastic wit was thought to be becoming in an advocate, but his excessive use of it offended many and earned him the reputation of being ill natured.

6. He was elected quaestor at a time when grain was scarce; and having Sicily allotted to him as his province he displeased the people at first by compelling them to send their grain to Rome. But afterward, when they had had experience of his diligence, justice, and clemency, they honored him more than any of their previous governors. And when several young men from Rome, of good and noble families, were charged with neglect of discipline and cowardice in war, and were sent to stand trial before the praetor of Sicily, Cicero undertook their defense, pleaded brilliantly, and got them acquitted. Accordingly, while traveling to Rome, and thinking highly of himself for these things, a funny thing happened, as he tells us himself. Meeting an eminent citizen in Campania, whom he considered his friend, he asked him what the Romans were saying and thinking about his accomplishments, imagining that he had astounded the whole city with the fame and glory of what he had done. In reply, his friend asked, "Where have you been all this time, Cicero?" At the time he was utterly mortified, perceiving that the report of his actions had sunk into the city as into a vast ocean, without any discernible effect on his reputation. But afterward he reasoned with himself and tempered much of his ambition, aware that the glory he contended for was an infinite thing, with no set limit. Yet the excessive pleasure he took in being praised and his passionate love for glory remained with him to the end, and very often impaired his judgment.

---

own murdered children. A later play on this theme, the *Thyestes* of Seneca, survives.

7. On applying himself more intently to public business, he considered it a shameful thing that whereas craftsmen, using vessels and instruments that are inanimate, know the name, place, and use of every one of them, the statesmen, whose instruments for carrying out public measures are *men*, were negligent and careless about knowing their fellow citizens. Hence he not only acquired the habit of remembering their names, but also knew the place where each of the eminent citizens lived, where he owned an estate, what friends he made use of, and who his neighbors were; and when Cicero traveled on any road in Italy, he could readily name and point out the estates and villas of his friends.

His own property, though sufficient to meet his expenses,[24] was quite small, and accordingly people found it surprising that he took neither fees nor gifts from his clients, and especially when he undertook the prosecution of Verres.[25] This man, who had been praetor of Sicily, and was prosecuted by the Sicilians for many wicked deeds, Cicero succeeded in getting convicted, not by speaking, but, in a way, by not speaking. For the praetors, favoring Verres, had by many postponements and evasions deferred the case until the last day,[26] since it was clear that a day's time would not be sufficient for the speeches to be heard, and the case to be brought to an end. But Cicero rose and said there was no need of speeches; and after

---

24 Like most upper-class Romans, Cicero owned villas in the countryside that produced revenue through farming and winemaking.

25 Gaius Verres had served as propraetor of Sicily in the late 70s BCE, and was accused upon his return to Rome in 70 of extortionate practices there. Cicero prosecuted him in the two speeches *Against Verres I* and *II*, only one of which was delivered; Verres went into voluntary exile before the second speech was needed. Both speeches survive.

26 The partisans of Verres succeeded in delaying the trial, hoping that a new set of magistrates, more favorable to Verres' cause, would take office before it began. Plutarch's implication that the trial took only one day reflects his experience of Greek, not Roman, judicial procedure; in fact the trial of Verres spread over weeks, with interruptions for state holidays.

bringing up and examining his witnesses, he told the jurors to cast their votes. Nevertheless, many witty sayings of his are on record in connection with that trial. For example, *verres* is the Roman word for "a castrated pig."[27] Accordingly, when a freedman named Caecilius, who was said to adhere to Jewish practices, wanted to thrust the Sicilians aside and conduct the prosecution of Verres himself, Cicero asked, "What has a Jew to do with swine?"[28] Furthermore, Verres had a young son whose conduct was thought unbecoming in a freeborn citizen. So when Cicero was reproached by Verres for effeminacy, he replied, "You ought to reproach your sons at home." Hortensius the orator, not daring to plead Verres' cause directly, was nevertheless persuaded to appear for him at the assessment of the fine, and received an ivory sphinx as his reward; and when Cicero made some oblique reference to him, and Hortensius declared that he was not skillful in solving riddles, Cicero said, "And yet you have the sphinx in your house!"[29]

8. When Verres had thus been convicted, Cicero, who set the fine at 750 denarii,[30] was accused of having accepted a bribe to lower the sum. But the Sicilians were grateful to him, and when he was aedile brought him all sorts of presents from their island; from these he

---

27 The word *verres* means only "boar" without reference to castration. It seems that Plutarch, hampered both by imperfect Latin and ignorance of Jewish practices, thought the joke that follows referred to circumcision rather than kosher dietary laws.

28 The pun cannot be reproduced by either Plutarch writing in Greek or a modern English translator.

29 In mythology the sphinx was famous for posing riddles to passersby, then killing those who failed to solve them.

30 Plutarch leaves the denomination of currency unspecified, perhaps because he was unsure whether his Roman sources were speaking of denarii or sesterces. Earlier (see chapter 3) Plutarch calculated a Roman sum in drachmas, evidently supposing that the original source was speaking of denarii, coins roughly equivalent to drachmas (whereas in fact sesterces were intended).

made no private profit, but used the Sicilians' benefactions only to reduce the public price of provisions.

He had acquired a pleasant country estate at Arpinum;[31] he also had a farm near Naples and another near Pompeii, neither very valuable. The dowry of his wife, Terentia, amounted to 120,000 denarii, and he had a bequest valued at 90,000. From these he lived in a liberal but temperate style with the learned Greeks and Romans who were his associates. He rarely, if ever, sat down to supper before sunset, not so much because of business, as because a weak stomach impaired his health. In other ways too, he was strict and fastidious in the care of his body, assigning himself a set number of massages and walks. Managing his health in this way, he kept himself free of illness and able to bear many great struggles and efforts. His father's house he made over to his brother, while he himself resided near the Palatine hill to spare his clients the trouble of a long walk.[32] And no fewer came daily to his door than came to Crassus for his wealth or to Pompey for his influence with the soldiery, these being the two most important and admired men among the Romans.[33] Even Pompey paid court to Cicero, and Cicero's public actions did a good deal to establish Pompey's influence and renown.[34]

9. Though many important men ran for the praetorship along with Cicero, he was elected in preference to them all; and he was thought to handle his cases with justice and integrity. It is related that Licinius Macer, a man who himself exercised great power in the

---

31 His hometown.

32 The Palatine hill was close to the Forum, where official and legal business was conducted.

33 Marcus Licinius Crassus and Gnaeus Pompeius Magnus, together with Julius Caesar, formed the unofficial alliance called the First Triumvirate and dominated Roman politics in the era 60–53 BCE. Both Crassus and Pompey are the subjects of Plutarchan lives.

34 In *Pompey* 46, Plutarch lays more emphasis on Pompey's later betrayal of Cicero.

city, and also had the support of Crassus, was tried before Cicero for fraud. Relying on his influence and the effort of his supporters, he went home while the jurors were still voting, quickly cut his hair and donned a white toga[35] (on the assumption that he had prevailed), and went out again to the Forum. But Crassus met him at the door of his house, and told him that he had been convicted unanimously, whereupon Licinius turned back, lay down on his bed, and died. The verdict brought Cicero the reputation of having managed the proceedings with diligence and aplomb. On another occasion, Vatinius, a man of rude manners (he was often insolent to the magistrates in court) who had large swellings on his neck, came before Cicero's rostrum and made some request; and when Cicero did not reply at once, but deliberated for a considerable time, Vatinius said that he himself would not have hesitated about the matter if he were praetor. At this Cicero turned to him and said, "But I haven't a neck such as yours."[36]

When there were only two or three days remaining in Cicero's term of office, someone brought Manlius before him on a charge of theft. This Manlius had the goodwill and support of the people, who thought he had been prosecuted only on Pompey's account (being a friend of Pompey). And when he asked for a number of days in which to make his defense, Cicero granted him only one, namely the day following. The people were offended, since it had been the custom for praetors to allow ten days at least to the accused. And when the tribunes called Cicero before the people and accused him, he, asking to be heard, said that he had always treated defendants with equity and kindness, so far as the law allowed, and thought it unfortunate to deny the same to Manlius; accordingly, since there was only one day left of which, as praetor, he was master, he had purposely appointed that day for the trial, for it was not the part of

---

35 As though about to celebrate a festival.

36 The untranslatable quip turns on the double meaning of "neck," which in Latin (*cervix*) can also denote "courage."

one who wished to help Manlius to hand the case over to another praetor.[37] These words effected a wonderful change in the people; commending him warmly, they asked him to undertake the defense of Manlius. This he willingly agreed to do, not least for the sake of Pompey, who was absent. And again taking his place before the people, he delivered a diatribe, attacking the oligarchical party and those who were jealous of Pompey.

10. Yet he was advanced to the consulship no less by the nobles than by the common people, and for the good of the city; both parties jointly promoted him for the following reasons. The change of government made by Sulla, which at first seemed strange, by time and familiarity had now come to be regarded by the people as no unreasonable settlement. But there were some who were trying to agitate and alter the present state of affairs, not from the best motives, but for their own private gain; and as Pompey was still engaged in the wars with the kings of Pontus and Armenia,[38] there was no sufficient force at Rome to oppose the revolutionaries. These had for their leader a man of bold, restless, and versatile character, Lucius Catiline, who, among other serious offenses, had once been accused of deflowering his own daughter and of killing his own brother.[39] Fearing to be prosecuted for this murder, Catiline persuaded Sulla to add the name of his brother, as if he were still alive, to the list of men who were to be put to death by proscription.[40] Choosing this man as their leader, the subversives gave pledges to one another, one of which involved sacrificing a man and tasting of his flesh. And

---

37 See note 26. Cicero here plays the same game that had been played against him in the proceedings against Verres.

38 Mithridates and Tigranes, respectively. Pompey, whose support for the senatorial party at Rome was considered crucial, was engaged in war with both sovereigns in the mid-60s BCE.

39 See *Sulla* 32. The alleged victim was in fact Catiline's brother-in-law.

40 See *Sulla* 32. This grim ruse was perpetrated fifteen years before the narrative present.

a great many of the young men in the city had been corrupted by him, as he constantly provided each of them with pleasures, drinking parties, and women, supplying without stint the expenses for these things. All Etruria, furthermore, had been incited to revolt, as well as a large part of Cisalpine Gaul.[41] But Rome itself was most dangerously inclined to revolt because of the unequal distribution of property, since men of the highest renown and spirit had impoverished themselves by shows, banquets, ambition for offices, and buildings,[42] and the riches had streamed into the hands of ignoble and lowborn men, so that only a slight impetus was needed to disturb everything, it being in the power of any daring man to overthrow the ailing commonwealth.

11. Catiline, however, wishing to procure first a strong base of operations, ran for the consulship; and he had high hopes that he would be elected with Gaius Antonius as his colleague, a man who, by himself, was unlikely to take the lead for good or ill, but would add strength to another's leadership. Most of the good and honest citizens were aware of this, and therefore promoted Cicero for the consulship; and as the people readily accepted him, Catiline was defeated, and Cicero and Gaius Antonius were elected. Yet among the candidates, Cicero was the only man descended not from a senator, but from a knight.[43]

12. Whereas Catiline's plans were not yet known to the public, serious preliminary troubles awaited the consulship of Cicero. On

---

41 Areas that had been despoiled by Sulla in the previous decades to furnish rewards for his troops.

42 Cicero's four surviving orations *Against Catiline* often mention the large number of debtors among Catiline's supporters.

43 The Roman populace was rigidly divided into classes based on wealth and descent, of which only the highest class was normally eligible for high political office. Class identity was normally inherited, but some mobility was possible; Cicero was considered a *novus homo* or "new man" in that he had advanced from his familial rank of *eques*, the second-highest property class, to the senatorial one above it.

one side, those who were disqualified by the laws of Sulla from holding office,[44] being neither weak nor few, ran for offices and sought to win the people's favor; and though many of the charges they made against the tyranny of Sulla were true and fair, they were disturbing the government improperly and at the wrong time;[45] and on the other side, the tribunes were proposing laws for the same purpose, appointing a commission of ten men, with absolute powers, who would have the right, as masters of all Italy, Syria, and the territories Pompey had recently added to the empire, to sell public lands, to prosecute and banish whomever they pleased, to found cities, to take money from the public treasury, and to levy and maintain as many soldiers as they wanted. Several of the prominent citizens favored this law, and the foremost of them was Antonius,[46] Cicero's colleague, who expected to be one of the ten. But what most alarmed the nobles was that Antonius was thought to be aware of Catiline's conspiracy and did not object to it because of his heavy debts.

Cicero, seeking first to allay this fear, saw to it that the province of Macedonia was allotted to Antonius, and then he himself declined the province of Gaul when it was offered to him; and by this favor he got Antonius to second, like a hired actor, whatever he said for the good of the country. As soon as Antonius had been caught and made tractable, Cicero attacked the revolutionaries with greater confidence. Then, declaiming in the Senate against the proposed law,[47] he so intimidated those who proposed it that they had nothing to reply. And when they tried again, and, after arranging matters beforehand, summoned the consuls to an assembly of the people, Cicero, fearing nothing, commanded the Senate to follow him, led the way, and not only got the law thrown out,

---

44 Principally, the offspring of those proscribed by Sulla.

45 That is, at a time when it was more gravely threatened by Catiline.

46 Not Marcus Antonius (Mark Antony) but his brother Gaius.

47 The three speeches *De lege agraria* survive largely intact.

but so overpowered the tribunes by his oratory that they renounced their other projects.

13. For this man, above all others, showed them how great a charm eloquence lends to that which is honorable, and that justice is invincible if it is well articulated, and that it is necessary for the conscientious statesman always in his actions to choose what is right instead of what is popular, and, in speaking, to remove from what is advantageous anything that might give offense. An incident during Cicero's consulship connected with the public spectacles illustrates the charm of his oratory. In former times the knights were mingled in the theater with the common people, and were seated among them as chance dictated. Marcus Otho, when he was praetor, was the first to assign them their own block of seats, which they retain to this day.[48] The common people took this as a sign of disrespect to themselves, and when Otho appeared in the theater they hissed him insultingly, while the knights received him with loud applause. The people repeated and increased their hissing, and the knights their applause. After this they turned upon one another with abusive words, and the theater was in an uproar. When Cicero, being informed of it, came to the theater, he summoned the people to the Temple of Bellona, where he admonished and exhorted them, after which, returning to the theater, they applauded Otho loudly, contending with the knights in showing him honor and respect.

14. Catiline and his fellow conspirators, at first cowed and afraid, began to take courage again. Coming together, they urged one another to pursue their project more boldly before Pompey returned (for he was now said to be marching home with his army).[49] But the old soldiers of Sulla, more than anyone, were prodding Catiline to act. They

---

48 Plutarch mistakenly names Marcus Otho instead of Lucius Roscius Otho, who, as tribune in 67 BCE, moved legislation to assign certain theater seats to the knights.

49 The death of Mithridates of Pontus in 63 BCE ended Pompey's major task in the East.

were everywhere in Italy, but the greatest number and the most warlike of them were scattered among the cities of Etruria and were again dreaming of plundering and robbing the riches that lay at hand.[50] These men, having Manlius as a leader, a man who had served with distinction under Sulla, joined themselves to Catiline and came to Rome to support his campaign for election. For he was again running for the consulship, having resolved to kill Cicero in the uproar that attended the elections. And even the divine powers seemed to foreshadow what was to come—by earthquakes, thunderbolts, and apparitions. In the human sphere there was also testimony that, though genuine, was not sufficient to convict a notable and influential man like Catiline. Cicero therefore postponed the day of the elections, summoned Catiline to the Senate, and questioned him about what was being said. Catiline, thinking there were many in the Senate who were eager for a revolution, and wishing to make a display of himself to the conspirators present, gave Cicero an insane reply. "What harm am I doing," he said, "if, when there are two bodies, the one lean and wasted but possessing a head, the other big and strong even though it lacks one, I myself put a head to the body that lacks one?"[51] Since these riddling words referred to the Senate and the people, Cicero was even more alarmed, and he donned a breastplate when all the nobles and many of the young men escorted him from his house to the plain.[52] There he purposely revealed the breastplate by loosening the tunic from his shoulders, and thus showed the spectators his danger. They were indignant, and gathered around him; and finally, when they voted, they again rejected Catiline and elected Silanus and Murena consuls.

15. Not long after this, when Catiline's soldiers were assembling in Etruria and forming themselves into companies, and the

---

50 See note 41.

51 This sneering remark deprecated the Senate as a useless, powerless "body" with Cicero himself perhaps cast as the "head."

52 Evidently the Campus Martius is meant.

day appointed for their attack was near, there came to the house of Cicero near midnight some of the principal and most powerful citizens of Rome—Marcus Crassus, Marcus Marcellus, and Metellus Scipio. Knocking at the door and summoning the porter, they commanded him to awaken Cicero and tell him they were there. Their business was this: after supper his porter had given Crassus some letters brought by an unknown man. They were addressed to a number of different persons, but one to Crassus, without a signature. Crassus read this one only; it informed him that there would be a great slaughter caused by Catiline, and advised him to leave the city. He did not open the others, but went at once to Cicero, since he was frightened by the danger and hoped to free himself of the accusations leveled at him for his friendship with Catiline.[53]

Cicero, considering the matter, convened the Senate at daybreak. Carrying the letters there, he gave them to those to whom they were addressed, and commanded them to read the letters aloud. All likewise told of a plot. And when Quintus Arrius, a man of praetorian rank, reported that soldiers were being formed into companies in Etruria, and Manlius was said to be hovering about in the cities there with a large force, constantly in expectation of some intelligence from Rome, the Senate passed a decree to place matters in the hands of the consuls, who were to accept the responsibility, undertake to manage everything, and do their best to save the city.[54] The Senate has not been accustomed to do this often, but only when it fears some great danger.

16. After Cicero had received this power, he entrusted all external affairs to Quintus Metellus, but he himself kept the city in hand, and went forth every day with a bodyguard so numerous that a large part of the Forum was filled with his escort when he entered it. Catiline, no longer able to endure the delay, decided to hasten away to

---

53 See *Crassus* 13, where the letter is cast as a forgery perpetrated by Cicero.

54 The reference is to the so-called *senatus consultum ultimum*, a vaguely worded decree that gave the consuls extraordinary powers to defend the state.

Manlius and the army, but he ordered Marcius and Cethegus to take their swords and go early in the morning to Cicero's door, as if to have a word with him, and then to fall upon him and slay him. But Fulvia, a woman of rank, divulged this plot to Cicero, coming to him by night and urging him to beware of Cethegus and his friends. They came at daybreak, and when they were denied entrance, they were angry and raised an uproar at the gates, which made them even more suspect. Then Cicero went forth and summoned the Senate to the Temple of Jupiter Stesius (or Stator, as the Romans say), which stands at the beginning of the Sacred Way as one goes up to the Palatine.[55] And when Catiline also came with the rest of his party, intending to make his defense, none of the senators would sit with him, but all of them left the bench where he had taken his seat. And when he began to speak he was interrupted with shouting. In the end Cicero stood up and commanded him to leave the city;[56] for since one of them governed with words and the other with weapons, the city wall should lie between them. Catiline, therefore, immediately left with three hundred armed men, and, assuming the fasces and axes and raising standards as if he were a magistrate,[57] he went to Manlius; and after collecting nearly twenty thousand men, he marched to the various cities, trying to persuade them to revolt. So now there was open war, and Antonius was sent forth to fight him.[58]

---

55 The Latin epithet Stator (in Greek, Stesios), usually translated "Stayer," refers to Jupiter's power to inspire troops in battle to stand their ground. The name and the shrine are significant given that Cicero is about to make a stand against Catiline.

56 The speech delivered on this occasion is the first of the four famous speeches *Against Catiline.* Plutarch's wording in this sentence paraphrases portions of the speech.

57 Certain high officials at Rome had the legal right to go about preceded by one or more lictors, each bearing bundles of rods surrounding an axe, symbolizing the right to use deadly force.

58 At the head of an army, that is.

17. The persons corrupted by Catiline who had been left behind in the city were kept together and encouraged by Cornelius Lentulus, surnamed Sura, a man of distinguished family, but one who had lived dissolutely, and for his debauchery had been expelled from the Senate; he was now serving as praetor for the second time, as is customary for those who seek to regain senatorial rank. He is said to have been given his surname of Sura for the following reason. In Sulla's time, while serving as quaestor, he lost and wasted a great quantity of the public moneys. Sulla was provoked at this and requested an accounting in the Senate; and Lentulus came forward, his manner very careless and contemptuous, and said he would not give an account, but would offer his leg,[59] just as boys do while playing ball, when they have missed. After this he was surnamed Sura; for *sura* is the Latin word for "leg." Prosecuted on another occasion, he bribed some of the jurors; and when he was acquitted by only two votes, he said the money given to the second had been wasted, since one would have been enough to acquit him.

Such by nature was the man who had been inflamed by Catiline, and he was further corrupted by the vain hopes held out by false prophets and fortune-tellers, who chanted fictitious oracles, supposedly from the Sibylline books,[60] to the effect that three Cornelii were fated to be monarchs in Rome, two of whom, Cinna and Sulla, had already fulfilled the prophecy, and that the divine powers were now bringing a monarchy to the third remaining Cornelius;[61] so he must by all means accept it, and not lose his opportunities by delaying, as Catiline had done.

18. Lentulus, therefore, was forming no mean or trivial plan, since

---

59 To be hit, evidently.

60 A collection of prophecies attributed to the Sibyl of Cumae, an oracular priestess.

61 Lucius Cornelius Cinna exercised supreme power at Rome in the mid-80s BCE, just before the dictatorship of Lucius Cornelius Sulla. Publius Cornelius Lentulus ("Sura") belonged also to the line of the Cornelii.

he meant to kill the entire Senate and as many of the other citizens as he could, to burn down the city itself, and to spare no one but the children of Pompey; these they intended to seize and keep in their own custody and hold as hostages for a reconciliation with Pompey. For there was then a common and reliable report that Pompey was on his way home from his great expedition. The night appointed for the attempt was one of the Saturnalia;[62] and they had carried swords, sulphur, and brimstone to the house of Cethegus and concealed them there. They had also appointed a hundred men, and had allotted to each the same number of Roman neighborhoods, so that within a short time, with many men kindling fires, the entire city would be engulfed in flames. Others were appointed to fence off the aqueducts and to kill those who tried to carry water.

While these preparations were in progress, two ambassadors happened to be visiting the city from the Allobroges, a tribe that was faring very poorly at the time and felt oppressed by the Roman government.[63] Lentulus and his associates, thinking these men would be helpful in stirring up Gaul to revolt, made them fellow conspirators. They also gave them letters to their own senate,[64] and letters to Catiline, promising that senate liberty and urging Catiline to free the slaves and march against Rome. They also sent as an escort to Catiline a certain Titus of Croton, who was to carry the letters to him. The conspirators were unsteady men who generally consorted with one another over wine and with women, whereas Cicero was watching their schemes with diligence, sober calculation, and remarkable sagacity. He also had many men abroad who were keeping an eye on the conspirators' activities and helping him track them down, and he

62 The Saturnalia, a ribald festival of misrule near the time of the winter solstice, in fact occupied only one day at this time, December 17. Later, and in Plutarch's time, it took place over several days.

63 The Allobroges, a Celtic tribe based in the southeast of modern France, had been Roman subjects for about fifty years by this time.

64 Some sort of tribal council, evidently.

conferred secretly and in confidence with men who were thought to be part of the plot, and through them learned of their conference with the strangers. Lying in wait for them by night, he seized the man from Croton with his letters, the ambassadors of the Allobroges cooperating with him in secret.

19. At daybreak, having convened the Senate in the Temple of Concord,[65] he read the letters aloud and cross-examined the informers. Junius Silanus also stated that certain persons had heard Cethegus say that three consuls and four praetors were to be murdered. Piso too, a man of consular rank, offered other similar reports. And Gaius Sulpicius, one of the praetors, on being sent to the house of Cethegus, found many spears and weapons, and an enormous quantity of swords and daggers, all of them newly sharpened. Finally, when the Senate had voted immunity to the man from Croton if he gave information, Lentulus was convicted, resigned his office (for he was then a praetor), and put aside his purple-bordered toga[66] in the Senate, changing it for another garment more suitable to his present circumstances. He and his associates, accordingly, were handed over to the praetors for custody without need of shackles.

By then it was evening, and the people were waiting in crowds around the temple, when Cicero came forth and told the citizens what had been done.[67] He was then escorted to the house of a friend and neighbor, since his own was occupied by the women who were celebrating with secret rites the feast of the goddess whom the Romans call Bona,[68] the Greeks Gynaeceia. A sacrifice is offered

---

65 This temple, on the side of the Capitoline hill rather than in the open ground of the Forum, was easier to protect than the regular Senate house.

66 The *toga praetextata* was the mark of rank worn by consuls and praetors.

67 The occasion of the speech *Against Catiline III*, which survives intact.

68 See *Caesar* 9. The Bona Dea, or "Good Goddess," was worshipped by gatherings of women from which men were excluded. These rites were customarily held at the house of a high magistrate, with the mistress of the household presiding.

to her every year in the house of the consul, either by his wife or mother, in the presence of the Vestal Virgins.[69] Cicero, accordingly, having gone to his friend's house, began to consider—only a few being present—how he should treat these men. For he dreaded to inflict the severest punishment (the only one fit for such crimes),[70] both from the kindness of his nature, and also lest he be thought to abuse his power and to trample too harshly on men who were of the noblest birth and had powerful friends in the city. And yet, if he treated them more leniently, he feared the danger they might pose. For if they suffered a punishment milder than death, he imagined that they would not rest content, but would rush into every sort of boldness, adding new rage to their former wickedness, while he himself, whom the multitude did not consider especially courageous, would be thought unmanly and weak.

20. While Cicero was in this quandary, a sign appeared to the women who were sacrificing. For the altar, where the fire seemed to have gone out, sent forth from the ashes and the burnt bark a great and brilliant flame. The other women took fright at this, but the sacred virgins urged Terentia, Cicero's wife, to hasten to her husband and tell him to carry out what he had resolved for the good of the country, since the goddess was giving him a great light for his safety and glory. Terentia, therefore, as she was otherwise neither mild nor timid by nature, but an ambitious woman (who, as Cicero himself says, would rather involve herself in his political affairs than share with him her domestic concerns), told him these things and provoked him against the conspirators. So also did Quintus, his brother, and Publius Nigidius, one of his philosophical friends, of whom he made the most and greatest use in his political enterprises.

The next day, when a debate arose in the Senate about the punishment of the men, Silanus, being the first who was asked his opinion,

---

69 The Vestal Virgins were a society of priestesses responsible for tending a sacred fire that was symbolically linked to the security of Rome.

70 The death penalty.

said they should be taken to the prison and there suffer the utmost punishment.[71] All the senators consented to this in order until it came to Gaius Caesar,[72] who afterward became dictator. He was then still a young man and at the outset of his rise to power, but in his policy and his hopes had already embarked on the course by which he changed the Roman state into a monarchy. Of this the others were still unaware; but to Cicero he had given many grounds for suspicion, though no sufficient proof. Yet there were some who were heard to say that Caesar had come close to being caught by Cicero, and just barely escaped him. Others, however, say that Cicero voluntarily overlooked and neglected the evidence against him through fear of his friends and power. For it was clear to everyone that the conspirators would share in Caesar's acquittal, rather than Caesar in their punishment.[73]

21. When, therefore, it was Caesar's turn to give his opinion, he stood up and proposed that the conspirators should not be put to death, but that their estates should be confiscated, and they themselves removed to whichever cities of Italy Cicero should approve, there to be shackled and guarded until Catiline was defeated.[74] To this proposal, as it was moderate, and its author an exceedingly eloquent speaker, Cicero himself added no small weight. For he stood up and considered the question from both sides, speaking partly in favor of the earlier sentence, and partly in favor of Caesar's. And

---

71 This phrase would usually imply the death sentence but was vague enough that Silanus might later claim otherwise (see next chapter).

72 Gaius Julius Caesar is known to the modern world as Julius Caesar.

73 Plutarch elsewhere (*Caesar* 7) claims not to know whether Caesar took part in the conspiracy of Catiline. His analysis here seems to imply that Caesar was a conspirator, but he may only be adopting the viewpoint of those who suspected this at the time. Those men believed Caesar's stature was such that, were he indicted along with the other conspirators, the whole group might be acquitted for his sake.

74 See *Caesar* 7.

all of Cicero's friends, thinking that Caesar's sentence was expedient for Cicero, since he would incur less blame if he did not put the conspirators to death, chose the second proposal, with the result that Silanus retracted his opinion, and said that he had not meant he favored a sentence of death, since "the utmost punishment" for a Roman senator was imprisonment. The first man who opposed Caesar's opinion was Lutatius Catulus. Cato[75] followed, and helped so vehemently to fix suspicion upon Caesar himself, and so filled the Senate with anger and determination, that a decree was passed for the execution of the conspirators. But Caesar opposed the confiscation of their goods, thinking it unfair that those who rejected the mildest part of his proposal should adopt the severest.[76] And when many insisted upon it, he appealed to the tribunes, but they would not listen to him. Cicero himself, however, gave way, and remitted that part of the sentence that required confiscation of property.

22. Then he went out with the Senate to the conspirators. These were not all in the same place, but the various praetors had different ones in custody. First he took Lentulus from the Palatine and brought him along the Sacred Way and through the middle of the Forum, the men of greatest authority surrounding and guarding him, while the people shuddered at what was being done, and passed along in silence, especially the young men, as if, with fear and trembling, they were undergoing a rite of initiation into some sacred mysteries of aristocratic power. When Cicero had passed through the Forum and reached the prison, he delivered Lentulus to the public executioner and commanded him to execute him; then after him he brought Cethegus, and so all the rest in order, and delivered them up to execution. And when he saw many of the conspirators

---

75 Marcus Porcius Cato (also known as Cato the Younger and Cato of Utica), the subject of another Plutarchan Life. For the episode recounted here, see *Cato* 22–23.

76 Since Caesar had earlier proposed confiscation of property *without* execution.

in the Forum, still standing together in companies, ignorant of what had been done, and waiting for the night, as if they thought the men were still alive and might be rescued, he called out in a loud voice, and said, "They did live." For thus the Romans, to avoid words of evil omen, indicate death.[77]

It was already evening when Cicero returned from the Forum to his own house, the citizens no longer escorting him in silence, nor in order, but receiving him, as he passed, with cries and applause, calling him the savior and founder of his country. Many lights illuminated the streets from the lamps and torches set up at the doors, and the women showed lights from the rooftops—to honor Cicero, and to behold him returning home with a solemn escort of the noblest citizens. Among these were many who had conducted great wars, celebrated triumphs, and added to the possessions of the Roman empire, both by land and sea. These, as they passed along with him, acknowledged to one another that though the Roman people were indebted to several officers and commanders of that period for wealth and spoils and power, yet to Cicero alone they owed their safety and security, for delivering them from so great and imminent a danger. For it was not his preventing the conspiracy and punishing the conspirators that seemed wonderful, but that he quelled the greatest of all revolutions with so little trouble, strife, and turmoil. For most of those who had flocked to Catiline, as soon as they heard what had happened to Lentulus and Cethegus, deserted him and departed, and he himself, with his remaining forces, on joining battle with Antony, was destroyed with his army.

23. Yet there were some who were ready both to malign Cicero and to injure him for what he had done; and they had for their leaders some of the magistrates-elect: Caesar as praetor, and Metellus and Bestia as tribunes. These men, assuming office a few days before

---

77 Plutarch uses a Greek translation of the Latin verb *vixerunt*, "they have lived," often used euphemistically to mean "their lives are over."

his consulship expired,[78] would not let Cicero address the people, but, placing their benches above the speaker's platform,[79] would not let him speak, urging him, if he liked, to take the oath of withdrawal from office, and then come down.[80] Cicero, accordingly, accepted these terms and came forward to pronounce the oath. And when silence fell, he recited, not the traditional oath, but a novel one of his own invention, swearing that he had saved his country and preserved her empire. And the entire people confirmed his oath with theirs. At this, Caesar and the tribunes, becoming even more exasperated, contrived new troubles for Cicero, and for this purpose introduced a law for calling Pompey home with his army, in order to put an end to Cicero's power. But Cato, who was then a tribune, was of great help to Cicero and to the entire city, and opposed the other tribunes' policies, having an authority equal to theirs, and a greater reputation. For he easily defeated all their other projects, and in an address to the people, so highly extolled Cicero's consulship that they voted him the greatest honors that had ever been conferred and called him the father of his country.[81] For it seems that Cicero was the first to be given this title,[82] when Cato bestowed it in this address to the people.

24. At this time Cicero wielded the greatest power in the city; but he made himself obnoxious to many, not by any wrongful action,

---

78 Tribunes took office on December 10 under the Roman system, consuls on the first of January.

79 The "benches" referred to here are *subsellia*, seats from which certain Roman officers presided. Metellus and Bestia evidently moved theirs so as to block Cicero when he was standing on the rostrum, the platform from which public addresses could be made.

80 That is, descend from the rostrum.

81 The Latin title was either *parens patriae* (Cicero's recollection in *Against Piso* 6) or *pater patriae* (*In Defense of Sestius* 121).

82 The title was later shared either with Julius Caesar or Augustus, depending on its exact wording.

but because he was always praising and magnifying himself. For there was no session of Senate, assembly, or court, in which one was not required to hear Catiline and Lentulus talked about. Indeed, he even filled his books and writings with his own praises, and made his style, in itself most agreeable and delightful, oppressive and irksome to his hearers, since this unpleasant habit always clung to him like a disease. Nevertheless, though he harbored an intemperate love of glory, he was free from envying others and most generous in praising his predecessors and contemporaries, as one may gather from his writings. And many such sayings of his are on record. For example, he said of Aristotle that he was a river of flowing gold, and of Plato's dialogues that if Jupiter were to speak, it would be in their style. And he used to call Theophrastus[83] his own private luxury. And being asked which of Demosthenes' orations he liked best, he replied, "the longest."[84] Yet some of those who pretend to imitate Demosthenes harp on a remark that Cicero made in a letter to one of his friends, to the effect that in some passages of his speeches Demosthenes nods. But they fail to mention the great and marvelous praises Cicero also bestows upon him, and the fact that those speeches of his own on which he lavished the most effort, namely those he wrote against Antony, he named *Philippics*.[85]

And as for the men of his own time who were eminent for eloquence or wisdom, there is not one of them he did not, by writing or speaking favorably of him, make more renowned. He obtained

---

83 An Athenian philosopher who succeeded Aristotle in leading the Lyceum in the late fourth century BCE.

84 For the eloquence of Demosthenes, see the Plutarchan Life of that great Athenian orator. The quip here may either be a generalized praise of Demosthenes' style or a specific reference to the speech *On the Crown*, Demosthenes' longest.

85 The speeches against Antony are discussed at 45 below. The *Philippics* of Demosthenes, directed at Philip of Macedon, were famed for the forcefulness of their invective (see *Demosthenes* 12).

from Caesar, then in power, the Roman citizenship for Cratippus the Peripatetic, and he got the court of the Areopagus to pass a decree requesting Cratippus to remain at Athens and converse with their young men, and thus be an ornament to their city.[86] There are letters from Cicero to Herodes,[87] and others to his son, in which he recommends the study of philosophy under Cratippus. But he blames Gorgias the rhetorician[88] for enticing the young man into pleasures and drinking parties, and forbids him his son's company. And this is almost the only one of his Greek letters (a second is addressed to Pelops of Byzantium) that was written in anger. In the first, he reproaches Gorgias—justly, if he were what he was thought to be, namely a worthless and dissolute character; but toward Pelops he expresses a petty and peevish rancor for having neglected to procure him a decree of certain honors from the citizens of Byzantium.

25. These complaints revealed his love of distinction, as did the fact that he was often carried away by the cleverness of his speech to ignore decorum. Once, for example, when he acted as advocate for Munatius—who, on being acquitted, immediately prosecuted a friend of Cicero, Sabinus—Cicero is said to have been so overcome with anger as to say, "Was it thanks to your own merits, Munatius, that you were acquitted, and not because I shed much darkness on the court when it was bathed in light?" When from the rostrum he won applause speaking in praise of Marcus Crassus, and within a few days just as publicly reproached him, Crassus said, "Did you not yourself, the day before yesterday, in this very place, commend me?" "Yes," Cicero replied, " for practice I declaimed on a bad

86 Cratippus was the leader of the Aristotelian (or Peripatetic) school during Cicero's time, and a man Cicero much admired. It's not clear what precise motive Cicero had for either of the benefactions mentioned here.

87 An otherwise obscure Athenian scholar.

88 Not the famous Gorgias of classical Athens, but a namesake.

subject."[89] On another occasion, Crassus had said that no member of his family in Rome had ever lived past the age of sixty, and afterward denied it and asked, "What put it into my head to say so?" "You knew," Cicero replied, "that the Romans would be glad to hear it, and by that means you sought to win their favor." And when Crassus said he liked the Stoics because they represented the good man as rich, Cicero said, "Consider whether it's not because they say that all things belong to the wise." (Crassus was generally accused of avarice.)[90] When one of Crassus' sons, who was thought to resemble a certain Axius, and thereby threw some suspicion on his mother's virtue, made a successful speech in the Senate, Cicero, when asked how he liked it, replied with the Greek words "Axius of Crassus."[91]

26. When Crassus was about to set out for Syria,[92] he wanted Cicero to be a friend rather than an enemy. Embracing him, he said he wished to dine with him, and Cicero readily received him. But a few days later, when some friends interceded for Vatinius, declaring that the man desired reconciliation and friendship (for he was an enemy), Cicero replied, "What, does Vatinius also wish to dine with me?"[93] Such was his way with Crassus. When Vatinius, who

---

89 Rhetorical schools in antiquity trained their students by assigning them difficult or improbable cases to defend.

90 Stoicism, the Greek philosophical school that was rising in popularity in late republican Rome, held that moral goodness was the only true wealth, but Crassus seems to have turned this into an endorsement of material riches. Cicero then takes the distortion a step further by implying that, in Crassus' view, the dictum "all things belong to the wise" would sanction any kind of acquisitiveness.

91 The untranslatable pun uses "Axius" both as a name and as the Greek word for "worthy." In one sense the reply means "worthy of Crassus," in another, "Axius, son of Crassus"—implying that Crassus' (unnamed) son was not his own offspring but another Axius.

92 To assume a proconsular post, in 55 BCE.

93 See chapter 9 for the enmity between Cicero and Vatinius. The point of Cicero's remark is the unpleasantness of sharing meals with men he detested.

had swellings on his neck, was pleading a case, Cicero called him a bloated orator. And when he heard that Vatinius was dead, and shortly thereafter learned that he was alive, Cicero said, "May the rascal perish, then, for his report not being true!" When Caesar proposed a law for the division of the land in Campania among the soldiers, and many of the senators opposed it, Lucius Gellius, who was one of the oldest among them, said that it would never pass while he lived. "Then let us defer the vote," said Cicero, "since Gellius does not ask for a long postponement." There was a certain Octavius, who was thought to be of African descent. He once said, at a certain trial, that he could not hear Cicero; to this the orator replied, "And yet your ear is not unpierced."[94] When Metellus Nepos said that Cicero had destroyed more men as a hostile witness than he had saved as an advocate, Cicero said, "I admit that my fidelity to truth is greater than my eloquence." To a young man who was suspected of having given a poisoned cake to his father, and who boasted of the abuse he meant to heap on Cicero, he said, "I prefer that to your cakes." Publius Sestius had retained Cicero, among others, as an advocate in a certain case, but then wanted to do all the pleading himself and would not allow anybody else a word; when it was clear that he would be acquitted by the jurors, and the vote was being taken, Cicero said, "Make use of your opportunity today, Sestius; for tomorrow you will be a nobody." He once summoned Publius Costa as a witness in a certain case (the man wanted to be a lawyer, but was ignorant and dull-witted); and when he kept on answering that he knew nothing, Cicero said, "Perhaps you think you are being questioned about points of law." To Metellus Nepos, who, in a dispute with Cicero, repeatedly asked, "Who is your father?," he replied, "In your case your mother has made the answer to this question more difficult." For Nepos's mother was thought to be a

---

94 Cicero's quip is based on an association of African descent with ear piercing. For Eurocentric Romans, the suggestion that Octavius came from Africa would be an insult.

loose woman, and Nepos himself a flighty character. At one point he suddenly resigned his office of tribune and sailed off to join Pompey in Syria, and then, with as little reason, returned. After giving his teacher, Philagrus, a funeral more elaborate than usual, Nepos set a stone figure of a crow over his tomb. "In this," said Cicero, "you have acted rather wisely; for he taught you to fly about rather than to speak." When Marcius Appius prefaced his speech in a case by saying that his friend had requested him to employ diligence, eloquence, and fidelity, Cicero asked, "Then how have you had the heart not to employ even one of the great virtues your friend requested?"

27. Now the use of this sharp mockery against enemies or legal antagonists seems to be an accepted part of rhetoric; but Cicero's tendency to attack anyone he met for the sake of a joke made many people hate him. I will set down a few instances of this. Marcus Aquinius, who had two sons-in-law in exile, he called Adrastus.[95] Lucius Cotta, who held the office of censor, was a great lover of wine. Cicero, when he was running for the consulship, got thirsty; and when his friends stood around him while he drank, he said, "You are right to be afraid, lest the censor be angry with me for drinking water." Encountering Voconius with his three very homely daughters, he said,

He begat children against Apollo's wishes.[96]

When Marcus Gellius, who was thought to be the son of a slave, had read some letters to the Senate in a shrill, loud voice, Cicero said, "Don't be surprised! He too is one of those who have called out their liberty."[97] When Faustus Sulla, the son of the dictator at Rome

---

95 Adrastus, a mythic king of Argos, also had two sons who were sent into exile. Both ultimately died in the expedition of the "seven against Thebes."

96 The quote is from an unknown Greek tragedy.

97 The untranslatable pun relies on a double meaning of "call out." Freed

who had posted bills proscribing and condemning many people to death,[98] had so squandered his estate and got into debt that he was forced to post bills for the sale of his household goods, Cicero said he liked these bills better than those of his father.

28. On this account he became disliked by many, and Clodius' partisans joined forces against him on the following occasion. Clodius was a man of noble birth, young in years, but in spirit bold and audacious. This man, being in love with Caesar's wife, stole into his house in secret, having donned the dress and ornaments of a lute-girl. The women were celebrating there that secret rite that men are not allowed to witness, and no man was present.[99] But being still a beardless youth,[100] Clodius hoped to reach Pompeia along with the other women without being detected.[101] But since it was night when he entered the large house he lost his way in the corridors; and as he wandered about, a maidservant of Aurelia, Caesar's mother, caught sight of him and asked him his name. Forced to speak, he said that he was looking for an attendant of Pompeia named Abra. At this the maid, perceiving that his voice was not a woman's, shrieked out and called the women together. And they, after shutting the doors, searched everywhere, and eventually found Clodius, who had taken refuge in the room of the girl with whom he had come in.[102] The

---

slaves in Rome, if maltreated by those who did not recognize their new status, could "call out" that they were in fact citizens.

98 See note 15.

99 See chapter 19 above and note 68.

100 An improbable statement, since in the next chapter Plutarch says that Clodius had played an important political role during the Catiline conspiracy, several years before this episode.

101 Pompeia was the second wife of Julius Caesar. On the episode related here, see also *Caesar* 9–10.

102 The role of this nameless girl in sneaking Clodius into the house is clearer in *Caesar* 10.

incident having become notorious, Caesar divorced his wife, and one of the tribunes indicted Clodius for sacrilege.[103]

29. Cicero was at this time a friend of Clodius, and in the conspiracy of Catiline had found him useful as one of his readiest assistants and protectors. But when Clodius, in answering the charge against him, insisted that he had not even been in Rome at the time, but was staying at country places far away, Cicero testified that he had come to his house and conversed with him about various matters; which was true, though Cicero was thought to testify to it not so much for truth's sake as to defend himself against the charges of his own wife, Terentia. For she bore a grudge against Clodius on account of his sister Clodia, whom Terentia thought wished to marry Cicero and was contriving this with the help of Tullus of Tarentum, a close friend of Cicero; and her husband's frequent visits to Clodia, who lived in their neighborhood, and the attentions he paid her had made Terentia suspicious. Being a woman of harsh temper, and having the upper hand over Cicero, she urged him to join the attack upon Clodius and testify against him. Many other good and respectable citizens also bore witness against him for perjuries, fraud, bribing the people, and seducing women. And Lucullus produced female slaves who testified that Clodius had slept with his youngest sister when she was Lucullus' wife; and there was a widespread belief that he had done the same with his other two sisters: Tertia, the wife of Marcius Rex, and Clodia, the wife of Metellus Celer. The latter was called Quadrantaria because one of her lovers had put bronze coins in a purse and sent them to her as if they were silver. (The smallest copper coin was called a *quadrans*.) It was on account of this sister in particular that Clodius was maligned. Yet when the people ranged themselves against the accusers and their supporters, the jurors were frightened and surrounded themselves with a guard, and most of them, when

103 The phrase "of the tribunes" has been inserted into the text following the emendation proposed by Ziegler.

casting their votes, wrote illegibly.[104] Nevertheless, those for acquittal seemed to be in the majority; and some bribery was reported to have been employed. Hence Catulus, when he met the jurors, said, "It was truly as a precaution that you asked for a guard, to prevent your money being taken from you." And Cicero, when Clodius told him the jurors had not believed his testimony, said, "By no means! Twenty of them trusted me and condemned you; and the other thirty of them did not trust you, for they did not acquit you until they got your money."[105] Caesar, though summoned, did not testify against Clodius, and claimed that he had not considered his wife guilty of adultery; he had divorced her, he said, because Caesar's wife should be free not only of shameful conduct, but even of the suspicion of it.[106]

30. Clodius, having escaped this danger, and getting himself elected tribune, immediately attacked Cicero, organizing everything and inciting all men against him. He won the common people over with beneficent laws, and to each of the consuls decreed large provinces: Macedonia to Piso, and Syria to Gabinius. He brought many of the poor into the citizen body, and kept a corps of armed slaves about him. Of the three men who were then most powerful, Crassus was an open enemy of Cicero, Pompey toyed with the other two, and Caesar was about to go out to Gaul with an army. Into Caesar's favor, therefore, Cicero sought to insinuate himself (though the man was not his friend, but had incurred his suspicions at the

---

104 Plutarch apparently misunderstood Roman juridical balloting. The scratching out of both the letters on a ballot ("A" for *absolvo* to acquit, "C" for *condemno* to convict) was a legitimate way for jurors to indicate abstention. According to a modern reconstruction of the vote in this case, about a quarter of the jury abstained.

105 Plutarch rounds off for effect; the original remark, in Cicero's letters (*Ad Atticum* 1.16), mentions twenty-five and thirty-one jurors, respectively.

106 The proverb "Caesar's wife must be above suspicion" comes from Shakespeare by way of this passage or a similar one in Plutarch's *Caesar* (chapter 10).

time of Catiline's conspiracy), and asked to be appointed a legate on his campaign. Caesar accepted him, and Clodius, seeing that Cicero would thus escape his tribunicial authority, pretended to be inclined to a reconciliation; and by laying the principal blame upon Terentia, and always making favorable mention of Cicero, and addressing him kindly, as if he felt no hatred or even ill will, but merely sought to present his objections in a moderate and friendly way, he altogether freed Cicero of his fear, so that he resigned his legate's post under Caesar and again devoted himself to political affairs. Vexed at this conduct, Caesar strengthened Clodius against Cicero, and wholly alienated Pompey from him, while he himself bore witness in an assembly of the people that he did not think it fair or lawful that Lentulus, Cethegus, and their associates should be put to death without a trial.[107] For this was the accusation made against Cicero,[108] and this the charge he was summoned to answer. And so, threatened by prosecution, he changed his dress, let his hair grow long, and went about supplicating the people.[109] But Clodius met him everywhere in the streets, having a band of insolent and daring men about him, who ridiculed Cicero for his change of dress, and often, by throwing mud and stones at him, interrupted his entreaties to the people.

31. First of all, however, almost the whole equestrian order changed their attire with him, and no fewer than twenty thousand young men followed him with their hair untrimmed, and joined in his entreaties to the people. Then the Senate met to pass a decree that the people should change their attire as in time of public sorrow. But the consuls opposed this, and when Clodius went about the Senate house with an armed escort, not a few of the senators ran out, tearing their clothes and crying out. But this sight awakened neither pity

---

107 In the events surrounding Catiline's conspiracy; see chapter 22.

108 That is, that he had presided over summary executions while consul.

109 The change of clothes mentioned here involved putting on mourning garb, and the long hair was also, customarily, a sign of mourning. Both displays were intended as a demonstration of distress and an implicit plea for support.

nor shame; and since Cicero must either go into exile or resort to force and the sword against Clodius, he appealed for help to Pompey, who had purposely got out of the way and was staying at his country estate in the Alban hills. First Cicero sent his son-in-law Piso to intercede for him; then he set out to go himself. But when Pompey was informed of his coming, he would not stay to see him, since he felt a terrible shame toward the man who had undergone many conflicts on his behalf and had often promoted political policies for his advantage.[110] But now, at Caesar's request (Pompey having become his son-in-law), he forsook Cicero's former kindness, slipped out by another door, and ran away from the encounter. Thus abandoned by him and left all alone, Cicero fled to the consuls. Gabinius was always rough with him, but Piso addressed him more courteously, advising him to yield and give way to the fury of Clodius, to bear with the change of times, and to become yet again a savior of his country when she was afflicted by strife and misfortune through Clodius.

Receiving this answer, Cicero consulted with his friends. Lucullus urged him to stay, thinking he would prevail in the end; but others advised him to go into exile, since the people would soon long for him again, once they were sated with the madness and folly of Clodius. This course seemed best to Cicero; but first he took the statue of Minerva that had long stood in his house and that he had honored above all others, and carrying it to the Capitol, dedicated it there, with the inscription, "To Minerva, guardian of Rome." Then, receiving an escort from his friends, he stole out of the city near midnight and proceeded on foot through Lucania, intending to reach Sicily.

32. But as soon as it was publicly known that he had fled, Clodius proposed a decree of exile, and issued an order that denied him fire and water,[111] and prohibited any man within five hundred miles of

---

110 See *Pompey* 46.

111 The Roman *interdictio aqua et igni*, denial of water and fire, was a symbolic

Italy from giving him shelter. Most people, however, out of respect for Cicero, paid not the least regard to this order, showing him every kindness and escorting him on his way. Yet at Hipponium, a city of Lucania now called Vibo, Vibius Sicca, who, among many other advantages he had enjoyed through Cicero's friendship had been made prefect of engineers when he was consul, would not receive him in his house, but sent him word that he would assign him his country estate as a residence; and Gaius Vergilius, the praetor of Sicily, who had been especially close to Cicero, wrote to him to keep away from Sicily. Disheartened at this treatment, he set out for Brundisium, and from there tried to cross to Dyrrachium with a favoring wind; but as he encountered a contrary wind at sea, he returned the next day, and then set out again. It is also reported that after he had come to shore at Dyrrachium and was about to disembark, an earthquake and a convulsion of the sea happened at the same time. Accordingly, the diviners guessed that his exile would not be prolonged, since these were signs of change. But though many visited him out of goodwill, and the cities of Greece vied with one another in sending him deputations, he nevertheless lived for the most part disheartened and dejected, gazing back toward Italy like an unhappy lover; and in his spirit he became very petty and humiliated in consequence of his misfortune, and more dejected than anyone would have expected in a man who had lived with such discipline. And yet he often asked his friends not to call him an orator, but a philosopher, because he had chosen philosophy as an occupation, and only used rhetoric as an instrument for attaining his ends in public life. But popular opinion has great power to wash reason, like a dye, from the soul, and to impress the feelings of the common people, by habit and association, on those who take a part in governing them, unless the politician takes great care, when engaging in external affairs, to interest himself only in

---

exclusion from communal life, often invoked (as here) against those who had fled from a trial before sentence was passed.

the affairs themselves, and not participate in the passions that arise from them.

33. Clodius, having thus driven Cicero away, burned down his villas, and afterward his house, and built on the site of it a temple to Liberty. The rest of Cicero's property he put up for sale, advertising it every day, though no one would buy anything. Clodius thereby became formidable to the patricians; and dragging along with him the common people, who indulged in much insolence and boldness, he went after Pompey, attacking some of the arrangements made by him in the course of his campaign. The disgrace of this made Pompey reproach himself for his desertion of Cicero; and having changed his mind, he and his friends now did all they could to bring about his return. And when Clodius opposed it, the Senate decided to ratify no measure in the meantime, and to do no public business unless Cicero were recalled. But when Lentulus was consul,[112] and the discord increased, so that tribunes were wounded in the Forum, and Quintus, Cicero's brother, was left for dead, lying unnoticed among the slain, the people began to change their minds, and Annius Milo, one of their tribunes, became the first who dared to bring Clodius to trial for acts of violence. Many from the people and from the neighboring cities formed a party with Pompey, and he went forth with them, drove Clodius from the Forum, and summoned the citizens for the vote.[113] And it is said that the people never passed any vote so unanimously. The Senate, also, vying with the people, wrote letters of thanks to all the cities that had sheltered Cicero during his exile, and decreed that his house and his villas, which Clodius had destroyed, should be rebuilt at public expense.

Thus Cicero returned sixteen months after his exile, and the cities

---

112 Publius Clodius Lentulus, nicknamed Spinther, a different man than the one known as Sura (see chapter 17); he was consul in 57 BCE.

113 The *comitia centuriata* that held this vote actually met in the Campus Martius, not the Forum.

were so glad, and people so eager to meet him, that what was said by Cicero afterward fell short of the truth. For he said that Italy had carried him on her shoulders and brought him to Rome. And Crassus too, who had been his enemy before his exile, now gladly met him and was reconciled, to please his son Publius, as he said, who was Cicero's ardent admirer.

34. Waiting only a short time, Cicero took advantage of Clodius' absence from the city, went with a large group to the Capitol, and there tore down and destroyed the tablets of the tribunes, on which their administrative acts were recorded. When Clodius censured him for this, and Cicero stated that it was illegal for Clodius, a patrician, to enter the tribunate,[114] and that therefore nothing done by him was valid, Cato was displeased and opposed Cicero. Not that he approved of Clodius—in fact he disliked his policies; but he pointed out that it was a terrible and violent step for the Senate to revoke so many decrees and acts, including those of his own administration in Cyprus and Byzantium. This led to an antipathy between Cato and Cicero; and though it never manifested itself openly, it weakened their friendship.

35. After this, Milo killed Clodius; and being indicted for the murder, he engaged Cicero as his advocate. The Senate, fearing that the trial of so notable and high-spirited a man might occasion a disturbance in the city, assigned Pompey to preside at this and other trials, that he might maintain security for the city and the courts of justice. Pompey, then, while it was still night, posted his soldiers on the heights overlooking the Forum, and Milo, fearing that Cicero, disconcerted by the unusual sight, might plead less effectively, persuaded him to be conveyed to the Forum in an enclosed litter, and to wait there quietly until the jurors had assem-

---

114 As one of the *optimates*, the Roman nobility, by birth, Clodius should have been excluded from the tribunate, but he had contrived to get himself adopted by a plebeian family.

bled and the court was filled. Cicero, as it would seem, not only lacked courage when armed, but was also fearful when he began to speak, and at many trials scarcely stopped shaking and trembling even when his eloquence had taken hold and was at its height.[115] When he was about to defend Licinius Murena against the prosecution of Cato, and was eager to surpass Hortensius, who had pleaded to great effect, he took no rest the night before, so that his anxiety and lack of sleep impaired his skill, and he was thought to argue less ably than usual.[116] And so on the present occasion, when he emerged from the litter to plead Milo's cause[117] and saw Pompey stationed on the heights as in a camp, and weapons gleaming all around the Forum, he was confused and barely able to begin his speech, since his body trembled and his voice faltered; whereas Milo appeared bold and intrepid at the trial, and had not thought fit to let his hair grow or to change into dark clothes.[118] And this seems to have been a principal cause of Cicero's condemnation. But his behavior led people to think him devoted to his friends rather than cowardly.

36. He also became one of the priests whom the Romans call augurs,[119] replacing the younger Crassus, who had died among the Parthians. Then he was allotted the province of Cilicia and an army of twelve thousand men-at-arms and twenty-two hundred horsemen, and set sail with orders to keep Cappadocia friendly and

---

115 This report seems out of step with the high regard Cicero's oratory obviously commanded among his contemporaries, and its source is unknown.

116 See *Cato* 21 for another, very different account of this trial.

117 Like most elite Romans, Cicero was carried in a litter about the streets of Rome.

118 See note 109.

119 The board of augurs at Rome was in charge of interpreting divine signs on behalf of the state.

obedient to King Ariobarzanes.[120] This he achieved and arranged impeccably without war. And perceiving that the Cilicians had become agitated by the Parthians' defeat of the Romans and the revolt in Syria, he soothed them by his gentle government. He would not accept gifts, even when the kings offered them, and he remitted the cost of public entertainments; he himself daily received the clever and accomplished men of the province, not extravagantly, but liberally. His house had no porter, nor did anyone ever find him lying in bed; but early in the morning, standing or walking before his room, he received those who came to meet him.[121] It is said that he never ordered anyone to be beaten with rods or to have their clothes torn off. He never swore at anyone in anger, or inflicted humiliating punishments. Finding that large sums of the public moneys had been embezzled, he recovered them and made the cities prosperous, and allowed those who made restitution to retain without further punishment their rights as citizens. He also engaged in war, routing the robbers who lived on Mount Amanus,[122] for which he was hailed by his soldiers as *imperator*.[123] And when Caelius the orator asked him to send him panthers from Cilicia for a spectacle at Rome, Cicero, pluming himself on his accomplishments, wrote to him that there were no panthers in Cilicia; for they had fled to Caria, offended that in so general a peace they had become the

120 Ariobarzanes was the name shared by three successive kings of Cappadocia in the first century BCE; probably Ariobarzanes III is the one meant here. The family had been installed by Rome as puppet rulers helping to safeguard the eastern frontier.

121 That is, he went out to greet visitors, rather than admitting them to his presence while seeming to be otherwise occupied or taking food and drink on a dining couch.

122 On the border between Syria and Cilicia.

123 An unofficial title that could at this time be awarded either by the Senate or by an army, giving a commanding general the right to request a triumphal procession.

only objects of attack. Sailing home from his province he touched at Rhodes, then lingered happily in Athens, eager to renew his old pursuits. After visiting with men of great learning, and greeting his former friends and companions, and receiving from Greece the honors that were his due, he returned to Rome, where the city's affairs, afflicted as it were by an inflammation, were breaking out into a civil war.

37. Accordingly, when the Senate was voting him a triumph,[124] he said he would rather follow in Caesar's triumphal procession if their differences could be resolved. He conferred with Caesar privately by letter, and made many appeals to Pompey in person, seeking to mollify and appease each of them. But when matters were past curing, and Caesar was marching against the city, Pompey did not stay, but left the city together with many honest men;[125] Cicero was left out of this flight, and was thought to be siding with Caesar. And it is clear that Cicero's views veered in both directions and that he was disturbed. For he writes in his letters that he was at a loss which way he should turn, since Pompey had fair and honorable grounds for the war, while Caesar managed his affairs better, and was more able to secure himself and his friends. He therefore knew *from* whom he should flee, but not *to* whom he should flee. Then Trebatius, one of Caesar's companions, wrote Cicero a letter saying that in Caesar's opinion Cicero should by all means embrace his cause and share his hopes, but if he declined on account of old age, then he should retire to Greece and live there quietly, out of the way of both parties. Cicero was amazed that Caesar had not written himself, and replied in anger that he would do nothing unworthy of his public career. Such is the drift of his letters.

38. But when Caesar had set out for Spain, Cicero immediately sailed to join Pompey. And he was welcomed by all but Cato, who,

---

124 See previous note. A conquering general's triumph, awarded by senatorial vote, conferred immense political advantage.

125 See *Caesar* 32–35 and *Pompey* 60–61.

when he saw him, chastised him in private for attaching himself to Pompey. In his own case, he said, it would have been dishonorable to abandon that role in the state that he had chosen from the beginning; but Cicero might have been more useful to his country and friends if he had remained neutral and stayed at home to moderate the outcome, instead of coming out to make himself, without reason or necessity, an enemy of Caesar and a partner in their great danger.

These words changed Cicero's attitude, as did the fact that Pompey made no great use of him. But for this Cicero was himself to blame, by not denying that he was sorry he had come, by belittling Pompey's preparations, by underhandedly finding fault with his plans, and by not refraining from jokes and sarcastic remarks about his fellow soldiers. Though he himself went about the camp with a grave and gloomy face, he made others laugh despite themselves. It may be well to mention a few instances. When Domitius was promoting to a command a man who was no soldier, and said he was a modest and prudent person, Cicero replied, "Why, then, did you not keep him as a tutor for your children?" And when certain people were praising Theophanes of Lesbos, who was prefect of engineers in the army, because he had consoled the Rhodians for the loss of their fleet, Cicero said, "What a good thing it is to have a Greek as prefect!"[126] And when Caesar was succeeding in most of his ventures, and in a way besieging Pompey, Lentulus said he had heard that Caesar's friends were gloomy, to which Cicero replied, "You mean they are ill disposed to Caesar?"[127] When a certain Marcius, who had just come from Italy, told them that a rumor prevailed in Rome to the effect that Pompey was besieged, Cicero asked, "Then did you sail out so that you might see it with

126 The remark seems to stress the ineffectiveness of a Greek military engineer as compared with a Roman.

127 The point of the joke seems to be that, since Caesar was winning at the time, the gloominess of his "friends" could be taken to imply that they secretly wanted him to lose.

your own eyes?" And after the defeat, when Nonnius said they should have good hopes, since there were seven eagles left in Pompey's camp, Cicero said, "Your advice would be good if we were fighting with jackdaws."[128] And when Labienus harped on some oracles, and said that Pompey must prevail, Cicero said, "Yes, and by employing this strategy we have now lost our camp."

39. But when the battle at Pharsalus[129] (in which Cicero took no part because of illness) was over, and Pompey had fled, Cato, who had a considerable force and a large fleet at Dyrrachium, asked Cicero to take the command, according to custom and on account of his superior consular rank. And when Cicero declined the command and was wholly averse to participating in the war, he came close to being killed (for the younger Pompey and his friends called him a traitor, and drew their swords upon him), except that Cato intervened and with difficulty rescued him and brought him out of the camp.[130] Afterward, landing at Brundisium, he remained there for some time waiting for Caesar, who was delayed by his activities in Asia and Egypt. And when it was reported that Caesar had arrived at Tarentum and was coming by land from there to Brundisium, Cicero hastened toward him, being not altogether without hope, but feeling somewhat ashamed to test the temper of an enemy and conqueror in the presence of many witnesses. But there was no necessity for him to either do or say anything unworthy of himself. For Caesar, as soon as he saw him coming far ahead of the others, dismounted and embraced him, and walked on for many stades, conversing with him alone. And from then on he continued to treat him with honor and affection, so that when Cicero wrote an oration

128 The "eagles" here are legionary standards, traditionally referred to by that name, but Cicero jokingly takes the word literally.

129 In 48 BCE, between Caesar's forces and those of Pompey and the Senate.

130 See *Cato* 55, where this story is relocated to Corcyra (modern-day Corfu). Pompey's elder son was named Gnaeus.

in praise of Cato, Caesar, writing a reply to it,[131] commended Cicero's eloquence and his life, declaring that he most resembled Pericles and Theramenes.[132] Cicero's oration was entitled *Cato*; Caesar's, *Anti-Cato*.[133]

It is also related that when Quintus Ligarius was prosecuted for being one of the enemies of Caesar, and Cicero had undertaken his defense, Caesar said to his friends, "What prevents us, after all this time, from hearing a speech from Cicero? For Ligarius has long been judged a wicked man and an enemy."[134] But when Cicero began to speak he moved his audience to an extraordinary degree, and his speech proceeded with such varied pathos and such remarkable grace that Caesar's face changed color often, and it was clear that all the passions of his soul were stirred up; and finally, when the orator touched upon the struggles at Pharsalus, Caesar was so affected that his body trembled and some of the papers he was holding dropped from his hands. At any rate, he was overpowered, and acquitted Ligarius.

40. After this, when the government had been changed into a monarchy,[135] Cicero abandoned public life and devoted his leisure to those of the young men who wished to study philosophy; and

---

131 See *Caesar* 54. Cato committed suicide after all hope of victory over Caesar was lost.

132 For Pericles, here used as a model of statesmanship and eloquence, see the Plutarchan *Life*. Theramenes, an Athenian political leader of the late fifth century BCE, was famous for his moderation and adaptability; he helped reconcile the two sides and resolve an Athenian civil war in 403 BCE, a role Caesar clearly hoped Cicero would emulate.

133 Neither treatise survives.

134 The flippant remark is tantamount to "We know the outcome but might as well hear the case." The speech Cicero delivered on this occasion, *Pro Ligario*, survives.

135 Plutarch uses "monarchy" loosely to describe various kinds of one-man rule. Caesar in fact had steadfastly rejected kingship but was instead appointed dictator, a constitutional office but in his case extended to a life term.

virtually by his intimacy with them, who were of the highest birth and rank, he again acquired great influence in the city. He made it his task to compose and translate philosophical dialogues[136] and to render into Latin the various terms of dialectic and natural science; for it was he, as they say, who first, or mainly, gave Latin names to *phantasia*, *syncatathesis*, *epoché*, *catalepsis*, as well as to *atomon*, *amerés*, *kenon*, and many other such terms, devising them partly by metaphors and partly by conveying their proper sense with words that were familiar and intelligible.[137] For his amusement he exercised his facility in poetry. For it is said that whenever he applied himself to it, he would compose five hundred verses in a night.

During that period he spent most of his time at his country estate in Tusculum, and he used to write to his friends that he was living the life of Laertes,[138] either in jest, as was his habit, or from an ambition for public employment, which made him impatient with the present state of affairs. He rarely went down to the city, unless to pay court to Caesar, and he was the first among those who advocated honors for Caesar and were eager always to be saying something novel about the man and his actions;[139] as, for example, what he said about the statues of Pompey that had been thrown down and removed, and were afterward by Caesar's orders set up again: namely that Caesar, by this act of humanity, had indeed set up Pompey's statues, but had also firmly established his own.

---

136 Among the works surviving from this period are *On the Nature of the Gods* and *Tusculan Disputations*.

137 The Greek words listed here derive from the philosophic schools, principally those founded by Plato and by Epicurus. The Latin language, being poorer than Greek in abstract nouns, often had a hard time coping with the vocabulary of Greek philosophy.

138 Laertes, father of Odysseus, is depicted in the *Odyssey* working quietly in his garden, far from the cares of state.

139 See *Caesar* 57, where Plutarch strives to mitigate the apparent capitulation by Cicero.

41. He intended, it is said, to write a comprehensive history of his country, combining with it much Greek history, and incorporating in it all the stories and tales that he had collected. But he was distracted by many public affairs, and by many unwanted private troubles and misfortunes, most of which it appears he had brought on himself. For first of all, he divorced his wife, Terentia, by whom he had been neglected during the war and sent off without the necessary supplies for his journey; nor did he find her well disposed to him when he returned to Italy. For she did not come to him herself, though he stayed a long time in Brundisium; and when their daughter, a young girl, made the long journey to join him, Terentia did not supply her with a suitable escort or adequate expenses; indeed, when Terentia left Cicero's house it was stripped, empty, and encumbered with many heavy debts.[140] These are the most plausible reasons alleged for the divorce. But Terentia denied them all, and her husband himself furnished her with an unmistakable defense when, not long afterward, he married a young girl. He did this, as Terentia proclaimed, for the love of her beauty; or as Tiro, Cicero's freedman, has written, for her money, so that he could clear his debts. For the girl was very rich, and Cicero had been left trustee of her estate.[141] And since he was many tens of thousands in debt, he was persuaded by his friends and relatives to marry the girl (though he was well past his prime) and to use her money to get rid of his creditors. But Antony, who mentions this marriage in his responses to the *Philippics*, says that he cast off a wife with whom he had grown old; and he pokes fun at Cicero's stay-at-home life, wittily deriding his idle and unsoldierlike habits.[142] Not

---

140 Plutarch is our only surviving source for this information; Cicero's many letters from this period give no hint of ill will on Terentia's part, but also do not suggest any other reason for the divorce.

141 By Roman law the girl (Publilia) could not inherit in her own name; her estate had to be held in trust for her until her marriage.

142 On the *Philippics*, directed against Antony, see 24 and 48. Antony's replies have not survived.

long after this marriage, Cicero's daughter Tullia died in childbirth at the house of Lentulus, to whom she had been married after the death of Piso, her former husband. The philosophers came from all sides to comfort Cicero; but his grief at this misfortune was so excessive that he divorced his newly married wife, because she was thought to be pleased at the death of Tullia.

42. Thus stood Cicero's domestic affairs. Yet in the plot then being laid against Caesar he took no part, though he was Brutus' closest confidant and was thought to be as distressed at the present and as desirous of the former state of affairs as anybody else. But the conspirators feared his nature, as lacking courage, and his old age, in which boldness fails even the strongest natures. And therefore, when the deed was done by the friends of Brutus and Cassius, and the friends of Caesar were leaguing themselves against the conspirators, and there was fear that the city would again be embroiled in civil wars, Antony, being consul, convened the Senate and spoke briefly about concord, whereupon Cicero, after delivering a speech appropriate to the occasion, persuaded the Senate to imitate the Athenians[143] and decree an amnesty for what had been done to Caesar, and to distribute provinces to Cassius and Brutus. But none of these things came to pass. For as soon as the common people, who were themselves moved to pity, saw the dead body of Caesar being carried through the Forum, and Antony showed them the clothes filled with blood and pierced everywhere with swords, they went mad with anger and conducted a search for the murderers, and with firebrands ran to their houses in order to burn them.[144] The conspirators, however, having taken precautions beforehand, escaped these dangers; and expecting many more and greater to come, they left the city.

43. At this Antony was at once elated, and everyone was alarmed at the prospect that he would make himself sole ruler, Cicero more than

---

143 See note 132 above. The regime of the Thirty at Athens was ousted in 403 BCE, but its members were allowed to leave the city under an amnesty.

144 Compare *Caesar* 68, *Antony* 14, and *Brutus* 20.

anyone. For Antony, seeing Cicero's influence reviving in the state, and aware that he was connected with Brutus and his party, was vexed to have him in the city. Besides, there had been some former suspicion between them, caused by the dissimilarity in their lives. Cicero, fearful of the outcome, was inclined to go as lieutenant with Dolabella into Syria. But the consuls who were about to succeed Antony, Hirtius and Pansa, good men and admirers of Cicero, entreated him not to desert them, undertaking to depose Antony if Cicero would stay in Rome. So Cicero, neither distrusting nor wholly trusting them, bade farewell to Dolabella, promising Hirtius and Pansa that he would spend the summer at Athens and return when they had assumed office. Accordingly, he set out on his journey; but when some delay occurred, fresh news, as often happens, came suddenly from Rome, to the effect that Antony had undergone an astonishing change and was doing everything and managing all public affairs at the will of the Senate, and that nothing but Cicero's presence was needed to bring things into the best possible state. And therefore, blaming himself for his excessive caution, Cicero returned again to Rome. At first he was not disappointed in his hopes; for an enormous crowd of people, stirred by joy and longing for him, flocked out to meet him, and the greetings and civilities that were addressed to him at the gates as he entered the city took up almost a whole day's time.

On the following day, however, when Antony convened the Senate and summoned him to attend, Cicero did not come, but lay in bed, pretending to be ill with exhaustion; but the true reason seemed his fear of a plot against him, arising from some suspicion and information given him on his way to Rome. Antony was incensed at the affront and sent soldiers with orders to bring Cicero or burn down his house. But when many interceded and entreated for him, Antony relented, satisfied to accept sureties. And from then on they continued hostile, silent, and on their guard, until the young Caesar,[145]

---

145 Octavian, who later took the honorific Augustus as his name, was Caesar's adopted heir.

arriving from Apollonia, assumed the inheritance of the elder Caesar and engaged in a dispute with Antony about twenty-five million drachmas that Antony was detaining from the estate.

44. After this, Philippus, who had married the mother of the young Caesar, and Marcellus, who had married the sister, came with the young man to Cicero, and agreed with him that Cicero should give Caesar the influence afforded by his eloquence and political prowess, both in the Senate and before the people, and that Caesar should give Cicero the security afforded by his wealth and arms. For already the young man had about him a considerable party of the soldiers who had served under the elder Caesar. It was also thought that Cicero had a stronger reason for gladly welcoming Caesar's friendship. For it would seem that while Pompey and Caesar were still alive, Cicero dreamt that someone was calling the sons of the senators to the Capitol, since Jupiter was going to declare one of them the ruler of Rome; and that the citizens eagerly ran and stood about the temple, while the youths, sitting in their purple-bordered togas,[146] kept silence. Suddenly the door opened, and the youths, rising one by one, passed around the god, who reviewed them all, and, to their sorrow, sent them away. But when the young Caesar was passing by, the god stretched forth his hand and said, "Romans, you will have an end to civil wars when this young man has become your leader." They say that Cicero, from some such dream, had formed an impression of the boy, and retained it clearly, but did not know who he was. The next day, however, as he was going down into the Campus Martius, the boys, who had just exercised there, were leaving it, and the first was the boy he had seen in his dream. Astonished, he asked him who his parents were. His father was Octavius, a man of no great eminence; but his mother was Atia, a daughter of Caesar's sister. Hence Caesar, who had no children of his own, made him by will the heir of his property and house. From then on, they say, Cicero took careful notice of the boy whenever they met, and

146 The dress of members of the senatorial class.

the young man kindly welcomed his civility; and by chance he happened to have been born when Cicero was consul.[147]

45. These were the reasons spoken of; but it was principally Cicero's hatred of Antony, and then his natural desire for honor, that attached him to Caesar,[148] since he imagined he would add Caesar's political power to his own. For the young man went so far in paying court to him as actually to call him father. At this Brutus was so displeased that in his letters to Atticus he attacked Cicero, saying that by his courting Caesar through fear of Antony he was clearly not seeking liberty for his country, but an indulgent master for himself. Yet Brutus took Cicero's son, who was then studying philosophy at Athens, gave him a command, and employed him on many occasions with excellent results.[149]

Cicero's own power in the city was then at its height, and as he could do whatever he pleased, he formed a faction against Antony, drove him out of the city, and sent the two consuls, Hirtius and Pansa, to wage war on him; he also persuaded the Senate to vote Caesar the lictors and ensigns of a praetor, arguing that he was his country's defender.[150] But after Antony was defeated,[151] and both consuls had died after the battle, the armies united under Caesar. And the Senate, fearing the young man, who had enjoyed such splendid good fortune, tried by honors and gifts to draw off his soldiers and to curtail his power, declaring that there was no further

---

147 In 63 BCE, the year that Cicero, as consul, faced down Catiline.

148 From this point forward Plutarch uses "Caesar" to refer to Octavian.

149 Brutus had at this time assumed command of the province of Macedonia (see chapter 47).

150 The lictors (officers bearing the bundled rods and axe called the fasces) and insignia came to Octavian as part of a grant of *imperium*, an essential prop to his military authority.

151 Not his final defeat at Actium but a smaller setback in 43 BCE. Antony and Octavian soon thereafter joined forces with Lepidus in the Second Triumvirate (see chapter 46).

need for defensive armies now that Antony had taken to flight. This frightened Caesar, and he privately sent some friends to entreat and persuade Cicero to procure the consulship for them both, but to manage matters as Cicero himself thought best after assuming office, and to direct a young man who only desired fame and glory. And Caesar himself later confessed that in fear of having his force disbanded, and in danger of being deserted, he had made timely use of Cicero's love of power, persuading him to run for the consulship and to accept his aid and cooperation in the campaign.

46. In this instance, more than in any other, Cicero let himself be carried away and deceived—an old man by a young one. Supporting Caesar's campaign, he gained him the goodwill of the Senate. He was at once reproached by his friends, and soon afterward saw that he had ruined himself and betrayed the liberty of the people. For the young man, as soon as he had exalted himself and obtained the consulship, bade farewell to Cicero; and after making friends with Antony and Lepidus and joining his power with theirs, he divided the leadership, like any other piece of property, among the three of them. They made a list of more than two hundred men who were to be put to death. But the proscription of Cicero caused the most contention in all their debates, Antony remaining irreconcilable unless Cicero should be the first man to be killed, Lepidus siding with Antony, and Caesar opposing them both. They met secretly and by themselves, for three days, near the city of Bononia. The place was at a distance from the camp, with a river surrounding it. Caesar, it is said, contended for Cicero for the first two days; but on the third he yielded and gave him up. They exchanged the following concessions. Caesar had to desert Cicero, Lepidus his own brother Paulus, and Antony his maternal uncle Lucius Caesar. Thus were they led by anger and madness to abandon their humanity, or rather, they showed that no wild beast is more savage than man in possession of the power to indulge his passion.

47. While these things were happening, Cicero was with his brother at his country estate in Tusculum. But when they heard of

the proscriptions they decided to depart for Astura, a place of Cicero's near the sea, and to sail from there to Brutus in Macedonia; for by then a report was going round that he was in power there. Overwhelmed by grief, they were conveyed in litters; and when they halted along the way, and had their litters placed side by side, they would console each other. But Quintus was the more disheartened when he reflected on his destitute state; for he said that he had brought nothing with him from home, and even Cicero had scanty provisions; so it was better, he said, that Cicero should hasten onward in his flight, but that he himself should get what he needed from home and then catch up with him. Having chosen this course, they embraced each other and parted with many tears.

Quintus, then, within a few days, was betrayed by his servants to those who came to search for him, and put to death, together with his son. But Cicero was conveyed to Astura; and on finding a vessel, he embarked immediately and sailed along the coast as far as Circaeum with a favoring wind. From there the pilots wished to set sail at once, but Cicero, either because he feared the sea, or had not altogether abandoned his faith in Caesar, disembarked and proceeded on foot for a hundred stades, as if heading for Rome. But again growing distraught and changing his mind, he went down to the sea at Astura. There he passed the night in terrible and helpless thoughts, and finally resolved to steal into Caesar's house, kill himself on the hearth, and thus bring divine vengeance upon him;[152] but the fear of torture put him off this course as well. After contemplating a variety of confused and contrary views, he turned himself over to his servants to be conveyed by sea to Caieta, where he had property and an agreeable refuge in summer, when the etesian winds[153] are most pleasant.

---

152 The killing of a suppliant at a guest's hearth was considered a violation of religious taboo and a source of ritual pollution, though the idea that one could use suicide to evoke such pollution seems to be a novel one.

153 The etesian (or "annual") winds in the Aegean region blow from the north in summertime.

The place also has a temple of Apollo, not far above the sea, from which a flock of crows flew with a scream toward Cicero's vessel as it was rowed to shore. Perching on both sides of the yardarm, some croaked, others pecked at the ends of the ropes, and everyone considered this a bad omen. Cicero therefore went ashore, entered his villa, and lay down to rest. Then most of the crows settled about his window, cawing raucously, but one of them flew down to the couch where Cicero lay with his head covered, and tried little by little to draw the clothes from his face. His servants, observing this, blamed themselves for waiting to be spectators of their master's murder, while brute creatures came to assist and take care of him in his undeserved misfortune, though they themselves did nothing to defend him. So partly by entreaty, and partly by force, they took him up and carried him in his litter toward the sea.

48. But in the meantime his assassins arrived—Herennius, a centurion, and Popillius, a tribune whom Cicero had once defended when prosecuted for the murder of his father; and they had underlings. Finding the doors shut, they broke them open; but Cicero was not to be seen, and the people inside claimed they did not know where he was. It is said that a young man who had been educated by Cicero in the liberal arts and sciences, a freedman of Cicero's brother Quintus (Philologus was his name), informed the tribune that the litter was being carried through the wooded and shady walks that led toward the sea. The tribune, taking a few men with him, ran around to the rear door, while Herennius went on the run through the walks; and Cicero, catching sight of him, ordered his servants to set the litter down where they were. He himself, stroking his chin with his left hand, as he used to do, gazed steadily at his murderers, his body covered with dust and his face ravaged by worries, so that most of those who stood by covered their faces while Herennius slew him. For Cicero stretched forth his neck from the litter and was slain, being then in his sixty-fourth year. Herennius cut off his head, by Antony's command, and his hands too, with which he had written his *Philippics*.

For Cicero himself gave this title to the orations he wrote against Antony, and so they are called to this day.

49. When Cicero's head and hands were brought to Rome, Antony was conducting an election; and when he heard of their arrival, and saw them, he cried out, "Now let there be an end to our proscriptions." He ordered them to be placed on the platform over the rostrum,[154] a sight the Romans shuddered to behold; for they believed they saw there not the face of Cicero, but the image of Antony's soul. Yet in the course of these actions Antony did justice in one instance, namely when he surrendered Philologus to Pomponia, the wife of Quintus. She, having got his body into her power, besides all the other punishments she inflicted on him, made him cut off his own flesh bit by bit, and roast and eat it. So some writers have reported; but Tiro, Cicero's own freedman, makes no mention at all of Philologus' treachery.

I have been told that Caesar, a long time after this, visited one of his daughter's sons; the boy, who was holding in his hands a book of Cicero's, was terrified and tried to hide it in his toga. Perceiving this, Caesar took it from him, read through a great part of it as he stood there, returned it to the boy, and said, "A learned man, my boy—learned and a lover of his country." And as soon as he had defeated Antony[155] (Caesar was then serving as consul), he chose Cicero's son as his colleague in office; and it was during that consulship that the Senate took down the statues of Antony, abolished the other honors that had been given him, and decreed that no Antony should ever again bear the name of Marcus. Thus it was through Cicero's family that the divine powers brought about the final acts of Antony's punishment.

---

154 The speaker's platform from which Cicero often addressed the people was adorned with *rostra*, or beaks of captured ships, and was often called the *rostra* or *rostrum*.

155 In the battle of Actium, in 31 BCE (see *Antony* 63–68).

BRUTUS

Marcus Brutus was descended from the Junius Brutus whose bronze statue, sword in hand, the ancient Romans set up on the Capitol amid those of their kings, in remembrance of his great resolution in deposing the Tarquins.[1] But that Brutus, like the cold-forged steel of swords, was of a severe nature and had never had his character softened by study, so that he was driven by his rage against the tyrants to slay his sons.[2] But *this* Brutus, whose life I now write, tempered his character with learning and the study of philosophy, and quickened his nature, which was grave and mild, by engaging in practical affairs, thus achieving a harmonious blend well suited for virtue. Hence even those who hated him for the conspiracy against Caesar attributed whatever was noble in the exploit to Brutus, and assigned to Cassius what was harder to accept, Cassius being a kinsman of Brutus, and a friend,

---

1 The Tarquins were the line of kings who ruled Rome in the seventh and sixth centuries BCE. The last of the line, Tarquinius Superbus, incurred the enmity of his people through his notorious rape of the noblewoman Lucretia, and was deposed after his nephew, Junius Brutus, led an uprising against him. These events took place, according to conventional Roman dating, in 509 BCE. Junius Brutus assumed the newly instituted office of consul in that year and the monarchy was abolished.

2 The two sons of Junius Brutus allegedly conspired with the exiled Tarquins to restore the monarchy, and their father, in his capacity as consul, presided over their executions.

but not equally straightforward and pure in character. Servilia, Brutus' mother, traced her descent to Servilius Ahala, who, when Spurius Maelius was plotting a tyranny and stirring up the people, took a dagger under his arm, went to the Forum, came close to the man as if he had some business to discuss with him, and when he turned to listen, struck and killed him.[3]

This much is generally agreed; as for his father's family, those who bear any hatred or ill will toward Brutus for the murder of Caesar deny that he was descended from the Brutus who expelled the Tarquins, arguing that none of that man's family was left after he slew his sons; they say that his ancestor was a commoner, the son of a steward named Brutus, and had only recently risen to office. But Poseidonius the philosopher[4] says that two of Brutus' sons who were adults were put to death, as the story relates, but that a third, still an infant, was left, from whom the family descended; he also mentions that in his own day there were some distinguished persons of that house whose looks resembled the statue of Brutus. So much for this subject.

2. Cato the Philosopher[5] was the brother of Servilia, Brutus' mother, and was the Roman whom Brutus most emulated, Cato being his uncle and later becoming his father-in-law.[6] Of all the Greek philosophers, there was virtually no one of whom Brutus had not been a student, or with whose work he was unfamiliar, though

---

3 Descent from Servilius Ahala gave Brutus a second famous tyrannicide as ancestor. The incident referred to took place in the fifth century BCE.

4 A Greek Stoic who took up residence in Rome in the early first century BCE and taught many prominent Romans. Fragments of his historical writings, chronicling the Roman world from 146 BCE on, have survived.

5 Also known as Cato the Younger, the subject of a Plutarchan Life. Plutarch calls him "the Philosopher" because of his staunch adherence to Stoicism, though Cato is better known as a political leader.

6 Brutus married Porcia, his first cousin (his mother's niece).

he especially admired the Platonists. Rejecting the New and Middle Academy, as they are called, he devoted himself to the Old, and continued to esteem Antiochus of Ascalon,[7] and made his brother Aristus his friend and housemate, a man who in his learning was inferior to many of the philosophers, but in good manners and gentleness could compete with the best. As for Empylus, whom Brutus and his friends often mention in their letters as living with him, he was a rhetorician, and has left a short but excellent treatise on the death of Caesar, entitled *Brutus*.[8]

In Latin, Brutus had by practice attained sufficient fluency for expositions or for trials; but in Greek he affected the epigrammatic and brief Spartan style, of which there are a number of striking examples in his letters.[9] For example, when he had already launched the war, he wrote to the Pergamenians, "I hear you have given Dolobella money; if willingly, admit that you have harmed me; if unwillingly, prove it by giving willingly to *me*."[10] And at another time to the Samians, "Your counsels are careless and your services slow; how do you think this will end?" And in another letter, "The Xanthians, disdaining my benefactions, have made their country a grave for their senselessness; the Patareans, entrusting themselves to me, enjoy in every respect their former freedom. Thus it is in your

---

7 Antiochus regarded his brand of Platonism as a return to the original tenets of the Academy. Two subsequent phases (the "Middle" and "New" Academies) had taken Plato's teachings in a more skeptical direction by questioning whether knowledge or truth could ever be attained.

8 The work has not survived.

9 The letters of Brutus have not survived, but Plutarch must have had access to them.

10 The war Plutarch refers to is the campaign in Greece and Asia Minor against the forces of Octavian and Mark Antony, described in more detail starting in chapter 23. Brutus was often short of funds to subsidize this war (see, e.g., chapter 30) and had to put pressure on the cities of the region, such as Pergamum, to support him. The quote that follows, addressed to the Samians, probably belongs to a similar context.

power to choose the judgment of the Patareans or the fate of the Xanthians."[11] Such is the style of his distinguished letters.

3. When he was still a very young man he traveled to Cyprus with his uncle Cato, who had been sent out against Ptolemy.[12] And after Ptolemy committed suicide, Cato, being forced to prolong his stay in Rhodes, had already sent one of his friends, Canidius, to safeguard the king's treasures; but fearing that Canidius would not refrain from theft, he wrote to Brutus, urging him to sail with all speed to Cyprus from Pamphylia, where he was recuperating after an illness. Brutus sailed, though very reluctantly, both because he respected Canidius, whom he felt had been ignominiously rejected by Cato, and also because he regarded such administrative cares and commissions as vulgar and ill suited to himself as a young man of letters. He nevertheless applied himself to the business, earned Cato's praise, and after turning the king's goods into money, sailed with most of it to Rome.[13]

4. But when the state split into two factions, Pompey and Caesar taking up arms against each other, and the leadership was thrown into disarray, it was believed that Brutus would choose Caesar's side; for his father's death had previously been arranged by Pompey.[14] But thinking it his duty to place the public good above his private feel-

---

11 Xanthus and Patara are two towns along the southern coast of Turkey. The context is once again Brutus' conduct of the war against Octavian and Antony in the Greek East. Xanthus' population set fire to their own town and destroyed themselves rather than submit to Brutus' demands; thereafter Brutus took steps to reassure the neighboring Patareans, and gained their trust.

12 Ptolemy of Cyprus, brother of the reigning Egyptian king Ptolemy XII, had offended various Roman senators; Cato's mission (see *Cato* 34–35) was to demand that he surrender his sovereignty. Ptolemy killed himself instead.

13 See *Cato* 36–37, where Plutarch gives credit for this sale to Cato rather than Brutus.

14 See *Pompey* 16 for Pompey's role in the death of the elder Brutus; see *Pompey* 60–72 and *Caesar* 33–47 for the war between Caesar and Pompey in the years 49–48 BCE.

ings, and judging that Pompey's grounds for war were better than Caesar's, he attached himself to Pompey. And though formerly he would not even speak to Pompey when he met him, believing it a sacrilege to converse with the murderer of his father, now, looking upon him as the general of his country, he placed himself under his command and set sail for Cilicia[15] as lieutenant to Sestius, who had been appointed governor of the province. But since there was no opportunity there of doing any great service, and Pompey and Caesar were now about to meet and engage in a battle on which everything depended, he came as a volunteer to Macedonia[16] to share in the danger. And it is said that Pompey was so surprised and pleased that, rising from his chair as Brutus approached, he embraced him as a superior as everyone looked on. During the campaign, except when he was in Pompey's company, he spent his time reading and studying, even on the day before the great battle.[17] It was the height of summer, and the heat was great, the camp having been pitched near marshy ground; and those who carried Brutus' tent were slow in coming. But though he was worn out, having by midday scarcely anointed himself and taken a little food, yet, while the others were either sleeping or occupied with thoughts of what lay ahead, he spent his time until evening arranging and composing a summary of Polybius.[18]

---

15 In the southeast corner of modern Turkey.

16 Pompey had brought his forces, including much of the Roman Senate, to Greece and Macedonia when Caesar invaded Italy in 49 BCE, thinking himself not strong enough to risk an immediate battle. Caesar pursued Pompey there the following spring.

17 The battle of Pharsalus, in which Caesar's forces defeated Pompey's; see *Caesar* 42–46 and *Pompey* 68–72.

18 The great Greek historian Polybius, who lived in the century before Brutus, left behind a voluminous history of Rome's rise to world supremacy, parts of which have survived. Brutus seems to have been engaged in summarizing the work, perhaps in Latin rather than the original Greek.

5. It is also said that Caesar took steps to protect Brutus, ordering his officers not to kill the man in battle but to spare him, and to take him prisoner if he surrendered voluntarily; but if he resisted arrest, to let him be and do him no violence. Caesar is said to have done this out of kindness to Servilia, Brutus' mother. For it seems that Caesar, when still a young man, was intimate with Servilia, who was madly in love with him; and as Brutus was born at the time when Servilia's passion was at its height, Caesar believed that the child was his own son. It is also said that when the great conspiracy of Catiline,[19] which came close to destroying the city, was being debated in the Senate, Cato and Caesar, who were of different opinions about the matter, were standing beside each other, at which moment a small note was passed to Caesar from outside, which he read in silence. At this, Cato cried out and accused Caesar of corresponding with and receiving letters from their enemies; then, when a great uproar arose, Caesar gave the note, just as it was, to Cato, who found, on reading it, that it was a love letter from his sister Servilia. Tossing it back to Caesar, he said, "Keep it, you drunkard," and returned to the subject of the debate.[20] So well-known was Servilia's passion for Caesar.

6. After the defeat at Pharsalus, when Pompey had escaped to the sea and his camp was being besieged, Brutus slipped out unnoticed by a gate leading to marshy ground full of water and reeds, and got away safe by night to Larissa. From there he wrote to Caesar, who was pleased that he was safe; and urging him to come, not only pardoned him, but made him one of his most highly honored companions. Since no one was able to say in what direction Pompey was fleeing, Caesar took a walk with Brutus alone and solicited his views. And as some of his conjectures about Pompey's flight struck Caesar as the soundest he had heard, he renounced all other courses

---

19 On the conspiracy of Catiline see *Cicero* 14–23, and see 21 in particular for the opposition of Cato and Caesar.

20 The same story is told at *Cato* 24.

and headed for Egypt. But Pompey, having reached Egypt, as Brutus guessed, there met his fate.[21] Meanwhile, Brutus tried to mollify Caesar with regard to Cassius. He also served as an advocate for the king of the Libyans;[22] and though he lost the case, owing to the magnitude of the charges alleged against the king, nevertheless, by his entreaties and supplications on his behalf, he preserved a large part of his kingdom for him. It is said that Caesar, when he first heard Brutus speak in public, said to his friends, "I know not what this young man wants; but whatever he wants, he wants vehemently." For the weight of Brutus' character, and the fact that he did not listen easily when anyone appealed to him for a favor, but achieved his goals by reasoning and the espousal of noble ideals, made his ventures, wherever he turned, vigorous and effective. He could not be flattered to listen to unjust petitions, and the inability to refuse shameless requests, which some call diffidence, he considered highly disgraceful in a great man, and used to say that those who could refuse nothing must not have behaved well in their youth.

When Caesar was about to cross over to Africa against Cato and Scipio,[23] he entrusted Brutus with Cisalpine Gaul, to that province's good fortune. For whereas the other provinces, thanks to the insolence and greed of their governors, were plundered as if they were taken in war, to the inhabitants of *his* province Brutus proved

---

21 In his generosity to his subject, Plutarch passes quickly over this rapprochement between Brutus and Caesar, and deflects any notion that Brutus had betrayed Pompey, his former ally, by describing his communications to Caesar about Pompey's whereabouts only as "conjectures" rather than inside information.

22 Plutarch probably meant to write "Galatians" here, not "Libyans" (or the error may have been introduced by copyists). In the aftermath of Pharsalus, Brutus pleaded before Caesar on behalf of Deiotarus, king of the Galatians, who had taken Pompey's side in the war and had fled from Greece with Pompey.

23 See *Caesar* 52–54. Cato and Scipio were the last remaining leaders of the faction Pompey had taken to Greece in 49 BCE; they had fled from the defeat at Pharsalus and taken refuge with King Juba in North Africa.

a respite and a consolation even for their earlier misfortunes. And he directed everyone's gratitude to Caesar, so that after Caesar's return, as he was traveling about Italy, the cities under Brutus' command were an exceedingly pleasurable sight, as was Brutus himself, who enhanced Caesar's honor and was a charming companion.

7. Now that several praetorships were vacant, it was expected that the most prestigious one, which is called the praetorship of the city, would be given to Brutus or Cassius; and some say that the two men, who were already somewhat at odds for other reasons, were even more estranged by this rivalry, though they were kinsmen; for Cassius was married to Brutus' sister Junia. Others say this competition was the work of Caesar, who had privately led each to hope for his support until, thus incited and provoked, they launched their campaigns. Brutus had only his reputation and his virtue to oppose to the many gallant exploits Cassius had performed in the Parthian War. But Caesar, after hearing each side and deliberating with his friends, said, "Cassius has the fairer plea, but Brutus must be given the first praetorship." So Cassius was appointed to another praetorship, but he was not as grateful for what he had gained as he was incensed over what he had lost.

And in all other things Brutus enjoyed as great a share of Caesar's power as he desired; for had he wished it, he might have been the foremost of Caesar's friends and exercised the greatest power; but Cassius and his associates drew him away from Caesar. Not that Brutus was yet wholly reconciled to Cassius after their rivalry; but he listened to Cassius' friends, who urged him not to let himself be softened and charmed by Caesar, but to shun the kindness and favors of a tyrant, which were bestowed upon him not to honor his merit, but to disarm him and undermine his spirit.

8. Now Caesar was neither wholly unsuspecting nor deaf to the accusations leveled at Brutus; but though he feared the man's proud spirit and his prestige, he had faith in his character. When he was told that Antony and Dolobella were plotting a revolution, he said it was not the fat and long-haired fellows who troubled him, but those

pale and thin ones, meaning Brutus and Cassius. And when some were maligning Brutus to him and urging him to beware of him, Caesar took hold of his own body and said, "What? Don't you think Brutus will wait for this bit of flesh?,"[24] hinting that no one but Brutus was fit to succeed him in his power. And it seems that Brutus might have been the first man in the city had he had the patience for a little while to be second to Caesar, allowing the man's power to decline, and the renown of his successes to fade. But Cassius, a hot-tempered man, and more a hater of Caesar for personal reasons than a hater of tyranny for patriotic ones, fanned Brutus' feelings and pressed him hard. Brutus is said to have disliked the *rule*, but Cassius to have hated the *ruler.* Among other things Cassius held against Caesar was the taking away of some lions Cassius had procured when he was about to be aedile. These had been left behind at Megara; and when the city was seized by Calenus, Caesar confiscated them.[25] These beasts, they say, brought great misfortune upon the Megarians; for just as their city was taken, they unlocked the lions' cages and removed their chains, so that they might hinder the approaching enemy; but the lions turned upon the unarmed citizens and attacked them as they ran about, so that even to the enemy the sight was pitiable.

9. On Cassius' part, then, they say this was the main reason he plotted against Caesar; but they are mistaken. For from the first Cassius had a natural hostility and rancor toward the whole class of tyrants, as he made clear when he was still a boy and attended the same school with Faustus, son of Sulla. For when Faustus boasted among the boys, and praised his father's sovereign power,[26] Cas-

---

24 See *Caesar* 62, where a similar remark is framed as a statement rather than a question.

25 The episode belongs to the period of Caesar's campaign against Pompey in Greece. Quintus Calenus was an officer serving under Caesar in the conflict.

26 Sulla had been appointed dictator in the previous generation and had used his power to destroy his enemies.

sius got up and pummeled him. When Faustus' guardians and relations wished to take the case to court, Pompey prevented them; and bringing the boys together, questioned them about the incident. And Cassius is then reported to have said, "Come on, Faustus, have the nerve, before this man, to say the words that provoked me, so that I may again smash your mouth." Such was Cassius.

But Brutus was stirred up and incited to the exploit by his friends' arguments and by many letters and proposals from his fellow citizens. For on the statue of his ancestor Brutus, who overthrew the government of the kings,[27] they wrote: "Would that we had you now, Brutus!" and, "Would that Brutus were alive!" And Brutus' praetorial rostrum was covered every day with messages such as these: "Are you asleep, Brutus?" and, "You are not truly Brutus." Caesar's flatterers were responsible for these things; and among other malicious honors that they invented for him they even crowned his statue at night with diadems,[28] hoping to induce the people to hail him as king instead of dictator. But the contrary came to pass, as I have described more fully in my *Life* of Caesar.[29]

10. When Cassius sounded his friends and solicited their participation in a conspiracy against Caesar, they all agreed to act if Brutus would be their leader. For the exploit required neither hands nor daring, but the reputation of a man like him, who by his very presence could consecrate the act,[30] as it were, and justify it; without him they would carry out the deed with less confidence, and afterward be under greater suspicion, since people would say that Brutus

---

27 See chapter 1 above and note 1.

28 The diadem, a simple band tied at the back of the head, had been used in the Greek world for centuries as a mark of royalty. The "flatterers" who devised these "malicious" honors were apparently trying to arouse popular mistrust of Caesar's designs on power.

29 See *Caesar* 61.

30 The Greek word Plutarch uses here compares Brutus to a priest presiding over an animal sacrifice.

would not have refused to act if their cause had been honorable. After considering these things, Cassius met with Brutus for the first time since their quarrel; and when they had agreed to forget their differences and resume friendly relations, asked him whether he planned to attend the session of the Senate on the Calends of March;[31] for Cassius had heard that Caesar's friends would then move to have him made king. When Brutus replied that he would not be there, Cassius asked, "But what if they summon us?" "It would then be my duty," Brutus replied, "not to remain silent, but to defend my country and die for her liberty." Elated, Cassius said, "But what Roman will let you die for her sake? Do you not know yourself, Brutus? Or do you think it was weavers and shopkeepers who left those messages on your rostrum, and not the first and most powerful men of Rome? From other praetors they demand gifts and spectacles and gladiatorial combats, but from you they claim, as an ancestral duty, the abolition of the tyranny; and they are ready to suffer anything on your account if you will show yourself to be what they think and expect you to be." So saying, he threw his arms around Brutus and embraced him, and thus reconciled they went to their friends.

11. Among Pompey's friends there was a certain Gaius Ligarius, who had been denounced as such, but whom Caesar had pardoned. This man, feeling no gratitude for having been forgiven, but rather oppressed by the power that had put his life in jeopardy, was an enemy of Caesar, and one of Brutus' closest friends. Once when he was ill, Brutus paid him a visit and said, "O Ligarius, what a moment for you to be ill!" At this, Ligarius raised himself on his elbow, took Brutus by the hand, and said, "Not at all, Brutus. If you have a plan worthy of yourself, I am well."

12. After this, they secretly tested the inclinations of the notable men whom they trusted, communicating their design to them, and enlisted not only their intimates, but all whom they knew were

---

31 In the Roman calendar, which was still partly lunar at this stage, the Calends corresponded to the new moon and thus the first of the month.

bold, brave, and contemptuous of death. For this reason they concealed the plot from Cicero, though as the foremost among them he was trusted and loved by all. But they were afraid, now that the caution of old age was added to his natural timidity and his tendency to weigh each step to ensure the greatest safety, that he might blunt the edge of their eagerness in an exploit that required speed. Among his other friends, Brutus left out Statilius the Epicurean and Favonius, the admirer of Cato. He did so for this reason: some time earlier, when he sought to test them in a roundabout way, and posed some such question as would be disputed among philosophers, Favonius had replied that civil war was worse than an illegal monarchy, and Statilius said that it was unseemly for a wise and sensible man to run risks and distress himself for the sake of worthless or foolish men. But Labeo, who was present, contradicted them both. Brutus, as if the question were rather difficult and hard to decide, held his peace at the time, but later imparted his design to Labeo, who readily embraced it. Then it was thought advisable to enlist the other Brutus, surnamed Albinus,[32] a man of no great boldness or courage, but considerable for the number of gladiators he was maintaining and the confidence Caesar had placed in him. When Cassius and Labeo discussed the matter with him he gave them no answer; but meeting with Brutus in private, and learning that he was their leader, he readily consented to join them. Among the others, most (and the best) were gained by the reputation of Brutus. And though they neither gave nor received any oaths or sacred pledges of fidelity, they all kept their plan so much to themselves, and were so silent in carrying it out, that though it was foreshadowed by the gods in prophecies and apparitions and sacrifices, no one found it credible.

13. Now Brutus, knowing that the Romans who excelled in courage, birth, and virtue depended upon him, and considering all the danger they would face, tried in public to keep his concern to him-

---

32 Decimus Junius Brutus Albinus, often referred to today as Decimus, was a senior officer in Caesar's army.

self, and his thoughts composed; but at home, and at night, he was not the same man: sometimes, against his will, his uneasiness would rouse him from his sleep; at other times he was more taken up with calculating and pondering his difficulties, so that his wife, who slept beside him, could not fail to notice that he was full of unusual trouble, and was revolving some perplexing and intricate question.

Porcia, as has been mentioned, was a daughter of Cato; and Brutus, who was her cousin, had married her very young, though she was not a virgin, but after the death of her husband, by whom she had a little son named Bibulus. (A little book written by him—*Memoirs of Brutus*—has survived.)[33] Porcia, being an affectionate woman, fond of her husband, and full of sensible pride, did not try to ask about his secrets until she had put herself to the following test. Taking a little knife of the kind that barbers use to cut nails, and sending all her servants out of her room, she made a deep gash in her thigh, so that there was a large flow of blood, and, in a little while, violent pains and a shivering fever caused by the wound. Brutus was dismayed, and she, at the height of her pain, spoke to him thus: "I, Brutus, being the daughter of Cato, was given to you in marriage, not like a concubine, merely to share your bed and board, but to be a partner in your good fortune, and a partner in your troubles. Now in all that concerns our marriage you are blameless; but what proof of my love or gratitude can I show you if I am to share neither your secret suffering nor any worries that need to be confided? I know that a woman's nature is thought to be too weak to keep a secret; but surely, Brutus, a good upbringing and a noble companionship impart strength to one's character; and it is my lot to be both the daughter of Cato and the wife of Brutus. Before this I had believed myself inferior, but now I have found myself to be superior even to pain." So saying, she showed him her wound and explained her test. And he, astonished, raised his hands to heaven, and prayed for the gods' help in his undertaking, that he

33 This treatise, like many of Plutarch's sources, has not survived.

might show himself a husband worthy of Porcia. Then he did all he could to restore his wife.

14. A meeting of the Senate being scheduled, which Caesar was expected to attend, they decided to attempt the deed there; for then they could all appear together without arousing suspicion, and would have in one place all the best and leading men, who, when the deed was done, would immediately lay claim to their common freedom. It was also thought that the place where the Senate would meet was divinely appointed to favor them; for it was one of the stoas near the theater, containing a hall in which there stood a statue of Pompey. The statue had been erected in his honor by the city when he adorned that neighborhood with stoas and the theater. It was to this place, then, that the Senate was summoned for the middle of March (the Romans call the day the Ides of March), as if some deity were leading the man to face Pompey's vengeance.

When the day came,[34] Brutus girded on a dagger, of which no one but his wife was aware, and went out; the others met at Cassius' house and escorted his son, who was about to put on the so-called manly toga, to the Forum.[35] From there they all entered the Stoa of Pompey and waited, expecting Caesar to come directly to the Senate. Anyone there who knew what was about to happen would have particularly admired the impassivity and composure of the men on the brink of a terrible exploit. Many of them, being praetors, and obliged to conduct official business, not only listened calmly to those who applied to them and pleaded against one another before them, as if they were at leisure, but made sure to give their verdicts in each case with great precision and judgment. And when someone refused to accept Brutus' verdict, and appealed loudly and with attestations to Caesar, Brutus looked about to those who were present and said,

---

34 For a slightly different account of the events that follow, see *Caesar* 66–67.

35 A Roman youth came of age at fourteen, when he donned an adult toga and was escorted to the Forum in a festive procession.

"Caesar does not, and will not, prevent me from acting according to the laws."

15. Yet there were many incidents that dismayed them. The first and most important was the delay of Caesar, as the day wore on; he was kept at home by his wife, and forbidden by the soothsayers to go forth, owing to unfavorable omens. Secondly, someone came up to Casca, one of the conspirators, took him by the hand, and said, "You concealed the secret from us, Casca, but Brutus has told me all." When Casca was utterly dumbfounded, the man burst out laughing and said, "How did you get rich so quickly, my dear fellow, that you could run for the aedileship?" So close did Casca come to revealing the secret, merely because of the man's ambiguity. Then Brutus and Cassius were greeted more warmly than usual by a senator, Pompilius Laenas, who whispered to them softly, "I pray with you that you may accomplish what you have in mind, and I advise you not to delay, for the thing is no longer a secret." So saying, he went away, and left them in great suspicion that their exploit had become known.

At that moment, someone from his house ran up to Brutus to report that his wife was dying. For Porcia, who was distraught about what was to come, and unable to bear the weight of her anxiety, could barely keep herself at home, and at every noise or cry, like the women possessed with the Bacchic frenzy,[36] would fasten on everyone who came in from the Forum and ask what Brutus was doing, and kept sending out one messenger after another. But finally, when the time grew long, her bodily strength could hold out no longer, but was exhausted and weakened, and her mind wandered, overcome by her perplexity. She had no time to get to her room, but faintness and a helpless amazement overwhelmed her, sitting as she was among her women, and her complexion changed, and her speech was quite lost. Her maidservants shrieked at the sight, and

36 Maenads or bacchants were female worshippers of Dionysus who danced ecstatically in celebration of the god.

since her neighbors came running to the door, a rumor soon spread that Porcia was dead. But she soon revived, came to herself, and was cared for by her women. When Brutus received this report, he was disturbed, naturally, but not so afflicted by his private concerns as to abandon his public duty.

16. It was now reported that Caesar was coming, conveyed on a litter. For in his dejection at the omens, he had decided not to authorize any important business that day, but to postpone it, giving the excuse that he was ill. As he came out of his litter, Popilius Laenas, who had lately wished Brutus success in his undertaking, came up and conversed with him for a considerable time, Caesar standing and listening attentively. The conspirators (let them be given this name) could not hear what he said, but guessing from their own suspicions that this conference was a disclosure of their plot, they were again discouraged; and glancing at one another, agreed by the looks they exchanged that they should not wait to be arrested, but should kill themselves at once. Cassius and some others had already clasped their daggers under their robes, and were drawing them out, when Brutus observed from Laenas's demeanor that the man was earnestly entreating and not accusing. He said nothing, since there were many among them who were not part of the plot, but with a cheerful look encouraged Cassius and his friends. And soon Laenas kissed Caesar's hand and went away, showing clearly that it was on his own behalf and on some business connected with himself that he had conversed with Caesar.

17. Now when the senators had entered the chamber ahead of Caesar, the rest of the conspirators placed themselves around his chair as if they intended to converse with him, and Cassius is said to have turned his face toward Pompey's statue and to have invoked it, as if it could hear his prayers, while Trebonius drew Antony to the door and kept him talking outside. When Caesar entered, the Senate rose, and as soon as he was seated the conspirators crowded round him, sending forward Tillius Cimber, one of their number, to intercede on behalf of his brother, who was banished; all the others

seconded his pleas, clasping Caesar's hands and kissing his head and his breast. At first Caesar simply rejected their entreaties, but then, when they would not desist, he rose violently to his feet, whereupon Tillius pulled Caesar's robe from his shoulder with both hands, and Casca, who stood behind him, drew his dagger and gave him the first wound, not a deep one, near his shoulder. Snatching the handle of the dagger, Caesar cried aloud in Latin, "Villainous Casca, what are you doing?" Then Casca, calling in Greek to his brother, urged him to come and help. By this time Caesar had received many blows, and was looking about to see if he could force his way through his attackers, when he saw Brutus with his dagger drawn against him. At this he let go of Casca's hand, which he had seized, and covering his head with his robe, gave up his body to their blows. The conspirators pressed so eagerly around the body, and struck it with so many daggers, that they wounded one another; Brutus received a wound in the hand as he joined in the murder, and all of them were covered with blood.

18. Caesar being thus slain, Brutus went to the center of chamber, wishing to speak, and encouraged the senators to stay.[37] But they fled in terror and disorder, and there was much jostling and crowding at the door, though no one pursued or followed them. For the conspirators had firmly resolved not to kill anyone else, but to summon and invite all the rest to their liberty. Now all the others, when they discussed their exploit, had been in favor of killing Antony, an insolent and monarchical man who had made himself powerful by fraternizing with the soldiery. And they urged this especially because at that time the prestige of being a consul and colleague of Caesar had only enhanced the arrogance and ambition of his nature. But Brutus opposed the plan, insisting, first, that they act with justice, and then suggesting that Antony might have a change of heart. For Brutus would not give up hope that Antony, a talented and ambitious man,

---

37 Fewer than two dozen senators had taken part in the plot, out of a body of several hundred.

and a lover of glory, might, with Caesar out of the way, be moved to emulate their noble attempt, and join them in restoring their country's liberty. Thus did Brutus save Antony's life; but Antony, in the general panic, put on plebeian dress and fled.[38]

Brutus and his associates marched up to the Capitol, showing their hands smeared with blood and their naked swords, and proclaiming the citizens' liberty. At first there were cries and shouts; and the running back and forth that followed the assassination increased the turmoil. But since no other bloodshed followed, and no plundering of property, the senators and many of the common people took courage and went up to the men on the Capitol. When the multitude had gathered, Brutus made a speech that was both popular and appropriate to the occasion. When his hearers applauded his words, and cried out to him to come down, Brutus and his friends took courage and descended to the Forum. The rest followed, mingling with one another, while many of the eminent citizens, surrounding and escorting Brutus with conspicuous honor, led him down and placed him on the rostrum. At the sight of him the crowd, though a ragtag lot and ready to raise a rumpus, was struck with awe, and awaited what he would say in orderly silence. And when he came forward, everyone listened with quiet attention. But that all were not happy with what had been done was made clear when Cinna began to speak and to denounce Caesar. For the crowd broke out into a rage, and reviled him so harshly that the conspirators went back to the Capitol. And there Brutus, fearing they would be besieged, sent away the best of those who had accompanied them, thinking that those who had taken no part in their crime should not share their danger.

19. But the next day the Senate met in the Temple of Gaea, and when Antony, Plancus, and Cicero spoke about amnesty and concord, it was decreed not only that there should be immunity for

---

38 See *Antony* 13, where Plutarch claims that the conspirators had been tempted to recruit Antony to their cause before the plot went into motion.

the men, but that the consuls should propose a measure to confer honors upon them. After passing these votes, the Senate adjourned. And when Antony had sent his son as a hostage to the Capitol,[39] Brutus and his associates came down, and greetings and salutations were exchanged among all who had gathered. Antony invited Cassius home and entertained him, Lepidus[40] did the same with Brutus, and the rest were invited and entertained by their acquaintances or friends. The next morning, the senators met again. They began by giving a vote of thanks to Antony for having checked the onset of a civil war; then there were commendations for Brutus and those of his associates who were present; and finally the provinces were distributed among them. They voted that Brutus should have Crete, Cassius Africa, Trebonius Asia, Cimber Bithynia, and the other Brutus Gaul near the Po.[41]

20. After this they took up the subjects of Caesar's will and his burial. Antony thought that the will should be read in public and that the carrying out of the body should not be concealed or lacking in honor, as this might further exasperate the people. Cassius strenuously objected, but Brutus yielded and consented, and thus was thought to have made a second mistake. For by sparing Antony's life he had been faulted for setting up against the conspiracy a dangerous and difficult enemy; and now, allowing the burial to be conducted as Antony saw fit, he fell into a fatal error. For first, when it appeared that in his will Caesar had left seventy-five drachmas to each Roman, and given to the public his gardens beyond the Tiber, where the Temple of Fortune now stands, a wonderful affection and yearning for him seized the citizens. Then, after the

---

39 In situations where pledges of safety were required by two parties holding a parley, one or both would put close relatives into the hands of the other.

40 One of Caesar's highest and most loyal officers, and a former consul.

41 The distribution of provincial governorships was intended both to secure the periphery of the empire and to give the conspirators a pretext to get out of Rome for a time.

body had been brought to the Forum, Antony made the customary eulogy, and when he saw that the multitude were moved by his speech, he changed his tone to one that expressed pity; and taking Caesar's bloody robe, he unfolded it, showing in how many places it had been pierced and Caesar wounded. Now all order was at an end; some shouted to kill the murderers, and others, as was formerly done in the case of Clodius the demagogue,[42] pulled the benches and tables from the shops, heaped them together, and built an enormous pyre; and having placed Caesar's body upon it, amid many temples, asylums, and sacred places, set it on fire. And when the fire blazed up, people flocked to it from all sides, snatched half-burnt brands, and ran through the city to set fire to the houses of Caesar's murderers.

These men, however, having fortified themselves well beforehand, repelled the danger. But there was a poet, Cinna, who had no share in the crime, but was in fact one of Caesar's friends. This man dreamt that he was invited to supper by Caesar, and that he declined to go, but that Caesar entreated and pressed him; and at last, taking him by the hand, led him into a dark and cavernous place, into which he followed, unwilling and dismayed. After this dream he had a fever throughout the night; nevertheless, in the morning, when Caesar's body was carried out for burial, he was ashamed not to be present, and came out into the crowd when it was already enraged. He was spotted, and being taken not for the Cinna who he really was but for the one who had recently inveighed against Caesar in the assembly, he was torn to pieces.

21. Fearing this incident more than anything (with the exception of the change Antony had effected[43]), Brutus and his partisans withdrew from the city. At first they spent time in Antium,

---

42 Publius Clodius Pulcher made various ambitious and unscrupulous bids for power in the late 60s and early 50s BCE. Parts of his bizarre career are recounted by Plutarch in *Cicero* 28–33.

43 That is, by his funeral speech.

thinking they would return to Rome once the people's anger had reached its peak and died down. This they expected would easily happen, since multitudes are apt to be carried away by sudden and unstable impulses. Furthermore, the Senate was well disposed to them: it had let those who tore Cinna to pieces go free, but had sought out and arrested those who had assaulted the houses of the conspirators. And by this time the people were disgruntled, aware that Antony had set up a kind of monarchy. They yearned for Brutus, and expected he would be present in person to conduct the spectacles that he, as praetor, had to produce. But when he became aware that many of the soldiers who had served under Caesar (from whom they had received land and cities) were plotting against him and stealing into the city in small bands, he lacked the courage to come. The people viewed the spectacles in his absence, however; and these were magnificent and sumptuous. For Brutus had purchased a great many wild beasts, and ordered that not one should be sold or left behind, but all should be used; and he himself went down to Naples and met with a great many theatrical artists, and wrote to his friends about Canutius, a successful actor, urging them to persuade the man to participate; for no Greek could fairly be compelled. He also wrote to Cicero, begging him by all means to attend the spectacles.

22. This was how matters stood when another change was made by the arrival of the young Caesar.[44] He was the son of the niece of Caesar, who had adopted him and made him his heir. At the time when Caesar was killed, he was studying in Apollonia[45] and was waiting for him there, since Caesar had decided to march at once against the Parthians. As soon as he learned of Caesar's death, he came to Rome; and as a first step toward ingratiating himself with the people, he assumed the name of Caesar and distributed among

44 Octavian, later known as Augustus. See *Caesar* n. 196.

45 In northern Greece.

the citizens the money that was left them in his will. He surpassed Antony in popularity; and by liberally dispersing money among the soldiers he assembled and gathered together many who had served under Caesar. When Cicero, in his hatred of Antony, sided with Octavian, Brutus castigated him sharply, writing that Cicero did not mind a despot, but only feared a despot who hated him; and that in calling Caesar a good man in his letters and speeches, he was advocating a benevolent slavery. "But our ancestors," he said, "could not abide even mild despots." For his own part, he added, he had not yet firmly resolved whether he should make war or peace; but there was one thing he *had* decided, which was not to be a slave; and he was astonished that Cicero feared the dangers of a civil war, but was not afraid of a shameful and disreputable peace, and that as a recompense for driving Antony from the tyranny he asked for the privilege of establishing Octavian as tyrant in his place.

23. Such was the tone of Brutus' first letters to Cicero. But factions were already forming, one about Octavian, the other about Antony, and the soldiers, as if at a public auction, were siding with him who would pay the most. Despairing altogether at these proceedings, Brutus decided to leave Italy; he traveled by land through Lucania and came to Elea at the coast. Porcia was about to return from there to Rome, and though overcome with grief she tried to conceal it. But a certain painting betrayed her, in spite of her noble forbearance on other occasions. It had a Greek subject: Hector parting from Andromache, who, while taking their little son from him, fixed her eyes on her husband.[46] When Porcia looked at this, the image of her own sorrow made her burst into tears; she went several times a day to see the picture, and wept before it. And when Acilius, one of Brutus' friends, recited the verses where Andromache speaks to Hector,

---

46 A famous scene from Book 6 of Homer's *Iliad*, from which the two quotes below are taken. Hector's departure from Andromache, to return to the battlefield, is in the end his final farewell to his wife.

But Hector, you are to me father and honored mother,
You are brother, and you are my loving husband.

Brutus smiled and replied, "But I cannot answer Porcia with Hector's words,

Ply your loom and distaff, and give orders to your maids,

for though her body is not strong enough to perform the brave deeds of men, yet in spirit she is as valiant in defense of her country as we are." This story is related by Bibulus, Porcia's son.

24. From there Brutus put to sea and sailed to Athens. The people welcomed him warmly, acclaiming and honoring him in public decrees. He lived there with a guest-friend,[47] attended the lectures of Theomnestus the Academic and Cratippus the Peripatetic,[48] shared their philosophical pursuits, and seemed to be wholly at leisure for study. But without arousing any suspicion, he was preparing for war. For he sent Herostratus to Macedonia, hoping to win over the commanders of the armies there, and he himself secured and enlisted the services of the young Romans who were studying in Athens. Among these was Cicero's son, whom he praises highly, and says that whether waking or sleeping he marveled at how noble the young man was and how great a hater of tyranny.

Eventually he began to act openly, and on being informed that Roman ships full of money were approaching from Asia, and that an able and respected man was in command of them, he went to meet him at Carystus. Finding him there and persuading him to hand

---

47 "Guest-friend" translates the Greek word *xenos*, a person living abroad who, owing to family connections or reciprocal bonds of obligation, can be counted on to give lodging and protection to a traveler.

48 Two prominent philosophers of the day, the first a Platonist, the second an Aristotelian. Brutus primarily followed the Stoic school, but like most Romans he sampled freely from all the Greek traditions.

over his vessels, he held an especially splendid entertainment; for it happened to be Brutus' birthday. Accordingly, when they came to drink, and raised their cups to pledge victory to Brutus and freedom for the Romans, Brutus, to animate them still more, called for a larger drinking bowl; and on receiving it, without any apparent reason, uttered this verse:

But it was baneful fate and Leto's son that slew me.[49]

Some historians add that when he was going out to fight his final battle at Philippi, the watchword he gave to his soldiers was "Apollo." They therefore conclude that the reciting of that verse presaged his downfall.

25. After this, Antistius[50] gave him fifty myriads[51] of the money he was conveying to Italy; and all of Pompey's soldiers who were wandering about Thessaly gladly streamed together to join him. He also took five hundred of the horsemen that Cinna was carrying to Dolobella in Asia. He then sailed to Demetrias, where he seized a large quantity of arms that had been manufactured at the late Caesar's command for the Parthian War and were now being sent to Antony. After Hortensius the praetor had handed Macedonia over to him, and all the neighboring kings and potentates were uniting and coming over to him, news was brought that Gaius, Antony's brother, having crossed over from Italy, was marching directly to join the forces that Vatinius commanded in Epidamnus and Apollonia. Wishing to anticipate him and to seize those forces,

---

49 *Iliad* 16.849, a passage in which Patroclus, dying at the hands of Hector, attributes his downfall to divine forces. "Leto's son" is Apollo.

50 Gaius Antistius Vetus was at this time in charge of Syria, and did come over to Brutus' side from that of Caesar, but Plutarch seems to have written his name in error; other sources indicate that Apuleius, quaestor of the province of Asia, gave the aid discussed here.

51 A myriad consisted of 10,000 drachmas.

Brutus suddenly set out with those he had with him, advanced over rugged terrain through snowstorms, and got far ahead of the troops conveying his provisions. Nearing Epidamnus, he was afflicted with bulimia[52] as a result of fatigue and the cold. This disorder mainly attacks men and beasts laboring through snow, whether because our natural heat, being trapped within when the body is seized with cold, consumes all its nourishment, or because a sharp and subtle vapor, coming from the melting snow, cuts the body and destroys the heat as it issues through the pores. For the body's sweat seems to be produced by its heat, which is quenched by the cold that meets it at the body's surface. But this I have discussed at greater length elsewhere.[53]

26. Brutus was growing faint, and since no one in the army had anything to eat, his servants were forced to appeal to their enemies. Going to the gates of the city, they begged bread from the guards on duty, who, as soon as they heard of Brutus' condition, came to him themselves, bringing food and drink; in return for this, Brutus, when he took the city, showed great kindness, not to them alone but to all the citizens, for their sake.

Meanwhile Gaius Antonius,[54] approaching Apollonia, summoned the soldiers who were nearby. But when they went to Brutus, and Gaius perceived that the people of Apollonia favored Brutus' cause, he left the city and went to Buthrotum. First he lost three cohorts of his men, who on their march were cut to pieces by Brutus; then, when he tried to wrest control of certain positions near Byllis that the enemy had seized earlier, he joined battle and

---

52 Literally, "the famine of an ox," a kind of ravening hunger. The modern medical term, though taken from the Greek word, has a somewhat different meaning.

53 A rare cross-reference to one of the *Moralia*. In *Table Talk* (*Symposiaca*), a miscellany of learned discussions, the eighth chapter concerns the causes of "bulimia," and Brutus' bout of it here is taken up as an example.

54 Mark Antony's brother, mentioned in the preceding chapter.

was defeated by the young Cicero.[55] For it was to him that Brutus gave the command, and through him achieved much success. Yet when he found Gaius in a marshy place, at a distance from the main body of his forces, Brutus would not let his own soldiers attack, but rode about ordering his men to spare the enemy, thinking they would soon be on his side. And that is what happened. For they surrendered themselves and their general, so that now Brutus had a considerable force. For a long time he held Gaius in honor, and did not deprive him of the ensigns of his office, though it is said that Cicero and many others wrote to him from Rome, urging him to put Gaius to death. But when the man began to converse in private with his officers, and tried to incite a mutiny, Brutus put him aboard a ship and kept him under guard. Meanwhile, the soldiers who had been traduced by Gaius retreated to Apollonia and invited Brutus to come to them there; Brutus replied that this was not the custom of the Romans, but that they should come themselves to their leader and try to allay his anger at their offenses. They came, accordingly, and when they begged his forgiveness he pardoned them.

27. But as he was about to cross over to Asia,[56] word reached him of the change that had taken place in Rome. For the young Caesar had been bolstered by the Senate in his opposition to Antony, and having expelled his rival from Italy, had himself become formidable, soliciting a consulship contrary to law, and maintaining large armies, of which the city had no need. But when he saw that even the Senate disliked this, and were looking abroad to Brutus and voting to confirm him in the command of his province, he grew alarmed. He sent word to Antony and invited him to an alliance; and then, posting his forces around the city, he gained the consulship, though he was a mere boy, being twenty years old, as he himself writes

---

55 Son of the orator, mentioned in chapter 24.

56 As often in this volume, "Asia" refers to the Roman province of that name, roughly the western portion of the Anatolian peninsula.

in his memoirs.[57] He immediately indicted Brutus and his associates for murder, charging that they had killed their foremost magistrate without a trial; and appointed Lucius Cornificius to prosecute Brutus, and Marcus Agrippa to prosecute Cassius. Accordingly, as none of the defendants appeared, the jurors were forced to condemn them. It is said that when the herald on the rostrum, as the custom was, summoned Brutus to appear, the people groaned audibly, and the nobles hung their heads in silence; and that Publius Silicius was seen to burst into tears, and for that reason was soon added to the list of the proscribed. After this, the three men, Octavian, Antony, and Lepidus,[58] were reconciled with one another, distributed the provinces among themselves, and sentenced two hundred men to death by proscription.[59] It was among these that Cicero perished.[60]

28. The news being brought to him in Macedonia, Brutus felt compelled to write to Hortensius, ordering him to kill Gaius Antonius, as he would thereby avenge his friend Cicero and his kinsman Brutus. It was for this reason, later on, that Antony, having captured Hortensius at Philippi, slew him at his brother's tomb. But Brutus says he was more ashamed at the cause of Cicero's death than grieved at the misfortune itself, and that he was forced to blame his friends at Rome; for they were more responsible for their servitude than their

---

57 The so-called *Res Gestae Divi Augusti*, a sketch autobiography first inscribed on Augustus' mausoleum in Rome and later copied and distributed elsewhere. The text, largely extant, opens with a list of the offices and honors Augustus (Octavian) attained.

58 The so-called Second Triumvirate. Pompey, Caesar, and Crassus had formed a similar alliance in the previous generation.

59 The procedure known as proscription, begun by Sulla in the 80s BCE, allowed the triumvirs to publicly list names of their enemies; the property of those listed was confiscated and a reward was offered to anyone who killed them.

60 The proscription of Cicero, demanded by Antony over Octavian's opposition, is condemned by Plutarch at *Cicero* 46.

tyrants were, and tolerated being present and seeing things that it should have been intolerable for them even to hear.

After crossing to Asia with his army, which was already a distinguished one, he fitted out a fleet in Bithynia and at Cyzicus, and he himself, advancing by land, restored order in the cities and gave audiences to the chieftains of the region. He also sent orders to Cassius in Syria, recalling him from his expedition to Egypt; for it was not to gain an empire for themselves, but to liberate their country, that they were wandering about assembling a force with which to depose the tyrants; they must therefore remember and persevere in their original purpose and not get too far from Italy, but should hasten there and aid their fellow citizens.

Cassius obeyed, and Brutus went to meet him as he was returning. They met at Smyrna, which was the first time they had seen one another since they had parted at Piraeus,[61] one for Syria, and the other for Macedonia. They were both overjoyed, and derived great confidence from the forces each of them now possessed. For they had set out from Italy like the most contemptible of exiles, without money or arms, without a ship or a single soldier or a city; but before very long they had met, having acquired a fleet, a land army, horses, and money, which made them fit to contend for the supremacy at Rome.

29. Cassius wished to give and to receive equal honor, but Brutus anticipated him, coming to *him* for the most part, since he was the older man and less able to bear hardships. Cassius was regarded as an able soldier but harsh in his anger, and inclined to command largely by fear, though among his intimates he was prone to laughter and fond of jesting. But it is said that Brutus, for his virtue, was loved by the people, adored by his friends, admired by the best men, and not hated even by his enemies. For he was exceptionally gentle and magnanimous, free from all anger, greed, and self-indulgence, and kept

---

61 Piraeus was the harbor town serving Athens; the parting here referred to must have occurred when Brutus left Athens at chapter 25.

his purpose steady and inflexible on behalf of what was honorable and just. And the greatest source of the goodwill and renown that he attained was the faith in his character. For it was never expected that Pompey the Great, if he overcame Caesar, could be relied upon to submit his power to the laws; instead it was assumed that he would retain control of the state, placating the people by using the name of consulship or dictatorship,[62] or some milder form of government. And they supposed that Cassius, a vehement and passionate man, and often driven by love of gain beyond the bounds of justice, was enduring all the dangers of wars and wanderings chiefly to establish some dominion for himself, and not liberty for his fellow citizens. For the men of an even earlier time, whether Cinnas, Mariuses, or Carbos,[63] made their country the booty or prize of their contests, and all but admitted that they fought to gain a tyranny. But we are told that even the enemies of Brutus did not accuse him of such inconstancy; in fact, many heard Antony declare that in his opinion Brutus was the only man who conspired against Caesar out of a sense of the glory and the apparent nobility of the action,[64] whereas all the others banded together against the man because they hated and envied him. Hence Brutus relied not so much upon his forces as upon his own virtue, as is clear from his letters. As he was nearing the moment of danger, he wrote to Atticus that his own affairs were

---

62 "Dictatorship" does not sound like a conciliatory term to modern ears, but under the Roman constitution, dictator was a legitimate and temporary office (see Appendix).

63 The plurals Plutarch uses here indicates he is referring to families rather than individuals, and indeed each of the families mentioned produced several leading statesmen in the late second and early first centuries BCE. That was the era that saw the rise of Sulla, a cruel military strongman, and members of these three families wrangled with him over control of the state. The most famous member of the Marius clan, Gaius Marius (died 86 BCE), is the subject of a Plutarchan Life.

64 The source of Shakespeare's portrayal of Brutus in *Julius Caesar* as "the noblest Roman of them all."

in the most fortunate state he could desire; for he would either prevail and liberate the people of Rome, or die and be freed from slavery; and that while everything else in their lot was safe and secure, one thing only was in doubt, namely whether they would live as free men or die. He adds that Mark Antony was paying a suitable penalty for his folly: for when he could have been numbered with Brutus and Cassius and Cato, he had given himself to Octavian as an appendage; and that if he should not now be defeated with him, he would soon be fighting against him. And in this Brutus seems to have been an excellent prophet.[65]

30. Now when they were at Smyrna, Brutus asked for a share of all the great treasure that Cassius had amassed; for he had spent all his own in fitting out a fleet large enough to keep the entire Mediterranean in their power. Cassius' friends tried to dissuade him from this, saying it was not right that the money he was safeguarding with such frugality, and had acquired at the cost of so much envy, should be taken by Brutus so that he might make himself popular and gratify his soldiers; nevertheless, Cassius gave him a third of all that he had. Then they parted again for their respective undertakings. Cassius, having taken Rhodes, showed no clemency, though on entering the city, when some hailed him as lord and king, he had replied, "Neither lord nor king, but the punisher and slayer of your lord and king." Brutus, on his part, asked the Lycians for money and an army.[66] But Naucrates, their popular leader, persuaded the cities to rebel, and the Lycians occupied a number of hills in order to hinder Brutus' passage. Brutus at first sent horsemen against them as they were taking their breakfast, and killed six hundred of them; then, capturing their towns and villages, he released all his prisoners without ransom, hoping to win over the entire nation by goodwill.

---

65 For the breakdown of the relations between Octavian and Antony, see *Antony* 30, 33, and 35.

66 On the incidents in this and the next two chapters, see chapter 2 and note 10.

But the Lycians were stubborn; they nursed their anger at what they had suffered, despising his clemency and generosity, until he drove the most warlike of them into Xanthus and besieged them there. They tried to escape by swimming underwater through the river that flows past the city, but were caught in nets that were let down deep into the channel; these had bells at the top, which gave immediate notice when anyone was entangled in them. After this, the Xanthians sallied out in the night and set fire to some siege engines; but these men were detected by the Romans and driven back to the walls. Then a strong wind carried the flames to the battlements, and some of the adjoining houses caught fire. Brutus, fearing for the city, ordered his men to lend aid and extinguish the fire.

31. But the Lycians were suddenly possessed by a strange, unspeakable, and desperate impulse, which one could best liken to a passion for death. For both free men and slaves of all ages, with their women and children, shot missiles from the walls at the enemy who were trying to aid them against the fire; they themselves, gathering reeds and wood and whatever combustible material they could find, were spreading the fire over the whole city,[67] stoking it with every sort of fuel and in every way exciting its fury. The flames, having dispersed and encircled the whole city, blazed out brilliantly, and Brutus, distraught at what was happening, rode round the walls, eager to lend aid, and with his outstretched hands begged the Xanthians to spare and save their city. But no one paid him any heed; instead they tried in every way to destroy themselves, not only the men and women, but even the little children with shouts and cries either leapt into the fire, or threw themselves from the walls, or fell under their fathers' swords, baring their throats and begging to be struck. After the city was destroyed, a woman was seen who had hanged herself, with her dead child fastened to her neck, and the torch in her hand with which she set fire to her own house. The sight was so tragic that Brutus could not bear to see it, but wept when he

67 Not the Lycians' own city but Xanthus, their place of refuge.

heard of it and proclaimed a reward for any soldier who could save a Lycian. But it is said that only one hundred fifty did not escape having their lives saved. Thus the Xanthians, after a long interval, as if the time appointed for their destruction had come, repeated by their desperate act the calamity of their ancestors, who, in the very same way, during the Persian Wars, burned down their city and destroyed themselves.[68]

32. When Brutus saw that the city of Patara was holding out against him, he hesitated to attack it and was at a loss, afraid it would be seized by the same madness; but as he held some of its women captive, he released them without ransom. They were the wives and daughters of eminent men; and when they described Brutus as a man of exemplary sense and justice, they persuaded their fellow citizens to yield and surrender the city. Thereafter, all the rest of the Lycians came and entrusted themselves to him, and found that his kindness and generosity surpassed their expectations. For at the very time that Cassius had forced the Romans to bring him all the gold and silver each of them possessed privately (from which he amassed eight hundred talents), and fined the city five hundred talents more, Brutus exacted only one hundred fifty talents from the Lycians. Having done them no other harm, he departed with his army for Ionia.

33. In awarding honors and imposing punishments on those who deserved them, he did much that was memorable. Here I will relate the one act that gratified him and the foremost Romans above all the rest. When Pompey, after being stripped of his great power by Caesar, had fled to Egypt and come ashore at Pelusium, the guardians of the young king held a council with their friends, and their views differed, some thinking they should receive Pompey, others that they should drive him from Egypt. But Theodotus of Chios, who attended the king as a paid teacher of rhetoric, and at the time was

---

68 As described by Herodotus (1.176), the inhabitants of Xanthus committed a similar self-immolation when attacked by Harpagus, a general of Cyrus the Great of Persia, in the mid-sixth century BCE.

thought worthy, in the absence of better men, to be admitted to the council, declared that both sides were mistaken—those who would receive Pompey, and those who thought he should be rejected; for under the circumstances the one expedient course was to receive him and put him to death. And he added, as he ended his argument, "A corpse does not bite." The council adopted his suggestion, and Pompey the Great lay dead, an example of the incredible and unexpected in human history. And this was the work of Theodotus and his clever rhetoric, as the sophist himself used to declare when boasting.[69] But shortly thereafter, when Caesar came, the other murderers paid the penalty, perishing miserably; as for Theodotus, having borrowed from fortune enough time for an inglorious, destitute, and wandering life, he did not escape the notice of Brutus as he passed through Asia, but was brought to him and punished, and gained more renown for his death than for his life.

34. Now Brutus summoned Cassius to Sardis, and went with his friends to meet him as he approached; and the whole army in array hailed both of them as *imperator.* But as usually happens in great undertakings that involve many friends and commanders, mutual accusations and charges had arisen, and thus, straight from their march, before doing anything else, they withdrew to a room by themselves; and when the doors were shut and the two men found themselves alone, they began first to assign blame, and then to rebuke and denounce each other. After this they were transported into passionate words and tears. Their friends, astonished at the harshness and vehemence of their anger, feared that some trouble might follow; but they had been forbidden to approach. Marcus Favonius, however, who had been an admirer of Cato, pursuing philosophy not so much by his reasoning as by his wild, impulsive manner, tried to go in to them, but was hindered by their attendants. It was hard work, however, to stop Favonius when he was rushing to act; for he was fierce and impetuous in all his behav-

---

69 See *Pompey* 77.

ior. That he was a Roman senator he regarded as the least of his attainments, and by the Cynic freedom with which he expressed himself[70] he often dispelled the rudeness and untimeliness of his remarks for those who took them in a humorous light. On this occasion he forced his way through the men guarding the door, and entered the room, declaiming in an affected voice the verses that Homer makes Nestor use:

But listen to me; you are both younger than I am;[71]

and those that follow. At this Cassius burst out laughing; but Brutus threw him out, calling him a *haplocyon*[72] and a counterfeit Cynic. Yet for the present they let this incident put an end to their quarrel, and parted at once. Cassius hosted a supper that night, and Brutus invited his friends to it. And when they had already sat down, Favonius, having bathed, came in among them. Brutus protested that Favonius was not invited, and told his servants to conduct him to the uppermost couch. But Favonius, violently forcing his way past them, lay down on the middle one;[73] and the revel passed in playful talk, lacking neither wit nor philosophy.

35. But the next day, on the accusation of the inhabitants of Sardis, Brutus disgraced and condemned Lucius Pella, a Roman who had

---

70 The Cynic philosophic school prided itself on unfettered freedom of speech, including the freedom to "bark" or carp at the objects of its scorn.

71 *Iliad* 1.259, where Nestor, the eldest member of the Greek high command, addresses Achilles and Agamemnon.

72 This rare Greek word, literally "single-dog," seems to be a jibe at Cassius' inauthenticity. Those who followed the Cynic (or "doglike") lifestyle normally doubled up their cloaks and wore no underlayer, thus subjecting themselves to greater discomfort. A Cynic with only a single fold in his cloak might be concealing a warm, soft garment beneath.

73 Seating arrangements at Roman dinners were formally arranged according to the relative importance of the guests.

served as praetor and been trusted by him, for having embezzled public funds; and this action vexed Cassius beyond measure. For only a few days earlier, when two of his own friends had been convicted of the same crime, he had admonished them privately, but in public acquitted them, and continued to employ them. Hence he reproached Brutus for being too strictly observant of law and justice at a time that required expediency and kindness. But Brutus urged him to remember the Ides of March, the day when they killed Caesar, not because the man himself plundered or pillaged mankind, but because he enabled others to do so; since, if there had been any good excuse for justice to be neglected, it would have been better to endure the wrongdoing of Caesar's friends than to sanction that of their own. "For in the former case," he said, "we would have had the reputation of cowardice only; whereas now, in addition to all our other dangers and hardship, we are liable to be deemed unjust." Such was the policy of Brutus.

36. When they were about to cross from Asia, it is said that a great sign was seen by Brutus. For he was naturally wakeful, and by practice and self-control had reduced his hours of sleep to very few, never napping in the daytime, and in the night only when it was not possible to transact business, and when, everyone else having retired to rest, he had no one to converse with. But at this time, when the war had begun and he had the whole of it to manage, and was pondering the future, he would doze in the evening after eating, and then spend the rest of the night settling his most urgent business. If he could finish early, he would read a book until the third watch, at which hour the centurions and tribunes used to visit him. One night, accordingly, when he was about to take the army across from Asia, he was up very late, his tent dimly lit, and all the rest of the camp was silent. As he was reflecting and reasoning about something, he had the impression that someone was coming in. Glancing toward the entrance, he saw a strange and terrible apparition of an unnatural and fearsome body standing silently beside him. Venturing to question it, he said, "What are

you, of men or gods, and on what business have you come to me?" The figure answered, "I am your evil destiny, Brutus; you will see me at Philippi." And Brutus, not at all disturbed, replied, "I will see you."[74]

37. As soon as the apparition vanished, Brutus summoned his servants; and when they declared that they had neither heard any voice nor seen any vision, he kept watch for the rest of the night. In the morning he went to Cassius and told him what he had seen. Cassius, who adhered to the views of Epicurus, and had been in the habit of debating with Brutus about such matters, said,[75] "It is our view, Brutus, that not everything we feel or see is real, but that sense perception is a slippery and deceitful thing, and the mind even quicker to set it in motion and transform the perceived thing, which has no real existence, into every sort of shape. For the sense impression is like wax; and the soul of man, which has within it both what imprints and what is imprinted on, can easily, by its own action, reshape and embellish it. This is evident from the changes that occur in our dreams, where the imagination, set in motion by some slight matter, transforms it into all sorts of different emotions and appearances. It is its nature to be in perpetual motion, and its motion is fantasy or thought. And in your case, the body, being exhausted by hardship, naturally works upon the mind and leads it astray. As for supernatural beings, it is neither credible that they exist, nor, if they do, that they have human shape or voice or power that reaches us. For my part, I could wish that there *were* such beings, so that we might rely not only on our arms, and horses, and ships, which are so numerous, but might also gain confidence from the assistance

74 The same anecdote is given at *Caesar* 69.

75 In this speech Plutarch seizes the opportunity to expound some ideas of the Epicureans, a school with which he was very much out of sympathy. Plutarch undermines these ideas by putting them in the mouth of Cassius, a figure who comes off poorly in the *Lives*, and by having them so clearly discredited by subsequent events.

of gods, since we are conducting the most sacred and honorable of exploits." With such arguments Cassius sought to reassure Brutus.

As the soldiers were embarking, two eagles perched on the first two ensigns and were carried along with them, accompanying the soldiers and being fed by them as far as Philippi. And there, only one day before the battle, they flew away.

38. Most of the peoples Brutus encountered on the march had already been subjugated. And now, if any city or potentate had been omitted, Brutus' soldiers brought them all over and advanced as far as the coast opposite Thasos. There Norbanus[76] and his forces had encamped at the so-called Narrows, and near Symbolum; but Brutus' army surrounded him and forced him to decamp and abandon his positions. They nearly captured his army, Octavian being delayed by illness; but Antony came to his rescue with such astounding speed that Brutus and those with him could hardly believe it. Octavian arrived ten days later, and encamped opposite Brutus, and Antony opposite Cassius.

The plain between the armies is called by the Romans the Campi Philippi. Never had such large Roman forces assembled to engage each other. In numbers the army of Brutus was far inferior to that of Octavian, but in the splendor of its arms it presented a marvelous appearance. For most of their armor was adorned with gold and silver, which Brutus had lavishly bestowed upon them, though in other things he had accustomed his officers to adopt a temperate and frugal way of life. But he thought that the riches they carried in their hands and on their bodies bolstered the pride of the more ambitious, and made the lovers of gain more warlike, since they clung to their armor as so much valuable property.

39. Octavian made a lustration[77] of his army within the camp, and distributed a little corn and five drachmas to each man for a sacrifice.

---

76 Gaius Norbanus Flaccus, a general supporting Octavian.

77 A ritual purification to cleanse the army in the eyes of the gods.

But Brutus, disdaining the enemy's poverty or parsimony, first made a lustration of the army in the open field, as the custom is, and then distributed a great number of beasts for sacrifice among the cohorts, and fifty drachmas to each soldier, so that in the goodwill and zeal of his soldiers Brutus had the advantage. But during the lustration it was thought that Cassius had an unlucky omen; for the lictor brought him his crown turned upside down. And it is said that some time before, in a solemn procession, a golden Victory[78] belonging to Cassius, which was being carried along, fell down when its bearer slipped. Furthermore, many birds of prey appeared daily about the camp, and swarms of bees were seen at a place within the trenches; this place the soothsayers shut off from the rest of the camp, to exorcise the superstitious fears that gradually began to distance even Cassius himself from his Epicurean doctrines, and had wholly subdued his soldiers.

Hence Cassius was not eager to have the outcome determined by battle at present, but thought they should protract the war, since they were well supplied with money, though inferior in the number of their arms and men. Brutus, on the contrary, had been eager even before this to have the outcome determined by the quickest of dangers, so that he might either restore freedom to his country, or release from their misery all who were harassed with the expenses and the service and exactions of the war. And now, seeing that his horsemen were doing well and prevailing in their preliminary skirmishes, he was even more elated. Furthermore, some desertions to the enemy, and accusations and suspicions about others to come, caused many of Cassius' friends in the council to come over to Brutus' way of thinking. But one of Brutus' friends, Atillius, opposed his resolution, urging that they should delay until the winter ended. And when Brutus asked him how he thought he would be better off a year later, Atillius replied, "If nothing else, I will have lived longer." Cassius disliked this answer, and the others

78 That is, a statue of the goddess Nike, signifying Victory.

were disgusted with Atillius for it. So it was soon decided to give battle on the next day.

40. Brutus was full of hope at supper, and after some discussion with his friends on philosophical topics, retired to rest. But Cassius, according to Messala,[79] dined privately with a few of his closest friends, and appeared thoughtful and silent, though he was not so as a rule. When supper was over, he took Messala warmly by the hand, and speaking to him in Greek, as was his custom when showing affection, said, "I call you to witness, Messala, that I suffer the same fate as Pompey the Great, compelled to risk the fate of my country on the outcome of a single battle. But let us be of good courage, and look to Fortune, which it would be wrong to distrust, even if our decisions are faulty." With these last words to him, says Messala, Cassius embraced him; Messala had already been invited to dine with him on the following night, it being Brutus' birthday.

In the morning, the scarlet cloak, the signal of battle, was set out in the camps of Brutus and Cassius, and they themselves met in the space between their armies. There Cassius said, "May we be victorious, Brutus, and all the rest of our time live together in prosperity; but since the greatest of human concerns are the most uncertain, and since we will not easily see each other again if the battle goes against us, what is your resolution about flight and death?" And Brutus replied, "When I was young, Cassius, and without experience of affairs, I was led, I know not how, to make a grandiose remark in philosophy. I blamed Cato for killing himself,[80] thinking it was impious and unmanly to evade the divine will, and not accept fearlessly whatever happens, but run away from it. But now in my present fortunes I feel differently; and if god does not decide the present

---

79 Marcus Valerius Messala Corvinus, a participant in the civil wars who later wrote an account of them (now lost).

80 Cato the Younger had committed a grisly self-disemboweling in North Africa some years before this, after losing a decisive battle to Julius Caesar (see *Cato* 70).

contest in our favor, I do not ask to put further hopes or preparations to the test, but will die praising my fortune. On the Ides of March, I gave up my life to my country, and have lived since then a second life for her sake, with liberty and honor." At these words Cassius smiled, embraced Brutus, and said, "With such thoughts let us go against the enemy. For either we will be victorious, or we will not fear the victors."

After this they conferred among their friends about the order of battle. And Brutus asked Cassius for permission to lead the right wing[81] himself, though it was thought more fitting for Cassius, given his experience and years, to hold that post. But Cassius granted him this favor, and ordered Messala with the most warlike of the legions to place himself in the same wing. Brutus immediately led out his horsemen, splendidly equipped, and as promptly brought up and arrayed his infantry.

41. Antony's soldiers, meanwhile, were running trenches across the plain from the marshes where they were encamped, and cutting off Cassius' communications with the sea. The army of Octavian was lying in wait, though he was not present himself, owing to illness; and his forces, not expecting that the enemy would give battle, assumed they would merely sally out to the works and harass the diggers with light missiles and loud cries. Accordingly, paying no attention to the troops drawn up opposite them, they were surprised when they heard the loud and confused shouting that reached them from the trenches. At that point, while the tablets conveying the password were on their way to Brutus' commanders, and while Brutus himself was riding along past the legions and encouraging the soldiers, only a few managed to hear the password, and most of them, not waiting to receive it, charged at the enemy with one impulse and war cry. This disorder made their line uneven, and

---

81 The right wing of an infantry line could easily be outflanked, and holding it steady required skill and nerve; hence it was deemed the place of highest honor.

the legions got separated from one another. Then Messala's legion first, and afterward those stationed with it, went beyond Octavian's left wing. Coming into brief contact with its outermost ranks, and inflicting only a few casualties, they outflanked the wing and dashed into the enemy camp. Octavian himself, as he writes in his memoirs,[82] had just been conveyed away, since one of his friends, Marcus Artorius, had seen a vision in his sleep that urged Octavian to get up and leave the camp; and he was thought to have been slain. For the litter, which was left empty, had been pierced by the spears and javelins of the enemy. There was a slaughter of those who were captured in the camp; and two thousand Spartans who had just arrived as auxiliaries were also cut to pieces.

42. The legions that had not gone to outflank Octavian's forces, but had engaged the ranks opposite them, easily overthrew them in their disorder, and massacred three legions in close combat; and being carried along with the momentum of victory, pursuing those who fled, they burst into their camp, keeping Brutus with them. But the conquered men now took advantage of what the conquerors did not consider. For they fell upon the section of the enemy line that had been left exposed and disrupted where the right wing had separated from them and rushed off in the pursuit; Brutus' center, however, would not give way, but resisted obstinately. Yet they routed his right wing, which was in disarray and unaware of what had happened, and pursued the men into their camp; this they sacked, neither of their commanders being present. For Antony, they say, having turned away at the start of the attack, retreated into the marsh, and Caesar was nowhere to be found after he had abandoned his camp; in fact some of the soldiers showed Brutus their bloody swords, and declared they had slain him, describing his appearance and his age. But by this time Brutus' center had driven its opponents back with a great slaughter, and Brutus was everywhere plainly victorious, as Cassius was plainly defeated. And this one mistake destroyed their

82 See note 57.

cause, namely that Brutus, thinking that Cassius too was victorious, did not go to his aid, while Cassius, thinking Brutus was dead, did not await his aid. For Messala regards it as a proof of Brutus' victory that he captured three eagles[83] and many ensigns from the enemy, whereas they took nothing.

As Brutus was returning after plundering Caesar's camp, he was surprised that he could neither see Cassius' tent standing tall as usual, and appearing above the rest, nor other things in their usual place. For most of the tents had been pulled down and plundered when the enemy burst in. But some of his companions whose sight was keener told him they could see many helmets gleaming, and many silver shields moving about in Cassius' camp, though they did not think either their number or armor was that of the men they had left to guard the camp; yet there were not so many corpses visible as it was probable there would have been had so many legions been defeated. This was what first made Brutus suspect Cassius' misfortune; and leaving a guard in the enemy's camp, he called back those who were in pursuit and rallied them for the purpose of lending aid to Cassius.

43. Cassius' fortune had been as follows. He had been displeased to see that the first sally of Brutus' troops had been made without a password or command; nor was he happy, after their victory, to see them rushing straight for plunder and spoils, and neglecting to surround the enemy. Furthermore, delaying and hesitating rather than acting with zeal and purpose, he found himself enveloped by the right wing of the enemy. His horsemen immediately broke away in a flight toward the sea, and when he saw his infantry also giving way he did all in his power to hinder their flight and bring them back. Snatching an ensign from a standard-bearer who fled, he planted it at his feet, though his own bodyguards were no longer inclined to stay together. Then he was forced to retreat with a small party to a hill that overlooked the plain. He himself, being weak-sighted,

83 The Roman "eagles" were military standards topped by eagle figurines, carried before each legion into battle.

could see little or nothing of the sacking of his camp; but the horsemen about him saw a large troop of cavalry approaching, whom Brutus had sent. Cassius supposed they were enemies in pursuit of him. Nevertheless, he sent Titinius, one of his party, to see who they were. When the horsemen saw him coming toward them, and knew him to be a faithful friend of Cassius, his friends shouted for joy, leapt from their horses, shook his hand and embraced him, while the rest rode round him singing and shouting, and thus, in their unbounded joy, did the greatest possible harm. For Cassius thought that Titinius had actually been taken by the enemy,[84] and cried out, "Too fond of life, I have allowed a friend to be seized by the enemy before my very eyes."

He then retired into an empty tent, dragging with him one of his freedmen, Pindarus, whom he had kept ready for such an occasion ever since the misfortune that befell Crassus.[85] From the Parthians he had come away safe; but now, pulling his cloak over his face, and baring his neck, he held it forth to be struck. For his head was found severed from his body. No one ever saw Pindarus again, from which some have suspected that he killed his master without his command. Soon afterward, the horsemen were clearly seen, and Titinius, whom they had crowned with garlands, came up to meet Cassius. But when he understood, by the cries and wailing of his distressed and weeping friends, his general's fate and his own error, he drew his sword, reproached himself harshly for his tardiness, and slew himself.

44. When Brutus learned of the defeat of Cassius he rode toward him, but heard of his death only when he had already drawn near his camp. He stood weeping over the body, and called Cassius "the last of the Romans," intimating that another man of so great a spirit would never again arise in the city. Then he laid out the body and

---

84 That is, because of his nearsightedness.

85 Crassus died among the Parthians in a melee caused by a misunderstanding; see *Crassus* 31.

sent it to Thasos, lest the funeral rites sow disorder in the camp. He himself gathered Cassius' soldiers together and comforted them; and seeing that they were destitute of all necessities, he promised every man two thousand drachmas to compensate him for what he had lost. The men took courage at these words and were amazed at the size of the gift; and they escorted him with shouts as he departed, exalting him as the only one of the four generals who had not been defeated in battle. And the action bore witness that he had been right to believe he would prevail in the battle; for with a few legions he had routed all who resisted him; and if he had used them all in the fighting, and most of them had not passed beyond the enemy in pursuit of the plunder, it seems likely he would have left no part of them undefeated.

45. On his side eight thousand men fell, including the servants of the army, whom Brutus called Briges;[86] on the other side, Messala says he thinks more than twice that number were slain. They were therefore more disheartened than Brutus, until Demetrius, a servant of Cassius, came to Antony in the evening, bringing him the robes and sword he had immediately taken from the dead body. They were so encouraged by the sight that at daybreak they led their forces out arrayed for battle. But both of Brutus' camps were wavering precariously. For his own was full of prisoners and required a strict guard; and that of Cassius was unhappy with the change of general,[87] besides which, those who were conquered bore some hatred and envy toward those who had been conquerors. He therefore decided to array his army, but to refrain from fighting. As for the multitude of slaves that had been captured, and who were fraternizing suspiciously among his soldiers, he ordered them to be put to death; but some of the free men he released, declaring that they had been more captured by his enemies than by him; for with *them* they were captives and slaves,

---

86 This was not in fact a name invented by Brutus, but a tribal name of local Thracians whom the army had employed as support staff.

87 Cassius was known to be a better general than the philosophic Brutus.

while with *him* they were free men and citizens. And when he saw that his friends and officers would not be reconciled with them, he saved them by hiding them and helping them to escape.

Among the captives were a certain Volumnius, an actor, and Saculio, a buffoon; to these men Brutus paid no attention. But his friends brought them before him and denounced them, saying that even now they did not refrain from their mockery and insulting language. Brutus, being preoccupied with other matters, had nothing to say; but Messala felt they should be whipped publicly, and then sent back naked to the enemy's generals, to let these men know what sort of fellow drinkers and companions they wanted on their campaigns. At this, some of the bystanders laughed, but Publius Casca, the man who first struck Caesar, said, "We do wrong to sport and make merry during the funeral of Cassius; and you, Brutus, will show what esteem you have for the memory of that general by the way you punish or protect those who mock and speak shamefully of him."[88] At this, Brutus lost his temper and said, "Why then, Casca, do you ask me about it, instead of doing what you think proper?" Taking Brutus' answer for his consent to the death of the wretched fellows, they were led away and executed.

46. After this, Brutus gave his soldiers their promised reward, and after gently scolding them for having leapt on the enemy without a command and in no sort of order, he promised that if they fought well now he would give them two cities for plunder and profit—Thessalonica and Sparta. This is the only accusation in the life of Brutus that admits of no defense, even though Antony and Caesar were much more cruel in the rewards they gave their troops after a victory, and drove the ancient inhabitants out of almost all of Italy in order that their soldiers might seize territory and cities that were not theirs by right. But for these men conquest and empire were the goals of the war, whereas Brutus, in light of his reputation for

---

88 The actor and the clown had evidently been poking fun at the dead Cassius.

virtue, could not allow himself to gain victory or safety except with honor and justice, especially after the death of Cassius, who was held to blame for leading Brutus into some acts of violence. But just as in a ship, when the rudder has been shattered, the sailors try to fit and nail on other pieces of wood to replace it, striving in their need not well but as best they can, so Brutus, not possessing in so great an army, and in so much uncertainty, a commander equal to his plight, was forced to make use of those he had, and to do and say many things that they approved. So he decided to do whatever they thought might make Cassius' soldiers better men. For these were very intractable—bold in their camp for want of a leader, and fearful of the enemy after their recent defeat.

47. But the affairs of Caesar and Antony were in no better condition; for they were short of provisions, and the hollow ground of their camp led them to expect a hard winter. They were crowded together near marshes, and the autumn rains that fell after the battle filled their tents with mud and water that immediately froze in the cold weather. While they were in this state, word reached them of the misfortune that had befallen their forces at sea. For Brutus' fleet, falling upon a large force being brought from Italy at Caesar's command, destroyed it; and the very few who escaped their enemies were forced by hunger to feed upon the sails and rigging of their ships. On hearing of this, Caesar and Antony were eager to have the outcome determined by battle before Brutus became aware of his great success. For it turned out that the conflicts on sea and land were decided on the same day. But by some misfortune, rather than any fault of his naval commanders, Brutus remained ignorant of their success for twenty days. Otherwise he would not have proceeded to a second battle, since he had sufficient provisions for his army for a long time, and occupied an excellent position, his camp being sheltered from the winter weather and inaccessible on the side facing the enemy,[89] while his secure control of the sea and the

89 That is, Brutus had no need to fight in order to keep his army supplied.

victory gained on land by the forces under his own command had made him hopeful and confident.

But since authority in Rome could no longer be exercised by many, but required a monarchy, the divine power, wishing to eliminate the only figure who stood in the way of the man who could be sole ruler, cut Brutus off from knowledge of his good fortune,[90] though it almost reached him in time; for the very evening before the battle, a certain Clodius, a deserter from the enemy, arrived and reported that Caesar had learned of the destruction of his fleet and was therefore eager to fight a decisive battle. But the man was not believed, nor was he even seen by Brutus; instead he was utterly despised. For it was thought that he had heard nothing sound, or was telling lies in order to win favor.

48. On that night, they say, the phantom appeared again to Brutus, in the same shape as before,[91] but departed without speaking. Publius Volumnius, however, a philosopher who had accompanied Brutus on his campaigns from the first, does not mention this omen, though he says that the foremost standard was covered with bees; and that the arm of one of the officers spontaneously sweated oil of roses, and though they repeatedly wiped and scraped it off, they could do nothing to stop it. He says that just before the battle itself two eagles attacked and fought each other in the space between the camps, and as everyone gazed at them, while an incredulous silence prevailed over the plain, the eagle on Brutus' side yielded and fled. And the story of the Ethiopian is widely known; for when the gate

---

and comfortable, whereas the forces of Antony and Octavian were rapidly deteriorating.

90 Plutarch here describes the victory of Octavian as the result of a divine plan for one-man rule. At *Pompey* 75 he places a similar idea in the mouth of a philosophic observer, again suggesting that the victory of a Caesar (Julius in that case) had been divinely ordained as the best outcome for Rome.

91 See chapter 36. Shakespeare, in his version of these episodes, made the phantom into the ghost of Caesar, but Plutarch leaves its identity more vague.

of the camp was thrown open, he met the standard-bearer and was cut to pieces by the soldiers, who regarded him as a bad omen.

49. After leading out his men and arraying them against the enemy, he waited a long time. For suspicions were aroused as he was reviewing his troops, and he heard some of them accused of disloyalty; he also saw that his horsemen were not at all eager to begin the battle, but were waiting to see what the infantry would do. Then, suddenly, an excellent soldier who had been conspicuously honored for bravery, charged past Brutus himself and went over to the enemy; his name was Camulatus. Seeing this, Brutus was deeply grieved; and partly out of anger, partly in fear of some greater desertion and treason, he led his forces at once against their opponents, at about three o'clock in the afternoon. He prevailed with the part under his own command, and advanced, pressing upon the left wing, which retreated; and his horsemen joined the infantry in attacking the disordered enemy. But the other wing, when its commanders extended the line to avoid being surrounded (their numbers being inferior), got drawn out too thin in the center and became too weak to withstand their opponents, but fled at the first onset. Those who had cut through this wing soon surrounded Brutus. He himself showed all the valor of a commander and a soldier in danger, exercising all his judgment and prowess to gain the victory; but what had been an advantage for him in the first battle was a liability in the second. For in the first, the conquered wing of the enemy had been slaughtered on the spot; but when Cassius' men had been routed, few were slain, and those who escaped, daunted by their defeat, infected the larger part of the army with their despair and disorder. Here Marcus, son of Cato,[92] fighting among the best and noblest of the young men, would neither flee nor yield when he was overpowered, but still wielding his weapon and declaring who he was and naming his father, he fell dead upon the many corpses of the enemy. Of the rest, the bravest lost their lives defending Brutus.

---

92 His character is sketched briefly by Plutarch at *Cato* 73.

50. Now among Brutus' friends there was an excellent man, Lucilius. This man, seeing some barbarian horsemen taking no notice of anyone else in the pursuit but charging headlong after Brutus, resolved to stop them, though at the risk of his life. Falling a little behind, he told them that he was Brutus. They believed him because he asked to be brought to Antony, as if he feared Caesar, but could trust Antony. They were overjoyed with their unexpected luck, and thinking themselves wonderfully fortunate, they took Lucilius along with them (by then it was dark), after sending messengers ahead to Antony. Antony himself was delighted and went out to meet them. All the others who heard that Brutus was being brought in alive ran there together, some thinking him pitiable for his fortune, others that he was unworthy of his renown, having become a prey to barbarians through his love of life. When they came near, Antony stood still, in doubt how he should receive Brutus; but Lucilius, being led up to him, said with great confidence, "No enemy, Antony, has taken or could take Marcus Brutus. May fortune never prevail so far over virtue! But he will be found, alive or dead, as becomes him. As for me, I have come here by cheating your soldiers, and am ready to suffer any fatal penalty for it." When Lucilius has spoken thus and everyone was amazed, Antony turned to those who had brought him and said, "I suppose, my fellow soldiers, that you are annoyed at your mistake and think yourselves insulted; but rest assured that you have caught a better prey than that you were seeking. For you were in search of an enemy, but have brought me a friend. For, by the gods, I know not how I should have treated Brutus, had you brought him alive; but I would rather have such men as this my friends rather than my enemies." So saying, he embraced Lucilius, placed him for the present in the charge of one of his friends, and forever after found him faithful and trustworthy.[93]

51. But Brutus, after crossing a stream that ran among trees and

---

93 Lucilius is found accompanying Antony to Egypt at *Antony* 69, where Plutarch cross-references this passage.

had steep banks, did not go much farther, as it was already dark, but sat down in a hollow place with a great rock in front of it, having a few officers and friends with him. First, looking up to the sky, which was full of stars, he recited two verses, one of which Volumnius has recorded:[94]

Zeus, may the author of these ills not escape you;

the other he says he has forgotten. After a while, naming each of his friends who had died defending him in the battle, Brutus groaned, especially at the mention of Flavius and Labeo.[95] Labeo was his lieutenant, and Flavius his chief of engineers. At that point, someone who was thirsty and saw that Brutus was in the same state, took his helmet and ran down to the stream. When a noise reached them from the other direction, Volumnius went with Dardanus, Brutus' shield bearer, to see what it was. They soon returned and asked about the water. Laughing very expressively, Brutus said to Volumnius, "It has been drunk; but more will be fetched for you." Then the same man was sent again; but he risked being captured by the enemy, was wounded, and barely got away safe. Since Brutus guessed that not many of his men were slain in the battle, Statyllius[96] undertook to cut through the enemy (for there was no other way), and to see what had become of their camp; and promised, if he found things there safe, to hold up a torch, and then return to him. Accordingly, the torch was held up, Statyllius having reached the camp; but when after a long time he did not return, Brutus said, "If Statyllius is alive, he will come back." But it happened that on his way back he fell in with the enemy and was slain.

---

94 Line 332 of *Medea*, a prayer spoken by Medea after she has learned of her banishment. Publius Volumnius fought at Philippi and accompanied Brutus in his last hours, and later published an account of the campaign, now lost.

95 Quintus Antistius Labeo, seen also in chapter 12.

96 Formerly a follower of Cato; see *Cato* 65.

52. As the night advanced, Brutus, as he was sitting, turned to chat with his servant Cleitus. But Cleitus could not speak; he merely wept. Then Brutus drew aside Dardanus, his shield bearer, and exchanged a few words with him in private. At last, speaking to Volumnius in Greek, he reminded him of their studies and training, and begged him to help grasp his sword, so he could run himself through. When Volumnius declined and the others did the same, and someone said they should not stay there, but should flee, Brutus rose up and said, "By all means, we must flee—not with our feet, though, but with our hands." Then, clasping each man by the hand, with a beaming face he said it gave him great joy that none of his friends had been false to him, and he blamed Fortune only for his country's sake. He considered himself more blessed than his conquerors, not only yesterday and the day before, but even now, as he was leaving behind a reputation for virtue that those who were superior to him in arms and money would never be able to acquire, since posterity would never believe that unjust and wicked men, who had destroyed the just and good, were fit to rule. Urging and entreating the others to save themselves, he withdrew to a distance with two or three friends; among them was Strato, who had been an intimate ever since they had studied rhetoric together. Placing this man next to himself, and grasping the hilt of his drawn sword with both hands, he fell upon it and died. But some say that it was not Brutus but Strato, who, at Brutus' earnest entreaty and averting his eyes, held the sword. Brutus then thrust himself upon it with such force that it plunged right through his breast, and he instantly died.

53. Messala, a friend of Brutus, after being reconciled with Caesar, once found a moment to introduce Strato to him, and said, with tears in his eyes, "This, Caesar, is the man who performed the last kind service for my beloved Brutus." Receiving him kindly, Caesar made use of him in his labors and at the battle of Actium,[97] Strato

---

97 The battle that in 31 BCE (eleven years after Philippi) decided the power struggle between Octavian and Antony (see *Antony* 61–68).

being one of the Greeks who fought bravely in his service. And it is reported that Messala himself was once praised by Caesar because, though at Philippi the man was his fiercest enemy on Brutus' side, at Actium he had been his staunchest supporter; to which Messala replied, "Indeed, Caesar, I have always been on the better and juster side."

Brutus' dead body was found by Antony, who ordered it to be cloaked in the richest of his own robes; and later, hearing that the robe had been stolen, he had the thief put to death. He sent the ashes of Brutus to his mother, Servilia. As for Porcia, Brutus' wife, Nicolaus the philosopher[98] and Valerius Maximus[99] write that, wishing to die, but being prevented by her friends, who watched her closely, she snatched up some burning coals from the fire, swallowed them, kept her mouth closed, and thus killed herself. But there is an extant letter from Brutus to his friends in which he laments the death of Porcia, and accuses them of so neglecting her that she chose to die rather than live as an invalid. It therefore appears that Nicolaus was mistaken about the time of her death; for this letter (if it indeed is genuine) shows Brutus' awareness of her illness, her love for him, and the manner of her death.

---

98 Nicolaus of Damascus, a Greek writer of the Augustan age whose *Universal History* is now lost.

99 A Roman writer of the first century AD, author of a collection of historical anecdotes that survives largely intact; for Porcia's death, see 4.6.5 in his collection.

ANTONY

Antony's grandfather was the orator Antonius, whom Marius put to death for joining the party of Sulla.[1] His father Antonius, called "the Cretan," was not very notable or distinguished in public life, but a kind and decent man, and especially remarkable for his liberality, as one may grasp from a single example. He was not very affluent, and was therefore prevented by his wife from indulging his philanthropic nature. When one of his friends came to him to borrow money, Antonius had no money to give him, but ordered a young slave to fetch some water in a silver basin. When the basin was brought in, he wetted his chin, as if he meant to shave. The slave was then sent off on another errand, whereupon Antonius gave his friend the basin and told him to dispose of it. Later, when a great search was made for it among the slaves, Antonius, seeing that his wife was angry and proposed to question them one by one, confessed what he had done, begged her pardon, and was forgiven.

2. Antonius' wife was Julia, of the family of the Caesars, and she could compete with the noblest and most discreet women of her day. It was by this woman that Antony, her son, was raised, and after his father died she married Cornelius Lentulus, who was put to death by Cicero for having been a member of Catiline's conspiracy.[2] This

---

1 Gaius Marius and Lucius Cornelius Sulla, both the subjects of other Plutarchan lives, grappled for power in the early 80s BCE, just before Marius' death. The tale of Antonius' murder is told in full at *Marius* 44.

2 Catiline's conspiracy is narrated in full in Plutarch's *Cicero* 10–22, with the

seems to have been the origin and cause of Antony's fierce hatred of Cicero. Antony, at any rate, says that not even the body of Lentulus was restored to them until his mother had begged Cicero's wife for it. But this is admittedly untrue, for no one who was punished at that time by Cicero was denied the right of burial.

Antony was a promising youth, they say, until the friendship and intimacy of Curio fell upon him like a plague. For Curio was unbridled in his pleasures, and in order to render Antony more manageable, involved him in drinking bouts, love affairs, and extravagant and unrestrained expenditures. As a result Antony incurred, at an early age, a debt amounting to two hundred fifty talents.[3] For this sum Curio became his guarantor, but Curio's father, when he heard of it, drove Antony out of his house. Then, for a short time, Antony consorted with Clodius,[4] the boldest and most rascally demagogue of his time, in the violent actions that were confounding the state; but he soon had had enough of the man's madness, and fearing the party that was forming against Clodius, left Italy for Greece, and spent his time in military exercises and in the study of oratory. He adopted the so-called Asiatic style of speaking,[5] which was then at the height of its popularity and bore a considerable resemblance to his own life, which was boastful and arrogant, full of empty bombast and overblown ambition.

3. When Gabinius, who had been consul, was sailing to Syria, he

---

death of Publius Cornelius Lentulus, nicknamed Sura, in 63 BCE a prominent episode in the last three of those chapters.

3 A vast fortune. Plutarch regularly translates Roman currency units, such as sesterces, into Greek units like the talent (consisting of six thousand drachmas) for the benefit of Greek readers.

4 On the bizarre career of Publius Clodius Pulcher, see *Cicero* 28–34.

5 Greek rhetorical styles were generally characterized as Attic or Asiatic, the former thought of as simple and austere, the latter as flowery and elaborate. Since Antony was studying in Greece, he was undoubtedly learning to declaim in Greek, not Latin; most elite Romans had command of that language.

tried to persuade Antony to join his expedition. Antony refused to go out with him as a private citizen, but being appointed to command the cavalry, he served in his campaign. And first, when sent against Aristobulus, who had incited the Jews to revolt, he was the first man to scale the largest of the fortifications, and drove Aristobulus out of all of them; then, joining battle and routing with his own small force an army many times more numerous than his, he killed all but a few of them. Aristobulus himself was captured along with his son.

After this, Ptolemy[6] tried to persuade Gabinius with an offer of ten thousand talents to invade Egypt with him and restore him to his kingdom. Most of the officers were opposed to the plan, and Gabinius himself was hesitant, though utterly captivated by the ten thousand talents. Antony, however, who desired great exploits and wished to gratify Ptolemy, joined in persuading and inciting Gabinius to undertake the expedition. But more formidable than the war itself was the march to Pelusium, since the route passed through deep sand, where there was no water, along the Ecregma and the Serbonian marshes. (These the Egyptians call Typhon's blowholes, though they appear to be a residue of the Red Sea, formed by infiltration where the isthmus that divides them from the Inner Sea is narrowest.[7]) Antony, being sent there with the cavalry, not only occupied the narrow pass, but actually seized Pelusium itself, a large city, and overpowered the garrison, thus rendering the march safe for the army and bolstering the general's hope of victory. And even the enemy reaped some benefit from Antony's love of glory. For when Ptolemy, after he had entered Pelusium, was moved by rage and hatred to slaughter the Egyptians, Antony hindered and stood up to him. And in all the

---

6 Ptolemy XII, ousted ruler of Egypt.

7 The term "Red Sea" here seemingly denotes the modern Red Sea, rather than the Indian Ocean as at *Pompey* 38. "Typhon's blowholes" refers to the hot sulfur springs of the region; Typhon was a mythological fire-breathing monster.

great and frequent battles and contests he gave many proofs of his valor and astute leadership; once in particular, by wheeling about and surrounding the enemy's rear, he gave victory to the troops in the front, and received for this service suitable rewards and honors. Nor did his humanity toward the deceased Archelaus[8] go unnoticed by the multitude. He had formerly been the man's friend and guest, and, as he was now compelled, he fought him bravely while alive; but when Archelaus had fallen, Antony found his body and buried it with royal honors. Thus he left behind him a great name among the Alexandrians[9] and was regarded by the Romans who served in that campaign as a most distinguished man.

4. He had also a princely dignity of form: his noble beard, broad brow, and aquiline nose were thought to convey the masculine traits found in the portraits and statues of Heracles. Furthermore, there was an ancient tradition that the Antonii were Heraclids, being the descendants of Anton, son of Heracles;[10] and Antony imagined that he gave credit to this tradition both by the shape of his body, as has been said, and by his attire. For whenever he was going to appear before large numbers he wore his tunic girt up to his thigh, a broadsword by his side, and a large coarse cloak.[11] And what others might find vulgar—namely, his boastfulness, his raillery, his drinking in public, his sitting beside a soldier who was taking his food, and his eating, as he stood, at a soldier's table—it was marvelous how much goodwill and longing for him these things aroused in his soldiers. Even his amorous exploits were endearing: he gained many friends

---

8 A usurper who had helped to oust Ptolemy from his Egyptian throne.

9 That is, the residents of Alexandria, the Hellenic city from which Egypt was governed.

10 No other references are found to this mythical Anton, and he may have been invented by Antony to give support to his claim of descent from Heracles.

11 The dress and weaponry were meant to suggest Heracles' primitivism.

by assisting them in their love affairs and took their teasing about his own with good humor.

And his liberality, his open and generous hand in conferring favors upon his friends and soldiers, furnished a splendid beginning for his advance to power, and after he had become great, exalted his influence even more, though it was hampered by countless missteps. One illustration of his generosity I will relate. He ordered that 250,000 drachmas[12] be given to one of his friends. (The Romans call this sum a *decies*.) His steward was amazed, and in order to show Antony the magnitude of the sum, laid the money in the open. Antony, passing by, asked what this was; and when the steward replied that it was the gift he had ordered, Antony, discerning the man's ill nature, said, "I thought the *decies* was more; this is too little; let it be doubled."

5. This, however, was at a later time. But when the Roman state broke apart into factions, the aristocratic party joining Pompey, who was in the city, and the popular party summoning Caesar from Gaul, where he was in arms,[13] Curio, the friend of Antony, who had changed party and was supporting Caesar, brought Antony over to his side. Curio had acquired great influence with the people by his eloquence; and by spending lavishly the money supplied by Caesar he got Antony elected tribune of the people, and thereafter had him made one of the priests known as augurs, who observe and interpret the flight of birds. As soon as Antony entered office he was of the greatest advantage to Caesar. First, when the consul Marcellus sought to put under Pompey's orders the soldiers who were

12 The sum was given in denarii, a Roman denomination, in Plutarch's sources, but Plutarch regularly translates such figures into Greek drachmas, the denarius and the drachma being roughly equivalent.

13 Plutarch's sketch of the factionalism leading to the civil war of the mid-first century is bare and simplified here. More detailed accounts of the war's outbreak, and Antony's choosing of sides, can be found in *Caesar* 28–31 and *Pompey* 56–59.

already collected,[14] and to give Pompey power to levy others, Antony hindered him by introducing a decree that the force already gathered should sail to Syria to reinforce Bibulus, who was making war with the Parthians, and that the troops Pompey was levying should not belong to him. Next, when the senators would not let Caesar's letters be received or read,[15] Antony, through the power of his office, read them himself, and changed the minds of many, since Caesar's demands, as they appeared in what he wrote, seemed just and reasonable. And finally, when two questions were put before the Senate, the one whether Pompey should dismiss his army, the other whether Caesar should dismiss *his*, and a few were for the former, but for the latter all but a few, Antony stood up and asked whether it would be agreeable to them that both commanders should lay down their arms and dismiss their forces. This proposal met with everyone's approval; Antony was applauded and the senators called for the question to be put to the vote. The consuls, however, would not allow this, and Caesar's friends again made demands that were thought reasonable. But these were strongly opposed by Cato;[16] and Lentulus, as consul, expelled Antony from the Senate. He departed, calling down many curses upon them; and after donning the clothes of a servant and hiring a carriage with Quintus Cassius, he went straight to Caesar. As soon as they reached the camp, they cried out that affairs at Rome were now conducted without any order, that tribunes were being denied their freedom to speak freely, and that everyone who spoke on behalf of justice was driven out and in danger of his life.

---

14 These soldiers had been taken away from Caesar's army in Gaul.

15 See *Caesar* 30 and *Pompey* 58, where it is made clear that the letters called for a mutual disarmament by Caesar and Pompey.

16 Cato the Younger, sometimes called Cato of Utica, was the subject of another Plutarchan Life. A senator and committed leader of the republican opposition to Caesar, he committed suicide after Caesar's decisive military victories over the forces of Pompey.

6. At this, Caesar took his army and marched into Italy. Hence Cicero, in his *Philippics*,[17] wrote that Antony was as much the cause of the civil war as Helen was of the Trojan. But this is patently false. For Caesar was not so reckless or weak as to let himself be carried away by the indignation of the moment to make war on his country—unless he had decided to do so long before—at the sight of Antony and Cassius, shabbily dressed and in a hired carriage, seeking refuge in his camp. Indeed, this merely furnished a cover and a plausible occasion for war to a man who had long desired a pretext for it. And the motive that led him to make war on all mankind was the same that formerly led Alexander, and Cyrus in ancient times,[18] namely an uncontrollable love of power, and a mad desire to be first and greatest, which he could not achieve unless Pompey were put down.

So as soon as Caesar had advanced and occupied Rome, and driven Pompey out of Italy,[19] he proposed first to go against the forces that Pompey had in Spain, and then, when he had prepared a fleet, to cross over and follow him, in the meantime entrusting the government of Rome to Lepidus, as praetor, and the command of the troops and of Italy to Antony, as tribune of the people. Antony immediately endeared himself to the soldiers, joining with them in their exercises, and for the most part living among them and making them as many presents as his means allowed; but with everyone else he was unpopular. He was too lazy to pay attention to the complaints of those who were injured; he listened with impatience to petitioners; and he had a

---

17 A set of speeches attacking Antony, named for the similarly polemical speeches of Demosthenes (the Athenian orator of the fourth century BCE, the subject of a Plutarchan Life) against Philip of Macedon.

18 Cyrus the Great founded the Persian empire after a campaign of conquest across Asia in the sixth century BCE. Alexander the Great of Macedon (the subject of another Life) conquered the empire of Cyrus, and other territory besides, some two centuries later.

19 These events are described more fully at *Caesar* 33–36 and *Pompey* 60–63.

bad name for his affairs with other men's wives. In short, the government of Caesar (which, as regarded his own behavior, appeared anything but a tyranny) got a bad reputation through his friends. And of these friends, Antony, who had the greatest power and committed the greatest errors, incurred the most blame.

7. But Caesar, on his return from Spain, overlooked the charges against Antony, and this was by no means a mistake, since in warfare Antony was energetic, courageous, and an able leader. Caesar, after crossing the Ionian Sea from Brundisium with a few troops, sent back the vessels with orders to Gabinius and Antony to embark their forces and proceed with all speed into Macedonia. Gabinius, however, afraid that a voyage would be dangerous in the winter season, started to lead his army around by the long land route; but Antony, fearing for Caesar, who was hemmed in among many enemies, beat back Libo, who was blockading the mouth of the harbor of Brundisium, by surrounding his triremes[20] with many small boats; he then embarked eight hundred horsemen and twenty thousand foot soldiers, and put to sea. And when he was seen by the enemy and pursued, he was rescued from this danger by a strong south wind that raised a great swell and forced the enemy triremes into a trough of the sea; he himself was carried with his own ships toward a steep and rocky shore, where there was no hope of safety. But suddenly a strong south wind blew from the bay, and the swell began to run from the land to the sea. Changing course and sailing fearlessly, he saw the shore covered with wrecks; for there the gale had driven ashore the triremes that were pursuing him, and many of these were destroyed. Antony seized many men and considerable booty, captured Lissus, and gave Caesar great encouragement by arriving at the critical moment with so large a force.

---

20 Triremes were Greek warships of the classical age (so named for their three banks of oars), and hence the word "trireme" became Plutarch's standard term for large warships, even when (as here) they were much larger than triremes.

8. The struggles that now arose were many and continuous, and in all of them Antony distinguished himself. On two occasions, when Caesar's men were fleeing headlong, he met them, turned them back, forced them to stand their ground and engage their pursuers, and gained the victory. Next to Caesar's, accordingly, his was the greatest reputation in the camp. And Caesar made clear what opinion he had of him. For as he began the final battle at Pharsalus, which determined everything, Caesar himself led the right wing, and gave the command of the left to Antony, as the best officer of all who served under him.[21] And after the victory, when he had been proclaimed dictator, he went in pursuit of Pompey, but chose Antony as his commander of cavalry[22] and sent him to Rome. This office is second in rank when the dictator is present; but in his absence it is the first and almost the only one. For when a dictator has been appointed, nearly all offices are abolished; only the tribuneship continues.

9. Dolabella, however, who was tribune at the time, being a young man and eager for change, introduced a measure for canceling debts, and tried to persuade Antony, who was his friend and always liked to please the multitude, to take part with him in this step. But Asinius and Trebellius were of the contrary opinion, and it so happened, at the same time, that a terrible suspicion fell upon Antony that Dolabella was taking liberties with his wife. Unable to bear this, he drove his wife from his house (she being his cousin, since she was the daughter of Gaius Antonius, Cicero's colleague in the consulship), embraced the faction of Asinius, and made war on Dolabella. For Dolabella had occupied the Forum, intending

---

21 The right wing of an infantry line could easily be outflanked, and holding it steady required skill and nerve; hence it was deemed the place of highest honor. The leftmost position was second. The battle of Pharsalus pitted the troops of Caesar against those of Pompey and the Senate; Pompey was defeated but escaped the battlefield and fled to Egypt.

22 *Magister equitum* was the Roman name for this post; see the Appendix on the Roman constitution.

to pass his law by force. But Antony, when the Senate had voted that arms should be used against Dolabella, came out against him, joined battle, killed some of his men, and lost some of his own. By this action he made himself odious to the common people, while to respectable and upright citizens his general way of life made him, as Cicero says,[23] utterly unacceptable; indeed, he was hated by them. They abhorred his drunkenness at all hours, his heavy expenditures, his wallowing in love affairs, his days spent in sleeping or walking about distracted and hung over, and his nights at revels, theaters, and the wedding festivities of mimes and buffoons. It is related, at any rate, that he once feasted at the wedding of Hippias the mime,[24] drank all night, and then, in the morning, when the people summoned him to the Forum, came forward still sated with food, and vomited, one of his friends holding his toga out of the way. Sergius the mime was one of those who had the most influence with him, and Cytheris, a woman of the same profession, whom he adored, and who, when he went to visit the cities, was conveyed alongside him (her litter being followed by as many attendants as followed the litter of his mother). And people were scandalized at the sight of golden cups carried about on his journeys as in processions, at the setting up of tents as he traveled, at the laying out of expensive meals near groves and rivers, at his having lions harnessed to his chariot, and at his quartering prostitutes and sambuca players[25] at the houses of decent men and women. And it seemed terrible that while Caesar himself, out of Italy, was encamping in the open and, with great effort and danger, mopping up the remainder of the war, others, by virtue of his authority, should insult their fellow citizens with their impudent luxury.

---

23 In his *Philippics* (see note 17).

24 Mimes at Rome performed a kind of low or bawdy theater.

25 The sambuca was a stringed instrument associated with shrill music suitable for raucous gatherings.

10. These things seem to have aggravated the discord, and to have encouraged the soldiers in acts of insolence and rapacity. Hence when Caesar came home, he pardoned Dolabella, and, on being chosen consul for the third time, took not Antony, but Lepidus, for his colleague. When Pompey's house was offered for sale, Antony bought it; but when the price was demanded of him he was vexed.[26] And he himself says that this was why he did not join Caesar's campaign in North Africa, since he had not been compensated for his former successes. But Caesar, by not allowing Antony's errors to pass unnoticed, seems to have cured him of much of his folly and extravagance. For Antony gave up his earlier way of life and turned his attention to marriage, wedding Fulvia, the widow of Clodius the demagogue.[27] She was a woman who had no interest in spinning or housekeeping, nor would she condescend to dominate a mere private citizen, but wished to rule a ruler and command a commander. Cleopatra,[28] since she took him over tamed, and trained from the outset to obey a woman, owed a large tuition to Fulvia for having schooled Antony in the dominion of women.

Yet Antony tried, by playful and boyish jests, to make even Fulvia more lighthearted. For example, when many were going out to meet Caesar after his victory in Spain, Antony joined them. Then, when a rumor suddenly fell upon Italy that Caesar was dead and his enemies were marching against the country, Antony returned to Rome. Donning the clothes of a servant, he came to his house by night, and on saying he was carrying a letter to Fulvia from Antony, was brought in to her, his head covered up. Then Fulvia, in great

---

26 Pompey had been killed by the Egyptians shortly after the defeat at Pharsalus. Evidently Antony felt his power was such that he would not be asked to pay for the house.

27 Clodius (see note 4) was far more dangerous than a mere "demagogue," but Plutarch uses *dēmagōgos* to denote various kinds of political striving based on appeal to the masses.

28 See chapters 25–29 below.

dismay, before taking the letter, asked if Antony were alive; and he, after handing her the letter in silence, threw his arms around her as she began to open and read it, and kissed her.

This little anecdote is one of many I have offered as an illustration.

11. On Caesar's return from Spain, all the foremost citizens traveled a journey of several days to meet him, but it was Antony who was conspicuously honored by him. For as Caesar rode through Italy he kept Antony in the carriage with him, while behind came Brutus Albinus[29] and Octavian, his niece's son, who afterward was named Caesar[30] and reigned for a great many years over the Romans. And when Caesar was proclaimed consul for the fifth time he immediately chose Antony as his colleague; he also wished to resign his office and entrust it to Dolabella, and informed the Senate of his resolution. But Antony vehemently opposed the plan, saying much that was bad against Dolabella and hearing as much in return, until Caesar, ashamed by their unseemliness, deferred the matter to another time. And thereafter, when Caesar came before the people to proclaim Dolabella, Antony cried that the auguries were unfavorable, until at last Caesar, much to the annoyance of Dolabella, yielded and gave him up. But it appears that Caesar found Antony as insufferable as he did Dolabella. For it is said that when someone was accusing both of them to him, he said he had no fear of these fat, long-haired men, but rather of those pale, thin ones, meaning Brutus and Cassius, by whom he would be plotted against and slain.[31]

12. And the fairest pretext for their conspiracy was furnished, unintentionally, by Antony himself. For the Romans were celebrating

---

29 Decimus Junius Brutus Albinus, a different Brutus than the senator who later helped kill Caesar.

30 Octavian preferred to be called "Caesar" after Julius Caesar's death, though modern historians refer to him by the honorific title later awarded by the Senate, Augustus. Plutarch uses "Caesar" to mean Julius up until chapter 16 of this Life, at which point "Caesar" refers to Octavian/Augustus.

31 See *Caesar* 62 and *Brutus* 8.

the festival of Lycaea, which they call the Lupercalia; and Caesar, dressed in a triumphal robe and seated above the rostrum in the Forum, was watching the runners. It is the custom at this festival for young noblemen and magistrates to run about, anointed with oil, and wielding leather thongs, with which they playfully strike everyone they meet.[32] Antony was among them; but, forgoing the ancient custom, he twined a laurel wreath around a diadem,[33] ran up to the rostrum, and, being lifted up by his fellow runners, tried to place it on the head of Caesar, thus hinting that he ought to be king. When Caesar, pretending to decline the diadem, leaned aside to avoid it, the people were delighted and loudly applauded him. Antony tried again to crown him, and Caesar again declined. This contest went on for some time, a few of Antony's friends encouraging him, but all the people applauding when Caesar refused. And it was certainly strange that the people were willing to behave like the subjects of a king, but disliked the title of king as if it spelled the destruction of their liberty. Caesar, displeased at what had happened, rose from the rostrum, pulled his toga back from his neck, and shouted that anyone who pleased might strike the fatal blow. When the wreath was placed on one of his statues, some of the tribunes of the people pulled it down. These men were escorted home by the people with praise and applause, but Caesar deposed them from office.

13. These incidents strengthened Brutus and Cassius and their followers; and when they were discussing which friends they could trust for their exploit, they considered Antony. The rest were in favor of including him, but Trebonius objected. For he told them

---

32 A partial description of the Lupercalia, an ancient fertility and purification ritual celebrated by the Romans on February 15. The connection to wolves, indicated both by the Latin name and by Plutarch's Greek equivalent, is obscure. See *Caesar* 61 for a different account of this whole episode.

33 The diadem or headband was worn by Hellenistic Greek monarchs as a mark of royal stature. Laurel wreaths were awarded to victorious athletes, musicians, or poets in various Greek competitions.

that Antony and he had traveled together and shared a tent on the journey to meet Caesar on his return from Spain, and that he had sounded Antony gently and in a cautious way; and that Antony had understood him but had not encouraged the overture. He had said nothing about it to Caesar, however, but had faithfully kept the secret. The conspirators then proposed that Antony should be killed after they had slain Caesar; but Brutus prevented this, insisting that an action taken in defense of law and justice should be kept pure and free of injustice. Yet as the conspirators feared Antony's strength and the prestige of his office, they appointed some of their number to deal with him, so that when Caesar entered the Senate house and the deed was about to be done, they might engage Antony outside in a conversation about some urgent matter and detain him there.

14. These things were done according to their plan, and Caesar fell in the Senate house. Antony at once donned the clothes of a servant and hid himself. But when he learned that the conspirators had assembled on the Capitol and were laying hands on no one, he persuaded them to come down, giving them his son as a hostage.[34] That night Cassius dined at Antony's house, and Brutus with Lepidus. Antony then convened the Senate and spoke in favor of an amnesty and a distribution of provinces among Cassius and Brutus and their partisans. The Senate passed these measures, and voted that no act of Caesar's should be altered. Thus Antony went out of the Senate house the most brilliant of men; for he was thought to have brought civil war to an end and to have managed difficult matters and extraordinary turmoil in the wisest and most statesmanlike way.[35]

But from these counsels he was soon dislodged by his popularity with the multitude and the expectation that he would surely hold first place if Brutus were overthrown. As Caesar's body was being

---

34 Children and close relatives were regularly handed over to rivals in the ancient world as guarantees of nonaggression.

35 See *Brutus* 19 and *Caesar* 67.

carried out for burial, Antony, according to the custom, was delivering his funeral oration in the Forum. And when he saw that the people were unusually affected and charmed by what he said, he began to mingle with his praises words of sorrow and horror at what had happened; and as he was ending his speech, he waved above his head the garments of the dead, all spattered with blood and pierced by swords, and called those who had done this villains and murderers. He thereby aroused such indignation in the people that they heaped together benches and tables and burned Caesar's body in the Forum;[36] then, snatching brands from the pyre, they ran to the conspirators' houses and assaulted them.

15. At this, Brutus and his partisans left the city, Caesar's friends joined together to support Antony; and Calpurnia, Caesar's wife, placing her trust in Antony, deposited with him most of the treasure from Caesar's house, which amounted to four thousand talents in all. Antony also obtained Caesar's papers, in which there were written notes of his decisions and decrees. Making insertions into these, Antony appointed many magistrates and senators of his own choosing; he also brought some men back from exile and freed others from prison, as if all this had been ordained by Caesar. This was why the Romans, in mockery, called all such beneficiaries Charonites; for to prove their claims they had recourse to the papers of the dead.[37] His behavior in general was autocratic, he himself being consul, and having his brothers in office as well: Gaius as praetor, Lucius as tribune of the people.

16. At that point the young Caesar[38] came to Rome—Caesar's niece's son, as has been said, who had been left heir to his estate and

---

36 See *Brutus* 20 and *Caesar* 68. A pyre had been made ready elsewhere by the senators, but the people felt impelled to honor Caesar by cremating him themselves.

37 The name plays on the mythical Charon, the ferryman of souls in Hades. The Roman term was in fact *orcini*, making a similar play on the figure of Orcus; it was applied to slaves freed by their masters' wills.

38 Octavian; see note 30 above.

had been living in Apollonia[39] when Caesar was killed. The young man greeted Antony as his father's friend and reminded him of the money deposited with him, since according to the terms of Caesar's will, every Roman was owed seventy-five drachmas.[40] But Antony, at first looking down on him as a mere boy, told him he was not of sound mind, and that, bereft of good judgment and of friends, he was taking on an unbearable burden in the succession of Caesar. When the young man would not listen to this and demanded the money, Antony continued to do and say many things to insult him. For he opposed him when he ran for a tribuneship, and when the young man sought to set up a golden chair in honor of his father, as had been decreed,[41] Antony threatened to haul him to prison unless he stopped courting the people's favor. But when Caesar offered his support to Cicero and all the others who hated Antony, and with their help gained the favor of the Senate, while he himself won the goodwill of the people and drew together the soldiers from the towns they had been settled in, Antony grew alarmed and came to confer with him on the Capitol, and they were reconciled.

Lying asleep that night, Antony had a strange dream; for he dreamt that his right hand had been struck by a thunderbolt. And a few days later a rumor reached him that Caesar was plotting against him. Caesar tried to defend himself, but Antony was not convinced. Their active hatred resumed, and both were rushing about Italy to obtain by high wages the old soldiers who were already settled on their allotted lands, and to be the first to secure the troops who were still in arms.

---

39 A town in Illyria (modern Albania) where Octavian had gone for study and military training.

40 The four thousand talents mentioned in the previous chapter, placed in Antony's hands for safekeeping but belonging principally to Octavian as Caesar's heir.

41 In life Julius Caesar had been awarded the use of such a throne; the empty seat now called to mind his absence.

17. Cicero was then the man of greatest influence in the city. He was doing all he could to incite everyone against Antony, and at last persuaded the Senate to declare him a public enemy, to send Caesar the fasces[42] and other praetorial insignia, and to send Pansa and Hirtius to drive Antony out of Italy. These men were the consuls at the time, and in an engagement with Antony near the city of Mutina[43] (Caesar was present and fought on their side), they conquered the enemy but fell themselves. Many hardships overtook Antony in his flight, the worst of which was famine. But it was his nature in misfortunes to be better than at any other time; in adversity he was most like a virtuous man. It is common for people to discern what is right when they have fallen into difficulties; but very few have the strength in such extremities to imitate what they admire and avoid what they condemn; some, indeed, are then even more likely, through weakness, to give way to their habits and to become incapable of reasoning. Antony, on that occasion, was a wonderful example to his soldiers. He who had lived in such luxury and extravagance was content to drink foul water and to feed on wild fruits and roots. Bark was even eaten, it is said, and in crossing the Alps they resorted to animals that had never been tasted before.

18. Antony's men were eager to join the troops beyond the Alps, whom Lepidus commanded, since he was thought to be a friend of Antony, and through him had enjoyed many advantages from Caesar's friendship. Antony came up and encamped nearby, but when he met with no friendly encouragement he resolved to take a great chance.[44] His hair was neglected, and he had let his beard grow since his defeat; and donning a dark cloak he came up to the camp of Lep-

---

42 The fasces was a bundle of rods surrounding an axe, signifying the power to impose corporal punishment. It was carried (by an official called a lictor) before the high magistrates of the Roman state as they walked through the city streets.

43 The modern Modena, in northern Italy.

44 Antony was at this point uncertain whether Lepidus' army would support

idus and began to speak. Many were moved by his appearance and touched by his words, whereupon Lepidus grew fearful and ordered all the trumpets to sound at the same time, so that Antony might not be heard. But the soldiers only pitied Antony the more, and conferred with him in secret, sending Laelius and Clodius[45] to him in women's clothes. They advised him to attack their camp boldly, assuring him that many would welcome him, and, if he wished it, would kill Lepidus. Antony, however, would not let them lay hands on Lepidus, but the next day proceeded to cross the river with his army. He himself was the first man to step in, and he made his way to the opposite bank, seeing already that many of Lepidus' soldiers were reaching out their hands to him and tearing down their barricade. After entering the camp and becoming master of everything, he treated Lepidus with the greatest civility. For he embraced him and addressed him as father; and though in fact he himself had everything under his control, he continued to preserve for Lepidus the name and honor of commander. This prompted Munatius Plancus, who was encamped not far off with a considerable force, to come over to him. Raised in this way to great power, Antony again crossed the Alps, leading with him into Italy seventeen legions of infantry and ten thousand horsemen. He also left a garrison in Gaul of six legions with Varius, one of his intimates and drinking companions, whom they used to call Cotylon.[46]

19. Caesar no longer paid heed to Cicero, seeing that the man favored liberty, and he invited Antony through friends to come to an understanding. And the three men,[47] meeting together on

---

him or Octavian and the Senate (who were at this point still allied). Lepidus himself had already become Antony's enemy.

45 Not the famous Clodius who had troubled the state two decades earlier, but an otherwise unknown soldier.

46 The nickname, formed from the Greek word *kotyle*, or "half-pint," refers to Varius' drinking habits.

47 Lepidus was also included, making up the so-called Second Triumvirate.

a small island in the middle of a river, sat in conference for three days. Everything else was equitably agreed upon, and they divided the entire empire among themselves as if it were a paternal inheritance; but the question of who should be put to death gave them the greatest trouble, each of them insisting on slaying his enemies and saving his friends. But at last, in their anger against those whom they hated, they abandoned respect for kinsmen and affection for friends. Caesar gave Cicero up to Antony, Antony gave up to Caesar his maternal uncle Lucius Caesar, and Lepidus was given permission to murder his brother Paulus (though some say that Lepidus gave his brother up to Antony and Caesar). Nothing, in my opinion, has ever surpassed the cruelty and savagery of this barter; for in this trading of murder for murder they were equally guilty of the lives they surrendered and of those they seized, though they were even guiltier in the case of their friends, whom they murdered without even hating them.

20. To conclude this resolution, the soldiers, surrounding them, demanded that Caesar bolster the friendship by a marriage, and that he marry Clodia, a daughter of Fulvia, Antony's wife. When this had also been agreed to, three hundred men were put to death by proscription.[48] When Cicero was slain, Antony gave orders that his head should be cut off and the right hand with which he had written the speeches against him.[49] And when these were brought to him he gazed at them joyfully, and actually burst out several times in exultant laughter. Then, when he had been sated with the sight of them, he ordered them to be placed over the rostrum in the Forum, as if he meant to insult the corpse, whereas he merely exposed his own insolence in good fortune and his shameless abuse of power. His uncle Lucius Caesar, being sought for and pursued, took refuge with his

---

48 Proscription at Rome involved the public posting of state enemies. Those whose names were so posted were subject to arrest or execution, and their property was forfeit; rewards were offered to any who helped kill them.

49 See *Cicero* 47–49.

sister.[50] And she, when the murderers arrived and tried to force their way into her room, stood at the door, spread out her hands, and cried out many times, "You will not kill Lucius Caesar unless you first kill me, who gave birth to your commander." And in this manner she succeeded in getting her brother out of the way and saved his life.

21. The government of the triumvirate was in most ways hateful to the Romans; and Antony bore most of the blame, since he was older than Caesar and more influential than Lepidus; and, as soon as he had shaken off the yoke of business, he threw himself again into his old life of pleasure and dissipation. To his bad reputation was added the considerable hatred caused by the house in which he lived, which had belonged to Pompey the Great,[51] a man who had been admired as much for his temperance and his orderly and public-spirited way of life as for his three triumphs. People were therefore pained to see that house closed for the most part against commanders, magistrates, and ambassadors, who were rudely thrust from its doors, and filled instead with mimes, jugglers, and drunken flatterers, on whom was spent most of the money that had been procured in the cruelest and most violent manner. For the three men not only sold the estates of those they slew, harassing the widows and families with trumped-up accusations,[52] and imposing every sort of tax; but when they learned that sums of money had been deposited with the Vestal Virgins both by foreigners and citizens, they went and took them. And since nothing was enough for Antony, Caesar demanded a share of the property. They also shared the army, and both marched into Macedonia to make war on Brutus and Cassius,[53] entrusting Rome to Lepidus.

---

50 Antony's mother, Julia.

51 See chapter 10 and note 26.

52 Since the property of those killed in proscriptions was already forfeit to the state, the triumvirs would not have needed these measures against their heirs.

53 Brutus' campaign in the east, where Antony was forced to pursue him, is

22. But after they had crossed the sea, engaged in combat, and encamped near the enemy (Antony opposite Cassius, and Caesar opposite Brutus), Caesar did nothing notable, whereas Antony was everywhere victorious and successful. In the first battle Caesar was decisively beaten by Brutus, lost his camp, and barely escaped his pursuers. (He himself writes in his memoirs that he withdrew before the battle because of a friend's dream.) Antony, on the other hand, defeated Cassius, though some have written that he was not actually present at the engagement, but arrived after it and joined in the pursuit. Cassius was killed, at his own request and order, by Pindarus, one of his trusted freedmen; for he was unaware that Brutus was victorious. After a few days, they fought another battle, and Brutus, when defeated, killed himself; but Antony got most of the credit for the victory, since Caesar was ill. Standing over Brutus' dead body, he reproached him a little for the death of Gaius, his brother, who had been executed by Brutus' own order in Macedonia to avenge Cicero; and declaring that Hortensius[54] was more to blame than Brutus for his brother's murder, he gave orders for Hortensius to be slain on his brother's tomb. But over Brutus' body he threw his own purple cloak, which was very valuable, and ordered one of his freedmen to take care of his burial. Learning afterward that this man had not burned the cloak with the body, and had kept most of the money to be spent on the funeral, Antony had him put to death.

23. After this, Caesar was conveyed to Rome, no one thinking that he would long survive, considering his illness, while Antony, intending to levy funds in all the eastern provinces, entered Greece with a large army. And since every soldier had been promised five thousand drachmas,[55] a more stringent policy was needed for raising

---

described in full at *Brutus* 24–37. The battles that now loom are those at Philippi in 42 BCE.

54 Governor of Macedonia, who had killed Gaius on Brutus' order.

55 As often, Plutarch converts Roman denarii into Greek drachmas, the two coins being roughly equivalent.

money and collecting tribute. To the Greeks, Antony's conduct was not at all out of place or vulgar, at least at first; for he amused himself by attending literary discussions, athletic games, and religious initiations;[56] in judicial matters he was also equitable, and delighted in being called a lover of Greece, and even more in being addressed as a lover of Athens, to which city he gave a great many gifts. But when the Megarians wished to show him something fine to rival Athens, and thought he should see their Senate house, he went up to view it; and when they asked him how he liked it he said, "It is both small and rotten." He also had measurements taken of the Temple of Pythian Apollo, as if he intended to complete it; for he promised the Senate that he would do so.[57]

24. Then, leaving Lucius Censorinus in charge of Greece, he crossed over into Asia,[58] and there laid his hands on its stores of wealth. Kings waited at his door; and wives of kings, vying with one another in their gifts and their beauty, welcomed his illicit advances. Thus, while Caesar in Rome was exhausting himself amid seditions and wars, Antony, enjoying abundant leisure and peace, let his passions carry him back into his former way of life. Lyre players like Anaxenor, flute players like Xuthus, Metrodorus the dancer, and a whole Bacchic revel of Asiatic performers, who surpassed in forwardness and buffoonery the pests from Italy,[59] streamed in and took possession of the court. (It was insufferable that everything was devoted to these frivolities.) The whole of Asia, like the city in Sophocles,

56 Certain Greek religious cults, such as the Eleusinian mysteries in Attica, required that adherents undergo a secret or mystical rite of initiation.

57 The temple referred to here seems to have stood at Delphi; it had been damaged by fire in an attack by invaders about four decades before this.

58 "Asia" refers here to the Roman province, roughly the western portion of modern Turkey.

59 Presumably, Antony had also been enjoying low or decadent entertainment in Rome before leaving for the East.

was filled alike with incense,
Alike with paeans and with groans of despair.[60]

When Antony made his entry into Ephesus, at any rate, women dressed like Bacchantes,[61] and men and boys like Satyrs and Pans, led the way, and the city was full of wands wreathed in ivy, harps, flutes, and pipes, the people calling him Dionysus, the Giver of Joy, and the Gentle. And so indeed he was to some, but to far more the Raw-Eater and the Savage.[62] For he would confiscate the fortunes of wellborn men and bestow them on rogues and flatterers. And men acquired the property of many persons who were still alive, having asked him for it on the grounds that the owners were dead. He gave the house of a Magnesian citizen to a cook, who is said to have acquired his reputation on the strength of a single supper. But at last, when he was imposing a second tribute on the cities, Hybreas, speaking on behalf of Asia, took courage and addressed him in forensic style, but wittily enough for Antony's taste, saying, "If you can take two tributes in one year, you can also give us a pair of summers and a double harvesttime." But he added, plainly and bluntly, that Asia had given him two hundred thousand talents. "If you have not received it," said Hybreas, "demand it from those who took it; but if you received it, and have it not, we are ruined."[63] These words cut Antony to the quick; for he was unaware of much

---

60 A quote from the opening of Sophocles' *Oedipus Rex* (4–5), describing Thebes at the time of its plague.

61 Female celebrants of Dionysus, who usually wore fawn skins and carried thyrsi, the "wands wreathed in ivy" described just below.

62 These cult titles of Dionysus represent the two sides of the god's nature. To those who welcomed him he brought pleasure and release from care, but those who resisted (like Pentheus in Euripides' *Bacchae*) might be destroyed or even torn apart so as to be consumed raw.

63 That is, the first tribute payment must have been either stolen in transit or spent, so that Antony now demands a new one.

that was happening, not because he was indolent, but because he was predisposed to trust those about him.

For there was a simplicity in his character, and a slowness of perception, though when he did perceive his mistakes his repentance was keen, as was his acknowledgment to the very men who had been unfairly treated, and there was an ampleness both in his amends and his punishments. Yet his generosity was thought to be more excessive than his severity. And his impudence in jokes and mockery contained its own antidote. For it was possible to return his mockery and insults, and he took no less pleasure in being laughed at than in laughing at others. And this ruined most of his undertakings. For he never imagined that those who spoke so freely in jest would flatter him in earnest, and as a result was easily taken in by their praises, being unaware that some men mix their flattery with boldness, as cooks do their desserts with something sharp, to take away its cloyingness. Such men employ their frank chatter over the wine to make their obsequious assent in weighty matters seem to be the mark not of those who seek to please, but of those who are persuaded by the stronger argument.

25. Such being Antony's nature, the crowning evil that befell him was his passion for Cleopatra, which awakened and roused to a Bacchic frenzy many of the drives that still lay hidden and dormant in him, and stifled and corrupted whatever good and sound elements still held their own. He was ensnared in the following way. While he was preparing for the Parthian War,[64] he sent to Cleopatra,[65] ordering her to meet him in Cilicia to answer an accusation that she had given great assistance to Cassius in the recent war. But Dellius, who was sent on this errand, when he beheld her face and appreciated her adroitness and subtlety in conversation, immediately grasped that Antony would not so much as think of doing such a woman any

64 Plutarch alludes only briefly to Antony's plans to invade Parthia, the powerful adversary on Rome's eastern frontier.

65 See *Caesar* 48–49 for some events of Cleopatra's life up to this point.

harm; on the contrary, she would be of the greatest importance to him. He therefore resorted to flattery and sought to persuade the Egyptian "to go to Cilicia, arraying herself beautifully," as Homer would say,[66] and not to fear Antony, who was the gentlest and kindest of commanders. She was convinced by Dellius, and judging by the effect her attractions had exerted earlier on Gaius Caesar[67] and Gnaeus, the son of Pompey, she had no doubt that she would more easily bring Antony under her power. For those men had known her when she was still a girl and ignorant of the world; but she was to meet Antony at the time of life when women's beauty is most splendid, and their intellects have fully matured.[68] Hence she furnished herself with many gifts, much money, and such adornments as a woman of so wealthy a kingdom might afford, but she went placing her surest hopes in herself, and in her own magic arts and charms.

26. Though she received several letters of invitation both from Antony and from his friends, she so scorned and laughed at the man as to sail up the river Cydnus in a barge with a gilded stern, its purple sails outspread, while its rowers plied silver oars to the music of flutes and pipes and harps.[69] She herself reclined under a canopy shot with gold, dressed like Aphrodite in a picture; and boys like painted Erotes[70] stood on either side to fan her. Likewise her fairest maids were dressed like Nereids and Graces, some stationed at the rudder, some at the ropes. Marvelous odors of incense wafted over the river-

---

66 Plutarch quotes a line from *Iliad* 14 but substitutes "Cilicia" for "Ida." In the Homeric passage, Hera is dressing herself seductively in an effort to distract her husband, Zeus.

67 That is, Julius Caesar.

68 At this point Cleopatra was twenty-eight.

69 The mockery Plutarch finds in this naval voyage consists in its grandeur. Ordinarily a summons from a Roman dynast would result in a quicker, humbler arrival.

70 The god Eros (the Roman god Cupid), son of Aphrodite, was often depicted as a young boy.

banks. Some of the inhabitants met her at the river and accompanied her on either side, while others came down from the city to see the sight. The throng in the Forum gradually dispersed,[71] and Antony at last, sitting on the rostrum, was left alone. And a rumor spread everywhere that Aphrodite had come to revel with Dionysus for the good of Asia.[72]

Antony sent to invite her to supper; but she thought it more appropriate that he should come to her. At once, then, wishing to show his good humor and courtesy, he obeyed and went. He found the preparations there beyond description, but was most amazed at the vast number of lights. For it is said that so many of these were lowered and displayed on all sides at once, and were so ingeniously arranged at angles to one another, some in squares, others in circles, that few sights have ever been so beautiful or worth seeing.

27. The next day Antony reciprocated her hospitality and was ambitious to surpass her both in magnificence and refinement, though he fell short on both counts; and when he found himself overmastered he was the first to scoff at the meagerness and inelegance of his own entertainment. Cleopatra, noting from Antony's jokes that he was very much the coarse-grained soldier, responded in kind, freely and boldly. For her actual beauty, it is said, was not, in and of itself, utterly beyond compare, or such as to astound those who beheld her; but her presence cast an inescapable spell, and her appearance, combined with the persuasiveness of her talk, and the personality that suffused all she said and did, had something bewitching about it. It was a pleasure merely to hear the sound of her voice; and she could readily turn her tongue, like a many-stringed instrument, to any language she pleased, so that she rarely conversed with foreigners through an interpreter, but could reply to most of them by herself, whether they were Ethiopians, Trog-

---

71 The scene shifts from the riverbank to the town of Tarsus, where Antony is awaiting Cleopatra.

72 See chapter 24 for Antony's association with Dionysus.

lodytes, Hebrews, Arabians, Syrians, Medes, or Parthians.[73] She is also said to have known many other languages, though the kings of Egypt before her had not even bothered to learn the local language, and some of them even abandoned their native Macedonian.[74]

28. Antony was so captivated by her that, while Fulvia his wife was waging war in Rome against Caesar on behalf of her husband's interests, and while a Parthian army was hovering around Mesopotamia (over which the king's generals had appointed Labienus Parthian commander-in-chief, and were about to invade Syria),[75] he let himself be spirited away by her to Alexandria. There, engaged in the pastimes and amusements of a young man of leisure, he squandered and lavished on pleasures that which Antiphon calls the most costly of valuables, namely time. For they had a sort of society that they called the Inimitables. And day by day they feasted each other with an extravagance of expenditure that defied belief or measure. Philotas, at any rate, the physician of Amphissa, used to tell my grandfather Lamprias[76] that he was at that time studying his profession in Alexandria, and that having become acquainted with one of the royal cooks, he was invited by

---

73 Members of all these nations would have appeared before her in Alexandria, where the language of the royal court was Greek. The Troglodytes lived on the coast of the Red Sea.

74 Ptolemy I, who founded the dynasty to which Cleopatra belonged, was a Macedonian, one of Alexander's senior staff; the language he spoke was probably a form of Greek but so different from other Greek dialects as to require an interpreter. Later Ptolemys evidently dropped their native speech in favor of standard Greek.

75 Plutarch follows standard Greek usage in referring to the head of the Persian or Parthian empire as "the king." Labienus was a Roman who had come to the Parthian court as an agent of the now defeated Brutus and Cassius, seeking support for the senatorial cause.

76 An interesting autobiographical note. The events of Antony's life preceded Plutarch's youth by about a century, so there would have been old men still alive in Lamprias's time who knew Antony personally.

him, being a young man, to come and see the sumptuous preparations for supper. So he was brought into the kitchen, and when he saw all the other abundant provisions and eight wild boars being roasted, he marveled at how many guests there must be. But the cook laughed and said, "There are not many dining; only about twelve. But every dish has to be set before them in a state of perfection, which a minute one way or the other may spoil. For Antony may ask for supper at once; but after a little while he may ask for wine, or fall into conversation, and postpone it. So not one," he said, "but many suppers must be arranged. For it is impossible to guess the precise moment." This was Philotas's story; he also said that as time went on he became one of the physicians who attended Antony's oldest son by Fulvia, and would regularly dine at his house with his other companions whenever the boy was not dining with his father. One day, when another physician was holding forth, and giving great annoyance to the company, Philotas stopped his mouth with some sort of sophistic syllogism as this: "To the somewhat feverish patient cold water must be given; but everyone who has a fever is somewhat feverish; therefore to everyone who is feverish cold water must be given." The man was utterly taken aback and struck dumb, and Antony's son was delighted and said with a laugh, "Philotas, I make you a present of all these things," pointing to a table covered with a great many large drinking cups. Philotas welcomed the boy's ardor but was far from thinking that someone so young had the power to give away so much. Soon after, however, one of the slaves brought him the cups in a sack, and told him to affix his seal to it.[77] When Philotas protested and was afraid to take them, the man said, "Why, wretched fellow, do you hesitate? Don't you know that the giver is Antony's son, who is free to give away so many golden cups? But take my advice and exchange all of them with us for money; for there may be among the rest some antique or admirable piece of

77 That is, to label it as his own property.

workmanship that his father might miss." These stories, according to my grandfather, Philotas used to recount on every occasion.

29. But Cleopatra distributed her flattery not into the four types admitted by Plato,[78] but into many. Whether Antony were serious or inclined to be playful, she had some new delight or charm with which to beguile him, and she kept him always under her wing, freeing him neither day nor night. She played at dice with him, drank with him, and hunted with him; when he exercised in arms, she would be there to see; and at night when he would stand at doors and windows and jeer at the people inside, she would wander about with him, dressed like a servant woman, since Antony also tried to disguise himself as a servant. And from these outings he always came home scorned, and often severely beaten, though most people guessed who he was. Yet the Alexandrians enjoyed his buffoonery and joined in his frolics in their decorous and refined way, saying they were very much obliged to him for using his tragic mask with the Romans, and his comic mask with *them*.[79]

Now it would be nonsensical to recount the greater part of his childish antics, but one instance must not be omitted. He went out one day to fish. Growing annoyed at his bad luck (since Cleopatra was present), he ordered his fishermen to dive down and secretly put on his hook some fish that had already been caught. He pulled up two or three, but the Egyptian detected the subterfuge. Feigning admiration, however, she told her friends how skillful Antony was and invited them to come as spectators on the following day. And when many of them had boarded the fishing boats and Antony had let down his line, she ordered one of her servants to anticipate him by swimming to the hook and fixing upon it a salted fish from the Black Sea. Then Antony, thinking he had caught

78 At *Gorgias* 462c–466a, Plato speaks of four arts that strengthen the health of the body and soul, each of which has a debased form that Plato refers to as "flattery."

79 A metaphor drawn from the theater.

something, pulled it up. And when, as was likely, great laughter ensued, Cleopatra said, "Surrender your rod, general, to the fishermen of Pharos and Canopus.[80] Your hunt is for cities, provinces, and continents."

30. While Antony was amusing himself with such child's play, two reports arrived: one from Rome, that his brother Lucius and his wife, Fulvia, after first quarreling with each other, had joined in war against Caesar, had lost their cause, and were in flight from Italy; and another, not at all more promising, that Labienus, at the head of the Parthians, was subjugating Asia from the Euphrates and Syria as far as Lydia and Ionia. Accordingly, as if roused from sleep after a debauch, he set out to attack the Parthians, and advanced as far as Phoenicia. But on receiving from Fulvia a letter filled with laments, he turned his course, with two hundred ships, to Italy. On the voyage, however, picking up his friends who had fled from Italy, he learned that Fulvia had been to blame for the war, since, being naturally meddlesome and bold, she hoped that an upheaval in Italy would draw Antony away from Cleopatra. But it happened that Fulvia, who was sailing to meet him, fell ill and died at Sicyon; and this made a reconciliation with Caesar even easier. For when Antony reached Italy, and Caesar showed no intention of bringing charges against him, and Antony himself shifted the blame for everything he was accused of onto Fulvia, the friends of both men would not allow the allegations to be looked into, but reconciled them, and divided up the empire, making the Ionian Sea a boundary, and assigning the eastern provinces to Antony, the western to Caesar; they left Africa to Lepidus.[81] They also agreed that when they preferred not to serve as consuls themselves, the friends of each would hold the office by turns.

31. These terms were considered fair, but it was thought that some

---

80 Two points along the shore of Egypt.

81 "Africa" in this case, as often in ancient usage, does not include Egypt.

stronger guarantee was needed, and this guarantee Fortune provided. Octavia was a sister of Caesar, older than he, but not by the same mother; for she was the child of Ancharia, and he, by a later marriage, of Atia.[82] Caesar was extremely devoted to his sister, who was, as the saying goes, a marvel of a woman. Her husband, Gaius Marcellus, had died not long before, and Antony was now thought to be a widower by the death of Fulvia, though he did not deny his passion for Cleopatra; but he would not acknowledge that she was his wife, his reason, on this point, still battling with his love for the Egyptian. Everyone was promoting this marriage, hoping that Octavia, who in addition to her great beauty had dignity and intelligence, would, when Antony came to know her, and she had won his heart (as such a woman naturally must), restore harmony between all parties and be their salvation. Accordingly, when both men had agreed, they went to Rome and celebrated Octavia's marriage, though the law did not permit a woman to marry until her husband had been dead for ten months. But in this instance the Senate decreed that the restriction should be waived.

32. Sextus Pompeius[83] was in possession of Sicily and was ravaging Italy, and, with many pirate vessels under the command of Menas the pirate and Menecrates, had made the sea unsafe for navigation. But he was believed to be warmly disposed to Antony (for he had received Antony's mother when she fled with Fulvia), and it was therefore thought best to make peace with him. The two men met near the promontory and breakwater of Misenum,[84] Pompey's fleet lying at anchor nearby, and the infantry of Antony and Caesar drawn up along the shore. When they had agreed that Pompey should have

---

82 Plutarch has confused two Octavias; the one discussed here was indeed Octavian's full sister.

83 Pompey's younger son, who was still leading the forces loyal to his father or unhappy with the leading triumvirate. Plutarch refers to him as "Pompey" throughout this chapter.

84 On the Bay of Naples.

Sardinia and Sicily, should keep the sea free of pirates, and should send a fixed amount of grain to Rome,[85] they invited each other to supper. By lot it fell to Pompey to give the first banquet. And when Antony asked him where it was to be held, "There," he replied, pointing to his admiral's ship with its six banks of oars, "for that is the ancestral house to which Pompey is heir." In saying this he was reproaching Antony, who was then in possession of the house that had belonged to Pompey's father.[86] After bringing his ship to anchor and forming a bridge connecting it to the promontory, he gave his guests a cordial welcome. When their party was at its height and jokes were being made about Antony and Cleopatra, Menas the pirate, coming up to Pompey, spoke low to him, so that the others might not hear. "Would you like me to cut the ship's cables and make you master not only of Sicily and Sardinia, but of the whole Roman empire?"[87] Pompey, after considering a little while, replied, "You should have done this, Menas, without speaking to me of it beforehand; let us now be content with things as they are, for I do not break my word." Then Pompey, after being feasted in turn by Antony and Caesar, sailed back to Sicily.

33. After the treaty was made, Antony sent Ventidius ahead into Asia to hinder the advance of the Parthians, while he himself, to gratify Caesar, was appointed priest of the late Caesar.[88] In their state affairs and matters of importance, Antony and Caesar acted in concert and in a friendly spirit; but their competitive pastimes annoyed Antony, since he always came off with less than Caesar. He had with him an Egyptian soothsayer, one of those who calculate natal horo-

---

85 That is, allow the grain to arrive. Sextus had used his huge fleet to cut off shipments to Rome.

86 See chapter 10 and note 26.

87 Since Sextus' fleet was in control of the seas, cutting the flagship's connection to the land would mean taking Octavian and Antony prisoner.

88 After Julius Caesar was officially deified, priests were appointed to supervise his cult worship, and Antony was one of these.

scopes. This man, either to pay court to Cleopatra or dealing honestly with Antony, spoke frankly to him, declaring that his fortune, though bright and glorious, was overshadowed by Caesar's; and he advised him to keep himself as far away as he could from that young man. "For your guardian deity," he said, "dreads his;[89] and though exultant and lofty when it is by itself, when his comes near, yours is humbled and abased by it." And events appeared to show that the Egyptian spoke the truth. For it is said that whenever, for any playful purpose, lots were cast or dice thrown, Antony came off the loser. They often held cockfights and quail-fights, and Caesar's contender was always the victor.

Secretly annoyed at this, Antony paid more attention to the Egyptian, and left Italy, entrusting the management of his home affairs to Caesar. He took Octavia, who had lately borne him a daughter, along with him into Greece. While he was passing the winter at Athens, he received news of the first successes of Ventidius, who had defeated the Parthians in battle and killed both Labienus and Pharnapates, the ablest of King Orodes' generals. To celebrate this, Antony feasted the Greeks and served as gymnasiarch for the Athenians.[90] Leaving his commander's insignia at home, he went forth with the rods of a gymnasiarch, in a tunic and white shoes, and when the young combatants had fought enough, he would take them by the neck and part them.

34. When he was about to set out for the war,[91] he took a wreath

---

89 The "guardian deity" is *daimōn* in Greek, a word impossible to translate because it means so many different things to Plutarch. Here, *daimōn* seems to be an individual deity keeping watch over a person's destiny and expressing its power in what we would call luck.

90 A ceremonial office involving supervision of athletic practices and games. The rods mentioned below allowed the gymnasiarch to enforce his judgments with beatings.

91 The offensive against the Parthians begun by Ventidius (see previous chapter).

from the sacred olive, and, in obedience to some oracle, filled a vessel with water from the Clepsydra to carry along with him.[92] Meanwhile Pacorus, the Parthian king's son, was again advancing with a large army into Syria; but Ventidius engaged and routed him in Cyrrhestica, and slew a large number of his men, Pacorus having fallen among the first. This victory, proving one of the most celebrated achievements of the Romans, fully avenged their defeats under Crassus,[93] and confined the Parthians, who had lost three successive battles, within the bounds of Media and Mesopotamia.[94] Ventidius decided not to pursue the Parthians further, since he feared Antony's jealousy;[95] but he went against those who had revolted from Rome, subjugated them, and besieged Antiochus of Commagene in the city of Samosata.[96] When Antiochus offered to pay a thousand talents and to obey Antony's commands, Ventidius told him to send word to Antony, who was already approaching and would not let Ventidius make terms with Antiochus, wishing that this one exploit at least might be ascribed to him, and that all his successes might not be due to Ventidius. But the siege was prolonged, and when the besieged despaired of a surrender on terms, they defended themselves vigorously. Antony, accomplishing nothing, and feeling ashamed and regretful, was glad to make peace with Antiochus for three hundred talents. Having arranged some minor matters in Syria, he returned

92 The sacred olive of Athena and the well known as Clepsydra were both important landmarks on the Athenian acropolis.

93 See *Crassus* 17–33 for a full account of the disastrous Roman defeat at Carrhae in 53 BCE. The "eagles," or army standards, that the Parthians had seized there had been demanded back on many occasions.

94 That is, east of the Euphrates River.

95 That is, the envy Ventidius might provoke in Antony by winning too great a glory.

96 Commagene was at this time a small Syrian kingdom that had resisted Roman demands for cooperation against Parthia.

to Athens; and after paying Ventidius appropriate honors, he sent him home to receive his triumph.

Ventidius is the only man, down to the present time, who has ever celebrated a triumph for victories over the Parthians.[97] He was of obscure birth, but by means of Antony's friendship he obtained an opportunity to perform great exploits; and by making such glorious use of it he confirmed what was said about Caesar and Antony—namely that they were more successful in campaigns conducted by others than by themselves. For Sossius, Antony's general, accomplished much in Syria, and Canidius, whom Antony left in Armenia, conquered the people there, as well as the kings of the Iberians and Albanians,[98] and marched as far as the Caucasus. And consequently the name and fame of Antony's power increased among the barbarians.

35. But Antony himself, provoked once more against Caesar by certain slanders, sailed with three hundred ships for Italy; and when the people of Brundisium would not admit his forces he brought his ships round to anchor at Tarentum. There, at her own request, he sent Octavia, who had sailed with him from Greece, to her brother. She was pregnant, having already borne her husband another daughter.[99] On her way she met Caesar, and after calling in his two friends Agrippa and Maecenas, besought him with many entreaties and lamentations not to allow her, who had been the happiest of women, to become the most wretched. For now all men's eyes were fixed upon her as the wife of one commander, and the sister of another. "But if,"

---

97 The Roman Senate awarded triumphs to Trajan in AD 115 for victories over the Parthians, so Plutarch must have written the Life of Antony before this date.

98 The people referred to here as Iberians and Albanians are today called Caucasian Iberians and Caucasian Albanians (that is, those dwelling near the Caucasus Mountains), to distinguish them from the separate but probably related groups in modern Iberia and Albania.

99 See chapter 33 for the birth of the first child. Both daughters were named for their father, so the first is referred to as Antonia the Elder, the second as Antonia the Younger.

she said, "the worse should prevail, and war should ensue, though it is not clear which of you will conquer, and which will be conquered, my own case will surely be miserable." Caesar was overcome by these entreaties, and advanced in a peaceable temper to Tarentum, where those who were present witnessed a most stately spectacle—a vast army calmly drawn up on shore, and many ships lying quietly in the harbor, while the commanders and their friends exchanged affectionate greetings. Antony entertained Caesar first, this being a concession on Caesar's part to his sister. And when an agreement was made between them that Caesar should give Antony two of his legions to serve in the Parthian War, and that Antony should give Caesar a hundred bronze-beaked ships, Octavia further obtained from her husband, besides this, twenty light ships for her brother, and from her brother a thousand soldiers for her husband. Having parted thus, Caesar went at once to make war on Pompey,[100] wishing to conquer Sicily, while Antony, entrusting to Caesar's care Octavia, their children, and his children by Fulvia, crossed over into Asia.

36. But the terrible mischief that had long been slumbering—namely his passion for Cleopatra, which was thought to have been lulled and charmed away by better thoughts—took fire again and gathered strength as he approached Syria. And at last, like Plato's restive and rebellious horse of the human soul,[101] he spurned all honorable and wholesome counsel and sent Fonteius Capito to bring Cleopatra into Syria. On her arrival, he made her a present of no small or trifling additions to her domain, namely Phoenicia, Hollow Syria,[102] Cyprus, a large part of Cilicia, the balsam-producing region

---

100 Not Pompey himself but his son, Sextus Pompeius.

101 In the dialogue *Phaedrus*, Plato configures the soul as a chariot drawn by two horses, one mild and tractable and the other, representing the appetites and passions, wild and rebellious. The charioteer, representing the reasoning faculty, must keep control of this second horse in order for the soul to remain healthy.

102 The region called Hollow Syria was distinct from Syria proper, corresponding

of Judaea, and that area of Arabia where the Nabataeans' land slopes toward the sea—gifts that particularly displeased the Romans. Yet he bestowed on many private citizens great governments and kingdoms, and deprived many kings of theirs, for example Antigonus of Judaea, whom he led forth and beheaded, though no other king had ever been punished in this way. Yet the shamelessness of the honors he paid to Cleopatra gave great offense. And he only worsened the scandal by acknowledging as his own the twin children he had by her, naming them Alexander and Cleopatra, and adding, as their surnames, the titles of Sun and Moon. But since he knew how to take pride in shameful deeds, Antony used to say that the greatness of the Roman empire was manifested not by what it acquired, but by what it bestowed; and that noble houses were expanded by the successive begetting of many kings. For in this spirit was his own ancestor begotten by Heracles,[103] who had not limited his succession to a single womb, or feared any laws like those of Solon, which regulate conception, but had indulged his nature and left behind him the beginnings and foundations of many families.

37. After Phraates had killed his father Orodes[104] and taken possession of his kingdom, many of the Parthians fled the country, including Monaeses, a man of distinction and authority, who sought refuge with Antony. Antony likened the man's case to that of Themistocles,[105] compared his own opulence and his magnanimity to those of the Persian kings, and gave him three cities—Larissa, Arethusa, and Hierapolis, which they used to call Bambyce. And when the king of the Parthians

---

roughly to modern Lebanon (the term "Hollow" perhaps referred to the Bekáa valley).

103 See note 10 on Antony's claim of descent from Anton, a seemingly invented son of Heracles.

104 The king of Parthia. His son then ruled as Phraates IV.

105 The Greek general who, after helping defeat the Persians at Salamis, later went over to the Persian side and served under the Persian king (see *Themistocles* 24–31), receiving three cities as the sources of his revenue.

offered to make terms with Monaeses, Antony gladly sent the Parthian back to him (having resolved to deceive Phraates into thinking there would be a peace), and demanded back the standards that had been seized when Crassus was slain, and the prisoners who had survived.[106] He himself, after sending Cleopatra off to Egypt, marched through Arabia and Armenia, where his own forces were joined by those of the allied kings. (Of these there were very many, but the greatest of all was Artavasdes, the king of Armenia, who furnished six thousand horsemen and seven thousand foot soldiers.) Here Antony mustered his army. There were, of the Romans themselves, sixty thousand foot soldiers, and the cavalry marshaled by the Romans, composed of ten thousand Iberians and Celts; of the other nations there were thirty thousand, including horsemen and light-armed troops.

Yet they say that this great preparation and power, which alarmed even the Indians beyond Bactria and set all Asia trembling, proved unprofitable to Antony because of Cleopatra. For he was so eager to spend the winter with her that he began the war prematurely and conducted everything in a confused manner. He was not governed by his reason; instead, as if under the influence of certain drugs or enchantments, he was forever glancing in her direction and thinking more of his speedy return than of conquering his enemies.

38. In the first place, then, though he ought to have wintered in Armenia and given his men a rest, exhausted as they were by a march of eight thousand stades, and to have occupied Media in early spring before the Parthians had left their winter quarters, he lacked the patience to wait so long, but marched onward, keeping Armenia on his left and invading and ravaging the province of Atropatene. Secondly, the engines required for siege warfare were sent after him on three hundred wagons, and among them was a ram eighty feet long; none of these devices, if destroyed, could soon be replaced, since the upper country produces no trees of adequate length or hardness. Nevertheless, he left these behind (on the grounds that

---

106 See note 93 and *Crassus* 17–33.

they would slow him down) in custody of a detachment under the command of Statianus the wagon master. He himself laid siege to Phraata, a large city, in which were the wives and children of the king of Media. But his actual need soon proved how great an error he had made in leaving the engines behind, and he was forced to approach the city and raise a mound against its walls, which entailed much labor and loss of time. Meanwhile Phraates, coming down with a large army, and hearing that the wagons carrying the engines had been left behind, sent a large party of horsemen against them. By these Statianus was surrounded, and he and ten thousand of his men were slain. The barbarians seized the engines and destroyed them. They also took many prisoners, including Polemo the king.[107]

39. This loss, occurring unexpectedly at the opening of the campaign, naturally discouraged all of Antony's men, and Artavasdes the Armenian, despairing of the Romans' prospects, took his own army and departed, though he had been the chief promoter of the war. The Parthians now showed themselves to the besiegers in brilliant array, threatening and insulting them. Antony, therefore, afraid that his soldiers' alarm and dejection would only increase if they remained inactive, took ten legions, three cohorts of heavy-armed praetorians, and all his horsemen, and led them out to forage, thinking that this would most likely draw the enemy into a pitched battle. After advancing a day's journey, he saw that the Parthians were surrounding him and seeking to attack him as he marched. He therefore gave orders for the signal of battle to be displayed in his camp, and after pulling down the tents, as if he meant not to fight but to retreat, he led his men past the line of the barbarians, which was crescent-shaped. He had given orders that whenever the enemy's front lines seemed to be within range of his infantry, his horsemen should charge them. To the Parthians drawn up opposite them, the discipline of the Romans seemed to defy description, and they watched the ranks marching past at equal distances, without uproar, and in silence, brandishing

---

107 Ruler of the Black Sea kingdom of Pontus.

their spears. But when the signal was given, and the Roman horsemen wheeled about toward the enemy, and with loud cries attacked them, the Parthians took the charge, though they were too near for bow shots; when, however, the infantry joined in the attack, with loud shouts and clashing of their arms, the Parthian horses shied and reared away, and the Parthians themselves fled without engaging.

Antony pressed hard in the pursuit, and had great hopes that in that battle he had put an end to the whole war, or to most of it. His infantry kept up the pursuit for fifty stades,[108] and the cavalry for three times that distance; yet when they counted those of the enemy who had fallen or been captured, they found thirty prisoners and eighty corpses. Then they were all filled with despair and dejection; for they considered it a terrible thing that when victorious they had killed so few, but if defeated they would be robbed of as many men as they had lost when the wagons were taken. The next day, after packing up, they marched back toward Phraata and their camp. On the way they met a few of the enemy at first, and then more of them, and finally the entire enemy army, which, as though fresh and invincible, challenged and attacked them from all sides, so that it was only with great difficulty and effort that they got safely to their camp. In the meantime the Medes had made a sally to the mound and put its defenders to flight.[109] Antony was enraged, and punished the shirkers with what is called decimation; dividing the entire force into groups of ten, he put to death the one from each group upon whom the lot fell. For the rest he ordered rations of barley instead of wheat.

40. The war was difficult for both sides, and what was to come was even more to be feared. Antony expected a famine, since it was no longer possible to forage without incurring many wounds and losses. And Phraates, knowing that his Parthians could endure anything rather than winter in the open, was afraid that if the Romans

---

108 About seven miles.

109 See chapter 38 for this mound, a cumbersome means of besieging a walled city in absence of siege engines.

were to persist and remain, his men might desert him, since the air was already growing brisk after the autumnal equinox. He therefore devised the following ruse. Those of the Parthians who were most familiar with the Romans accosted them more gently when they met them foraging, allowed them to carry off some provisions, and praised their valor, saying they were excellent fighters and justly admired by the Parthians' own king. After this, riding up closer and drawing up their horses beside the Romans, they would abuse Antony for his stubbornness, saying that whereas Phraates wished to make peace, and to spare the lives of so many brave men, Antony would give him no opportunity, but sat awaiting the arrival of harsh and powerful enemies—famine and winter—which would make it hard for them to escape even if the Parthians offered to escort them. Many reported this to Antony, who, in hope, began to relent; but he would not send heralds to the Parthian until he had inquired of these friendly barbarians whether what they said reflected the thinking of their king. When they declared that it did, and urged him to have no fear or distrust, he sent some of his companions to demand once more the standards and prisoners, lest he be thought overeager to escape in safety. But the Parthian[110] urged him not to press the point, and declared that if he departed he would at once obtain peace and security. So Antony, within a few days, packed up his baggage and broke camp. But though he was persuasive when addressing a multitude, and surpassed any of his contemporaries in carrying soldiers with him by the force of words, out of shame and sadness he could not find it in his heart to encourage the men himself, but ordered Domitius Ahenorbarbus to do so. Some of the men resented this, thinking Antony despised them, but most were moved to pity when they saw the true cause, and thought it even more incumbent upon them to revere and obey their commander.

41. When he was about to return by the same way he came, which was through a treeless plain, a certain Mardian who was con-

110 Phraates, evidently addressing Roman envoys.

versant with the habits of the Parthians, and whose fidelity to the Romans had been proved in the battle over the siege engines, came to Antony and urged him to keep close to the hills on his right as he fled, and not to expose his men, heavily armed, in a broad and open tract of land, to the attacks of a large force of mounted archers. For this was the very course Phraates had devised when persuading him with friendly promises to raise the siege; the Mardian said that he himself would lead the army by a route that was shorter and supplied with a greater abundance of provisions.

On hearing this, Antony deliberated. He did not wish to seem to distrust the Parthians after their treaty, but since he preferred to take a shorter and more inhabited route, he asked the Mardian for a pledge of good faith. The man offered himself to be bound until he had brought the army safe into Armenia; and upon being bound he led them for two days without incident. But on the third day, when Antony had given up all thought of the Parthians, and was marching at his ease in loose array, the Mardian noticed that a dam of the river had been recently broken down, and that the water released was overflowing the road by which they had to march. He understood that this was the work of the Parthians, who had diverted the river to hinder their march, and he advised Antony to look sharp and be on his guard, since the enemy was nearby. And no sooner had Antony begun to put his men in formation, and arranged for the javelin men and slingers to sally out through them against the enemy, than the Parthians appeared and began to ride round the army in order to encircle and throw it into disarray from all sides. When the light-armed troops sallied out against them, the Parthians inflicted many wounds with their arrows, but sustained just as many from the sling bullets and javelins, and beat a retreat. Soon after, coming up again, they were attacked and scattered by the Celts' cavalry, and their fear deterred them from fighting again that day.[111]

---

111 The translation here reflects the textual emendation of Christopher Pelling.

42. Having learned from this what he should do, Antony not only posted the javelin men and slingers as a rear guard, but also protected both flanks with them, and thus led the army in a square formation; he also ordered the horsemen to drive off the enemy when they attacked, but not to pursue them as they retreated. As a result the Parthians, for the next four days, inflicted no greater losses than they suffered, grew less zealous, and made the winter an excuse to think of returning home.[112]

But on the fifth day Flavius Gallus, a brave and energetic officer of high rank, came to Antony and requested more light-armed troops from the rear, and for some of the horsemen from the front, confident he would achieve a great success. When Gallus obtained the troops and the enemy attacked, he beat them back, not withdrawing, as before, and leading them toward the infantry, but resisting and engaging them more intrepidly. The leaders of the rear guard, seeing that he was being cut off from them, sent to call him back; but he took no notice of them. They say that Titius the quaestor[113] snatched the standards and tried to turn back, reproaching Gallus for risking the lives of so many brave men. But Gallus reproached him in turn and commanded the men with him to stand firm, at which point Titius withdrew. Gallus then thrust his way into the enemy facing him, without noticing that many of them were encompassing him from the rear. But when missiles came flying at him from all directions, he sent and asked for help. Then the leaders of the infantry, including Canidius, a man of the greatest influence with Antony, seem to have made a serious mistake. For whereas they ought to have wheeled the entire phalanx against the enemy, they sent only a few men at a time to assist Gallus, and when these few were overwhelmed they sent out others, so that by their negligence the rout might have spread through the whole army. But Antony

112 That is, used the oncoming winter weather to justify a cessation of hostilities.

113 See the Appendix.

himself soon came up from the vanguard to confront the fugitives, and thrusting through them to reach enemy, he hindered any further pursuit.

43. No fewer than three thousand men died, and five thousand wounded were carried back to their tents, including Gallus, who was pierced with four arrows. He did not recover from his wounds, but Antony went to visit and comfort all the rest, his eyes filling with tears at the sight of them. They, however, with beaming faces, seized his hand and urged him to go and take care of himself and not worry about them, calling him *imperator*,[114] and saying that if he were well they were safe. In short, no other commander of that period seems to have assembled an army superior to his in valor, endurance, and youthful vigor; but the respect, obedience, and affection they felt for their leader, and the unanimous feeling among the renowned and the obscure alike, officers and private soldiers, to prefer his good opinion of them to their own lives and safety, could not have been surpassed even by the ancient Romans. The reasons for this were many, as I have said before: his noble birth, his eloquence, the simplicity of his manners, his munificent generosity, and his lively and gracious conversation; and at the present time, by sharing the toils and sorrows of those suffering, and giving them whatever they needed, he made the sick and wounded more eager for duty than the healthy.

44. The enemy, however, who were worn out and ready to give up, were so encouraged by their victory and felt such contempt for the Romans that they even spent the night near their camp, expecting that they would soon be plundering the empty tents and the baggage of deserters. In the morning, many more forces gathered, and there are said to have been no fewer than forty thousand horsemen, their king having sent those who always surrounded his person, so confident was he that the battle would be a clear and resounding

---

114 The honorific was normally awarded to victorious generals by their troops, but in this case to a defeated one.

success; for he himself was never present at an engagement. Then Antony, wishing to address his soldiers, asked for a mourning robe, that he might appear more pitiable to them, but was dissuaded by his friends; so he came forward in the purple cloak of a general and made his speech, praising those who had been victorious, and chastising those who had fled. The former urged him to take heart, while the latter, making their apologies, offered themselves for decimation or for any other punishment he wished to impose.[115] They asked only that he cease to be anxious and distressed. At this, Antony lifted up his hands and prayed to the gods that if any retribution should follow his former successes, it might fall only upon him, and that the rest of his army might be granted victory and deliverance.

45. On the following day they advanced under better protection; and the Parthians met with a great surprise when they attacked them. For they thought they were marching for plunder and spoils, not battle; and when they encountered many missiles and saw that the Romans were vigorous, fresh, and eager to engage, they themselves began to lose heart. But where the Romans were descending a hill, the Parthians attacked and shot at them as they moved slowly down. Then the Roman shield bearers, wheeling round, enclosed the light-armed troops within their array, while those in the first rank, dropping on one knee, held their shields before them. The rank behind held their shields over the first, and the next rank did the same. The arrangement resembles a roof, and affords a splendid appearance and a perfect defense against arrows, which glance off.[116] The Parthians, however, assumed that the Romans' dropping down to their knees indicated fatigue and exhaustion; so they laid down their bows, took up their spears, and attacked. But the Romans, with a great war cry, leapt to their feet, and striking with their jave-

115 Presumably those who had tried to run off had been apprehended and brought back to camp.

116 The distinctively Roman *testudo* or "tortoise" formation. It was unfamiliar to the Parthians, as is revealed below.

lins slew the foremost Parthians and put the rest to flight. This happened every day thereafter, as the Romans gradually proceeded on their march.

Famine also afflicted the army, which could procure little grain even by fighting and was not well supplied with implements for grinding it. For these had for the most part been left behind, since some of the pack animals died, and the others were carrying the sick and wounded. It is said that an Attic choenix of wheat sold for fifty drachmas,[117] and barley loaves for their weight in silver. And when they turned to vegetables and roots, they found few they were familiar with, and so were forced to try those they had never tasted before, including an herb that produced madness and then death. He who ate it remembered nothing, and thought of nothing but one task, that of moving and turning over every stone, as if he were doing something of the greatest importance. The plain was full of men bowed down to the ground and digging at the stones and moving them from place to place. Finally, vomiting bile, they died, since the only antidote, wine, was no longer available. When many were perishing in this way, and the Parthians would not relent, Antony was often heard to exclaim, "O the Ten Thousand!" as if marveling at Xenophon's army, which made an even longer journey from Babylon, fighting with an army many times as large, and yet came away safe.[118]

46. The Parthians, finding that they could not entangle the Roman army or even disrupt its line of battle, and having already been so often defeated and put to flight, began again to mingle

117 The Attic choenix was about the equivalent of a liter. The price given here is several hundred times the normal cost of grain.

118 The reference is to the march of the ten thousand Greek mercenaries who were stranded deep inside Persian territory after their employer, Cyrus the Younger, was killed in battle (401 BCE). Xenophon, one of the leaders of the expedition, later wrote an account of it (the *Anabasis*) after most of the troops had fought their way back to Greece.

peaceably with those who came out to forage for provisions; and pointing to their unstrung bows, they said that they themselves were going home and that this was the end of their retaliation, though a few of the Medes would follow for one or two days, not to give them any trouble, but to defend some of the villages farther on. These words were accompanied by embraces and a great show of friendship, so that the Romans again took heart, and Antony, on hearing of it, was more disposed to take the road through the plains, since the route through the mountains was said to be waterless. But as he was preparing to do so, a man reached their camp from the enemy, Mithridates by name, a cousin of the Monaeses who had been with Antony and had received the three cities as a gift. Mithridates asked that someone come to converse with him who could speak the Parthian or Syrian language. And when Alexander of Antioch, a friend of Antony, was brought to him, Mithridates, explaining who he was and mentioning Monaeses as the person who wished to do the favor, asked Alexander if he saw in the distance a range of lofty hills. When Alexander replied that he did, Mithridates said, "Under those hills the Parthians, with all their forces, are lying in wait for you. For these hills border the great plain, and the Parthians expect to trick you into turning in that direction and abandoning the route through the mountains. It is true that the mountain route involves thirst and toil, to which you have become accustomed; but let Antony know that if he passes through the plains he must expect the fate of Crassus."

47. So saying, the man departed, and Antony, alarmed by what he had heard, called together his friends and the Mardian guide,[119] who was of the same opinion as Mithridates. For he knew that even without enemies the lack of roads through the plains would likely cause them to wander blindly and lose their way; whereas the other road, though rough, had no difficulty other than lack of water for a single day. Antony therefore took this route and led his army along

119 The same Mardian who appeared in chapter 41.

it by night, after commanding his men to carry water with them. But as most of them had no vessels, some filled their helmets with water and carried them, while others filled skins.

But as soon as they started, the news was brought to the Parthians, who followed them, contrary to their custom, while it was still night. At sunrise they attacked the rear-guard of the Romans, who were exhausted by sleeplessness and toil. For they had covered two hundred forty stades[120] in the night, and were disheartened by the swift and unexpected approach of the enemy. And the struggle only increased their thirst; for they had to defend themselves and make their way forward at the same time. The foremost ranks arrived at a river, the water of which, though cool and clear, was salty and poisonous. On being drunk it produced instant pains, cramping of the bowels, and an inflammation of one's thirst. Of this the Mardian had also forewarned them, but nonetheless the men forced away those who tried to stop them, and drank. Antony went around and begged them to hold out for a little while; for not far ahead was a river of potable water, and the rest of the way was too rough for the cavalry, so that the enemy would certainly turn back. At the same time, he called back those who were fighting, and gave the signal to make camp, that the soldiers might at least get the benefit of some shade.

48. The Romans set about pitching their tents, while the Parthians, according to their custom, began at once to withdraw. Then Mithridates came back to the Romans, and after Alexander had joined him he advised Antony to give the army no more than a brief rest, and then to set it in motion and hasten to the river, assuring him that the Parthians would not cross it, but would pursue them only so far. After relaying this message, Alexander brought out many of Antony's golden drinking cups and bowls. Mithridates took as many as he could conceal in his clothes and rode away. While it

---

120 A distance of thirty miles, too great to be covered by exhausted troops over rough terrain.

was still day, the army broke camp and set off on their march. The Parthians did not harass them; but that night, by their own doing, was the most wretched and terrible that they passed. For they set about killing and robbing those who had gold or silver, and ransacked the goods from the beasts of burden. At last, laying hands on Antony's baggage carriers, they cut to pieces all his costly tables and cups, distributing the fragments among themselves.

Antony, hearing such confusion and movement here and there throughout the army (for it was thought that the enemy had attacked and was routing and dispersing them), called for Rhamnus, one of his freedmen, then serving as one of his guards, and made him swear that whenever the order was given he would run his sword through Antony's body and cut off his head, that Antony might not be taken alive by the enemy, nor, when dead, be recognized. Antony's friends burst into tears, but the Mardian sought to cheer and encourage them, insisting that the river was near: for a breeze wafting from it was moist, and the air, growing cooler, was easier to breathe; and the time that had elapsed during their march confirmed his estimate of the distance, since the night was almost over. At the same time, others came to report that the confusion in the camp arose only from their own violence and robbery among themselves. Antony, therefore, wishing to bring the throng back into some order after their wandering and distraction, commanded that the signal be given for a halt.

49. Day was already dawning, and the army was starting to assume a certain order and tranquility, when Parthian arrows began to fall upon the rearmost ranks, and the light-armed troops were ordered to battle. The heavy-armed infantry, again covering one another as they had done before with their shields, withstood their attackers, who did not dare to come any closer. The front ranks advanced slowly in this manner, and the river came into view. Arraying his horsemen on its bank to confront the enemy, Antony sent his sick and wounded over first. By now even those who were fighting were able to drink at their ease. For when the Parthians saw the river,

they unstrung their bows and urged the Romans to cross over freely, offering many compliments in praise of their valor. Having crossed without trouble, they rested awhile and then marched onward, placing no trust at all in the Parthians. On the sixth day after their last battle they arrived at the river Araxes, which divides Media and Armenia, and which seemed, both by its depth and turbulence, to be hard to cross; a rumor also spread among them that the enemy was lying in ambush there and would attack them as they were trying to cross. But when they got safely to the other side and set foot in Armenia, they kissed the ground, just as if they had caught sight of that land from the open sea, and fell to weeping and embracing one another in their joy. Yet as they advanced through that prosperous country they gorged themselves after great scarcity, and fell sick with dropsies and dysenteries.

50. There Antony held a review of his forces, and found that twenty thousand foot soldiers and four thousand horsemen had perished, not all at the hands of the enemy, but more than half from diseases. They had marched twenty-seven days from Phraata and had beaten the Parthians in eighteen battles, though their victories were not decisive or lasting, since the pursuits were brief and ineffective. And this made it perfectly clear that it was Artavasdes the Armenian who had robbed Antony of the goal of that war.[121] For if the sixteen thousand horsemen whom he had led back from Media had been present, equipped like the Parthians and accustomed to fighting them, and if those horsemen, when the Romans had routed the enemy, had slain the fugitives, it would not have been possible for the enemy to have rallied after their defeats and renewed their attacks so often. The entire army, therefore, in their anger, tried to incite Antony to take vengeance on the Armenian. Yet Antony, employing his reason, chose not to reproach Artavasdes for his treachery, but continued to express his former affection and respect, since his army was now exhausted and in need of provisions. Afterward, however, when

121 The Armenian cavalry departed from Parthia in chapter 39.

he again invaded Armenia, and with many invitations and promises prevailed upon Artavasdes to meet him, Antony arrested him and brought him in shackles to Alexandria, where he celebrated a triumph. And in doing so he greatly offended the Romans, who felt that for Cleopatra's sake he was bestowing all the honors and rites of his own country upon the Egyptians. This, however, occurred at a later time.

51. But now, marching in haste in the dead of winter through continual snowstorms, he lost eight thousand of his men. He himself came down to the sea[122] with a small party, and in a place called the White Village, between Sidon and Berytus, he awaited the arrival of Cleopatra. When she was delayed he grew fretful and distraught, and soon gave himself up to wine and drunkenness, though he could not endure to remain at table for long but would often leap up to see if she were coming. At last she put into port, bringing plenty of clothing and money for the soldiers (though some say that Antony received only the clothes from her, and distributed his own money in her name).

52. A quarrel now arose between the king of the Medes and Phraates the Parthian. It began, as they say, over the division of the Roman spoils, but it made the Mede suspicious and afraid that he would lose his kingdom. He therefore sent word inviting Antony to come, promising to join him in the war with his own force. Antony, accordingly, was full of hope. For the one thing that he thought had prevented him from subjugating the Parthians previously—namely, his lack of a large number of horsemen and archers—he now saw offered to him, and he would be granting and not requesting a favor. He therefore made immediate preparations to march inland through Armenia, where he would join the Medes at the river Araxes and then launch the war.

53. But in Rome Octavia was eager to sail to Antony, and Caesar

122 The Mediterranean, at the Levantine coast (the Berytus mentioned later in the sentence is modern Beirut).

gave her permission to go to him, not so much, as most writers say, to gratify her, as to obtain a reasonable pretext for war in the event she were mistreated or neglected. When she arrived at Athens, she received letters from Antony in which he urged her to remain there and informed her that he was marching inland. And she, though disappointed, and aware that this was a pretext, nevertheless wrote to him to learn where she should send the things she was bringing to him. For she was conveying a great quantity of clothes for his soldiers, many pack animals, money and gifts for his friends and officers, and two thousand picked soldiers equipped with splendid armor, to form praetorian cohorts. This message was brought from Octavia to Antony by Niger, one of his friends, who added to it praises that were appropriate and well deserved.

But Cleopatra, sensing that Octavia was coming to challenge her at close quarters, feared that if her rival added to the nobility of her character and the power of Caesar the pleasure of her companionship and her devotion to Antony, she would become irresistible and acquire complete mastery over her husband. So she pretended to be madly in love with Antony herself, and made herself slender by a light diet. Her glance, when he entered the room, was rapturous, and when he left, seemed downcast and despondent. She took care to be often seen weeping, and then would quickly wipe the tears away and try to conceal them, as if she wished him to be unaware of them. Such was her conduct while he was planning to go up from Syria to the Mede. And her lackeys, busy on her behalf, would reproach Antony for being hard-hearted and unfeeling, and for destroying a woman who depended on him and him alone. For Octavia, they said, had married him for the sake of her brother's affairs, and enjoyed the name of wedded wife; but Cleopatra, the queen of so many nations, was called Antony's beloved, and did not shun or scorn the name while she could see him and live with him; but if she were deprived of this, they said, she would not survive the loss. And finally, they so melted and unmanned him that, believing she might throw her life away, he returned to Alexandria, putting off the Mede until the summer, though the Parthians were said to be roiled by internal strife. Nevertheless, he eventually journeyed into Media and made an alliance with the king; and after engaging one of his sons by Cleopatra to the king's daughter, who was still very young, he returned, his thoughts taken up with the civil war.

54. When Octavia, who was thought to have been poorly treated, returned from Athens, Caesar ordered her to live in her own house. But she refused to leave the house of her husband, and even entreated Caesar—unless he had already, on other grounds, resolved to make war on Antony—to ignore Antony's treatment of her, since it would be ignoble even to hear it said of the two greatest commanders in the world that they had involved the Romans in a civil war, the one out of passion for a woman, the other out of resentment of her. These were her words, and her deeds proved them to be sincere. For she lived in Antony's house as if he were at home in it, and took the finest and most generous care of his children, not only of those by her, but of those by Fulvia as well. She also received all the friends of Antony who were sent to Rome to seek office or on business, and helped them to obtain from Caesar what they requested. But without her intending it, this behavior damaged Antony: he was hated for injuring such a woman. He was also hated for the distribution that he made to his children in Alexandria, which seemed theatrical, arrogant, and contemptuous of Rome. For after filling the exercise ground with a throng, and having two golden thrones placed on a platform of silver, one for himself and the other for Cleopatra, and other lower thrones for their children, he began by proclaiming Cleopatra Queen of Egypt, Cyprus, Libya, and Hollow Syria;[123] and she was to share the sovereignty with Caesarion, who was thought to be the son of the former Caesar—the man who had left Cleopatra pregnant. Secondly, he proclaimed his own sons by Cleopatra Kings of Kings; to Alexander he allotted Armenia, Media, and Parthia (as soon as it should be conquered); to Ptolemy, Phoenicia,

123 See note 102.

Syria, and Cilicia. At the same time Alexander was brought out in Median dress, which included a tiara with upright peak,[124] Ptolemy in boots, short cloak, and *kausia* adorned with the diadem; for this was the dress of the kings who succeeded Alexander,[125] as the other was of the Medes and Armenians. And when the boys had embraced their parents, the one received a bodyguard of Armenians, the other of Macedonians. Cleopatra was then, as at other times when she appeared in public, dressed in a robe sacred to Isis; she used to give audiences as the New Isis.[126]

55. Caesar, by reporting these things to the Senate, and often complaining to the people, tried to excite the multitude against Antony, and Antony also sent countercharges against Caesar. The gravest of his charges were these: first, that after taking Sicily from Pompey, Caesar had not given a share of the island to him; second, that after borrowing ships from him for the war, he had kept them for his own use; third, that after deposing and dishonoring his colleague Lepidus, he was keeping for himself the army, territory, and revenues that had been assigned to Lepidus; and lastly, that he had parceled out almost all Italy among his own soldiers, and left nothing for Antony's. Caesar replied to these charges by saying that he had deposed Lepidus for misconduct in office; and that what he had acquired in war he would divide with Antony as soon as Antony gave him a share of Armenia. For Antony's soldiers had no claim on Italy, being in possession of Media and Parthia, the countries they had added to the Roman empire by their brave struggles under their commander.

---

124 The tiara or felt hat, when worn upright, symbolized royal status in Media.

125 The so-called Diadochs or Successors, former generals of Alexander who made themselves kings, wore a diadem or headband as a crown, in imitation of Alexander. The *kausia* was a distinctive Macedonian cap.

126 The Ptolemaic queens had long been associated with the Egyptian goddess Isis, but the title "New Isis" carried this association to an unprecedented level.

56. Antony was in Armenia when this answer reached him, and he immediately sent Canidius with sixteen legions toward the sea.[127] He himself, with Cleopatra, went to Ephesus, where his naval forces were converging from all quarters—eight hundred warships with merchant vessels, of which Cleopatra furnished two hundred, together with twenty thousand talents and provisions for the whole army during the war. Antony, however, on the advice of Domitius and some others, urged Cleopatra to sail to Egypt and there await the war's outcome. But she, fearing that Octavia would effect some new reconciliation, persuaded Canidius with considerable sums to speak in her favor with Antony, pointing out that it was neither just to drive away from the war a woman who was making such generous contributions, nor expedient to discourage the Egyptians, who were so large a part of his naval forces; nor was it easy to see how Cleopatra fell short in prudence of any of the kings who were serving with him, since she had long governed a great kingdom by herself, and from long association with Antony had learned to manage public affairs. These arguments carried the day, since everything was destined to fall into Caesar's hands;[128] and when all their forces had met, they sailed together to Samos, where they gave themselves up to merrymaking. For just as all the kings, potentates, governors, nations, and cities between Syria, Lake Maeotis, Armenia, and Illyria had been ordered to send or convey their equipment for the war, so were all the theatrical artists required to make an appearance at Samos; so that while nearly all the world around was filled with groans and lamentations, this one island for many days resounded with piping and harping, theaters filling, and choruses competing. Every city sent an ox for the sacrifice, and kings vied with one another in their mutual feasts and presents. And men

127 That is, the Mediterranean. The objective was to confront Octavian militarily.

128 As he does at *Demosthenes* 19 and elsewhere, Plutarch here suggests that the course of history is somehow predetermined or guided by divinity.

began to ask themselves how the conquerors would celebrate their victories, when they held such extravagant festivities at the opening of the war.

57. These festivities over, Antony gave Priene to Dionysus' Artisans[129] as a place to live, and sailed to Athens, where he occupied himself again with amusements and spectacles. Meanwhile Cleopatra, jealous of Octavia's honors in the city (for Octavia was deeply beloved by the Athenians), tried with many benefactions to gain the people's favor. They, in turn, decreed her public honors, and sent ambassadors to her house conveying the decree; among them was Antony, since he was now a citizen of Athens. Standing before her, he made a speech on behalf of the city; and to Rome he sent men to have Octavia removed from his house. They say she departed and took all of Antony's children with her except his eldest son by Fulvia (for he was with his father), weeping and grieving that she might be looked upon as one of the causes of the war. But the Romans felt pity not for her but for Antony, and particularly those who had seen that neither in beauty nor youth was Cleopatra superior to Octavia.[130]

58. When Caesar heard of the speed and scale of Antony's preparations, he was distressed, afraid that he might be forced to fight the decisive battle that summer. For he lacked many necessities, and people resented the collecting of taxes, free men being required to pay a fourth part of their income, and freed slaves an eighth of their property; so there were loud outcries against Caesar and disturbances throughout Italy. Hence people consider Antony's postponement of the war to be one of his greatest mistakes, since he allowed Caesar time to make his preparations and for the disturbances to die down. For while people were having their money levied, they were provoked; but once they had paid it, they were quiet. Meanwhile Titius and Plancus, friends of Antony who were of consular rank, finding

---

129 The name of a theatrical society or guild. Members of such guilds often lived together in small settlements.

130 The two women were at this point both about thirty-seven.

themselves maligned by Cleopatra (for they had been vehemently opposed to her taking part in the expedition), ran away to Caesar and informed him of the contents of Antony's will, with which they were familiar. This will had been deposited with the Vestal Virgins, who would not give it to Caesar when he asked for it; they told him that if he wanted it he should come and take it himself, which he did. First he read through it by himself and marked certain blameworthy passages; then, convening the Senate, he read it aloud, though most of the senators were aghast at his doing so, thinking it strange and dreadful to call a man to account for what he wished to have done after his death. Caesar drew particular attention to what Antony had said in the will about his burial. For he had ordered that even if he died in Rome, his body, after being carried in state through the Forum, should be sent to Cleopatra in Alexandria. Calvisius, a companion of Caesar, brought the following charges against Antony in connection with his behavior toward Cleopatra: he had given her the libraries of Pergamum, which contained twenty thousand separate scrolls;[131] at a banquet attended by many he had stood up and rubbed her feet, to fulfill some pact or promise; he had permitted the Ephesians, in his presence, to hail Cleopatra as mistress; and frequently, while seated on the tribunal and hearing the cases of princes and kings, he would receive love notes from her written on tablets made of onyx and crystal, and would read them openly; and once when Furnius was speaking, a man of great prestige and the cleverest orator in Rome, Cleopatra was carried in a litter through the Forum, and Antony, when he saw her, started up and left the trial, clinging to her litter and attending her on her way.

59. Calvisius, however, was thought to have invented most of these stories. The friends of Antony went about in Rome entreat-

---

131 The library at Pergamum, in what is now Turkey, was far smaller than that at Alexandria, but Alexandria's had suffered losses in a fire of 48 BCE. As master of Rome's Asian provinces, Antony apparently (if the will described here is genuine) felt he had the right to dispose of the Pergamene library's contents.

ing the people on his behalf, and sent one of their number, Germinius, to beg him not to allow himself to be voted out of his office and proclaimed an enemy of Rome. But Germinius, after sailing to Greece, was looked upon with suspicion by Cleopatra, who thought he was acting in Octavia's interests. He was always made the butt of jokes at supper and was given the least honorable places at table; but he bore all of this well and waited for an opportunity to speak with Antony. Commanded at supper to say what business had brought him there, he said that everything else had better wait until he was sober, but there was one thing he *could* say, whether sober or drunk—namely that all would be well if Cleopatra were sent to Egypt. And when Antony lost his temper at this, Cleopatra said, "You have done well, Germinius, to admit the truth without being put on the rack."[132] So Germinius, after a few days, ran away to Rome. With their drunken behavior and buffoonery, Cleopatra's flatterers drove away many other friends of Antony, including Marcus Silanus and Dellius the historian. Dellius says he was afraid of a plot against him by Cleopatra, of which he had been informed by Glaucus the physician. For he had offended Cleopatra at supper by saying the present company was being served sour wine, while Sarmentus, at Rome, drank Falernian.[133] (Sarmentus was one of Caesar's little boyfriends—his *deliciae*, as the Romans call such a person.[134])

60. When Caesar had made sufficient preparations, a decree was enacted to wage war against Cleopatra and to deprive Antony of the authority that he had handed over to a woman. Caesar added that

---

132 The comment refers to the custom at Rome of torturing slaves to get legal testimony from them. Thus Cleopatra demeans Germinius by reducing his status to that of a slave.

133 Falernian wine, produced on the slopes of Mt. Falernus in central Italy, was a highly prized vintage.

134 Plutarch here transliterates into Greek a Latin term of endearment that has distinct sexual overtones.

Antony was under the influence of drugs and not even master of himself,[135] and that the war against the Romans would be conducted by Mardion the eunuch, and Potheinus, and Eiras, Cleopatra's hairdresser, and Charmion, by whom the chief affairs of state were administered.

The following signs are said to have been observed before the war. Pisaurum, a city colonized by Antony near the Adriatic, was swallowed up after chasms opened up beneath it. Sweat dripped from one of the marble statues of Antony at Alba for many days, and though wiped away, it did not cease. When Antony himself was staying in Patrae, the Heracleium was struck by lightning, and at Athens the figure of Dionysus in the Battle of the Giants, buffeted by the winds, tumbled down into the theater.[136] (Antony associated himself both with Heracles, from whom he professed to be descended, and with Dionysus, whose way of life he imitated, as I have said; and he was called the young Dionysus.) The same storm fell upon the colossal statues of Eumenes and Attalus at Athens, which were inscribed with Antony's name[137] and were the only ones, among many, to be overturned. And on Cleopatra's flagship, which was called the *Antonias*, a dreadful omen occurred. Some swallows had built their nest under the stern; but other swallows came, drove the first away, and destroyed their nestlings.

61. When the forces gathered for the war, Antony had no fewer than five hundred battle-ready ships, including many eighters and tenners,[138] proudly and showily arrayed; he also had a hundred thou-

---

135 The implication here seems to be that Cleopatra had used love potions on Antony.

136 The sculpture group at Athens, affixed to the south wall of the Acropolis, depicted a mythic battle between gods and giants. The Heracleium at Patrae was a temple dedicated to Heracles.

137 Eumenes and Attalus were kings of Hellenistic Pergamum. Antony may have inscribed his name on the bases of their statues to claim them as his own memorials, a regular practice at this time.

138 "Eighters" and "tenners" here presumably refer to the number of men

sand foot soldiers and twelve thousand horsemen. Of the subject kings who fought on his side there were Bocchus of Libya, Tarcondemus of Upper Cilicia, Archelaus of Cappadocia, Philadelphus of Paphlagonia, Mithridates of Commagene, and Sadalas of Thrace. These were with him in person; from Pontus Polemo sent an army, as did Malchus from Arabia, Herod the Jew, and Amyntas, the king of Lycaonia and Galatia; the king of the Medes also sent an auxiliary force. Caesar had two hundred fifty warships, eighty thousand foot soldiers, and about as many horsemen as his enemies. Antony's empire extended from the Euphrates and Armenia to the Ionian Sea and Illyria; Caesar's, from Illyria to the western ocean, and from the ocean back to the Tyrrhenian and Sicilian Seas.[139] Of Africa, Caesar had the coastal territories opposite Italy, Gaul, and Spain as far as the Pillars of Hercules, and Antony the provinces from Cyrene to Ethiopia.

62. But Antony was now to such an extent a mere appendage of the woman that though he was far superior to the enemy on land, he wanted the victory to be gained at sea, to please Cleopatra, even though he could not fail to see that for lack of crews his captains were pressing every sort of person into service from a Greece "that hath suffered much":[140] wayfarers, mule drivers, reapers, and boys; and that even then their ships were not filled, but remained for the most part undermanned and poorly sailed. Caesar, on the other hand, had ships that had been built not for grandeur or show but for service, being maneuverable, swift, and fully manned. Keeping this fleet at Tarentum and Brundisium, Caesar sent messages to Antony urging him not to prolong the war but to come out with his forces; he himself would provide him with safe

---

pulling each oar in the galleys of the ships, but it's not clear just how the terms should be interpreted.

139 The Tyrrhenian Sea refers to the Adriatic, not to the modern-day Tyrrhenian.

140 The short quote, from Euripides' tragedy *Heracles* (line 1250), adds to the portentousness of the moment before battle.

roadsteads and harbors for his fleet, and would withdraw his forces inland from the sea to a distance a horseman can cover in a day, keeping them there until Antony had safely disembarked his army and pitched his camp. Antony, matching this bold language, challenged Caesar to single combat, though he was older than Caesar; and if Caesar declined the challenge, Antony proposed that they fight at Pharsalus, as Caesar and Pompey had done before.[141] But while Antony was lying at anchor off Actium, where Nicopolis now stands, Caesar anticipated him by crossing the Ionian Sea and occupying a place at Epirus called the Ladle. And when Antony and his friends were disturbed by this, since their land forces had been delayed, Cleopatra, in mockery, said, "What is so awful about Caesar sitting on a ladle?"[142]

63. But Antony, seeing the enemy sailing up at daybreak, and afraid that his ships might be captured for lack of soldiers on board, armed the rowers and stationed them on the decks to make a good show; he had the rows of oars spread like wings on either side[143] and drew the ships up at the mouth of the gulf near Actium, their prows toward the enemy, as if they were properly manned and ready for an engagement. And Caesar, deceived by this stratagem, withdrew. Antony was also thought to have shown considerable skill in cutting off the drinking water from the enemy by certain barriers, since there was little water elsewhere in the neighborhood, and its quality was poor. And his conduct toward Domitius, despite Cleopatra's

---

141 For the battle of Pharsalus in 48 BCE, see *Caesar* 44–49 and *Pompey* 68–72.

142 There may be an obscene pun in Cleopatra's comment, since the Greek word she uses for "ladle" is occasionally found as a slang term for penis. It is not clear that Plutarch was aware of the double meaning.

143 Antony's warships would normally have had armed soldiers on deck for boarding enemy vessels, but these seem not to have embarked or were not available. Since the rowers were used in their place, the oars were "spread like wings" to disguise the fact that they were not manned.

opposition, was generous. For when Domitius, already in a fever, got into a little boat and went over to Caesar, though Antony resented it, he nevertheless sent after him all his baggage with his friends and servants. And Domitius, as if the exposure of his faithlessness and treachery had prompted a change of heart, instantly died.

There were also defections of kings, Amyntas and Deiotarus going over to Caesar. And since his fleet was unfortunate in all its undertakings and always unready to offer assistance, Antony was again forced to give his attention to the land forces. Canidius too, who commanded the land army, when he saw its danger, changed his mind and advised Antony to send Cleopatra away, then withdraw to Thrace or Macedonia and let a battle on land decide the issue. For Dicomes, the king of the Getae, promised to aid them with a large army, and it would be no disgrace to yield the sea to Caesar, who had gained such expertise fighting at sea in the Sicilian War; but it would be strange for Antony, who in land battles was the most experienced commander of his day, to make no use of the strength and equipment of his numerous infantry, but to disperse and squander his forces by parceling them out in the ships.

Cleopatra, however, prevailed with her view that the war should be decided in a sea battle, since she already had her eye on flight and was disposing her own forces not where they would be helpful for gaining a victory, but where they could escape with the greatest ease in the event of a defeat.

There were two long walls extending from the camp to the station of the ships, and between these Antony used to pass back and forth without suspecting any danger. But a slave told Caesar that it would be possible to catch Antony as he went down between the walls, and Caesar sent men to lie in ambush for him. These men nearly succeeded, but they caught only the man who came just before Antony, since they rose up too quickly. Antony himself narrowly escaped by running.

64. When it had been decided to fight at sea, Antony set fire to all

the Egyptian ships except sixty;[144] of these he manned the best and largest (ranging from triremes to tenners),[145] and embarked twenty thousand heavy-armed soldiers and two thousand archers. It was then, they say, that an infantry centurion, who had fought in many of Antony's battles and whose body was covered with scars, cried out to Antony as he was walking by, and said, "Commander, why do you distrust these wounds and this sword, and pin your hopes on these rotten timbers? Let Egyptians and Phoenicians fight at sea, but give us the land, where we are accustomed to take our stand, and either conquer or die." To this Antony made no answer, but merely urged the man by a gesture and a look to take heart, and passed on. Yet his hopes were not high; for when the pilots wished to leave their sails behind, he forced them to put them aboard, saying that not one of the enemy should be allowed to escape.[146]

65. That day and the three following, the sea was so agitated by a gale that the fleets could not engage; but on the fifth the wind dropped, the sea grew calm, and they joined battle. Antony commanded the right wing with Publicola, Coelius the left, and in the center were Marcus Octavius and Marcus Insteius. Caesar assigned his left wing to Agrippa, keeping the right for himself. As for the land forces, Canidius commanded for Antony, Taurus for Caesar, both armies drawn up in order along the shore. And as for the leaders themselves, Antony visited all his ships in a rowboat, advising his soldiers, in view of the weight of their ships, to stand firm and fight as steadily as if they were on land. He ordered the captains to receive the assaults of the enemy

---

144 Antony did not have enough crewmen to row these ships, and did not want them to fall into Octavian's hands.

145 Triremes were smaller warships propelled by 170 oars.

146 Warships would normally leave their sails on land when putting out to sea for a battle, trusting only to oar power. Plutarch assumes Antony was planning his own flight when he kept sails on board while pretending that he meant to speed the pursuit of a fleeing Octavian.

as if they were at anchor, and maintain their position at the entrance of the port, which was a narrow and difficult passage.

It is related that Caesar, leaving his tent and going round to visit his ships while it was still dark, was met by a man driving an ass and asked him his name. The man, who had recognized Caesar, replied, "My name is Fortunate, and my ass's name is Conqueror." Hence when Caesar afterward adorned the place with the beaks of the ships, he erected a bronze statue of this man and an ass. After inspecting the rest of his array, he went in a boat to his right wing and marveled at the enemy lying perfectly still in the narrows, looking as if they were riding at anchor. For a long time, convinced that this was actually the case, he kept his own ships at a distance of eight stades from the enemy. But about midday a wind rose up from the sea, and Antony's men, chafing at the delay, and trusting to the height and size of their own ships, as if they were invincible, put their left wing in motion. Seeing this, Caesar was overjoyed, and ordered his own right wing to backwater, wishing to draw the enemy even farther from the gulf and the narrows, and then to surround them with his own more maneuverable vessels and fight at close quarters against ships that, owing to their size and their smaller crews, were slow and hard to manage.

66. When they engaged, there was no ramming or even crushing of ships, since Antony's, on account of their great bulk, lacked the momentum that chiefly made the blows from beaks effectual; while Caesar's not only guarded against charging hard bronze armor[147] head-on, but did not even dare to ram the sides of the enemy's ships. For the beaks of his own ships would easily have been shattered by colliding with vessels built of enormous square timbers bound together with iron. The struggle therefore resembled an infantry battle; or, to speak more accurately, an assault on a walled city. For three or four of Caesar's ships would converge on one of Antony's, and the

147 That is, the bronze-reinforced prows.

soldiers used wicker screens, spears, poles, and flaming projectiles; and Antony's soldiers fired their catapults from wooden towers.[148]

And when Agrippa extended the left wing with the intention of surrounding the enemy, Publicola, being forced to advance against him, was cut off from the center, which fell into disarray and engaged with Arruntius.[149] But the outcome was still undecided, and the battle equal, when suddenly the sixty ships of Cleopatra were seen hoisting sail for a full flight out to sea, right through the ships that were engaged. For her fleet had been stationed behind the large ships, and threw them into disorder as it broke through. The enemy watched in amazement as her ships sailed off with a favoring wind toward the Peloponnese. Here it was that Antony made clear that he was governed by the motives not of a leader or of a brave man, or even by his own judgment; instead, just as someone jokingly said that the soul of a lover lives in someone else's body, he was dragged along by the woman as if he had been born part of her, and must go wherever she went. For as soon as he saw her ship sailing away he forgot everything, betrayed and ran away from those who were fighting and dying for him, and went aboard a quinquireme,[150] taking with him only Alexas of Syria and Scellius, to pursue the woman who had already begun his ruin and would in due course complete it.

67. Recognizing his vessel, Cleopatra raised a signal on her ship; and as soon as Antony came up he was taken on board, though he neither saw her nor was seen by her, but went forward to the bow and sat down by himself in silence, holding his head in both hands. At that point some Liburnian ships[151] were seen pursuing them from

---

148 Ship-mounted catapults stood atop wooden platforms, hardly the "towers" Plutarch refers to here; he had no clear understanding of military technology.

149 Arruntius commanded the central section of Octavian's fleet.

150 An especially large warship.

151 Small, light vessels designed for rapid pursuit.

Caesar's fleet; but Antony, giving orders to face about, repelled all of them except that of Eurycles the Spartan, who attacked violently, brandishing a spear from the deck, as if he meant to hurl it at Antony. And when Antony, standing at the prow, said, "Who is this that pursues Antony?," the man replied, "I am Eurycles, son of Lachares, blessed by Caesar's fortune to avenge my father's death." (Lachares, condemned for a robbery, had been beheaded by Antony.) Eurycles did not attack Antony's ship but rammed the other admiral's ship (for there were two) with his bronze beak, spun it around, and seized it as it turned sideways, along with one of the other ships, in which there were costly household goods. When Eurycles departed, Antony resumed the same posture and sat silent. He spent three days by himself at the prow, either because he was angry with Cleopatra or ashamed to see her. At the end of that time they put in at Taenarum.[152] Here Cleopatra's chambermaids first got them to speak to each other and afterward persuaded them to eat and sleep together.

And before long, several of their transport ships and some of their friends began to assemble around them after the defeat, reporting that the fleet had been destroyed, but that the land army, they thought, still stood firm. Antony sent messengers to Canidius, commanding him to march the army with all speed through Macedonia into Asia. He himself, planning to cross from Taenarum to Libya, chose one of the merchant ships that was carrying plenty of coined money and valuable royal trappings in silver and gold, and gave it to his friends, urging them to divide up the treasure and save themselves. When they refused his kindness with tears in their eyes, he comforted them and entreated them with great goodness and humanity, and then sent them off, having written to Theophilus, his steward in Corinth, that he should provide for their security and keep them concealed until they were able to make their peace with Caesar. This Theophilus was the father of Hipparchus, who had the

---

152 At the southern tip of the Peloponnese, the last way station in mainland Greece before the crossing to Egypt.

greatest influence with Antony, but was the first of his freedmen to go over to Caesar. Hipparchus settled afterward at Corinth.

68. Such, then, was Antony's own situation. Meanwhile, at Actium, his fleet, after resisting Caesar for a considerable time and being badly damaged by the high sea that rose up against it, gave up the contest, though reluctantly, at four in the afternoon. There were no more than five thousand dead, but three hundred ships were captured, as Caesar himself has written.[153] Only a few were aware of Antony's flight; and those who were told of it could not at first believe that he had gone away and left nineteen legions of undefeated foot soldiers and twelve thousand horsemen, as though he had not often experienced both good and evil fortune and were not trained by reverses in countless struggles and wars. His soldiers had a longing for him and an expectation that he would soon appear from some place or other; and they showed such fidelity and courage that even after his flight had become evident they kept together for ten days, ignoring the messages sent to them by Caesar. But finally, when Canidius their general had run away by night and abandoned the camp, the soldiers, bereft of everything and betrayed by their commanders, went over to the conqueror.

After this, Caesar sailed to Athens, where he made a settlement with the Greeks and distributed among their cities what remained of the provision of grain after the war; these cities were in a miserable condition, despoiled of their money, slaves, and beasts of burden. My great-grandfather Nicarchus,[154] at any rate, used to relate that all his fellow citizens were required to carry a certain measure of wheat on their shoulders to the sea at Anticyra,[155] and were hurried along

---

153 Augustus published an autobiography (now lost) about a decade after Actium. The number of captured ships Plutarch gives here conflicts with chapter 64, where Antony burned all but sixty; there is no clear way to reconcile the two passages.

154 Presumably, this story was passed down through Plutarch's family, though perhaps it was told directly by Nicarchus to a young Plutarch. See also note 76.

155 Anticyra, on the Gulf of Corinth, lies over twenty miles from Chaeronea, across rough terrain.

by men with whips. They had made one trip of this kind, and when the second load had been measured out and they were about to put it on their shoulders, news came that Antony had been defeated, and this saved the city; for Antony's stewards and soldiers immediately fled, and the citizens divided the grain among themselves.

69. When Antony had reached the Libyan coast, he sent Cleopatra on from Paraetonium into Egypt, while he himself enjoyed a boundless solitude, roaming and wandering about with two friends, one a Greek—Aristonocrates, a rhetorician—and the other a Roman—Lucilius—of whom I have written elsewhere. Lucilius was at Philippi, and in order to give Brutus time to escape, pretended to be Brutus and surrendered to his pursuers. For this his life was spared by Antony, and he remained true and faithful to him to the end.

When the general to whom Antony had entrusted his forces in Libya deserted to Caesar, Antony resolved to kill himself, but was hindered by his friends. And on reaching Alexandria he found Cleopatra engaged in a bold and important enterprise. The isthmus that divides the Red Sea from the Egyptian Sea and separates Asia from Africa measures three hundred stades across at the place where it is most hemmed in by the two seas and has the smallest width.[156] Over this neck of land Cleopatra proposed to haul her fleet, set it up in the Arabian Gulf, and settle outside Egypt with her soldiers and her considerable wealth, thus escaping war and slavery.[157] But since the Arabians near Petra were burning the first ships that were hauled over, and Antony assumed that his army at Actium still held

---

156 The isthmus of Suez, today cleft by the Suez Canal, is in fact more than twice as wide as Plutarch here supposes (three hundred stades are about thirty-eight miles). Ships could theoretically be hauled across such distances after being broken up into sections.

157 The waters of what was then termed the Arabian Gulf (the modern-day Red Sea) were known to connect with the Indian Ocean, but few Roman ships had as yet operated in either body of water.

together, she desisted, and guarded the approaches to Egypt. But Antony, leaving the city and the companionship of his friends, built himself a dwelling in the sea near Pharos,[158] on a causeway he threw out across the water. And there he lived, an exile from mankind, and said he was content to live the life of Timon,[159] since his experience was the same; for he too had been wronged by his friends, who had treated him with ingratitude, and he therefore hated and distrusted all mankind.

70. Timon was a citizen of Athens, and lived at the time of the Peloponnesian War, as one may gather from the plays of Aristophanes and Plato,[160] in which he is lampooned as an ill-tempered misanthrope. But though he avoided and repelled all fraternizing, he would kiss Alcibiades, who was then young and bold, and show him great affection. And when Apemantus expressed surprise at this, and asked the reason for it, Timon replied that he knew this young man would do great harm to Athens.[161] This Apemantus was the only man Timon would occasionally admit into his company, since Apemantus was like him and tried to adopt his way of life. And once, during the Choes festival,[162] when these two feasted together, and Apemantus said, "What a fine party we're having, Timon," Timon

---

158 Pharos was a small island in the seas off Alexandria, famous for its magnificent lighthouse.

159 A famous hermit of classical Athens, as explained below.

160 The Plato mentioned here is a comic playwright of the fifth century BCE, not the philosopher. Aristophanes' extant comedies have two mentions of Timon: *Birds* 1549 and *Lysistrata* 809–15. The more detailed account of Timon that Shakespeare relied on for *Timon of Athens* came from the dialogue *Timon* by the Greek satirist Lucian of Samosata, Plutarch's contemporary.

161 See chapter 16 of Plutarch's *Alcibiades* for another version of the story. Timon's misanthropy here leads him to take delight in greeting the agent of Athens' downfall.

162 The "festival of pitchers," held on the second day of the Anthesteria, a festival devoted to Dionysus.

replied, "It would be if you weren't here." It is also reported that once when the Athenians were holding an assembly, he went up to the speaker's platform, and the strangeness of this spectacle produced silence and great expectation; then he said, "I have a small plot of ground, men of Athens, and in it grows a fig tree, on which many of my fellow citizens have hanged themselves. So now, as I am planning to build on that site, I wish to announce it publicly, so that any of you who wish to do so may hang yourselves before the fig tree is cut down." When he had died and was buried at Halae, near the sea, the stretch of shore in front of his tomb slid away, and the sea, flowing in and surrounding it, made it inaccessible to man. It bore this inscription:

Here, after ending a luckless life, I lie.
You won't learn my name; but go, you wretches, and wretchedly die!

This epitaph he is said to have composed himself; the one that is more generally known is by Callimachus:[163]

Here dwell I, Timon the misanthrope.
Go past my grave and lament me, stranger—only go.

These are a few of many anecdotes about Timon.

71. Canidius now came in person to report the loss of the forces at Actium, and Antony received word that Herod of Judaea had gone over to Caesar with some legions and cohorts, and that the other princes were likewise deserting him, and that nothing remained of his power outside Egypt. Yet none of these things disturbed him;

---

163 Poets in antiquity often composed fictional epitaphs, almost always in elegiac couplets (as is this one), for famous people. Callimachus, a Greek poet of the second century BCE, may have written an epitaph for Timon, but the one Plutarch quotes here is in fact elsewhere attributed to a different writer, Hegesippus. The speaking voice in these epitaphs is usually that of the dead person, addressing those visiting his or her tomb.

instead, as if he were glad to put away all hope, that he might also put away all worry, he abandoned his residence by the sea, which he called Timoneum, and when he had been received into the palace by Cleopatra, diverted the city with feasts, drinking bouts, and distributions of gifts, registering among the ephebes the son of Cleopatra and Caesar, and bestowing upon Antyllus, his son by Fulvia, the toga without the purple border,[164] in honor of which Alexandria was occupied in banquets, revels, and festivities for many days. Antony and Cleopatra dissolved their famous Order of the Inimitables and founded another, not inferior in splendor, luxury, and extravagance, calling it that of the Partners in Death. For their friends enrolled themselves as those who would die together, and spent their time enjoying a regular succession of banquets. Cleopatra, meanwhile, was occupied in collecting all sorts of deadly poisons and testing them for painlessness by having them administered to prisoners condemned to death. When she saw that the quick-acting ones induced painful deaths, while the gentler ones acted slowly, she next tried wild animals, observing them as they attacked one another. This she did every day; and by testing nearly all of them she found that only the bite of the asp brought on a sleepiness and lethargy, without convulsions or groans, producing only a gentle sweat on the face, while the faculties were easily relaxed and clouded, and resisted all efforts to arouse and revive them, as happens with those who are fast asleep.

72. At the same time they also sent ambassadors to Caesar into Asia,[165] Cleopatra asking for the sovereignty of Egypt for her chil-

---

164 Antony marked the coming of age of the two boys, both now in their teens, in different ways: Ceasarion (reportedly the son of Julius Caesar) was accorded a Greek-style ritual, Antyllus a Roman one. In chapter 54, Antony had treated his sons by Cleopatra as heirs to different parts of the world and had dressed them accordingly.

165 "Asia" refers here (as it often does in Plutarch) to the Roman province so named, consisting largely of the western portion of Anatolia. Octavian had moved his fleet to Samos and Ephesus after Actium.

dren, and Antony proposing that he live as a private man in Athens if he were not welcome to do so in Egypt. But because of their lack of friends and the distrust aroused by desertions, Euphronius, the children's teacher, was sent on this embassy. For Alexas the Laodicean,[166] who had become acquainted with Antony in Rome through Timagenes and had more influence with him than any other Greek, and who had been Cleopatra's most forceful instrument against him and had undermined any notions that might arise in his mind in Octavia's favor, had been sent to dissuade Herod from deserting; but after remaining there and betraying Antony he had the temerity to come into Caesar's presence, relying on Herod's support. Herod, however, was unable to help him, for Alexas was immediately taken into custody and sent in shackles to his own country, where, by Caesar's orders, he was put to death. Such was the penalty he paid for his disloyalty while Antony was still alive.

73. Caesar would not listen to any proposals about Antony, but he replied to Cleopatra, saying that there was no reasonable treatment she would fail to obtain if she put Antony to death or cast him off. Along with the messengers he sent one of his own freedmen, Thyrsus, a man of no little intelligence, and not at all incompetent to convey messages from a youthful general to a woman who was haughty and astonishingly proud of her beauty. This man, who was granted longer audiences with Cleopatra than anyone else, and received special honors from her, aroused the suspicion of Antony, who had him seized, whipped, and sent back to Caesar with a written message to the effect that Thyrsus, by his insolence and impertinence, had irritated him at a time when his misfortunes made him easily irritated. "But if this offends you," he wrote to Caesar, "you have my freedman Hipparchus; hang him up and whip him, and we'll be even." Thereafter Cleopatra, to absolve herself and allay Antony's suspicions, lavished extraordinary attentions upon him. Her own birthday she held modestly, in keeping with their circumstances; but his

---

166 Evidently a different person than the Alexas mentioned in chapter 67.

she celebrated with outstanding splendor and extravagance, so that many of the guests invited to the supper sat down poor and went away rich. Meanwhile, Caesar was being called home by Agrippa, who wrote him frequently from Rome, saying that his presence was urgently required there.

74. And thus there was a pause in the war. But when the winter was over, Caesar himself set out again through Syria, his generals through Libya.[167] When Pelusium[168] was taken, there was a rumor that Seleucus had given it up, not without Cleopatra's consent.[169] But Cleopatra permitted Antony to have Seleucus' wife and children put to death. She had caused to be built, near the Temple of Isis, a number of tombs and monuments of surpassing loftiness and beauty; there she collected the most valuable of the royal treasures, gold, silver, emeralds, pearls, ebony, ivory, and cinnamon, as well as a large quantity of torch wood and tow, with the result that Caesar feared for the treasures. Concerned that the woman might, in a fit of desperation, set fire to these riches and destroy them, he regularly sent her certain assurances that she would be treated kindly, even as he advanced with his army toward the city. But when he took up a position near the hippodrome, Antony came out against him, fought brilliantly, routed Caesar's cavalry, and pursued them as far as their camp. Glorying in the victory, he entered the palace, still in his armor, kissed Cleopatra, and presented to her the soldier who had fought with the greatest zeal. She gave him as a prize of valor a golden breastplate and helmet. The man accepted the gifts, but deserted that night to Caesar.

75. Antony again challenged Caesar to single combat, but Caesar

---

167 The army and fleet Octavian had used at Actium had wintered in Anatolia, and now proceeded south down the Levantine coast toward Egypt; fresh troops were brought east through North Africa.

168 At the mouth of the Nile.

169 Plutarch neither endorses nor rejects the idea that Cleopatra was planning to join Caesar's side and abandon Antony.

replied that Antony had many ways to end his own life.[170] Then Antony, reflecting that there was no better death for him than by battle, decided to attack by land and sea at the same time. And at supper, it is said, he ordered his servants to pour out more freely and feast him more generously, since it was unknown whether tomorrow they would be doing the same, or whether they would be serving other masters, while he himself lay on the ground, a dried corpse and a nothing. Seeing his friends weeping at these words, he said he would not lead them to a battle in which he sought an honorable death rather than safety or victory.

It is said that on that night, near the middle of it, when the city was quiet and despondent, anxiously awaiting what was to come, the sound of all sorts of instruments was suddenly heard, and the roar of a crowd, accompanied by joyous cries and satyric leapings, as if a tumultuous band of revelers were leaving the city. They seemed to be making their way through the middle of the city to the gate that faced the enemy, and there the uproar became loudest, and then passed out. Those who sought to interpret the sign believed that the god whom Antony had always tried most to copy and imitate had now deserted him.[171]

76. At daybreak, Antony posted his infantry on the hills in front of the city and watched his ships advancing to attack the enemy; and there he remained, waiting to see what they would accomplish. But as soon as the fleets drew near to each other, his men saluted Caesar's troops with their oars, and when their salute was returned, they changed sides, so that all the ships, forming into a single fleet, sailed toward the city. No sooner had Antony seen this than he was deserted by his cavalry, which went over to Caesar; and after his infantry had been defeated, he retired into the city, crying out that

---

170 That is, Antony should not recklessly throw his life away in a single fight with Octavian.

171 The sounds suggested a Bacchic procession like the ones that followed the god Dionysus.

he had been betrayed by Cleopatra to those against whom he had fought for her sake. She, fearing his anger and his madness, fled to her tomb and let down its doors, which were fortified with bars and bolts, and then sent messengers to tell Antony that she was dead. He, believing it, and saying to himself, "Why delay any longer, Antony? Fate has taken away your only remaining pretext for desiring to live," went into his chamber. And there, loosening and undoing his armor, he said, "O Cleopatra, I am not troubled to lose you, for I shall soon be with you; but I am distressed that so great a commander should be found inferior to a woman in courage."

Antony had a faithful servant named Eros, whom he had formerly engaged, should the need arise, to kill him, and now he asked him to fulfill his promise. Eros drew his sword, and held it out as if he meant to strike, but instead, turning his face away, slew himself. When he had fallen at his master's feet, Antony said, "Well done, Eros! You teach me how to do what you could not do yourself"; and striking himself through the belly, he dropped to the couch. But the wound was not immediately fatal. And since the blood stopped flowing when he lay down, he soon came to himself and entreated those who were there to strike the death blow. But they fled from the chamber, and left him crying out and struggling, until his secretary, Diomedes, came from Cleopatra with orders to bring him into her tomb.

77. When he realized that she was alive, Antony eagerly ordered his servants to raise him up, and he was carried in their arms to the door of her building. Cleopatra would not open the door,[172] however, but showed herself from a window, and let down ropes and cords. To these Antony was fastened, whereupon she and her two women, whom alone she had admitted with her to her tomb, pulled him up. Those who were present say that nothing was ever more pitiable than that sight. Smeared with blood and struggling against death, he was drawn up, stretching out his hands to her even as

172 Probably in fear that she would be taken alive by traitors.

he was hanging from hers. It was no easy task for the women; and Cleopatra, clinging to the rope, the strain visible in her face, with great difficulty pulled him up, while those below encouraged her with their cries and shared her agony. When she had thus got him up and laid him on the bed, she tore her clothes over him, beat and lacerated her breasts with her hands, wiped some of his blood on her face, called him master, husband, and commander, and nearly forgot her own sorrows in her pity for his. Antony, stopping her lamentations, asked for a drink of wine, either because he was thirsty, or in the hope that it would speed his demise. When he had drunk, he advised her to look to her own safety, if this could be done without disgrace, and, among the friends of Caesar, to rely most on Proculeius; and he urged her not to pity him for his last reverses, but to consider him blessed for the happiness he had known, since he had become the most illustrious of men, had attained the most power, and in the end had fallen not ignobly, a Roman conquered by a Roman.

78. Just as he died, Proculeius arrived from Caesar. For when Antony had wounded himself, and was being carried to Cleopatra, one of his bodyguards, Dercetaeus, took Antony's sword, concealed it, and slipped away; running to Caesar, he was the first to bring him word of Antony's death, and showed him the bloodied sword. At this, Caesar retired into his tent and wept for a man who had been related to him by marriage, his colleague in office, and companion in many struggles and undertakings. Then, taking the letters they had exchanged, he summoned his friends and read the letters aloud, showing how reasonably and fairly *he* had written, and what coarse and arrogant answers he had always received. After this he sent Proculeius to do all he could to get Cleopatra alive into his power; for he was fearful about her treasures[173] and thought it would enhance the glory of his triumph if she were led

---

173 Octavian thought Cleopatra was preparing to destroy the treasures (see chapter 74).

in the procession. She, however, refused to put herself in Proculeius' hands; but she conferred with him when he had approached her monument and posted himself outside a door that was on a level with the ground. The door was strongly barred, but they could hear each other's voice. Thus they conversed, she requesting that sovereignty be given to her children, he urging her to take heart and trust Caesar in everything.

79. After inspecting the place, he brought word back to Caesar, and Gallus was sent to have a second meeting with her. Coming to the door, he purposely prolonged the conversation, while Proculeius placed a ladder and went in by the window through which the women had received Antony. Then, with two servants, he went straight down to the door where Cleopatra was conversing with Gallus. One of the two women who were confined with her cried out, "Wretched Cleopatra, you are taken prisoner!" At this the queen turned around, saw Proculeius, and tried to stab herself; for she had in her girdle a pirate's dagger. But Proculeius ran up to her quickly, threw both his arms around her, and said, "Cleopatra, you are wronging both yourself and Caesar by trying to rob him of a great occasion to show his clemency, and by misrepresenting the gentlest of commanders as a faithless and implacable enemy." He took the dagger from her, and at the same time shook out her dress to see whether she was concealing any poison. Thereafter Epaphroditus, one of Caesar's freedmen, was sent to her with orders to take the strictest precautions to keep her alive, but otherwise to do all he could to promote her ease and pleasure.

80. Caesar himself now drove his chariot into the city, conversing with Areius the philosopher, to whom he had given his right hand, so that the man might at once be conspicuous among the citizens and admired for the splendid honor paid to him by Caesar. After Caesar had entered the gymnasium and mounted the rostrum that had been specially built for the occasion, the people were stricken with fear, and prostrated themselves before him. Ordering them to stand, he said he acquitted the people of all blame, first, for the

sake of Alexander, their founder;[174] second, because he admired the beauty and size of the city; and third, to gratify his friend Areius. This honor Areius received from Caesar, and at his request Caesar pardoned many other men, including Philostratus, a man whose ability to speak extemporaneously surpassed that of any sophist who ever lived, though he improperly tried to pass himself off as belonging to the Academy.[175] Caesar therefore detested the man's character, and refused to hear his entreaties. So Philostratus, growing a long white beard and donning a gray cloak, would follow behind Areius, forever intoning this verse:

The wise save the wise, if they are wise.[176]

When Caesar learned of this, he issued a pardon, more from a desire to free Areius from ignominy than Philostratus from fear.

81. As for Antony's children, Antyllus, his son by Fulvia, was betrayed by his tutor Theodorus and put to death; and after the soldiers had cut off his head, the tutor stole the precious stone the boy wore around his neck and sewed it into his own belt; and though he denied the fact, he was convicted and crucified. Cleopatra's children, with their attendants, were kept under guard and treated handsomely. Caesarion, on the other hand, who was said to be the son of Julius Caesar, was sent by his mother with a large sum of money through Ethiopia into India;[177] but Rhodon, another tutor

---

174 Alexander the Great had chosen the site for Alexandria and ordered its construction about three centuries before this. Alexander's mummified body had lain in state in the city since shortly after his death.

175 The reference is probably to the Platonic Academy at Athens. Philostratus evidently had pretensions to philosophic wisdom, even though he was in fact merely a talented rhetorician.

176 The meter suggests this line came from a lost tragedy, but its source is unknown.

177 An unlikely route; perhaps Cleopatra intended that some intrepid ship

like Theodorus, persuaded him to go back, declaring that Caesar intended to make him king. But when Caesar was pondering the matter, Areius is said to have remarked,

Not a good thing is a multitude of Caesars.[178]

82. So afterward, when Cleopatra was dead, Caesarion was put to death by Caesar. As for Antony, many kings and generals asked to give him funeral rites; but Caesar would not take his corpse from Cleopatra, and it was buried by her hands with royal splendor, since she had been permitted to arrange everything as she pleased. But as a result of her great grief and pain (for her breast was inflamed and ulcerated by the blows she gave herself) she fell into a fever, which she welcomed as a pretext to abstain from food, and thereby release herself from life without interference. She had a physician in her circle, Olympus, to whom she told the truth, and asked his advice and help in making her body waste away, as Olympus himself has related in a narrative of these events that he published. But Caesar, suspecting her intention, proceeded to assail her with threats and fears about her children, and by these she was overpowered, as if by siege engines, and submitted her body to those attending her to be treated and nourished as they wished.

83. A few days later, Caesar himself came to visit and comfort her. She was lying on a shabby pallet, wearing only her tunic, but leapt up as he entered and flung herself at his feet, her hair and face in wild disarray, her voice trembling, and her eyes sunk in her head. Many marks of the blows she had given herself were visible about her chest, and altogether her body seemed no less afflicted than her

---

would take Caesarion through the Red Sea and Arabian Sea and along the coast of Iran, but the journey was a long and perilous one.

178 The quote is a clever spoof of a line of Homer's *Iliad*, in which Odysseus declares that a multitude of *leaders* is a bad thing; the word *polukaisariê* has been substituted for Homer's *polukoiraniê*.

spirit. Yet her famous charm and the boldness of her beauty were not entirely extinguished, but, in spite of her present condition, still shone out from within, and manifested themselves in the play of her features. When Caesar had urged her to lie down[179] and had sat down beside her, she launched into a justification of her actions, attributing what she had done to the necessity she was under, and to fear of Antony. But when Caesar, on each point, made objections, and she found herself refuted, she quickly changed her tone and sought to arouse his pity by entreaties, as one who at any cost clings to life. And at last, as she had with her a list of all her treasures, she gave it to him; and when Seleucus, one of her stewards, pointed out that she was concealing and attempting to steal some of them, she sprang up, caught him by the hair, and showered many blows on his face. And when Caesar smiled and tried to stop her, she said, "Is it not a terrible thing, O Caesar, that, when you have deigned to visit and speak to me in my sorry state, my slaves should denounce me for setting aside a few women's trinkets, not meant, surely, to adorn my wretched self, but so I may give some little gifts to your Octavia and Livia,[180] that by their intercession I may find you more mild and merciful?" Caesar was pleased with her words, being now altogether assured that she wished to live. And therefore, telling her that he would entrust these ornaments to her, and that in other matters his honorable treatment of her would exceed her every hope, he went away, thinking that he had deceived her, but in fact was himself deceived.[181]

---

179 Apparently Octavian felt concern that Cleopatra, in her depleted condition, was overexerting herself. His primary objective at this stage was to keep her alive so that she could be displayed in his triumph back in Rome.

180 Octavian's sister and wife, respectively.

181 The deception lay not in the false motive for keeping the treasures but in the false impression Cleopatra gave that she wished to live. Plutarch perhaps implies that the whole episode involving the treasures had been staged by Cleopatra to make Octavian less vigilant in his suicide watch.

84. Now among Caesar's companions there was a distinguished youth named Cornelius Dolabella. He was not on bad terms with Cleopatra and now sent word to her in secret, as she had asked him to do, that Caesar was about to march with his infantry through Syria, and had decided to send her and her children off[182] within three days. On hearing this, she entreated Caesar to let her pour libations for Antony; and when the request was granted, she had herself conveyed to the tomb, and there, accompanied by her women, she embraced his coffin and said, "Beloved Antony, I buried you just lately with hands that were still free, but now I pour libations[183] as a captive, and am closely guarded, lest with blows or lamentations I mar this body of mine—that of a slave—and make it less fit for the triumph that will mark your fall. Do not expect other honors or libations. These are your last from the captive Cleopatra. Nothing could part us while we lived, but in death it seems that we will change places: you, the Roman, lying here, I, the wretched woman, in Italy, having got only that much of your country.[184] But if any of the gods below have might and power—those above have betrayed us—do not abandon your wife while she lives, do not let me be led in the triumph over you, but hide me here with you and bury me beside you, since not one among all my countless misfortunes is so great and awful as this brief time that I have lived apart from you."

85. Having made these lamentations, she wreathed and kissed the coffin, and gave orders to prepare her bath. After bathing, she

---

182 That is, to Rome, to be exhibited in a triumphal procession.

183 Pouring small offerings of wine or honey to the dead was a Greek rite of mourning, more typical in settings where the deceased had been buried beneath the earth than, as here, interred in an aboveground sarcophagus.

184 There seems to be an evocation here of an idea, stressed by other authors but not by Plutarch, that Cleopatra meant to be queen in Rome; instead of possessing the whole land, she will now have only a grave-sized portion.

reclined and took a splendid meal. Someone arrived from the country bringing her a basket; and when the guards asked him what it contained, he opened it, took out the leaves, and showed them a bowl full of figs. When the guards admired the beauty and size of the figs, the man smiled and invited them to take some; and they, trusting him, told him to carry them in. After her meal, Cleopatra sent to Caesar a tablet that was already written and sealed; and then, dismissing everyone but her two women, she shut the doors.

When Caesar opened the tablet and found mournful prayers and entreaties that he bury her with Antony, he soon guessed what had happened. At first he thought to go himself and give aid; then he sent others to investigate. But the death had been quick. For though his men came on the run, and found that the guards were unaware of anything amiss, on opening the doors they found her lying dead on a golden couch, arrayed in her royal ornaments. Of her women, the one called Iras was dying at her feet, while Charmion, already tottering and hardly able to hold up her head, was adjusting the diadem around her mistress's head. And when someone said angrily, "Fine work, Charmion," she replied, "The finest indeed, and becoming to the descendant of so many kings." Saying nothing more, she fell there beside the couch.

86. It is said that the asp was brought in with those figs and covered with the leaves, in accordance with Cleopatra's orders, so that the creature might bite her before she was aware of it. But when she took away some of the figs and saw it, she said, "So here it was, after all," and held out her bare arm to be bitten.[185] Others say that the asp was kept in a water jar, and that she provoked and irritated

185 All ancient writers who attributed Cleopatra's death to an asp bite believed she had been bitten on the arm. Shakespeare, in *Antony and Cleopatra*, indicated two snakebites, one on the arm and the other on the breast; perhaps he relied on testimony by Galen, the Greek medical writer, that in Alexandria it was common to execute criminals by applying a venomous snake to the chest.

it with a golden spindle until it sprang and seized her arm. But no one knows the truth, since it was also said that she carried poison in a hollow hairpin, which she kept hidden in her hair. Yet no discoloration or other sign of poison appeared on her body. Nor was the creature seen inside the chamber, though people said they saw something like the trail of it near the sea, at a place visible from the chamber's windows. And some relate that Cleopatra's arm was seen to have two faint puncture marks; and this is the account Caesar appears to have believed. For in his triumph there was carried an image of Cleopatra, with an asp clinging to her. Such are the various accounts.

But Caesar, though disappointed by the death of the woman, admired her nobility of mind, and gave orders that her body should be buried beside that of Antony with regal splendor and magnificence. Her women also received honorable burial by his orders. When Cleopatra died, she had lived thirty-nine years, during twenty-two of which she had reigned as queen, and for more than fourteen had been Antony's partner in power. Antony, according to some, was fifty-six, according to others, fifty-three years old. His statues were all thrown down, but those of Cleopatra remained in place; for Archibius, one of her friends, gave Caesar two thousand talents to save them from the fate of Antony's.

87. Antony left seven children by his three wives, of whom only Antyllus, the eldest, was put to death by Caesar. Octavia took the rest and brought them up with her own. Cleopatra, his daughter by Cleopatra, was given in marriage to Juba, the most accomplished of kings;[186] and Antony, his son by Fulvia, attained such high favor that, while Agrippa held the first place with Caesar, and the sons of Livia the second,[187] the third both was, and was thought to be,

---

186 Juba II was king of Mauretania, a Roman client state in North Africa.

187 Livia, wife of Octavian (later called Augustus), had two sons from a previous marriage, Tiberius and Drusus.

held by Antony. (Octavia had two daughters by Marcellus and one son, also named Marcellus, whom Caesar made both his son and his son-in-law;[188] he gave one of Octavia's daughters to Agrippa. But when Marcellus died soon after his marriage, and Caesar was at a loss to find among his other friends a son-in-law he could trust, Octavia proposed that Agrippa should divorce her own daughter and marry Caesar's. Caesar was persuaded first, then Agrippa, at which point Octavia took back her own daughter and married her to the young Antony, and Agrippa married Caesar's daughter.[189]) Of the two daughters Octavia had borne to Antony,[190] one was married to Domitius Ahenobarbus, and the other, Antonia, famous for her beauty and prudence, was married to Drusus, the son of Livia and stepson of Caesar. Of these parents were born Germanicus and Claudius. Claudius later reigned; and of the children of Germanicus, Gaius, after ruling in an illustrious manner[191] for a short time,

---

188 That is, Octavian (by then known as Augustus) both adopted Marcus Claudius Marcellus and married him to his daughter, Julia. Octavia, sister of Octavian, who has been encountered elsewhere in this *Life* as the wife of Antony, had first been married to the elder Marcellus (Gaius Claudius Marcellus).

189 These complex marital arrangements were part of Augustus' efforts to establish a line of succession ("find . . . a son-in-law he could trust") following the death of Marcellus, his most promising heir, in 23 BCE. Having begotten no sons, Augustus married his top general, Agrippa, to his daughter, but this move required that Agrippa first divorce Augustus' niece (Octavia's daughter). That niece was then remarried to Antony, son of Mark Antony, perhaps in an effort to make that young man a potential successor, should the two more obvious candidates—Agrippa and Augustus' stepson Tiberius—not survive. In the end both Agrippa and Antony predeceased Augustus, and Tiberius succeeded.

190 Both named Antonia (see note 99), though Plutarch, to avoid confusion, gives only one (Antonia the Younger) that name.

191 Gaius Caesar is better known to modern readers by his nickname, Caligula. Plutarch's characterization of his reign may seem surprising, but

was killed with his wife and child, and Agrippina, who had a son by Ahenobarbus,[192] Lucius Domitius, was married to Claudius Caesar. And Claudius, having adopted Domitius, gave him the name of Nero Germanicus.[193] He, becoming emperor in our time,[194] killed his mother, and by his madness and folly came close to ruining the Roman empire. He was fifth in descent from Antony.[195]

Gaius did indeed govern ably, and with huge popular support, for two years, before his madness began to emerge. Some editors, however, emend the text slightly here such that it reads "in an insane manner."

192 Son of the Domitius Ahenobarbus mentioned just above.

193 Known to us as Nero.

194 Nero reigned from AD 54 to 68, during Plutarch's teens and early twenties.

195 This family tree of descendants extends over a far longer span of time than other closing chapters of Plutarch's *Lives*. Plutarch seems intrigued by the fact that Marc Antony's line included three Roman emperors, two of whom became destructively insane.

APPENDIX: THE ROMAN CONSTITUTION

J. E. LENDON

The intricacy of the Roman constitution of the late Republic is the result of the conservatism of the Romans, who layered new institutions over old while discarding as little as possible of what they had before. The powers of the magistrates (the collective terms for various high officials) can be imagined as evolving from those of Rome's early kings, who possessed *imperium*, the semimagical absolute power to lead their people in war. Those kings were also priests or magi with *auspicium*, the power to investigate the will of the gods on matters of state. Finally, they also served as judges in disputes between their subjects. The kings were advised by a body called the Old Men—the Senate—drawn from the elderly heads of families. But in 509 BCE, the Romans expelled their kings and split the royal power between two annual elected officials, the consuls, who were elected by the army voting in its military units (this was the origin of the *comitia centuriata*, one of the Republic's four assemblies). The consuls retained the king's religious functions related to warfare, but his other sacred duties were distributed among the senators, who could serve in one of several colleges of priests, of which the most important were those of the *pontifices* (led by the *pontifex maximus*) and the augurs. The consuls also inherited the king's judicial functions, which they exercised especially on military campaigns; but, because they were so frequently on campaign, the Roman legal system that evolved subsequently came to rely upon other magistrates—praetors—as well.

A short time after the expulsion of Rome's kings, a small number of the oldest Roman families secured acceptance of their claim that they alone could perform the sacred rites of the city: this gave these patricians, as they were called, exclusive access for a period to the consulship and Rome's important priesthoods, and allowed them to become a ruling caste, scorning marriage with outsiders. But soon the rest of the population, the plebeians, and especially the rich and prominent among them, agitated for greater participation and pressed their claims by departing not infrequently from the city to inhabit a nearby hill, where they ruled themselves with institutions of their own: an assembly of the plebeians (the *concilium plebis*) and plebeian officers, the tribunes of the plebs (eventually ten in number). This assembly, unlike the *comitia centuriata* (the army assembly), voted by territorially based tribes, of which the Romans by 241 BCE had thirty-five; its decrees were called *plebiscita* (plebiscites).

This "conflict of the orders" between patrician and plebeian was gradually resolved by admitting plebeians (slowly, because of genuine religious anxiety) into offices and priesthoods previously limited to patricians, by allowing intermarriage between the two groups, and by simply adding the plebeian institutions and officers to the existing patrician constitution and authorizing them to speak for the entire Roman *populus*. In this way plebiscites were (by a law of 287 BCE) decreed to be binding on all Romans and the intercessory powers of the tribunes of the plebs came to protect any citizen threatened by a magistrate and to have the capacity to freeze, by veto, any matter of public business. Early on, the Romans also met and voted in a tribal assembly, the *comitia tributa*, in which both patricians and plebeians participated. The distinctions among these three assemblies (*comitia centuriata*, *comitia tributa*, and *concilium plebis*) and a fourth, the ancient curiate assembly (*comitia curiata*, used in the late Republic for religious purposes only) are rarely noted, much less understood, by Greek authors of the imperial period such as Plutarch.

The patrician magistracies multiplied over time, but in each case came to be opened to plebeians as well. The mid-fourth century BCE saw the election of two censors to establish a list of Roman citizens and their property, award public contracts, revise the membership of the Senate, and rebuke the immoral. Censors were elected every five years and served only as long as it took to complete their duties; the office was confined to patricians for its first century.

The same generation saw the first election of a patrician praetor, to whom *imperium* was granted to lead armies, as the consuls could, but whose legal role in the city gradually came to dominate the definition of the magistracy. The praetor himself could judge, but in accordance with Roman legal tradition usually "spoke the law" through his edict, laying out the legal principles and procedures to be followed during his year in office, and functioned more as a gatekeeper and director of legal traffic, defining the legal and factual matters at issue and sending litigants to private judges, rather than judging cases in his own right. Soon this office too was opened to plebeians, and a century later a second praetorship was established, dividing legal business into cases between Romans, presided over by the city praetor—the *praetor urbanus*—and those between Romans and non-Romans, seen to by the peregrine praetor (*peregrinus* being the Latin for "foreigner"). After Rome won the first Punic War against Carthage (264–241 BCE) and established Sicily as its first territorial province, a third praetor was created and sent to govern it, and thus, as the size of Rome's directly governed dominions increased, so did the number of praetors, eventually rising to eight under Sulla and sixteen under Julius Caesar.

Quaestors, who existed under the kings, were probably also initially patrician, but by the middle of the fifth century BCE the function of the office was reconstrued as financial (especially to assist a consul as quartermaster) and four quaestors were thenceforth elected in the *comitia tributa*. Sulla would raise their number to twenty, Julius Caesar to forty. In contrast, only one plebeian office was added, and like the tribunate could never be held by a patrician. This was the plebeian aedileship, established in the early fifth century, two "building wardens" who, in addition to attending to the upkeep of shrines, came to have wide authority over the markets, streets, and grain supply of Rome. The addition in the middle of the fourth century of two patrician curule aediles—so-called for the special curule on which they sat, a stool to which consuls and praetors were also entitled—was probably meant to balance these plebeian aediles, although these curule offices were also, gradually, opened to plebeians.

By the beginning of the first century BCE, then, Rome had around twenty-five elected magistrates (two consuls, six praetors, four aediles, at least ten quaestors, and—every five years—two censors), plus ten elected tribunes of the plebs (not technically considered magistrates, and with no insignia of office); four assemblies, which always had to be summoned by one of these elected officials; and a Senate of around three hundred members.

In principle, Rome's wars were supposed to be fought by her consuls and praetors, with their powers of *imperium* and *auspicium*. But when Rome's wars became great, multiple, distant, or long, two or even four men, replaced yearly, failed to answer these military needs. To meet acute crises, early Rome appointed, for the strictly limited term of six months, a dictator, who in turn appointed a second-in-command, the master of horse (*magister equitum*), to both of whom *imperium* was granted. The consuls continued in office, but the dictator outranked them and usually led the army to handle the emergency that had called him into being. This conventional use of dictators at Rome lapsed after the Second Punic War (218–201 BCE), but the office was for a short time (82–81 BCE) revived by Sulla, the victor in Rome's first round of civil wars, and then again by Julius Caesar, who, after his victory in renewed civil war, was authorized in 44 BCE to hold the dictatorship for life, in ultimately fatal unconcern for the traditionally limited tenure of the office.

But mid- and late-republican Rome's preferred way of fighting a long war was to appoint a former consul as a proconsul, allowing him to keep his *imperium* for this specific purpose even though he had formally passed out of office; for lesser wars propraetors could also be appointed. By the age of Caesar, almost all wars were fought by these promagistrates, and the consulship itself was held in the city, where political life was absorbing, thrilling, and sometimes even dangerous: during his consulship in 63 BCE, for example, Cicero had to suppress the conspiracy of the disgruntled patrician Catiline.

By the late Republic this mass of magistracies had been reduced to a competitive career, the *cursus honorum* or "racetrack of honors," and to the tenure of each of three offices, held in sequence, was assigned a minimum age (at the beginning, thirty for quaestor, thirty-nine for praetor, and forty-two for consul). The offices whose holders could command armies (consuls and praetors) continued to be elected by the *comitia centuriata*, those from the plebeian tradition were elected in the *concilium plebis*, and all others were elected in the *comitia tributa*. Actual legislation could be passed in all three of these assemblies. This baroque constitutional complexity was not the result of a rational differentiation of function but of the agglutinative and reluctant-to-throw-anything-out process by which Rome's constitution evolved. In practice, as the distinctions between patrician and plebeian became virtually meaningless, all candidates for Roman magistracies came from the richest stratum of society, the "equestrian" census class, derived from the citizen cavalry (defunct by the first century BCE) that had been made up of Rome's wealthiest citizens.

Once a man had served as quaestor, he was conventionally admitted to the Roman Senate by the next board of censors and stayed a member for life: that is how the Senate reproduced itself. While the Roman assemblies were fully constitutional voting bodies, and while Roman magistrates were fully constitutional elected officials, the Senate was neither. Normally that did not matter: any good Roman would leap to obey a formal expression of the Senate's opinion, a *senatus consultum*, backed as it was by the massed social authority (*auctoritas*) of the former holders of high offices and doers of great deeds. But a *senatus consultum* was just that, an "opinion of the Senate" given to a magistrate in response to a question (the *senatus consultum ultimum* or "supreme opinion of the Senate" merely gave a magistrate senatorial support to do what he thought best, usually to suppress an uprising in the city); it was not a law and could not compel by force of legal authority. As a consequence, the Senate's numerous traditional prerogatives and spheres of responsibility could be invaded or even taken away by law, as increasingly happened in the late Republic. Thus, although admired as Rome's guiding force for hundreds of years and a highly significant element in the Roman unwritten constitution, the Senate as an institution was peculiarly vulnerable to attack. The Greek historian Polybius saw the Roman constitution as perfectly balanced between its three elements of magistrates, assemblies, and Senate, but in truth the balance itself was traditional and conventional rather than constitutional, and the balance was first destabilized and then destroyed by the tremendous personalities of the late Republic.

ACKNOWLEDGMENTS

The editor and translator would like to warmly thank copy editor Prudence Crowther for the many improvements she has made to this book. We thank as well our Norton editor, Steve Forman; our cartographer, Kelly Sandefer; our agent, Glen Hartley; Louise Mattarelliano and Travis Carr at W. W. Norton, and copy editor Trent Duffy, for shepherding the book into production; and the various Plutarch scholars we have consulted along the way, in particular Christopher Pelling, who generously shared his insights and expertise.

INDEX